Light & Strength:

Mother Cécile Bruyère,
First Abbess of Sainte-Cécile of Solesmes

by

Dom Guy Marie Oury, O.S.B.

Translated by M. Cristina Borges

Abbey Editions
Our Lady of Clear Creek Abbey
Hulbert, Oklahoma

Abbey Editions
Our Lady of Clear Creek Abbey
5804 West Monastery Road
Hulbert, OK 74441
www.clearcreekmonks.org
© 2012 Our Lady of Clear Creek Abbey
All rights reserved. Published 2012
16 15 14   1 2 3

Cover Design: Michaela Harrison

ISBN: 978-0-615-86225-5

Originally published as *Lumière et force:*
Mère Cécile Bruyère, première abbesse de Sainte-Cécile
© Éditions de Solesmes, 1997

Printed in the United States of America

Table of Contents

Preface

IN A CONFERENCE TO the nuns of Sainte-Cécile of Solesmes in 1948, Dom Germain Cozien, third successor of Dom Guéranger, recommended that they always unite the present to their past and to the traditions of their monastic family—that they preserve the legacy of their abbesses. In this context, he described the substantive contribution of Mother Cécile in two most significant words: light and strength. The present biography responds to the legitimate desire of the nuns, monks, and all the friends of the Solesmian family to become better acquainted with Mother Cécile Bruyère, foundress and first abbess of Sainte-Cécile of Solesmes, indebted as they are to her for such a legacy. These pages are more than a simple narration of the events that make up the fabric of an existence. They reflect and testify to the action of God in a life that was given over entirely to Him and which He, in turn, filled up entirely.

An abbess at age twenty-five, Jenny Bruyère—who chose Cécile for her confirmation name in 1858 at Chantenay—possessed remarkable qualities and a no less admirable gift for governing, which were recognized and refined by the extraordinary spiritual father who directed her from childhood. Dom Guéranger came to know her when she was eleven, having agreed to prepare her for her First Communion. He retained her as his spiritual child and continued to impart to her a spiritual education founded on equilibrium and common sense, aimed at bringing to full fruition the abundant supernatural gifts that he had discerned in this chosen soul. He insisted, in particular, on docility to the will of God and the need to quiet and control her temperament, which could be characterized as strong and independent. While eschewing certain debatable aspects of the spirituality of those times, he helped her above all to grow in the love of Christ and in the desire to belong to Him, always stressing gentleness and suppleness.

In the course of the several sections of this book, the reader will be able to trace the different stages by which the Lord forged the work that He had envisioned. On October 12, 1861, after a year of "novitiate," Cécile Bruyère took a private vow of chastity before Dom Guéranger. Shortly afterwards, she confided to him her desire to embrace a life entirely consecrated to God. It was then Dom Guéranger's turn to take a leap of faith, and in 1863 he began pointing Cécile toward Benedictine spirituality.

The outbursts of wrath of her father, the settling of the foundresses in their first Solesmian home, named "Sainte-Cécile-la-Petite," the daily conferences given by Dom Guéranger to the members of the infant community, all are woven into a moving story in which the anecdotes of daily life blend with an admirable submission to the ways of God.

Dom Guéranger's spiritual direction, conducted with tact, wisdom and firmness, fashioned an exceptional personality. Mother Cécile Bruyère assimilated the teachings of her mentor as much with her heart as with her mind, while the abbot placed great importance on liberty of the spirit in directing souls. In the long years of her abbacy, the foundress of Sainte-Cécile revealed the pure light of solid monastic doctrine, accentuated by specific tenets that went immediately to the essentials. This light strengthened her faith and that of her daughters, leading their souls to be ever immersed in adoration.

It is noteworthy, in particular, that Mother Cécile's mind and heart were constantly directed toward the person of Christ, loved as the Divine Spouse. When she pronounced her vow of virginity on her sixteenth birthday, Jenny Bruyère delivered herself entirely to the divine power. She had no other support, no other succor than God in the midst of the tempests of this world. This divine power would accompany her all her life, which was not exempt from many trials and sufferings, but throughout which she always radiated a profound peace.

The contemplative life to which she was called from her youth would always be for her quite simply an anticipation of the beatific vision, just as participation in the liturgy was always for her a foretaste of the liturgy that is celebrated in heaven. What will be remembered, above all, are her teachings on prayer, outlined in a book that was widely disseminated: *The Spiritual Life and Prayer in Holy Scripture and Monastic Tradition*. Concealed behind the didactic language of this work one can often detect the experiences of a profound life of union with God, which Mother Cécile's discretion revealed only to her spiritual father.

May the pages of this biography unfold for the reader the beauty and fullness of an existence that never had any purpose other than to remain always and entirely ready before the presence of God, a presence that fulfills the desires of a soul, a presence that radiates the love of charity. In these pages, monastic life, that is, a life consecrated to prayer, is fully validated; as Mother Cécile so magnificently summarized in a conference to her nuns: "The spirit of prayer, as the foundation of monastic life, is a willingness to live unceasingly before God, having the habitual consciousness of His presence in us, around us, with us, in such a way that, be it consciously or be it in a general manner, we never leave His gaze."

Solesmes, March 18, 1997
Dies natalis[1] of Mother Cécile Bruyère

+ fr. Philippe Dupont, Abbot of Solesmes

---

[1] The "day of her birth" into eternity.

Introduction

OF ALL THE DIFFICULT YEARS traversed by Dom Guéranger in his labors for the creation of Solesmes, 1845 seems to have been the most tragic. In that year, his foundation, established in the midst of so many obstacles, was shaken to its very base and seemed doomed to disappear forever.

Firstly, in the beginning of the year, the French government communicated to the Holy See, through its ambassador, that the exempt status of the "so-called Jesuits" and the "so-called Benedictines" of Solesmes was absolutely contrary to the Concordat,[1] which recognized only the jurisdiction of bishops. To avoid the worst, the Congregation of Bishops and Regulars suspended the concessions of 1837[2] for an undetermined period of time and placed the monastery under the close supervision of the bishop of Le Mans, who, for the circumstance, was appointed apostolic delegate (January 1845). Thus was undone one of the principal objectives of Dom Guéranger, that of affirming the independence of religious life within the common law of the Church, which would enable him, as well, to avoid being controlled by Gallican legislation.[3]

Then, in September of the same year, he was forced, with a bleeding heart, to close the priory of Saint-Germain in Paris. The monastery, which had been founded four years earlier, was literally

---

[1] The French Concordat was a convention ratified on July 16, 1802, between Napoleon Bonaparte and Pope Pius VII, following the devastation of the French Revolution, which restored some of the rights of the Roman Catholic Church in France, while the state retained most of its control. Among other things, it declared that Catholicism was the religion of the majority of Frenchmen and that the papacy had the right to depose bishops, while the state continued nominating them. — Trans.

[2] On July 14, 1837 Rome approved the Constitutions of the Benedictines of Solesmes presented by Dom Prosper Guéranger, and, on its own initiative, raised the priory of Solesmes to the status of an abbey with the charge of reintroducing the Benedictine Order in France — as the Benedictine Congregation of France — and the power to establish other foundations without need of further approval. — Trans.

[3] This refers to the fact that in France the bishops were appointed by the state, as well as to the whole struggle between those among the clergy with Gallican tendencies, suspicious and defiant of Rome's supremacy, and the Ultramontanists loyal to Rome, among whom Dom Guéranger was a prominent figure. — Trans.

crumbling under debt and any prospect of saving it seemed impossible. Along with itself, Saint-Germain dragged the second Solesmian house in the area of Paris to its ruin—Bièvres, in the diocese of Versailles. The financial abyss threatened to swallow up even the abbey of Solesmes itself, which was only narrowly saved thanks to the eventual formation of an aid committee.

Lastly, Dom Groult d'Acy, the depositary of a substantial fund which had been destined for the re-establishment of the Order of Saint Benedict in France, had died in Vichy on August 18, 1843, leaving the monies to another institution: the Picpus Society, created under the Rule of Saint Benedict during the French Revolution by Father Coudrin. The society was chosen by Dom d'Acy to be the recipient of the estate because its future seemed better assured than that of the small Benedictine Congregation of France. Dom Guéranger could no longer expect anything from this erstwhile prospect.

The hour was tragic. Dom Guéranger was facing the imminent collapse of his work. He did not even know whether it would be possible to salvage anything from the shipwreck. It was with these sentiments that, on October 12, he celebrated the great feast of the dedication of the abbatial church, perhaps for the last time.

Omnis illa Deo sacra
Et dilecta civitas,
Plena modulis in laude,
Et canore jubilo . . .[4]

On that very day, October 12, 1845, was born at the rue d'Alger in Paris, little Jenny-Henriette Bruyère, who would be the first abbess of Sainte-Cécile of Solesmes, "she who is among all, the heiress of the spirit (of Dom Guéranger)," as Dom Charles Couturier[5] would state in his preface to *The Spiritual Life and Prayer*.[6]

---

[4] "Entirely consecrated to God, this city which He loves, full of harmony, praise and joyous song."—Trans.

[5] Second abbot of Solesmes.—Trans.

[6] Mother Cécile Bruyère's book on the spiritual life and prayer, *La vie spirituelle et l'oraison d'après la Sainte Écriture et la tradition monastique* (Solesmes, 1895), translated to English by the Benedictines of Stanbrook as *The Spiritual Life and Prayer According to Holy Scripture and Monastic Tradition* (London, 1900) and reprinted in 2002 by Wipf and Stock Publishers (Eugene, Oregon).—Trans.

Part I

The Preparation Years
1845–1866

Chapter 1

The Family

IN 1845, PARIS COUNTED one million residents, double the number living there at the turn of the century. During the July Monarchy[1] alone (1830–1848), 350,000 souls had migrated into the city. About a third of the population was made up of artisans and craftsmen, more so than laborers. Living conditions for these were difficult; it was rare that a workshop or studio would have more than ten paid employees.

For some years, the government had been building a vast system of defense for Paris, surrounding the city with a wall that also encompassed some of the neighboring villages: Grenelle, Vaugirard, Issy, and others. The wall was secured by a hundred bastions protected by seventeen fortresses. From 1841 to 1845, whole armies of stonemasons, quarry workers, cart drivers, etc., labored at this colossal project. The massive wall, which outlined the present-day limits of the city, was built thirty feet high with grass-covered embankments, topped by a walkway.

The family of the future foundress of the Abbey of Sainte-Cécile had been in Paris for only half a century. Her grandfather, Louis Bruyère (1758–1831), was born in Lyon and had begun his career as an engineer in Le Mans prior to the eruption of the French Revolution, working on urban development projects for the city. Among these was the planning and design of the Promenade des Jacobins.

In 1811, Louis Bruyère was appointed director of public works in Paris by the Napoleonic government, and was inducted, at that time, as Knight of the Empire. Upon the restoration of the Bourbon dynasty,[2] he became general inspector of bridges and roadways. He committed his long and vast experience to writing in a treatise entitled *Études relatives à l'art des constructions* (Studies on the art of

---

[1] The liberal monarchical rule of Louis-Philippe d'Orléans, from 1830 to 1848, following the overthrow of the Bourbon monarchy in the "July Revolution" of July 1830. —Trans.

[2] The restoration of the Bourbon dynasty occurred in 1814, with the accession of Louis XVIII to the throne, brother of Louis XVI.—Trans.

construction), which quickly became a classic. The work was published as a series between 1822 and 1829.

Louis Bruyère wedded Élise (or Elisabeth) Le Barbier (1776–1842), the daughter of a painter of historical themes.[3] Élise herself was an artist of distinction, securing a prize at the Salon de Paris[4] in 1827; her own salon was frequented by writers and artists. Some of her paintings are preserved in the Fine Arts museums in Lyon and Valenciennes. According to her own children, she had a difficult character and her belief system was akin to that of Jean-Jacques Rousseau. Fortunately, her household was cared for by her sister, Henriette Le Barbier, a good Christian soul who had remained single and who was a second mother to Élise's children.

Louis Bruyère and Élise Le Barbier were married in 1797 and had five children—two sons and three daughters. One of their daughters would marry Jacques Mallet who, in 1866, was made Count of the Empire. The father of the future abbess of Sainte-Cécile was the younger of the two sons. Named Léopard, he was born on July 1, 1810, around the time that the "King of Rome"[5] came into the world. Being a son and grandson of artists, architects and engineers, he pursued his schooling at the École des Beaux-Arts (School of Fine Arts) in Paris, which was not exactly known for producing exemplary well-behaved young men. Accordingly, his language, his choice of reading, and his social life were, at times, reflective of his student days. He had a foul mouth.

Lively, gifted with great ease of expression, a natural writer, cultivated, witty, and rather bawdy, he did also have his bouts of anger when he was too strongly opposed. He was very proud—and rightly so—of his family, of the accomplishments of his father, and of his ancestry. His artistic temperament and his cultivation had rendered him a highly sensitive person. Still, he was often capricious and unpredictable, and, on occasion, despotic toward his own. His

---

[3] Jean-Jacques-François Le Barbier (1738–1826).—Trans.

[4] The "Salon de Paris" or simply "Salon," was the official art exhibition of the Académie des Beaux-Arts (Academy of Fine Arts) in Paris, beginning in 1725. Between 1748 and 1890 it was the greatest annual or biannual art event in the western world.—Trans.

[5] Napoléon François Joseph Charles Bonaparte (1811–1832) was the son of Napoleon Bonaparte and his second wife, Marie Louise of Austria. As heir-apparent, he was accorded the titles "King of Rome" and "Emperor of the French."—Trans.

relationship with his daughter—whom he much admired though without saying so, and for whom he had a tender and protective love—was not always easy.

Léopard's competency as a professional was beyond dispute. Upon leaving the École, he at first worked for the city of Paris at the department of monument inspection. Then, as was commonly the case with young artists and architects in France, he went on an artistic tour of Italy, returning from there with a great many pencil drawings and watercolors. He did honor to his lineage. In 1852, his entry at the competition of the École des Beaux-Arts was a house plan employing metal frame construction. This construction technique was an area of research given luster by the likes of Henri Labrouste, Louis Auguste Boileau, and Victor Baltard,[6] while Léopard's own father had already preceded them in treating of the subject in his works.

His wife, Félicie Huvé, thirteen years his junior, was born at the end of the reign of Louis XVIII, on October 3, 1823. Félicie's father and grandfather were also architects of great talent with impressive careers. Her grandfather, Jean-Jacques Huvé (1742–1808), had studied with Jacques François Blondel (1705–1774). Some of his drawings can be found in public art collections in America. Her father, Jean-Jacques-Marie Huvé (1783–1852), worked on the construction of La Madeleine,[7] starting in 1808 under Pierre-Alexandre Vignon[8] and becoming the sole head of the project in 1828 upon Vignon's death. Jean-Jacques-Marie Huvé and his wife, Cécile Caillat (1789–1840) had four children: two sons, who, like their father, had no faith, and two

---

[6] Henri Labrouste (1801–1875), Louis Auguste Boileau (1812–1896), and Victor Baltard (1805–1874) were illustrious French architects who had studied in Rome and whose career had unfolded in Paris. All three had experimented with and employed frame construction using metals such as iron and steel.—Trans.

[7] The site where La Madeleine stands had been the location of a church dedicated to St. Mary Magdalen since the twelfth century. The current building was originally commissioned by Napoleon Bonaparte in 1806 as a "Temple to the Glory of the Great Army." This purpose was changed by Louis XVIII, whose intention was that the edifice be a church. His plan was interrupted, in turn, by the accession of Louis-Philippe d'Orléans to the throne in 1830, who at first made it a monument of national reconciliation. However, in the end, La Madeleine was consecrated a church in 1842 upon completion of its construction.—Trans.

[8] Pierre-Alexandre Barthélemy Vignon (1763–1828), French architect of the Revolutionary and Napoleonic periods.—Trans.

daughters, Félicie and Louise, who were imbued with the deep faith of their mother.

For the profoundly religious Félicie, God was truly above all and took precedence over all. She was very exacting of herself, and would be so, as well, of her children, devoting herself to providing them with an unwaveringly Christian education.

The young woman's health was never good after her marriage to Léopard Bruyère on February 23, 1843. She suffered some serious crises when her daughters were still small, as described in her own words: "In 1851, I suffered from a nervous condition that at times twisted, and at other times temporarily paralyzed, my limbs. The doctor prescribed treatment at the thermal springs of Enghien.[9] At that time I was living at Montmorency, at the top of the hill. As part of the therapy, the doctor had directed that I go on foot every day to Enghien for my bath and shower treatment, so I would leave every morning at four o'clock in order to avoid having to wait in line."[10] Then again in 1862 she went through yet another bout of ill health about which no details have been left.

At first the young couple settled at 9 rue d'Alger. There it was that Jeanne-Henriette, "Jenny," was born on October 12, 1845—the future Mother Cécile, Abbess of Sainte-Cécile. The house stands in the beautiful district along the right bank of the Seine, midway between the Place Vendôme and the Palais des Tuileries, destroyed in 1871. The street, no more than three hundred feet long, is situated between the rue de Rivoli and the rue Saint-Honoré in the parish of Saint-Roch, where the remains of Pierre Corneille, André Le Nôtre, Guillaume Cardinal Dubois, and Marshal François de Créquy[11] are entombed.

---

[9] Montmorency is a northern suburb of Paris, located on a hill. From 1689 to 1789 it was known as Enghien, after one of the titles of the princes of Condé, who had inherited the land from the Montmorency family. While the town ceased to be named Enghien at the formation of the communes during the French Revolution, the local lake retained the family name, as well as the nearby thermal baths discovered in 1766.—Trans.

[10] "Récit de madame Bruyère sur l'enfance de sa fille Jenny" (Account by Madame Bruyère about the childhood of her daughter Jenny), p. 18.

[11] Pierre Corneille (1606–1684), considered creator of French classical tragedy; André Le Nôtre (1613–1700), landscape architect and the gardener of King Louis XIV; Guillaume Dubois (1656–1723), a cardinal and prime minster of Louis XV; François de Créquy (1625–1687), Marshal of France.—Trans.

Madame Bruyère would have liked her daughter's baptism to have taken place immediately following her birth. However, to her great chagrin, this was not possible. The child, deemed too fragile to be taken out-of-doors, did not receive the baptismal waters until eleven days later, on October 23. Mother Cécile would later emphasize the importance of baptism: "All Christians may attain union with God, without any other call to it than that given in their baptism; they can do so in virtue of their simple title of children of God."[12]

Altogether, the family into which the child was born did not make for a profoundly Christian environment. As was frequently the case among the grand bourgeoisie of France at that time, religion was a matter for women. One might well allow them to practice their faith to a certain point, but far be it from men to adhere to what was taught to their wives and children. Even those men who had received their education at good Catholic schools were wont to take permanent holidays from their faith and its practice once their schooling had been completed. This was the case with Jeanne-Henriette's father, who had been educated at the Collège de Juilly under the direction of Fathers Louis-Antoine de Salinis and Olympe-Philippe Gerbet, adepts of Lammenais's ultramontanism.[13] Illustrative of this state of affairs was the book *Du prêtre, de la femme et de la famille* (On priests, women and the family) by Jules Michelet (1798–1874), published the same year Jenny was born. In this book Michelet attacks what he deems the intrusion of the priest into the intimacy of the family through the confessional, an intolerable state of affairs as far as he was concerned. There were many who agreed with Michelet and shared his annoyance and irritation over this perceived power exerted over souls.

---

[12] Cécile Bruyère, *The Spiritual Life and Prayer According to Holy Scripture and Monastic Tradition*, trans. Benedictines of Stanbrook (Eugene, OR : Wipf and Stock, 2002) p. 28.

[13] Félicité de Lamennais (1782–1854), born in Brittany and ordained a priest, was, for an entire generation of clergy, the defender of religion in face of the revolutionary spirit, and of Catholicism in face of Gallicanism. Later, his liberal pronouncements and insubordination brought about his condemnation by Rome. He ended by leaving the priesthood and renouncing religion altogether. Fathers Salinis and Gerbet, who were under Lamennais's influence prior to his tragic transformation and apostasy, eventually became bishops, respectively of Amiens and Perpignan. — Trans.

Jeanne-Henriette lived closely to her mother, whose affection for her had something of possessiveness (which would explain certain reactions of the girl once she was past her first few years). Madame Bruyère had a very high opinion of her daughter and often felt less gifted than she.

Thanks to the insistence of Dom Prosper Guéranger, we have two invaluable documents about Jenny's childhood and youth: a type of "Story of a Soul,"[14] written at his request when she was nineteen (1864), and notes he asked for from her mother, upon Jenny's entrance to religious life in 1867. In the former document, Jenny shows herself to be a severe—nearly merciless—judge of her own behavior, which necessitates that the reader be on his guard against taking too literally what she says about her own bad character. On the other hand, the latter document, memoirs of an admiring mother, has the tendency of overlooking those more difficult traits of the girl's personality. The two sources are thus mutually corrective. Some of Jenny's letters written starting at age six have also been preserved, and the prolific correspondence with Dom Guéranger provides abundant information about her adolescence.

Certain autobiographical memoirs, written in the genre of "confessions" as addressed to God, provide glimpses into the early formation she received from Madame Bruyère. "My first recollections go back to when I was somewhere between eighteen months and two years of age. I was beginning to think, to talk, and I already had a precise notion (my Lord) of Your presence everywhere. When I was taken to church, although the hour was quite early, I would be very still and quiet, in great tranquility, for as long as we remained there."[15]

The said church is Saint-Roch, where Jenny had been baptized. Already as a little toddler, she became well familiar with its three-part structure encompassing three sanctuary areas, one behind the other: the main nave and sanctuary leading to a rotunda—the chapel of Our Lady—behind which was the Calvary chapel at the apse. The

---

[14] Reference to the autobiography of St. Thérèse of Lisieux (1873–1897), Carmelite saint.—Trans.

[15] "Enfance et jeunesse de Mère Cécile Bruyère" (Childhood and youth of Mother Cécile Bruyère, autobiographical notes), p. 8.

rotunda, dedicated to the Blessed Virgin Mary, had been designed by Jules Hardouin-Mansart[16] after the Église du Dome at Les Invalides.[17] The layout and location of this chapel were intended to encourage frequent communion at a time when the influence of Jansenism made this practice rare among the faithful.

The parish of Saint-Roch had been severely affected by the French Revolution. Its pastor set about repairing the damage as soon as he was able, under the Napoleonic Empire (1804–1814) and the Bourbon Restoration (1814–1824). He sought to refurbish the building, enriching its interior with numerous paintings and sculptures obtained from monasteries in the area that had been either suppressed or destroyed.

"Very early on, my mother gradually taught me the principal obligations of a Christian, and I could not conceive of these ever being neglected. ... I was most intrigued and attracted by the ceremonies of the Church, and I unceasingly pestered my mother with questions about the meaning of everything. Sermons would arouse yet another form of curiosity. My mother, with untiring patience and great prudence, would not let a single one of my questions go unanswered. Also, it was of no one else but her that I asked for the explanations my inquiring mind desired. Thus, I never had any of the ridiculous and false notions that children might absorb from the most well-intentioned of servants. There was no subject that stumped my intellect and even when I innocently encountered things that might have been dangerous to me because of my tendency to observe everything, my mother did not avoid my questions. Without arousing my imagination, while at the same time not rejecting its inquisitiveness, she explained all with gravity, evoking within me thoughts of Your sovereign rule."[18]

---

[16] Jules Hardouin-Mansart (1646–1708) was Louis XIV's chief architect whose work is considered the apex of French Baroque architecture. Besides his extensions to the royal palace at Versailles, among his best known works are the Place Vendôme, the Place des Victoires, the Pont-Royal, the Church of Saint-Roch, and the great domed royal chapel dedicated to Saint Louis, the Église du Dome, at Les Invalides, all in Paris. —Trans.

[17] Les Invalides, built in 1680 in Paris, was originally the royal veteran's hospital. In our day it is a complex of buildings containing museums and monuments related to France's military history, as well as a hospital and retirement home for war veterans. —Trans.

[18] "Enfance et jeunesse," p. 8.

Thus, Jenny was unaffectedly introduced at an early age into the artistic milieu of her parents, where the human body and the facts of life were taken for granted, so that she was never disturbed by what she might have seen or heard. "I never sought any information beyond that which my mother had given me because her explanations were always clear and true. Even now, as I reflect upon the past, I can see that never did my mother dissimulate or lie to me in the least of things. . . . Was it not You, my Lord, who gave her such prudence and temperance? Do I not owe You immense gratitude for having prepared for me such a firm and thorough formation?"[19] Among the bourgeoisie of the time, the introduction of young women to the facts of life was often left to the last moments before their wedding. In this respect, the education given by Madame Bruyère to her daughter was quite extraordinary.

In the future, when still at a young age Jenny would ask to take a vow of virginity, she would do so not in bewilderment or fear of an unknown reality, but fully conscious of its meaning. It is well that her elders never had recourse to circumlocutions with her and never avoided dealing with fundamental matters. Her father's unrestrained conversation combined with her mother's clarity and prudence both helped Jenny to arrive at an equanimity regarding this point which would never be disturbed. She spoke uninhibitedly.

But we anticipate her adolescence. Let us return to Jenny's early years, through certain childhood memories she loved to recall or which she confided to only a few.

"Thus, I grew in tranquility," she continues in the same narrative, "spending long days at my mother's side, without looking for or desiring any other company than her own. . . . It was in our conversations, as well, that I learned sacred history, some of the history of France, and, above all, the catechism. I understood in depth the mystery of each liturgical feast, but, above all, my mother was intent on instilling in me a profound conviction of, and high esteem for, Your sovereign rule above all creatures and Your presence in all places. She showed me sin as being always hideous and repulsive, and the good as being beautiful and attractive; and she so strongly

---

[19] Ibid., p. 10.

impressed upon my soul the notion of duty that I could not conceive of anyone hesitating on this point once the word 'duty' had been pronounced. I noted that at least with her this was always the case, and that never once were her actions guided by whim. While she was extremely tender, her tenderness was never touched by weakness. . . . She often repeated to me: 'My child, God will never fail you; He alone is all, no one but He is necessary. The only necessary thing is to please Him and to fear nothing but displeasing Him, everything else is of no value at all.'"[20]

Madame Bruyère recounts that one Sunday at Saint-Roch's the front door of the church closed on Jenny's fingers as they were entering the building. The pain was awful, but Jenny said not a word, hiding her hands in her coat. No one noticed the incident until after Mass: one of her nails was black and blue. She was then about five (Jenny relates this same event, but places it at a yet younger age).

Before she was able to read, Jenny learned numerous fables from her mother, whose side she never left. (Fables by Jean-Pierre Claris de Florian were perhaps easier for a child her age than those by Jean de La Fontaine). Madame Bruyère would take the time to explain to her daughter what each difficult word meant. The girl, in this way, acquired a marked taste for literature at a very young age. Often, when alone, she would pick up a book and simulate reading while reciting the text; little did it matter that the book was upside-down.

However, Jenny did not have a docile character, something in which she closely resembled her father. She had a fierce pride, and was unflinching when she thought herself to be in the right; no one could overcome her resolve. She refused to humiliate herself by asking forgiveness, which secured for her not a few spankings from her father. But punishment had no result except to exacerbate her resistance, so that Monsieur Bruyère would often exclaim in dismay: "I really do not know what will ever subdue this child!"[21]

Her mother usually knew how to better handle the situation: "Be on your guard," she would say, "you are behaving like a pagan, and you are thinking like a pagan; Our Lord is so ashamed of you. You

---

[20] Ibid., p. 10.
[21] Ibid., p. 15.

are acting like those Romans who were capable of great feats, but weren't able to conquer themselves. They were less guilty than you, since they did not know the Gospel."[22]

To conquer oneself so as to obey the Gospel, so as to be more like Jesus, crowned with thorns, nailed to His Cross for the love of men . . . only these thoughts would succeed in bringing Jenny back to composure. The crisis would fade away and give place to a torrent of tears of repentance. The child battled against her own difficult character so that, beginning at the age of reason, she made great progress in improving her behavior.

Nevertheless, when she did not like something, she promptly sulked. It was difficult for her to suffer stupidity and fickleness. She inevitably discovered the weak side of those with whom she came into contact, and it cost her great effort to overcome her repugnance. From this trait followed her tendency to isolate herself, to avoid those who displeased her, to withdraw into her hidden life. It was not an easy thing to have her uniformly maintain a smile for everyone. Her father's friends were amused by her distant attitude which kept them at bay: "What a unique little girl, with this very observant pair of eyes!"[23] Her verdicts were always without appeal. Her nature was so repulsed by mediocrity under any form and so thirsted for purity and integrity that she instinctively revolted against the ugly, the bad, or the simply imperfect.

She was the leader among her playmates, arbitrating disagreements and imposing her will by dint of her force of character, even with older friends. The vast garden at the Tuileries, in front of the palace, was the only place in her neighborhood where children could play, located only a little further from the Church of Saint-Roch. The much smaller garden at the Royal Palace was likewise close by. Here in these gardens she would meet her little friends and proceed to lead the games.

Born, as she was, into a family of artists, Jenny displayed great aptitude for painting. Her musical talents also blossomed, and she did well at the piano. She was precocious beyond her years in all

---

[22] Ibid., p. 14.
[23] Ibid., p. 19.

areas, and this was as true of the awakening of her faith as of her intelligence. She wanted to know and understand everything. Her lively spirit easily absorbed all that was presented to her.

From the moment she understood that the Eucharist is the real, actual presence of Jesus in a wafer, she conceived of a great desire to receive It. But at that time children had to wait until nearly their adolescence before they could receive First Holy Communion, instead of at the age of reason, which Jenny had achieved much earlier than most children. "I felt an immense desire of uniting myself to You in Holy Communion. Sometimes I could barely keep myself at my seat. If it were not for concern that my small stature might be detected, I certainly would have presented myself at the communion rail. The only way I was consoled was by snuggling up to my mother on the days she received You, so that I could find You in her."[24]

These words reveal that Madame Bruyère received Holy Communion frequently according to the custom of those days, that is, on Sundays and feast days. They also indicate that she attended the early morning Mass at the parish, because it was not customary to distribute communion at the High Mass or at Masses offered later in the morning. The early Mass was celebrated in the chapel of Our Lady, under the grand rotunda created by d'Hardouin-Mansart, which had been designed specifically for this purpose. Above the altar of the chapel rests the famed marble Nativity Group sculpted by Michel Anguier[25] (1665), expressing admiration before the mystery of Bethlehem while announcing the mystery of the Eucharist, the "living bread come down from Heaven."

---

[24] Ibid., p. 20.
[25] Michel Anguier (1613–1686), sculptor trained in his native Normandy, as well as in Rome. The Nativity Group is considered his masterpiece and was originally created for the high altar of the Church of Val-de-Grâce in Paris, having been transferred to Saint-Roch after the French Revolution.—Trans.

Chapter 2

Upheavals in Paris

AS PRECOCIOUS AS Jenny Bruyère might have been, she was not so much so as to be able to follow and understand the events that so brutally shook Paris from 1848 to 1851. She was only two years and four months when the student and worker demonstrations against François Guizot[1] erupted and barricades were raised along the streets of the city on February 22, 1848. But she remembered well the flight of the family from their home at the rue d'Alger—too exposed to the violence due to its proximity to the Tuileries Palace—to take refuge in a quieter area of Paris. Here is how Madame Bruyère recalls the incident:

"Her father took her in his arms, our dear little one, and as we distanced ourselves from the rue du Marché-Saint-Honoré, we felt bullets whizzing over our heads. I positioned myself so as to protect little Jenny's head. All the while she smiled at me."[2]

On December 3, 1851, one day after the coup d'état of the Prince-President,[3] when members of the working class again raised barricades at the faubourg Saint-Antoine,[4] she had only just turned six.

Nonetheless, the uncertainties with which her family lived and the instability of the political scene could not have escaped the girl,

---

[1] François Guizot (1787–1874), French statesman, was successively Minister of Education, Ambassador to England, Foreign Minister and Prime Minister to Louis-Philippe d'Orléans.—Trans.

[2] "Récit de madame Bruyère," p. 10.

[3] Louis-Napoleon Bonaparte (1808–1873), nephew of Napoleon Bonaparte, was elected President of the Second Republic in December 1848, following the ouster of King Louis-Philippe. During this period he was referred to as the "Prince-President." As the end of his four-year term approached, he effected a coup d'état on December 2, 1851 with the support of the army, seizing dictatorial powers. One year later he would make himself Emperor, establishing the "Second French Empire."—Trans.

[4] Following Louis-Napoleon's seizure of power, protests again erupted in Paris. Most symbolic of this uprising were the barricades raised at the neighborhood of Sainte-Antoine, where a young doctor, Jean-Baptiste Baudin, who had published a manifesto against Louis-Napoleon, was shot to death by a government troop. This incident kindled yet more unrest and violence.—Trans.

despite her young age. She was too intuitive not to perceive what went on about her. She also had ears to hear, and the gunfire in the narrow streets of the city resounded from neighborhood to neighborhood. In this situation, one could but remain indoors and take all necessary precautions.

In August 1830, following the Revolution of the Three Glorious Days,[5] Victor Hugo had noted in his *Journal des idées et des opinions d'un révolutionnaire de 1830:* "After July 1830, what we need is the reality of a 'republic,' under the name of 'monarchy.'"[6] On February 24, 1848, Louis-Philippe departed France for England by carriage, after having abdicated his rule to his grandson, the Count of Paris. The populace had preferred the name 'republic,' and no one saw much wrong with that.

Louis Veuillot[7] wrote in a letter dated March 14, 1848, at a time when he was being considered for a deputy seat for the Loiret region: "There is only one class of people for us to fear—those who hate God and liberty. In the name of France, in the name of humanity, it is these whom we must combat regardless of their political allegiance. There are plenty of them, even among the republicans. As to those who do not have religion but firmly love liberty, I do not despair of them. A liberated religion will bring about such beautiful, such great things that these people will end up laying down their weapons. Do not dismiss them. Prefer them even over those narrow-minded and timorous Catholics who believe that the Church's life depends on the goodwill of governments."

---

[5] The "Three Glorious Days" were the three days in which the "July Revolution" was effected: July 27, 28, and 29 in 1830. Within these three days the Bourbon monarchy was overthrown and Louis-Philippe d'Orléans installed as "King of the French," inaugurating his liberal monarchical rule which would last until 1848, when he in turn was ousted.—Trans.

[6] Journal of the ideas and opinions of a revolutionary of 1830. The original phrase in French, which is deemed ambiguous by some scholars, reads: "Après Juillet 1830, il nous faut la chose *république* et le mot *monarchie.*"—Trans.

[7] Louis Veuillot (1811–1883), French journalist, satirist, devotional writer and newspaper editor whose conversion back to the Catholic faith of his childhood occurred upon a visit to Rome during Holy Week in 1838. He became a staunch defender of the ultramontane position and an ardent champion of Catholicism. He was a vehement critic not only of anti-Catholic republicans but also of Catholics who sought to work with the government and accommodate the tenets of the Revolution. Pope St. Pius X styled him a "model for the Catholic laity."—Trans.

Unfortunately, following the abdication of Louis-Philippe in February, the situation deteriorated very quickly. The first signs of unrest and discontent among contingents of the National Guard broke out on March 16. These were countered March 17 by demonstrations of the people. On April 16, the protests took on a violent turn. On May 15, the Palais Bourbon was invaded by the populace. However, members of the General Assembly refused to be swayed by the mob, prompted by memories of the chaos unleashed during the Great Revolution. Thus came about the terrible days in June,[8] which took on the semblance of a civil war: 1,500 dead and 2,500 wounded according to official figures.

Then followed the presidential election of Louis-Napoleon Bonaparte, whose name, because of his uncle, was popular among the working class. But he was not so among traditional republicans. Other political parties unenthusiastically rallied to the new president, mockingly nicknamed "Badinguet" after the name of the laborer whose clothes he had borrowed when escaping from the fortress in Ham, in 1846. He seemed quite mediocre and unimpressive. "He is a moron," Adolphe Thiers[9] is known to have said. However, Louis-Napoleon obtained 72% of the vote (58% in Paris). Charles de Montalembert[10] was a better judge of the man's mettle and political ambitions, however. Three years after his election as head of state,

---

[8] Between June 23 and June 26, in what came to be known as the "June Days Uprising," the National Guard executed a systematic assault against the revolutionary Parisian citizenry, targeting the blockaded areas of the city. The casualties were many, as described.—Trans.

[9] Marie-Joseph-Louis-Adolphe Thiers (1797–1877) was a key figure in the liberal monarchy of Louis-Philippe d'Orléans, holding, among other posts, that of Prime Minister. He opposed Louis-Napoleon's government and was temporarily imprisoned and exiled to England. With the dissolution of Louis-Napoleon's Second Empire, Thiers was elected first president of the Third Republic in 1871.—Trans.

[10] Charles Forbes René, Count of Montalembert (1810–1870), journalist, historian, hagiographer and politician, held legislative posts in both the Second Republic and the Second Empire. Scion of an ancient noble family that had fled to England during the Terror, he favored a constitutional and liberal monarchy, and advocated the rights of the Catholic Church in collaboration with de Lammenais and Lacordaire, favoring a politically liberal view while staunchly defending the supremacy of Rome against Gallican tendencies held by much of the French clergy. He founded a short-lived Catholic political party, and supported the restoration of religious orders in France, including the work of Dom Prosper Guéranger.—Trans.

came the coup d'état of December 2, 1851, followed exactly one year later by the re-establishment of the Empire.

Even before his power was completely consolidated, Louis-Napoleon launched upon his massive renovation project of the city of Paris, clearing out wide spaces and establishing construction sites. Napoleon Bonaparte (Napoleon I) had already undertaken the demolition of the crumbling neighborhood that stood between the Louvre and Tuileries palaces, but there were still entire blocks of buildings that needed to be torn down before the two palaces could form a unified monumental complex.

As Prince-President, in 1851 and 1852 Louis-Napoleon moved to complete the Louvre (the north wing of the Palais-Royal and the Cour Napoléon); he commissioned the extension of the rue de Rivoli and had the area around the Hôtel de Ville[11] opened up. Then, in June 1853, now as Emperor, Napoleon III appointed Georges-Eugène Haussmann[12] to be prefect of the Seine Département[13] and entrusted the program of transformation of the city to him. The means of financing the enterprise were not entirely orthodox, since making a direct appeal to obtain funds from taxpayers was out of the question. There was plenty of opposition to the project. However, at the cost of unrelenting labor and of destruction at a scale that could well be classified as irresponsible vandalism, Paris became the city of human dimensions and bourgeois elegance of today, where broad spaces and wide boulevards are filled with air and light. For the duration of the Second Empire, a great many Parisians lived amidst demolition sites and construction projects, having to take long detours in order to avoid rutted streets, wreckage and debris. The rue d'Alger was not very far from the area that had been cleared so that the Louvre could be completed and joined, on the north side, to the Tuileries Palace.

---

[11] The Hôtel de Ville has housed the administration of the City of Paris since 1357.—Trans.

[12] Georges-Eugène Haussmann (1809–1891) was born in Paris to a Protestant family from Alsace. On mandate from Louis-Napoleon, he transformed Paris from a medieval town with narrow winding streets into the city of our days, with wide, tree-lined boulevards and expansive gardens. He also furnished the city with a new water supply, a gigantic system of sewers, new bridges, the opera house, and other public buildings.—Trans.

[13] Département—beginning with the remapping of France by the Revolutionary government—is an administrative division of land, akin to a county in the United States and Ireland, or a district in England.—Trans.

At the Bruyère home, a second daughter was born on June 29, 1849. Louise-Charlotte—who would go by Lise—was Jenny's junior by four years. The delivery had been very difficult and greatly draining for Madame Bruyère, so the father decided that they would have no more children, despite the desire of his wife to have a boy. She would have named him Paul.

In 1848, prior to the arrival of Lise, the family had left their home at the rue d'Alger to take up residence at the home of Monsieur Huvé, Madame Bruyère's father, at 15, rue du Helder. Her younger sister, Louise, had just married Henri Bertin (July 11, 1848) and left Paris to live in Roye, in the region of Picardie. The rue du Helder is situated in the same neighborhood as the rue d'Alger, still close enough to the church of Saint-Roch, between the future Opéra de Garnier and the Bourse.

Jenny, who was distant with everyone except her mother and did not easily relate to people, deeply regretted having left the familiarity of the house where she had been born. She did not feel at home at her grandfather's, whose life was far from being that of a model Christian. When Madame Bruyère became ill, anxiety took hold of the small girl. Would her mother die? What, then, would become of her? A few memories from that period have been preserved by Madame Bruyère:

"My father was very severe with Jenny. But whenever she behaved well he would give her some coins, which she kept for the poor. One day, he had just given her a 50 cent coin (a fortune at that time) when, shortly afterwards, Jenny had a temper tantrum. Her grandfather said to her: 'I haven't rewarded you just for you to turn around and be a bad girl!' Well, she took her coin and returned it to him saying, 'You shouldn't be giving advance payments. I didn't promise you that I would never be a bad girl again. I know very well that I cannot control myself. Keep your coin. It isn't for money that I behave well.' And never again was it possible to have her accept a coin as a reward."[14] These are astonishing words for a small child. Jenny was not afraid to be insolent, and how highly did she prize her liberty!

---

[14] "Récit de madame Bruyère," p. 21.

At the rue du Helder, the young girl became "more difficult," her mother tells us, and it was necessary to be severe with her. However, it is true that she was not always at fault. "One evening," continues Madame Bruyère, "she did not want to say goodnight to her grandfather. Having refused several times at our insistence, her father, who would not countenance resistance, gave her a severe beating with a ruler. The beating left marks that remained for two weeks. After crying for a long time, the poor child fell asleep. The next day she said to me: 'Mama, I fell asleep last night, but I did not give in because father beat me!'" [15] Through what is known from Jenny's recollections, she had good reason for her refusal.

From the vantage point of her wisdom of four years, she analyzed all those about her, rarely to their advantage. This was not particularly appreciated. Her mother alone found favor in her eyes. It was necessary to be constantly preaching patience to her, along with sweetness, humility and indulgence towards others.

But this difficulty of communication conversely led Jenny to lead a very intense interior life. Since the time she had begun reading, she would immerse herself in her books, with a marked preference for those that spoke to her of God. She very much liked the lives of the saints, and, even more so, the lives of women saints wherein she could find models for herself. Having always been called Jenny, instead of Jeanne-Henriette, she searched far and wide for a life of Saint Jenny and was inconsolable at not finding one. Thus, she made up her mind to become Saint Jenny herself so that all little girls to come named Jenny would have their own patroness. There was still a very long way to go before she would become a Saint Jenny, but this goal served as stimulus to fight against her defects, for the child felt called to live close to God and she had a profound conviction of His tenderness.

Her mother taught her to love the poor and to give them alms from her own funds. For example, on the way back from a long walk in Paris, she might propose to Jenny that they continue on foot instead of hiring a carriage: "If you'd like to continue on foot, I will

---

[15] Ibid., p. 15.

give you the money we would spend to hire a carriage for your alms fund."[16]

The Bruyères remained at the rue du Helder for about four years, during the entire length of the Second Republic. When Jenny's grandfather died, on November 23, 1852 (the year of the restoration of the Empire), they left the house to take up residence at 25, rue Louis-le-Grand, in an area that Haussmann's reforms would soon turn inside out. The rue Louis-le-Grand is just east of the rue de la Paix, which runs from the Place Vendôme to the Opera. It begins at the place du Marché-Saint-Honoré and ends at the boulevard des Capucines, by the Chaussé d'Antin.

The death of Monsieur Huvé was the first family bereavement that the girl experienced. His passing made a deep impression on her. Her mother writes about this episode: "When my father died (she was seven years old) ... I could not bring myself to let her in to see my poor deceased father one last time, although had I done so, the prayers of my dear little one would have been yet more fervent. Instead, she knelt at the doorway of his room and, seeing me cry, she comforted me: 'Mother, he was so good to those in need that he is in heaven, do not worry!' The spectacle afforded by the distribution of his belongings was most upsetting to her. She could not understand how they could so laugh and talk inside her grandfather's quarters and show no respect when handling things that had belonged to him."[17]

Living with her parents and sister alone once more, far away from an environment where the behavior of guests and servants often disturbed her, Jenny's smile and affability returned. "My dear child changed quickly, she became cheerful and at ease ... ,"[18] writes Madame Bruyère.

Madame wished that her eldest daughter be brought up firmly. She watched closely after her fragile health, and made sure precautions were taken accordingly. However, she did not permit the child to complain about heat, cold, thirst, or fatigue. This helped Jenny to practice and appreciate concrete mortification as a matter of

---

[16] "Enfance et jeunesse, " p. 23.
[17] "Récit de Madame Bruyère," p. 22.
[18] Ibid., p. 24.

course, following the example of Saint Genevieve, whose life story she had recently discovered. Comparing her comfortable situation to the deprivation of the poor was also a stimulus to Jenny's practice of mortification. "When you deprive yourself of something," her mother would say, "there is no great merit in it, because you know that you could choose otherwise. On the other hand, truly destitute people are always that way, in health and in illness, when they want to and when they do not want to."[19]

Sometimes her mother's firmness was rather severe. One day, a dreadful soup—the sight of which turned Jenny's stomach—was served at breakfast and then again at the midday meal. The child refused to touch it at each turn. "I had an empty stomach until three o'clock in the afternoon, which was when I usually had a snack. At snack time the disagreeable soup made its reappearance, but my hunger was so great that I went ahead and swallowed the soup. . . ."[20]

Monsieur Bruyère was both a stern and a very affectionate father. His daughters knew well the depth of his tenderness and loved him very much. On Holy Thursday in 1874, Mother Cécile confided to Dom Guéranger one of her childhood memories: "I told him [Dom Guéranger] that I had been singing the Lamentations of Jeremiah for a very long time, since practically when I first knew how to speak. On the three days when the Lamentations were sung at Church,[21] my father would take me upon his knees and prompt me to sing in a plaintive tone: *Jerusalem, Jerusalem, convertere ad Dominum Deum tuum* (Jerusalem, Jerusalem, return to the Lord your God.) When I had sung the phrase well, my father—for whom this no doubt evoked old memories and holy stirrings of the soul—could not keep the tears from welling up in his eyes."[22]

The letters Jenny wrote her father when on vacation show the same tenderness of affection: "I'd be so happy to see you and hug

---

[19] "Enfance et jeunesse," p. 38.

[20] Ibid., p. 39.

[21] The "Lamentations of Jeremiah" were sung at the office of Matins during Holy Week, originally in the early hours of Thursday, Friday and Saturday, and later were moved to the preceding night, that is, Wednesday, Thursday and Friday. The text consists of the five chapters of the Book of Lamentations.—Trans.

[22] "Souvenirs de 1875 sur dom Guéranger" (Memories of Dom Guéranger, 1875), pp. 103–104.

you; it seems such a long time since I last saw you. I hope you are not tiring yourself too much. I am enjoying myself here with my cousin and my sister. I have not been sweet all the time, but I hope that by the time you come, Mama will be happy with me. Farewell my dear father, I kiss you with all my heart, as well as granddaddy."[23]

"My dear little father. I am having great fun swimming with Julie; I love being at the beach, and when the tide is down we go fishing for mussels; the other day with Mama we fished a big dishful of mussels for dinner and also found other shellfish; I will be very happy to see you here; we will all go together to the cliffs. Lise is always kind, the only thing is that she hit her nose and now it's bruised. We get along very well with Julie and we make an effort to be good. Good-bye, my dear little father, I hug you tightly with all my heart, how I love you."[24]

At age seven, Jenny prepared herself for her first confession (end of 1852 or beginning of 1853). She went to catechism lessons at La Madeleine parish. She was terrified at the idea of going to confession, and made a mountain out of the whole thing. But in due course she overcame her apprehension, and after her confession, felt a great joy and profound peace. It seems that the custom then for children of that age consisted only of an avowal of sins, followed by a simple blessing from the priest.

Some time afterwards, perhaps toward the end of 1853 when she had turned eight, Jenny went through a painful period of scruples. One Sunday morning she woke up late and took her time to rise up and dress, so that Madame Bruyère went to early Mass without her; Jenny attended a later Mass. But she had learnt that missing Mass on Sundays was a grave sin, and her laziness had put her in danger of committing that fault. She thought she was lost. She accused herself of her laziness in confession, but the priest took the thing lightly, thinking it best to put at ease a conscience that was too rigid. This only aggravated the crisis which took on considerable proportions. Jenny thought herself damned. Her mother, who was aware of the

---

[23] Summer 1852. She was six and a half years old.
[24] August 12, 1852.

incident without realizing the extent of the young girl's anxiety, did not succeed in reassuring her.

These scruples lasted for a long time. The child was counting on the occasion of a jubilee celebration at the parish to obtain a true absolution in confession, but she fell ill and had to stay in bed for three months, thus missing the opportunity. The resolution of the crisis only finally came about in Lent of the following year (1855?). Both mother and daughter went to church for confession. The priest at first hesitated, but then gave Jenny her penance and absolution. At long last the girl had the certainty of having been forgiven and went away in peace. But the crisis had been severe and the child was left with the impression that she had not been understood by the priests who had charge of her. Nonetheless, the experience had imprinted in her a horror of sin which helped her fight even more effectively against her bad tendencies.

The young girl did not attend school. Her mother preferred to teach her the first rudiments herself and then guide Jenny in her readings, as her own health permitted. Because she also took care of the education of the younger daughter Lise, Madame Bruyère later entrusted Jenny to a tutor with whom the child got along famously. This was Gabrielle Chamagne, who later entered the Congregation of Mary Reparatrix[25] and was sent to India as a missionary. It was she who completed the primary education given by Madame Bruyère.

---

[25] Founded in 1855 by the Belgian Blessed Emily d'Oultremont, Baroness of Hooghvorst.— Trans.

Chapter 3

Coudreuse in Chantenay

LOCATED IN THAT AREA OF the Haut-Maine called Champagne-Hommet, Coudreuse commands a wide view from its elevated vantage point. The manor overlooks a valley where a small stream, the Deux-Fonts, meanders its way from its source in the village of Chantenay to the Sarthe River, into which it flows some miles to the south, at the town of Avoise.

There are vestiges of a fortress on the property. Its bastions on the southeastern walls, including embrasures pierced with arrow slits, and the sentinel turrets at the corners of its northwestern wall, together indicate that the structure was designed to be a defense fortification that dates most likely to the fifteenth century. The transformation of the property into a country mansion dates from the sixteenth and seventeenth centuries. There are several drawings of the ruins by Monsieur Bruyère, done when he first bought the property, prior to its restoration. These show that the two angled towers and walls that used to enclose the courtyard were demolished in the process. He preserved the chapel, which had been neglected for a long time; its former chaplains are mentioned several times in the registers of Chantenay.

The de Bastard family, originally from the area of Nantes, lived at one time at the Dobert castle in Avoise, and then, in 1478, at La Salle in Chantenay, moving later to Fontenay. In the fifteenth century, the junior members of the family became lords of Roche-Paragère and of Coudreuse. There is an entry in the parish registers of Chantenay dated March 27, 1596—from the period of conflicts that marked the later years of the reign of Henry IV—regarding five men from the area who were "killed in the taking of Coudreuse, on the day of Our Lady."[1] Some time earlier, the manor had been assaulted by a band of Protestants who had imprisoned its lord, Guillaume de Bastard, for ransom.

---

[1] The "day of Our Lady" being March 25, feast of the Annunciation.—Trans.

At the end of the seventeenth century, Coudreuse passed by inheritance to the Hardouin de la Girouardière family. Anne-Renée de la Girouardière was born there on August 25, 1740. She devoted herself to the service of the poor and, in 1784, founded a hospice—the Hospice des Incurables de Baugé—using of her own funds. Later, in 1790, she established a new congregation of religious, the Sisters of the Holy Heart of Mary. Her brother, Armand-René, left the property at Coudreuse upon his marriage in 1768, to take up residence at the Château de la Freslonnière in Souligné-sous-Ballon. The old deserted manor subsequently served as a dwelling for farmers. However, at the time Monsieur Bruyère purchased the property at the suggestion of his brother-in-law, it had lain completely abandoned for three-quarters of a century.

In November 1841, Madame Bruyère's eldest brother, Félix Huvé (1816–1887), established residence at Sablé. Though at first he had studied architecture with his father, the latter arranged for him to take up the management of mines so as "to remove him from the capital, where his penchant for prodigality and his easily swayable character made him more susceptible to trouble than others in Paris would be."[2] The area of Sablé was undergoing a vigorous industrial expansion at this time, which eventually came to an abrupt end, but for the moment seemed very promising, attracting many families to the area. It boasted marble quarries, marble workshops, furnaces, and tile factories. The landscape is still strewn with the ruins of industrial buildings, whose tall brick chimneys once served as reference points for the wayfarer. There was the Maupertuis mine in Sablé, the Sanguinière mine in Juigné, and the Monks' mine in Solesmes! . . .

Félix began his career in the mine business as director of administration for the mines of Sablé. Life in the country settled his ways. He developed an intimate friendship with Dr. Rondelou-Latouche, the monks' physician, who was very close to Dom

---

[2] "Annals: Origins," p. 2. The Annals are the account of the history of the Abbey of Sainte-Cécile. "Origins," which begins with the arrival of the Bruyère family in the Sarthe region, along with "First Year" and "Second Year," which give an account of the foundation of the monastery, were all written by Mother Cécile Bruyère herself and reveal her ease of expression. The other chapters of the Annals were written much later by another nun.—Trans.

Guéranger and had been converted by him. The doctor appreciated the young man and introduced him to his sister Rose. By the end of September 1842, Félix and Rose were married. They had four children: two who died at a very young age; then Jeanne, born in 1851, who would die at the age of twelve; and finally a son, Jules, who came into the world the following year.

The young Monsieur Huvé bought a property in Saint-Brice, the Genouillerie, a beautiful house in classical style located about six miles northwest of Sablé. The Bruyères, who did not own a country house and spent their vacations at Tréport by the sea, occasionally came to visit at Genouillerie. Madame Bruyère's brother had returned to the practice of his faith through contact with his brother-in-law and Dom Guéranger. His daughter Jeanne was baptized by the abbot of Solesmes.

From director of mines in Sablé, Monsieur Huvé was eventually elected mayor of the town in 1858. However, four years later he resigned from office because of the failure of a bank he had established, which came to ruin thanks to the maneuvers of a swindler. Monsieur Huvé had to sell Genouillerie.

It was thus that Dom Guéranger entered into relations with the Huvé family, and, indirectly, with the Bruyères. He also came into the confidence of Madame Bruyère's father, Jean-Jacques-Marie Huvé, who was not pleased, at first, with the marriage his son had entered into—in a forgotten corner of the world with the sister of a country doctor—not a good match in his eyes. The abbot of Solesmes, after having succeeded with the son, began to work on the conversion of his father.

In the summer of 1853, Félix Huvé learned that the Coudreuse manor was to be sold at auction. He wrote about this to his brother-in-law in Paris, as he nurtured hopes that the family might someday come live close to Sablé. He did not expect much from his letter, having sent the information more in the way of a jest. To his great surprise, however, Léo Bruyère bit the bait. He came to Sablé with the entire family on August 7, and went to visit the property that was to be auctioned seven days later in Le Mans, on August 14. The manor house was in great disrepair; nonetheless, Monsieur Bruyère succumbed to the property's charm.

While the two men were in Le Mans for the auction, Madame Bruyère took little Jenny, aged seven, to First Vespers of the Assumption at the Abbey of Solesmes. The abbey church had not yet been enlarged, so that it still looked as it had since its restoration in 1833. Thus, the monks were in choir at the back of the sanctuary, the abbatial throne was set before the Sepulcher Chapel for the pontifical office, and the faithful sat at the Chapel of Notre-Dame-La-Belle.

This first contact with the monks left a lively impression in the young girl. She could not take her eyes off of the venerable head of the abbot, whose white hair, fused with the clouds of rising incense, seemed to form a luminous halo. The impression of beauty and fervor was intense, and a sense of deep longing welled up in the child.

After the office, Rose Huvé and Madame Bruyère asked to see Father Abbot, who welcomed them in his small parlor. Jenny was struck with a bit of panic at the thought of accompanying her mother and aunt to see the abbot, but unnecessarily so, as in the end she was sent to play with the Landeau children, whose family were good friends of the abbot and of the Huvés. Monsieur Léon Landeau was director of the marble workshops at Sablé and Solesmes. He had been brought back to the faith by Dom Guéranger and a great friendship developed between the two. The abbot of Solesmes when referring to the Landeau home, located in the valley, would jokingly call it the "monastery down below."

That night Monsieur Bruyère did not return from Le Mans until after midnight. The child had been sent to bed, despite her desire to know whether her father had succeeded in buying Coudreuse. The following day, when she learned that indeed Coudreuse was theirs, she wept with deep emotion without knowing the reason why.

But the manor lacked much and needed considerable work before it could be the proper dwelling of a family accustomed to the comforts of the city. Nonetheless, the Bruyères moved in that same summer, under rather primitive conditions. The restoration of the house would not begin until the spring of 1854:

"I am with you in all your labors, with you in all the difficulties that must beset you in this work, and also in your joys when seeing yet a few more stones moved into place each day," Madame Bruyère wrote in a letter to her husband during the restoration. "I understand with my heart how you must find the courage, and I love you all the more for it; all this that you tell me about your problems with lodging there, that is precisely what worried me about doing the work in the middle of summer. I've seen Félix and he told me that you've accomplished a near miracle by being able to gather so many laborers around you. Lise said that everything is topsy-turvy, that you have to go up the staircase on all fours because of all the rubble. And she finds our room to be too small; you know that it is impossible to please everyone."[3]

In 1856, Monsieur Bruyère left his architectural practice to his associate Eugène Chauvet—who was also related to him by marriage to his niece, Jeanne Dausse (daughter of his sister Louise Bruyère)— and retired from his profession. This enabled him to be away from the capital for long stretches of time and to dedicate himself to the restoration of Coudreuse. Unfortunately, he was never interested in restoring the chapel, which he simply turned into a utility shed. Having fallen into ruins, it was demolished in 1946.

Thus it was around the time Jenny turned ten that the family began the custom of passing the long summer and autumn months until after Christmas at the old house. The winter season was left for Paris. This was the usual practice among the gentry of the Second Empire, who would come to the capital at the beginning of winter and, when the social season was over, would repair to their country estates—the "maison des champs"—in April or May.

The Bruyère estate was only relatively close to Solesmes, especially during the middle of the nineteenth century. There were about ten miles from Chantenay to Port-de-Juigné. Then, to arrive at the abbey it was necessary to take a ferry ride across the river Sarthe. The ferryman's old house (recently destroyed) lay below the rock where the old guest house of the monastery sits, named *"La Rose"* because of the color of its plaster. There were no bridges at that point, and in bad weather the rough waters made for a difficult ride. Several times the ferryboat came very close to foundering. There is an account by Dom Dépillier[4] about a very dangerous ferry crossing in

---

[3] Spring 1854.

[4] Dom Pierre Dépillier (1821–1890) was the prior of a failed foundation of the Benedictines of Solesmes, made at his property in Acey, an ancient Cistercian abbey in the Jura region. Dom

which his cool head did marvels to save the monks that were with him! The Bruyères, therefore, were much closer to the abbey when they were staying with the Huvés in Sablé. They would be even closer some years later, when Félicie Bruyère's second brother, Adrien Huvé (1819–1873), upon retirement from a brilliant career in the navy, purchased a property in La Grange facing the monastery just across the river Sarthe. He is the one who built the large bourgeois house that stands there today surrounded by cedars.

It would be well worth including all the letters that Jenny wrote to her father during vacation time when the family was apart. However, we must content ourselves with only a few extracts. On September 6, 1853, she wrote to her father from Tréport: "I am enjoying myself very much. The sea is so beautiful. Today I've already played in the water several times and I enjoy that very much. We went to the pier to watch the arrival of the "Empereur" [a ship], but it never came and we were drenched. . . ."

Letters that date from 1854, when she was eight, are already more significant. For example, on June 5, 1854 she sent him the following words from Roye: "You know me well, and you know that once I start playing it is always difficult for me to stop. That is why I haven't written you before, but surely you realize that I haven't forgotten you; I love you too much for that. I am not as happy with myself as I would like to be, and it hurts me to have to tell you this. I hope that this week all of this will be fixed; I really do wish so. Mama always helps me much when I am a bad girl, and I know that without her I would not know what to do."

This small note was accompanied by an explanatory—and very affectionate—letter from Madame Bruyère to her husband: "The letter from your daughter, my dear love, has cost her much. She was very upset that she could not report to you that she had behaved well. And I did not want her to leave the letter for another day. This was the only punishment that I wanted to give her. As Sunday was a very bad day, I had to do this in order to get her out of the rut. She cried a little from shame, and much at the thought of causing you

---

Guéranger later removed his monks from Acey and parted ways with Dépillier, who eventually was suspended from the priesthood by the Church.—Trans.

displeasure. But I sat close to her and calmed her down ever so gently. I believe I was not mistaken about the outcome of this strategy; yesterday was a good day. Now, dear friend, your letter has done me much good. I have read it over and over again and sweet tears come to my eyes when I think of the treasure of affection that surrounds me: a husband and two children. . . . I will come back home to you this time much better than I have in a long time; the idea of embracing you when I arrive makes me anticipate this return with great delight. I will not miss the woods and fields or the sun, since I cannot enjoy them without you. We have much to look forward to, and if we can refresh ourselves for one month *together* at Coudreuse this year, I think that we will be able to bear the winter in Paris. . . ."[5]

Another letter from Jenny to her father is written at Coudreuse in the fall of the same year, October 8. The child already shows her great compassion for the poor: "We worked together until four o'clock, then I went to do some knitting at the home of Madame Dugast [the wife of the caretaker at Coudreuse]. At a certain point we saw Monsieur Dugast coming in with three small children, and Madame Dugast said to them: You must be cold! Warm yourselves up here. They were freezing because they did not have a sweater and their clothes were all torn. When I saw them, I went to tell Mama, who gave them each a piece of bread. Their father, who was ill, was with them and they had a small cart pulled by a donkey. And Madame Dugast gave them some of her soup, which warmed them up. Then Mama and I went to see if we could find a few old things to give them, and it happened that we had brought some knit dress parts that weren't assembled yet, so we stitched them together as best we could and after dinner we went back to dress them with these clothes. The older girl, who was ten, did not want to take off her dress because she did not have any slip on, so Madame Dugast gave her one that belonged to her daughter. After the girl had put this on, Mama slipped the knit dress on her and did the same for the two smaller children, except that they had undershirts that only reached to their tummies. Afterwards, they were sent to the barn to rest on the hay, and I am told that they slept very well. Mama made an

---

[5] Letter dated June 5, 1854.

undershirt for the littlest one and when he put it on he was very happy indeed. And after they had eaten, they hitched up the donkey. Mama told Madame Dugast to place two loaves of bread in their cart. They were very happy and they left."

When Jenny turned eleven, she began to attend catechism classes on a regular basis at the parish of Saint-Eugène in Paris. After each class, the teacher would ask the children to write down whatever they had retained from the lesson and to add a personal resolution and a short prayer to their text. Jenny's notes from 1854 to 1858 have been preserved.

In 1855 the Bruyères had moved yet one more time, establishing their new residence at the rue de Paradis, not far from the Gare de l'Est. Their new parish was Saint Eugène-Sainte Cécile, located at rue Sainte-Cécile. The church, newly built in 1855, was designed by Louis Boileau (1812–1896) in neo-Gothic style using metal frame construction.

First Communion at Saint-Eugène-Sainte-Cécile in 1857 was set to take place on April 30. Though Jenny had not yet reached the required age, the priests of the parish agreed to let her participate because of her precocity and her great desire to receive Holy Communion.

For the occasion, Madame Félix Huvé (Rose Rondelou) asked Dom Guéranger for a gift for her niece. The abbot was in possession of some cloth from Saint Cecilia's tomb, which he had brought back with him from Rome. He had a fragment of it placed inside a reliquary, then sealed the reliquary and prepared the relic's authenticating document. Along with the relic, he sent an image of the Blessed Virgin Mary depicted as a girl, plucking a lily close by Saint Anne, who is seated holding a scroll with some words.

This beautiful gift resonated exactly with Jenny's secret desires. She loved the name "Cécile," the same as her maternal grandmother's. She would have liked to have been called by that name and had already chosen it for her Confirmation, whenever that day should arrive. As to the image, it was something of a response to the foremost desire of her heart. Since reaching the age of reason, Jenny had wished to preserve her virginity and to consecrate it to God some day. The story of little Saint Genevieve of Nanterre, patroness of Paris, had consolidated this aspiration. Upon receiving the gift on April 26, Jenny was utterly astonished. How is it that, without ever having had any particular contact with her, he could have guessed at all this?

However, the long expected First Communion did not take place, after all, in Paris on April 30, the feast of St. Catherine of Siena. Lise had contracted the measles and it seemed to be reaching a dangerous stage. The contagious disease infected Jenny on April 29 and on the thirtieth she lay prostrate in bed with a high fever. It was a tremendous disappointment to her, to the point that her physician feared complications from the emotional blow. Nonetheless, she accepted God's decision in her regard and her mother helped her bear the trial, pointing out to her the benefit of being able to undergo a yet more thorough preparation. "I wasn't a good enough girl, I wasn't prepared enough," Jenny kept dolefully repeating.[6]

By the middle of May, the child was back on her feet. Madame Bruyère was well acquainted with the vicar of the neighboring parish, Saint-Louis d'Antin, and asked him if Jenny could join the group of first communicants there. But he was afraid that the young girl might still pass on the disease, and, besides, he didn't think it necessary to have her make her First Communion at all cost that same year.

Concurrently, the doctor sent Jenny to the country to finish off her convalescence there. When they arrived in Coudreuse they learned that First Communion at the local parish was to occur the very next day. It was impossible to include Jenny: there wasn't enough time. "And the following day I assisted at the First Communion ceremony in Chantenay, all covered in tears."[7]

Aunt Rose Huvé let Dom Guéranger know that the gift had duly reached its recipient, but that First Communion had been delayed. The abbot was aware of the great desire that the child had to receive the Eucharist and was of the opinion that it should not be left for the following year, which was too far away. The ceremony at the parish in Sablé had been scheduled for the end of May. The abbot of Solesmes accepted to prepare little Jenny himself for the great day.

---

[6] "Récit de madame Bruyère," a copy, p. 8 (the original is damaged in two places).
[7] "Enfance et jeunesse," p. 60.

The prospect of receiving First Communion was a great joy to the child; the prospect of finding herself face-to-face and alone with the monk terrified her. She had only seen this great personage from afar and had always shied away from meeting him whenever her mother attempted to introduce her. Here is how she describes her first interview with Dom Guéranger in her memoirs about him written in 1875:

"It was 1857. He had had the kindness of taking me under his charge. Around five in the afternoon of Tuesday, May 19, we returned to Coudreuse by way of Sablé. When our carriage was passing by the Saint-Clément factory, we saw the monks coming out in formation for their walk, with Father Abbot at the center. I was sitting next to my father, who was driving the carriage. When we came close to the monks, my father halted the carriage, got off and exchanged some polite words with the Right Reverend Father, while the monks passed on to await their abbot at a short distance. My father and my mother warmly thanked the Right Reverend, while I looked on with wide gaping eyes. I was very impressed because he seemed to me as luminous here as when at the altar, and I felt an extraordinary pull toward him. I kept as quiet as a tombstone, while rejoicing greatly at what they were saying about me without my yet having been introduced. But, after a few words, the Right Reverend said to my mother: 'Madame, which of the two will be my dear little daughter?' At my mother's reply, our Right Reverend approached the carriage and looked at me with his beautiful eyes, clear and penetrating, saying: 'Isn't it so, my dear child, that we will get along very well?' I let out a solemn 'Yes, Father.' 'At least you are not afraid of me, are you?' he came back, with his good and gracious smile. I replied with a 'No' that undoubtedly was betrayed by my tone of voice. However, I must say that these simple words effectively disbanded the fear that had nearly made me faint two years earlier at his Mass. . . ." This conversation took place at the other side of the river, before the very spot where, nine years later, the Abbey of Sainte-Cécile would rise.[8]

---

[8] "Souvenir sur dom Guéranger, " p. 359.

Fear had given way to trust and an admiring affection, but there was still need for self-abandonment. For a long time, Jenny would not utter a word when she was in the parlor. A clam. Dom Guéranger nicknamed her "my little mute one." In any event, she believed that the abbot read her soul like an open book and had no need of her confidences in order to understand her. It took some time before communication was established between the two, as Dom Guéranger by habit did not compel reticent souls into opening their hearts to him.

Before the great day arrived, she made her general confession and the floodgates of tears burst open, mingling repentance and joy. Her habitual stiffness disappeared. The First Communion ceremony took place at the old church of Notre-Dame du Sablé, the church where the abbot of Solesmes had been baptized, on the main street of the island where the Place Dom Guéranger now lies. It was May 28, 1857.

The day was filled with abundant graces. The child promised complete fidelity to the Lord who had deigned to come to her, having at the same time the presentiment that this gift of self would entail suffering. But in the evening, at Benediction of the Blessed Sacrament, anxiety took hold of her. Would she be unfaithful as so many others? Would Satan triumph over her weakness? The tears flowed again, but no longer for joy. The other communicants kneeling close to her stared in bewilderment. Light returned when a sense of reassurance took hold of her: the Lord is the party most interested in this alliance and never abandons those whom He draws to Himself. Peace once again descended into the child's heart, along with the desire to belong completely to God.

Jenny wanted to make the pilgrimage to the Chapelle-du-Chêne on foot with her mother on the following day. Accordingly, they departed Sablé the next morning at five o'clock in order to attend early Mass at the small seventeenth-century chapel, which still stood in those days.

It was decided that the child would continue communicating with Dom Guéranger and also that during the family's sojourn at Coudreuse she would come each month to make her confession to him. With time, the monthly confession became a semi-monthly confession, with the agreement of Monsieur Bruyère, for this entailed setting aside a whole afternoon for the trip by carriage to and from the monastery: two hours there and two hours back to Coudreuse. It was a veritable expedition. The meetings were short, not long enough to loosen Jenny's lips.

Léo Bruyère was none too displeased that Dom Guéranger was interested in his family. The abbot of Solesmes was an impressive personality, known to have a superior intelligence, and he had the prestige of his rank within the monastery. The proprietor of the Coudreuse manor, a newcomer to the area, did not mind at all receiving some recognition in the person of his wife and his daughter. He himself did not have much sway over Jenny, always so secretive and rather withdrawn.

Dom Guéranger began by providing some structure to the girl's readings, up to then chosen rather haphazardly. He had her give a regular account of her readings, prescribed a daily schedule, gave her counsel, and proposed a rule of life. The latter was given in 1858.

Around this time Madame Bruyère once again took upon herself the education of her daughter, as Gabrielle Chamagne, Jenny's tutor, had left a while before to enter religious life. This did not last long, however, because she also had to take care of Lise. Thus, she secured the services of a niece of Madame de la Corbière, a neighbor from Chantenay, who was as much a friend as a teacher to the child.

"The dear little one" writes Madame Bruyère, "gave herself over to work at her studies with remarkable resoluteness and dedication. She was very attracted to history, she learned English, and her teacher told me that she had never encountered such great ease in a child so young. . . . What made the task of teaching her so pleasant was that she reasoned and deduced things for herself; rote learning would never have succeeded in teaching her anything."[9]

Jenny received the sacrament of Confirmation the following year, on April 15, 1858, at the church in Chantenay. According to the desire which she had nurtured for a very long time, she took the name Cécile. After the ceremony, Bishop Nanquette,[10] who knew the great

---

[9] "Récit de madame Bruyère," p. 42.

[10] Jean-Jacques Nanquette (1807–1861), bishop of Le Mans from 1855 to 1861.—Trans.

devotion that Dom Guéranger had for Saint Cecilia, came upon the abbot of Solesmes and remarked:

"Today I have confirmed a young girl who is yours."

"But, Monseigneur, how do you know that?"

"Oh, it is very simple. There were about three hundred children there, but only one Cécile, and while I was confirming her I thought to myself, this child here is a daughter of the abbot of Solesmes!"[11]

For Dom Guéranger, Jenny's name was now Cécile, and henceforth he would call her by no other name.

---

[11] "Annals: Origins," p. 17. (In several countries of Europe, members of the hierarchy are addressed as "Monsignor," meaning "My Lord." Thus, in France, "Monseigneur" is used in reference to bishops and cardinals. In Britain this usage is still preserved in formal address, "My Lord, the bishop of . . ." —Trans.)

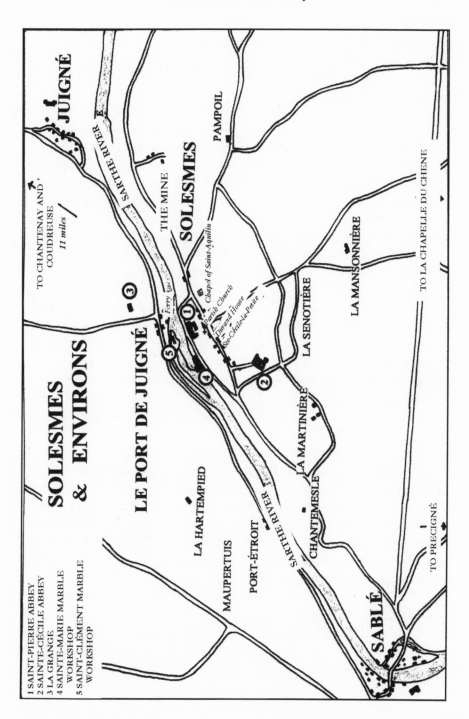

SOLESMES & ENVIRONS

LE PORT DE JUIGNÉ

1 SAINT-PIERRE ABBEY
2 SAINTE-CÉCILE ABBEY
3 LA GRANGE
4 SAINTE-MARIE MARBLE WORKSHOP
5 SAINT-CLÉMENT MARBLE WORKSHOP

JUIGNÉ

SARTHE RIVER

TO CHANTENAY AND COUDREUSE
11 miles

THE MINE

SOLESMES

PAMPOIL

Chapel of Saint-Aquilin

Parish Church
Durand House
Ste-Cécile-la-Petite

LA MANSONNIÈRE

LA SENOTIÈRE

LA MARTINIÈRE

TO LA CHAPELLE DU CHÊNE

LA HARTEMPIED

MAUPERTUIS

PORT-ÉTROIT

SARTHE RIVER

CHANTEMESLE

SABLÉ

TO PRECIGNÉ

Chapter 4

Under the Direction of Dom Guéranger

WHEN STAYING IN PARIS, Madame Bruyère and her daughters used to frequent the parish of Saint-Roch at first, and later, that of Saint-Eugène. During their yearly sojourn in Coudreuse, from Easter until the end of December, their church was Saint-Jean-Baptiste in Chantenay. There is a little over a mile between the manor and the town: half that distance up to the divide where the roads to Chevillé, Poillé-sur-Vègre and Asnières part, and the other half down the small valley and then up the hill upon which the village sits. The church in Fontenay-sur-Vègre is only a little beyond that, through unpaved byways.

The town of Chantenay hangs tightly onto the flanks of the hill. The church, perched at its top, presents an austere exterior with its tall walls and its massive tower capped by a pyramid-like roof that resembles the top of a Louis XIII pavilion more than the belfry of a church. But once inside the building, one is taken by the beauty and quality of the architecture of the choir and the sanctuary, their vaulted ceilings in Angevin style reposing upon striking Romanesque capitals. The nave itself dates from no earlier than the Renaissance period. It had just recently been enlarged by the addition of a second aisle to the south, and the old fir wood wainscotting originally added in 1660 had been replaced. Three matching altars were erected in the eighteenth century, crafted in black marble from Sablé, with white marble inlay used for highlighting and to trace the Maltese cross. To Jenny their design and build were reminiscent of the high altar of the abbatial church of Solesmes where so many times she saw Dom Guéranger officiating with such majesty.

The population of Chantenay at this time—between 1850–1860—was sizeable, having doubled by the annexation of the parish of Villedieu. The latter village still had its own church, a mile and a half to the north of the town on the way to Saint-Christophe-en-Champagne. The parish of Chantenay was among those that had remained faithful[1] and, thus, attendance at Sunday Mass was high. Religious and priestly vocations were able to flourish there more than elsewhere.

Jenny, Lise, and their mother, easily settled into the communal life of the parish. As to Monsieur Bruyère, he set foot into church only very rarely, when some social obligation required it of him. It was easier to forge relationships here in the church square after Sunday Mass than in Paris, where parishioners largely ignored one another, lost in the anonymity of the large city. Jenny accompanied the singing at church from the harmonium. She loved music very much. On Thursdays, she would come from Coudreuse to give lessons to little girls in the town. She visited the sick with her mother. She was loved by the people of Chantenay.

But the Bruyères, nonetheless, were still city people from Paris, a bit lost in the countryside. It was largely out of affection for his wife and children that Monsieur Bruyère had forfeited his profession, in which he was enjoying much success, and had come bury himself in the country, though still keeping an apartment in Paris for the winter months. As for himself, he would much rather have lived in the capital.

The family established itself within the social life of the bourgeoisie of Sablé and the landed gentry of the area. Manors, châteaux, and country houses were not wanting in the environs of Chantenay: Thomassin and Chanteloup in Chantenay, Cheneru and La Baluère in Pirmil, Moulin-Vieux in Asnières, La Rougeollière and Dobert in Avoise, to mention only those that were in close proximity. But Jenny detested worldly life and rarely felt comfortable at social gatherings.

Only very slowly did Dom Guéranger come to know the child. It was not an easy thing to forge a conduit into the heart of her interior fortress, protected as it was by her silence. This, not because of ill will on her part, but because of her long-standing habit of not opening herself up and keeping her own secrets to herself. Since it was difficult to communicate with her in conversation, the abbot of Solesmes encouraged her to write to him instead.

---

[1] During the repression of the Church by the French Revolution. —Trans.

At the time of her first Holy Communion she had started to keep written notes of the more significant experiences in her spiritual life— certain graces of understanding that had marked her, her sorrows at having offended God, her self-reproaches, her resolutions.

Children at the catechism classes Jenny attended were required to put what they had retained of their lessons and their resolutions into writing, and to compose their own prayers. The archives of the Abbey of Saint-Cécile have preserved her catechism notebooks from the years she was at Saint-Eugène (1854–1858). But she also wrote another series of journals, of a more personal nature, entitled "Notebooks of Reflections" (November 1, 1857 to August 18, 1866). Dom Guéranger asked Jenny to describe in writing what transpired within her, so as to help her overcome her silence and difficulty in expressing herself. Whenever the texts were not sufficiently clear or hovered in vagaries, he required her to re-write them. It was in this way that he was able to discover, little by little, the graces with which God had favored the child since her early childhood.

The great desire that the girl had for her father's conversion resurfaces with a remarkable consistency upon the preserved pages of these notebooks. She suffered at seeing him so indifferent to God and prayed ardently that some day he would find the light of faith. "She had only one goal and one desire," writes Madame Bruyère, "the conversion of her father, and she offered everything up for this intention."[2] She would have to pray for a very long time before her prayers would be answered.

At twelve and thirteen, Jenny was no longer the stubborn and independent little girl of her first years. She had gained greater control over herself, and continued her efforts to act with greater docility. But she had not succeeded in becoming more sociable— perhaps never really making the effort, taking too literally the ideal traced by the life of St. Cecilia, her patroness of choice: "Amidst concerts of musical instruments, the virgin Cecilia sang to God alone

---

[2] "Enfance et jeunesse," p. 44.

in her heart, saying: That my heart and my senses remain pure, O my God, that I may not be confounded!"[3]

Marie Eynaud, daughter of Lise and a nun, described Jenny and her sister in this way: "The two children formed a perfect contrast. One was reserved, serious, profound, with an intelligence and maturity well beyond her years. Her cold exterior concealed a highly impressionable nature, an ardent soul, faithful, generous, passionate for all noble causes, and extremely sensitive. The other was lively, gay, witty and mischievous, having a quick repartee. Along with a spirit at the same time frivolous and perspicacious, she carried a heart of gold. There was not a trace of selfishness in her."

But that which her relatives and acquaintances might have taken for unsociability, was in Jenny a need for solitude and silence, a need for the desert. It is no wonder, then, that she so loved Coudreuse. God was calling her to another mode of life, different from that of those near to her. No sooner was she in contact with God and His silence, in contact with souls who also wished to belong to Him, than her personality shone forth. She lost her tautness and that tendency to retire within, of which she could not undo herself completely when in Parisian society. The life to which she aspired was so different!

When Jenny joined a group at social gatherings, the conversation would immediately lose the spontaneity that had animated it a few moments before her approach. In an unpublished biography, Dom Paul Delatte, third abbot of Solesmes, writes about Jenny: "Her rectitude was demanding, her very silence carried a certain air of condemnation, a nuance of offended gravity would cloud her countenance, inhibiting the conversations she joined. People did not feel at ease with her, nor was she at ease in society."[4] This was not quite the ideal defined by St. Francis de Sales in his *Introduction to the Devout Life*.[5]

---

[3] Embellishment of the first antiphon of Lauds for the feast of St. Cecilia: "Cantantibus organis, Cæcilia Domino decantabat dicens: Fiat cor meum immaculatum, ut non confundar." — Trans.

[4] Dom Paul Delatte, "Vie de madame Cécile Bruyère," manuscript, 1915–1916, chap. 1. (Parts of this work are available online at www.domgueranger.net. — Trans.)

[5] St. Francis de Sales (1567–1622), a master of the spiritual life, is known in particular for the emphasis he placed on using one's duties in everyday life as means of attaining sanctity. Born of a noble family in Thorens, Savoy, he rejected what promised to be a brilliant career in

But Jenny was like this only in her external relations, so to speak. Around her mother, Lise, and her intimate friends, she regained her ease and good humor. It must be said that the social milieu frequented by her family in Paris, and with which she had become acquainted as a young child, exasperated her. She had developed an attitude of self-defense, which gave her an air of rigidity. This, in turn, caused some to dislike her, thus provoking further suffering for Jenny.

Nonetheless, we must keep in mind that it is Jenny herself who is the source of most of the accounts of her childhood. The majority of witnesses to her young years have not left any written testimonies. If some of them had done so, it is probable that the image given would be that of a more tranquil and captivating child. Jenny was not without her own charm and did not solely keep others at a distance. She also had a charism capable of attracting others to her and evoking great affection and unconditional fidelity; her heart could easily be conquered, showing what treasures it contained.

Jenny's monthly visits to the abbey gave Dom Guéranger the opportunity to know her better and gradually to topple her defenses. On December 7, 1858, she told the abbot for the first time of her great desire to belong only to God and to serve him alone: "Dom Guéranger having asked her what sentiments God inspired in her on this great solemnity,[6] she replied with a firmness that left no room for doubt: '... that God loves purity and that she would never be married.'"[7]

---

law and public life to become a priest, despite the great opposition of his father. His first priestly work was as a missionary in the region of Chablais, where the population was staunchly Calvinist. With a combination of charity, gentleness (a trait that he had to labor to acquire during his years of formation, being naturally volatile), and brilliance in expounding the truths of Catholicism, he brought thousands back to the Catholic Church, having to escape and elude several attempts against his life occasioned by his great success. In 1602 he was appointed bishop of Geneva in exile, as the city was the center of Calvinism. With St. Jane Frances de Chantal, one of his spiritual daughters, he founded the Order of the Visitation for nuns in 1610. His best known works are the *Introduction to the Devout Life* (1609), written for a lay directee, and *Treatise on the Love of God* (1616), for the nuns of the Visitation. St. Francis de Sales was canonized in 1665 and declared a doctor of the Church in 1877. He was made patron of journalists in 1923.—Trans.

[6] Eve of the feast of the Immaculate Conception.—Trans.

[7] "Annals: Origins," p. 18.

However, these pithy words did not quite constitute a momentous revelation or a recital of her interior life. Dom Guéranger had to question her further. He discovered that Jenny had harbored a desire to consecrate her virginity to God since the awakening of reason. He encouraged her in this resolve and pointed out to her that the times of Saint Genevieve were not something of the past. In our days it was also still possible to give oneself in this way to God. This date— December 7, 1858—was a watershed for the girl, and she long cherished its anniversary: ". . . [this] day when, despite my young age and my excessive timidity, I dared to tell you of the extreme yearning I had had since my earliest years to belong to God alone." She wrote these lines at age seventeen, on October 26, 1862, when she began to read the *Exercises* of St. Gertrude.[8]

Thirteen. St. Agnes's age! The abbot helped her make this desire for total purity of soul and body the principal instrument of her soul in its progress toward God. He also proposed the possibility of a fuller commitment through a vow of chastity that she could take upon reaching her sixteenth birthday. This seemed too long a wait for the young girl, so exactly did it correspond to her aspirations. As for Dom Guéranger, he was convinced of the very particular calling God had for this child and of His designs upon her soul.

Madame Bruyère had taught her daughter that, once an authority had spoken, she was to accept what was said and keep quiet. Jenny's silence, which at times astonished Dom Guéranger—by nature so spontaneous—was in part due to the type of upbringing she had received. This did not help the dialogue needed in spiritual direction. On the other hand, this avoided any hesitation on the part of the child upon an order pronounced by the abbot, or even when he simply expressed his opinion.

At the close of 1858, Jenny assessed the status quo: "During this year that is ending I have made very little progress, my Father, in comparison to the graces received. The only area in which I may have made some progress is in never committing a voluntary fault and falling less often into a bad mood. And still, Father, even this little

---

[8] Letter to Dom Guéranger.

progress I owe to the grace of God and to your good counsels, without which I would have achieved less than nothing."[9]

In Chantenay, the little Parisian had become a country girl. Her good spirits would fade away, however, as soon as there was question of leaving the silence and peace of Coudreuse to once again take the road back to Paris. She viewed the bourgeoisie of the capital through the same lenses as Honoré Daumier.[10] The great city at that time resembled what Louis Veuillot described in his *Odeurs de Paris*.[11] But that is too negative a portrait, one that does not render justice to all that Paris has of the beautiful and good.

On the eve of one of these departures for Paris, Dom Guéranger drew up for Jenny a program designed to guide her behavior: "The most important thing for Cécile is to act so as to never lose her calm, and always preserve peace in her soul. When we allow ourselves to be troubled, we no longer belong to ourselves and we cease to hear the interior voice of God. . . . Many things will shock you during your life. Will it then be necessary for you to lose your peace each time? Most certainly not. Whatever does not take God away from our hearts is not an evil to us; therefore let us remain serene. There is a way of profiting from many things that may be harmful to others and which we cannot avoid ourselves—it is never to internalize them, but to analyze them with the discernment that God has been pleased to give us. By this means, Cécile will acquire experience, her good judgment will be formed and broadened, and she will understand more things. She will better comprehend how much she owes to the goodness of God and she will be the better for it, as well as more fit to do good by her example and her influence when she no longer is a child."[12]

However, once arrived in Paris there was no longer enough time for God. A short prayer in the morning and another in the evening, Low Mass on Sundays furtively squeezed in at the early morning hours! The tension between the interior need for silence and prayer,

---

[9] Letter to Dom Guéranger, December 31, 1858.
[10] Honoré Daumier (1808–1879), French printmaker, caricaturist, painter, and sculptor, whose works offer commentary on social and political life in nineteenth-century France.—Trans.
[11] Published in 1867, a critical commentary of Parisian secular society.—Trans.
[12] Note from Dom Guéranger to Jenny sent upon one of her departures to Paris.

and the "crushing weight of the nothing" as Joseph de Maistre[13] describes it, was often too great and stretched her patience to the limit, provoking her to irritation. Against this tendency to become irritated, the abbot of Solesmes alerts her to be on her guard:

"You should be neither sullen nor mute, but possess your own soul and let it be possessed by Him who deigns to live within it. Be sweet and serene in all circumstances. . . . My child, reflect often on the inequality of distribution of the gifts of grace. God does not refuse anyone the graces they need, but there are chosen souls. What have you done to be one of these, my poor little naughty girl? Nothing. And still Our Lord bestows so much upon you. Be aware of this, and take refuge in the shelter of humility. Be humble and humiliate yourself. Otherwise, you could very well be capable of turning those very gifts that God has granted you against Him. Beseech Him unceasingly to continue sustaining you in your weakness. Be good and indulgent towards those who have received less than you and who, perhaps, would profit more than you if they felt what you have been given to feel."[14]

Dom Guéranger had no difficulty recognizing the special dispensations of God upon this soul that had been entrusted to him. He made no mystery of it and did not see any danger in letting her know about it. However, this was only in order to impress upon Jenny the total gratuity of these gifts and to put her on her guard against a tendency of her nature—heightened by awareness of her own superiority over those about her—the tendency to pride.

During these years, Jenny was always ready for an argument and she would continue so for some time. In many cases, one would have found fault with her. She reacted each time someone in her presence indulged in facetious remarks about the Jesuits, the clergy in general, and the Church, or when the conversation turned dubious. The "esprit gaulois" is not a thing confined to the present. At that time

---

[13] Joseph-Marie, Comte de Maistre (1753 – 1821), of French extraction, was a Savoyard philosopher, writer, lawyer and diplomat serving the kingdom of Piedmont-Sardinia. Writing at the time of the French Revolution, he was a defender of the monarchy as a divinely instituted system of government, as well as an apologist for papal infallibility. He also wrote works on mysticism and the tenets of the Christian faith.—Trans.
[14] Letter dated February 18, 1860.

racy quips were, perhaps, more veiled and light-hearted. But that did not make them any more attractive to Jenny. In Christian families, many a well brought-up young woman knew nothing and suspected nothing up to her wedding day, at times. But at the Bruyères, among their relatives and friends, all sorts of subjects were freely discussed even in the presence of the children. Often things went beyond what Jenny could bear—the measure was full:

"If I were to contract a deadly disease, I would not complain. Not because I am weary of life—that would amount to being ungrateful toward God. But I am surrounded by so many threats to purity; I would much rather die than lose my innocence."[15] The ermine is the symbol of purity that absolutely refuses to let itself be soiled. However, all in all, it is not a fragile animal. It is a carnivore that knows how to defend itself, and lacks neither claws nor teeth.

Jenny had no desire to remain in the world under the circumstances she knew, even if leading a celibate life. No record exists of when her vocation to a life of solitude and silence first emerged, but it was latent. Once Jenny came to know of the existence of organized communities formed to facilitate such a calling, the inclination of her heart bore her in this direction.

The first datable sign of this leaning of hers is a prayer to St. Teresa of Avila[16] penned on October 15, 1859. "Great Saint Teresa, you know how much I venerate you, and perhaps someday you will count me among your daughters; will I perhaps find a place of refuge from this world in one of the holy havens you founded? Since I know nothing, I beg you to take me under your protection and keep me at

---

[15] Delatte, "Vie," chap. 1.

[16] St. Teresa of Jesus (1515–1582), known also as St. Teresa of Avila, great Spanish mystic and reformer of the order of Carmel; she was canonized in 1622 and declared a doctor of the Church in 1970. As a Carmelite nun, she brought about a return to the observance of the original constitutions of the Order of Carmel, restoring greater austerity, including strict enclosure, silence and poverty, all directed toward facilitating a more profoundly contemplative life. Her reform—which became a new order within the Carmelite family, the Discalced Carmelite Order—began with the foundation of the convent of St. Joseph in her native town of Avila in 1563. St. Teresa subsequently established sixteen other monasteries for nuns and two for friars, St. John of the Cross being her first recruit for the reform of the men's branch. Her writings are masterpieces of mysticism and prayer, and had a powerful influence on many, including another doctor of the Church and master of the spiritual life, St. Francis de Sales. Her feast day falls on October 15.—Trans.

all times, for one can never have enough protection when one belongs to the Church Militant, and above all when committed to fighting Satan, the world and oneself." [17]

---

[17] "Cahiers de réflexions," (Notebooks of Reflections), vol. 2.

Chapter 5

Longing for the Monastic Life

"I AM NOW GOING TO MAKE a request which may astonish you, Father, but that does not matter. I have always had a great desire to know Latin so as to be able to understand the prayers of the Church said in this language; and the other day I was thinking that, if you would give your permission, I would work on this during my recreation," wrote Jenny to Dom Guéranger during this period.[1]

Normally, young girls were not taught Latin. It was not until the end of the nineteenth century, when the first state schools were created, that the full classical curriculum was adopted in schools for young girls and that the course of studies at these schools became identical to that used for boys. But there were exceptions, and Dom Guéranger had no objections to giving the consent asked of him. Jenny, perhaps with a calculated diplomacy, had spoken about her desire to "understand the prayers of the Church." An irresistible argument.

But her fifteenth year was a particularly difficult time in her life. Up to this point, Jenny's mother—whom she loved with a kind of fierce exclusivity—had been her harbor and support. The crisis of adolescence, however, would make the relationship more difficult. Until then, Jenny believed she had nearly conquered her pride and checked her great thirst for independence and autonomy. She realized now that the victory which, by dint of dedication and will power, she had gained over herself beginning at the age of reason, was not definitive. Everything was in danger of collapsing again.

Madame Bruyère's authority hovered over everything and anything. With her, the line between good and bad was confused with the distinction between the more perfect and the less perfect. She demanded much, and much became at times too much. Her approach lacked the moderation needed to allow for a harmoniously balanced development. She wanted to make saints out of her daughters, but it

---

[1] Letter dated November 13, 1859.

seems that she did not allow enough liberty to Jenny, who was growing.

Thus, around the age of fourteen or fifteen the authority of her mother started to weigh upon Jenny. She began to regret the isolation and austerity of her education, carried out at home, without allowing her the possibility of breaking away at certain points of the day, as would have been the case had she gone to school. Confronted with this situation, Madame Bruyère, instead of relaxing her control somewhat, pulled the reins even more tightly, mindful of the special vocation she discerned in her daughter. Later, Mother Cécile would admire her mother's firmness and perseverance and appreciate how much her formation had prepared her for the work that would be her lot. But at the time, she highly resented the severity of her mother. And there was another factor that no doubt had bearing. Jenny was not an ordinary young girl, as Dom Guéranger had noticed immediately upon making her acquaintance. She was exceptionally gifted and highly intelligent. Madame Bruyère had a formidable being in her hands and was aware of her daughter's superiority, which compelled her to be overly exacting, whereas in certain instances Jenny's judgment was more astute than her own.

This critical phase of life for most young girls coincided with an interior trial in the case of Jenny. "It seemed to her that the heavens had turned into sand," writes Dom Delatte, "and that the bitter dryness that assailed her was an indication of the degree of indignation and distance that her secret pride provoked in God."[2]

Temptations to discouragement were always looming on the horizon: "Even when desiring the good, we can be incapable of accomplishing it!" continues Dom Delatte's account. "Wouldn't it be better to take things more at ease? Instead of aspiring to the heights of perfection, wouldn't it be simpler to reduce Christian life to that prudent minimum that is acceptable to the world? For life was becoming oppressive. Always to have to bow, always to break oneself, always to submit, without hope of ever being free, without even being able to satisfy a mother's demands—even at the cost of

---

[2] Delatte, "Vie," chap. 1.

much effort and suffering! They ask me for cheerfulness and warmth; how can this be possible?"[3]

The prospect of an entire existence in this mold was not particularly attractive. Was this really the calling for which she had consecrated herself to God? Entering a monastery would require even further sacrifices—a rupture more complete, a renouncement more absolute. This was not a life!

This new crisis lasted one full year. Jenny did her best to continue her efforts, despite all; to submit herself regardless of the repugnance she felt and to accept her mother's imperiousness, which she found too onerous to bear. But her health suffered for it. She had frequent migraines and bouts of neuralgia. Dom Guéranger helped her as best he could, following from afar the difficulties of the girl entering upon her adolescence, without being sure about how much she revealed to him of her plight.

Shortly after the family returned to Paris in February 1860, the abbot wrote Madame Bruyère with some advice: "How much I would like the dear child to profit from her stay in Paris by learning a bit, visiting the monuments that are in such close proximity. She is at an age to make a thousand interesting observations. It is impossible to see everything at one time. But since she returns to Paris every year, it would be enough to let her see at times this, at times that."[4] What he had in mind for Jenny was a discovery of the cultural and spiritual patrimony of Paris, visits to religious and civil landmarks, to museums, and among these, above all, to the Louvre.

1860 was a moment in nineteenth-century history when the Roman Question was passionately being discussed in Parisian salons. Everyone spoke about it. With the defeat of the Austrian army by the troops of Napoleon III, Parma, Modena and Tuscany were annexed to Piedmont. Then there followed the invasion of the States of the Church brought about by the victory at Castelfidardo, close to Ancona. The regions of Romagna, the Marche, and Umbria came under the control of Napoleon III, while the Pope was left with a mere coastal strip of 105 by 30 miles surrounding Rome.

---

[3] Ibid.
[4] Letter dated February 19, 1860.

Napoleon III succeeded in alienating everyone by his political policies. He favored Italian unity and the ambitions of Cavour.[5] However, twelve years earlier France had secured a military presence in Rome in order to protect the Holy See from the revolutionaries of Rome, as well as the revolutionaries of Rome from the Holy See. It would not be possible now to recall the military detachment deployed there and simply abandon to the Italian crown the little that was left of the Papal States.

The majority of French liberal newspapers considered the existence of the patrimony of St. Peter as a remnant of feudal times destined to disappear, without considering the international implications of such a prospect. Monsieur Bruyère was one of the rare men in his circle to uphold the legitimacy of an independent state of the Church—independent in the full sense of the word. Jenny was most proud of her father for this and told Dom Guéranger about it.

The abbot, for his part, saw in this stance of Monsieur Bruyère's a favorable sign for the future of this soul whose conversion had such a prominent place in the prayers and concerns of the young girl. In the same letter he added: "I trust, my dear child, that you are profiting from your Holy Communions to obtain victory over your defects and to acquire vigilance over all the interior and exterior movements of your soul, and that sweet spirit of docility that gives fortitude to the soul and so helps it love Jesus. . . ."[6]

On another occasion, when Jenny was staying in Roye with her aunt Louise Bertin, he told her what strength she is to rely upon, and what lever will more effectively help her to find a solution to the problem of the ambiguities she was forced to live in the world: "Dear child, one single Holy Communion would be more than sufficient to sustain you. Think well on this and have greater diligence in safeguarding the fruits of those Communions that you do make. Our Lord tells us in the Gospel: 'The kingdom of God is within you.' Given that, then why are you afraid of what is outside of you? Keep yourself within, while giving yourself exteriorly to all that is not bad.

---

[5] Camillo Paolo Filippo Giulio Benso, Count of Cavour, of Isolabella and of Leri (1810–1861) was a leading figure in the movement toward Italian unification and Prime Minister of the Kingdom of Piedmont-Sardinia.—Trans.

[6] Letter dated February 28, 1860.

Willingly let yourself be contradicted, and be assured that Jesus Who is within you will reward you. Our nature rebels against the interior life. We would prefer to rest in leisure and hold on to our independence. But Our Lord finds that a soul develops more fully under these constraints, detaching itself from the sweetness of piety. Therefore, we must desire that which He wills, remaining recollected on the inside, and very supple on the outside."[7]

Even when Jenny was at Coudreuse, she could not always count on her relative proximity to Solesmes. Monsieur Bruyère did not consistently appreciate the abbot of Solesmes at all times, and believed that his wife and daughter saw him much too frequently. A bit of religious piety renders women devoted to their duties and faithful to their husbands, but enough is enough. This was Monsieur Bruyère's general attitude and he acted accordingly. He kept it as a principle not to allow too many visits to Solesmes. Thus, great diplomacy was required, since he was the absolute master of the means of transportation when he was at Coudreuse. For a very long time Jenny remembered that afternoon of Pentecost spent in La Grange, when it had been impossible to escape for Vespers. The adolescent girl exerted great self-control on that occasion, even if she did not always succeed in hiding her disappointment when it was too keen. Her efforts were not without cost. On the following day she fell ill.

And even when she did go to Solesmes, her time with Dom Guéranger was very limited. Something might come up that would cut short her visit with the abbot, or the family might arrive too late to see him before the office. Disappointments were frequent, and all that could be done was to accept them with a good disposition.

Two years had passed since Jenny's first meetings with Dom Guéranger and his discovery, on December 7, 1858, of her great desire to consecrate herself to God. On October 12, 1860 she attained her fifteenth year. It was decided that she would begin a secret novitiate, and that after a year, on her sixteenth birthday, the abbot would receive her private vow of chastity, made for the period of one year.

---

[7] Letter dated March 27, 1860.

The plan was to renew the vow and eventually enter Carmel when circumstances would permit.

"I am in such a good disposition, Father, to begin my trial," writes Jenny on October 2, 1860. "Thinking of what will happen on the twelfth of this month so transports me beyond myself, that everything takes an almost humorous aspect. . . . Moreover, Our Lord shows me clearly the difficulties that I will have to overcome and, for me, this is always a good sign. In any case, and whatever may happen, I am in His hands and I will take refuge in His Sacred Heart when difficulties arise. . . . I am firmly convinced that we will be able to come see you on that beautiful day which will usher in a year yet even more beautiful for me. Oh, Father, if you could only know how sweet this prospect is. It moves me to such a degree that when I think of it I can no longer pray, for there are no words that can convey my gratitude, and I find silence more eloquent. At these moments, how all the things of this world seem artificial and indifferent!"

Dom Guéranger composed a "rule" for this novitiate that was to be carried out in the world, unperceived by all who surrounded Jenny, except Madame Bruyère. The rule did not include the recitation of the Divine Office, as it was impossible to fit it into the daily routine of a young girl whose schedule at that time was too dependent on her family's affairs. However, the abbot insisted that all efforts be directed toward those critical aspects he had discerned in Jenny's temperament:

Absolute docility in everything
An effort to be continuously indulgent with others
Habitual readiness to break her will

From these points, one can deduce the character of the adolescent—a strong and often imperious will; a demand for rectitude and perfection in others that kept her from accepting their limitations, their half-heartedness and sluggishness; a thirst for independence.

"The famous day has finished its course," Jenny wrote on October 14, "and it was with delight that I told myself that when it returns next year, it will most likely be associated with the happiest occurrence in my life. Here I am, then, entering upon this important

year, which I had been so impatiently awaiting! I try to observe my
rule as best I can. . . . I will not be able to receive Holy Communion on
the feast of St. Teresa (the fifteenth) which I regret somewhat, as I
have a truly filial devotion to this saint."

Dom Guéranger had given her the autobiography of the saint of
Avila as a reading assignment: "The fruit that you should gain from
this first reading is to understand to what degree Our Lord loves
souls. He desired that all of this be written so that we may learn what
He is for his poor creature. I ask you, my child, did He have any need
of St. Teresa? Undoubtedly no need whatsoever, He Who has all! Still,
see what courteousness, what kindness, what patience! Reflect on
this, Cécile, and apply it to yourself. What fidelity should we not
have in responding to the advances of such a Lord? . . . What would
Teresa be if He hadn't gone after her, brought her back, set her
aright? And what would Cécile be if He did not accomplish
everything in her? I understand that Cécile would be happy to live
entirely for Him. Then, as of today, let her give Him her will; let her
work diligently on this, always vigilant to correct even her desires
and submit them to Our Lord's good pleasure, Who wishes to be the
Master. . . . My child, see how time flies, it already is December! You
find that the months go by slowly. Fill them well and they will pass
quickly enough. Work on your education, develop your intelligence,
become a fine lady who no longer makes orthographical mistakes and
who takes the time to finish her sentences."[8]

Jenny-Cécile would become a great abbess, but she would retain
this penchant for orthographical errors, falling subject to many a
taunt from Dom Guéranger, who himself did not always perceive his
own mistakes.

After Christmas at Coudreuse there followed the worldly season
in Paris, which Jenny detested above all, but toward which her father
tended more and more as she became older. "Courage, my dear
Cécile," wrote Dom Guéranger to her on January 9, 1861. "Continue
the good work of self-reform. Above all, be humble, practice
humility; consistently do the will of others; willingly give of yourself
to others; be amiable with a sweet hint of gravity; be indulgent with

[8] Letter from Dom Guéranger dated December 2, 1860.

all, keeping in mind the different measures of grace in each. In this way you will profit from your sojourn away from Coudreuse. You will come back more supple, more detached from yourself; and Jesus, Who lives in your heart, will feel more comfortable therein. Live with Him, my child. Listen to Him and do not spare yourself. . . . Act so as to arrive at complete dominion over the first movements of your soul."

Madame Bruyère was appointed novice mistress of sorts for this first year of training. The abbot delegated to her a certain measure of his authority and counseled her as appropriate. No doubt, her tendency was to exaggerate on the side of authoritativeness and severity. Indeed, it was necessary to help Jenny triumph over her ardent nature, but always with tact and discernment. Dom Guéranger encouraged her in his letters:

"With regards to the advice you ask about Cécile, I have only one thing to tell you, and that is that I wholeheartedly approve of the system of firmness of which you speak. She needs it, and it is for her good. Thus, do not weaken your stand. In this way you will render her service and will prove your tenderness to her. She knows well how much you love her; but it is high time that she become strong against herself."[9]

He showed himself severe and recommended that his directee be highly demanding of herself, because he perceived that she was called to sanctity. At least she now opened herself more easily to him and communication flowed between them:

"The time is pressing for you to let Our Lord be your Master. He will not be so until your self-will is forever trampled underfoot; not until you are supple, open and amiable, considerate, gentle, attentive to please, in short, not until you come out of this absorption that is more rudeness than it is recollection. Courage, my dear Cécile; your Communions and your spiritual exercises are for this very end. It will be only then that Our Lord will truly reign in you, over the ruins of your difficult nature. I constantly entreat Him for this grace."[10]

---

[9] Letter dated May 11, 1861.
[10] Letter dated May 11, 1861.

Jenny was still far from being a model of sweetness. If God already favored her with graces which Dom Guéranger considered extraordinary, she still had to rid herself of whatever might hamper the Lord's action in her and weaken the influence she would be called to exert. If she was to enter Carmel, she should be prepared for everything.

Chapter 6

The Vow of Chastity

FOUR MONTHS IN PARIS, interrupted by a sojourn in Roye at the Bertins, and then eight months at Coudreuse. It is remarkable that Jenny—born in the capital and brought up in the capital—would so enjoy Chantenay and the small valley of the Deux-Fonts. In those days of the Second Empire, the countryside was not outfitted for ease of travel and communication, and conditions around the manor were still primitive. Once beyond Asnières, there were no longer any signs of the small industrial developments that populated the district of Sablé, lending it a semi-urban air. Chantenay was in the district of Brûlon, the country of the peasantry.

At that time, around 1860, many of the houses in the district were still covered with thatched roofs. Roofing tiles had only just begun to replace thatch, at the prompting of insurance companies that made tile-covered roofs a condition *sine qua non* for coverage. The insurance companies, which were just starting to emerge, effected what the government authorities had not been able to accomplish when seeking to bring about a change that would have diminished the risk of fire. Scattered just about everywhere were the *ballets* or the *lorgeaux*, huts built of heather and brush following a technique of two thousand years. They served as miniature barns or workshops, and some of them as homes for families too poor to afford anything else. Wheat was still threshed with flails, and the land still measured in *hommées* or *journaux*.[1] For the peasant of that land, self-sufficiency remained the ideal—a life in which people purchased as little as possible and provided for themselves in more or less all their needs.

Artists had begun to develop an interest in real life as it was lived by the people of the land, not as they had romantically imagined it in the pastoral artistic tradition of the seventeenth and eighteenth

---

[1] Archaic measures of land. The *journal* (from *jour*, day) was equivalent to the area that a pair of oxen could till in the course of one day. The *hommée* (from *homme*, man) corresponded to the area that one man could farm in one day. Equivalent exact measures varied from province to province.—Trans.

centuries. It is the true peasant that is depicted by Jean-François Millet, Adolphe-Louis Hervier, Théodore Rousseau and Constant Troyon, all active during those years.[2]

Jenny, who in Paris became tense and distant as soon as she approached social company, was relaxed and at ease in this rural setting. The curate of the church in Chantenay had grouped some of the young women of his congregation into a schola that provided the music for May devotions and on feasts of Our Lady. (Sundays and other feast days were out of the question, as the zealous members of the men's choir would never have consented to ceding their place). Jenny was invited to join the schola and was joyfully received by its members. She conceived of forming a small group of young women in her choir that would engage in prayer and good works and submitted the plan to Dom Guéranger, who approved of it forthwith. Made up of some of her friends, peasant girls and daughters of well-to-do families, this small association would later play an important role in Jenny's life. Five years hence, some of its members would become lay sisters[3] of the newly founded monastery of Sainte-Cécile. We will return to this further on.

Even in Coudreuse, where Jenny was more at ease because there were less demands than in Paris, the intransigence of Madame Bruyère still made it difficult for her to be obedient: "When Mama makes a simple observation, a tempest immediately explodes in my heart," Jenny wrote to Dom Guéranger on May 31, 1861, "and it is impossible that it doesn't show. If my mother's rules prescribe that I do one thing, at these moments something in me makes me feel like doing another thing. If she talks to me about whatever it may be, I feel an urge to contradict her, despite myself. . . . My mother has become to me the image of strict severity, so that I fulfill my duties only very grudgingly. This well-merited severity towards me pierces my soul through and through and puts a muzzle on my mouth — I dare not speak anymore once I see Mama."

---

[2] All artists of the Barbizon school (*circa* 1830–1870), who drew inspiration directly from nature, whereby realistic natural and rural scenes were the actual subjects of their paintings rather than mere backdrop for romantic or dramatic themes. — Trans.

[3] Lay sisters are those members of the community dedicated to more manual labor, having less choir duty than the choir sisters. — Trans.

These difficulties, most normal at her age, made her suffer intensely as her will to act correctly remained intact. Unbeknownst to Jenny, she was being trained in patience and understanding, in preparation for that time when she herself would be charged with the role of a mother, as abbess of Sainte-Cécile. Above all, she was afraid that Dom Guéranger would deem her not ready for her vow, planned for October 12: "There is one thought, my Father, that compounds my distress. It is the excessive fear I have right now that the beautiful day I so eagerly await will be postponed until next year. In any event, my Father, my heart is completely torn at seeing myself as I am, and I have no courage to write you any further."[4]

This was not her usual state, however. The prospect of the quickly approaching commitment she would be making in the fall filled her with joy. In her, the thought of God became increasingly habitual. That which has been called the state of continuous prayer was second nature to her, amidst the most diverse occupations of the day.

The abbot encouraged her along. He also reminded her of the importance of interior peace, beyond the impetuous movements of an overly sensitive soul: "Do you not have a center of peace within you? Do not leave it so easily, then, and do not trouble yourself about everything. When your emotions are just and legitimate, always temper them by bringing them into this divine center that will purify them and ensure that they do not affect your health. It will be good neither for your body nor for your soul if you let go too much of the reins bridling your excessive sensitivity. I would be sorry if you were not a sensitive person, but there must be a measure to everything."[5]

The imminence of the great day brought a profound peace to her soul. Jenny felt calm and happy. She could not understand how she could have been assailed that year by so many movements of rebellion in her heart, starting in July and growing more and more intense in the course of the summer. At the beginning of October, Dom Guéranger had her make a retreat in preparation for the approaching event. Her sentiments were fervent. She would have

---

[4] Letter dated May 31, 1861.
[5] Letter dated September 3, 1861.

liked all the past to have been blotted out, to have been different; she would have wanted her selfishness and pride never to have existed.

Dom Guéranger wished to bring Madame Landeau into the secret—the good friend of the Huvés and the Bruyères. She was very close to Madame Bruyère and Jenny, but it pertained to the latter to give her consent. "I thank you for having guessed at one of my secret wishes," the young girl responded, "which I had not presumed to reveal to you thinking that you would know much better than I what you should do. I am very glad that, by sharing in our secret, Madame Landeau will be forced, in a certain way, to pray for me."[6]

On October 11, the Bruyères were in La Grange visiting Monsieur and Madame Adrien Huvé who had just moved to their new home. In the evening, Jenny went for a walk along the paths of the beautiful garden leading down to the stream. Under the stars, wandering below the cedar trees through which she could discern the Abbey of Solesmes, the young girl dreamed of the consecration she would make the very next day, on her sixteenth birthday. God Himself had prepared everything. He had planted in her heart a desire like little Genevieve's, the virgin of Nanterre. He had brought Father Abbot into her life, who had accepted to espouse her to the Lord.

> Saint Germain dit à Geneviève :
> Douce fille, ne me celez vous mie,
> Mais dites-moi si vous voulez
> Être sacrée à Dome Dieu.
> Plait vous il
> A tenir comme sa fille ?
> Celle qui est épousée
> Et jointe à Dome Dieu
> Ne doit avoir nulle accointe au siècle.[7]

The family spent the night at La Grange. Jenny did not sleep much. In the morning, she attended the pontifical Mass at the Abbey

---

[6] Letter dated October 8, 1861.

[7] Mazarine Library, MS 1032. ("Saint Germain said to Geneviève: / Sweet daughter, do not deceive me, / But tell me if you wish / To be consecrated to the Lord God. / Does it please you / To be His daughter? / She who is espoused / And joined to the Lord God / Must have no attachments to the world." The manuscript source is dated 1306.—Trans.)

of Solesmes, celebrated by Dom Guéranger in the chapel of Notre-Dame-la-Belle.

Three years later she committed her sentiments of that day to writing: "Was I still of this world? Was I still aware of what went about me? I do not think so. The Holy Sacrifice followed its course, and the moment for Communion arrived. I received You, my Lord and my Spouse, and I pledged my love and fidelity to You. All was consummated; I felt it in the innermost recesses of my soul. I had fully abandoned myself into Your hands, entirely and loyally, and, in turn, I received You as my only good. We together were but one; I not only knew this, I felt it! Oh, if I could properly tell of the ineffable rapture of my soul at the moment I crossed the threshold of the sacred *thalamus*;[8] if I could speak of the new heart that was given to me, the spousal love that kindled my entire soul. This recital would be for Your glory, my King and my Spouse, but for that I would need the tongue of angels, which I lack. Until that moment I thought I knew You, I thought I loved You. But then I saw that Your incomparable beauty surpasses anything that the imagination can conceive of and aspire to in the created order. I was bewildered in admiration, as I felt blossoming within me that intimate familiarity which exists between the Bridegroom and the Bride. I understood that from then on I had a right over Your Person, at the same time as I had abandoned all my rights to You. In an instant You made me realize that the cross would be my lot, and that You would do me the honor of communicating to me all that You Yourself had embraced. I felt also that You would be my strength, my joy, my center, my life, my all! No trial would ever frighten me again; and I could foresee that I would have many. But I pressed myself tightly and sweetly against You, savoring the thought that nothing in the world could take me from Your arms."[9]

This account was asked of her by Dom Guéranger in 1864, when she was nineteen and spoke to him during her spiritual direction of particular graces received in prayer. He wanted to be able to judge the authenticity of these communications from God so as to better

---

[8] "Bridal chamber," mystical terminology.—Trans.
[9] "Enfance et jeunesse," p. 91.

guide Jenny. He did not want to see her stray from the right path or plunge into delusion, taking her own imagination for divine revelation—thus the origin of the texts that have come down to us. They were written to make herself known and to provide her spiritual director with a means for discernment. The young girl did not compose them for herself in the way of a spiritual journal such as she had done at the time of her First Communion. Dom Guéranger had explicitly required these reports from her.

The vow of chastity Jenny made on October 12, 1861, and accepted by Dom Guéranger for one year's time, was akin to a monastic profession. It has correlations with the ritual consecration of virgins that she would make after her canonical novitiate at Sainte-Cécile. Jenny kept nothing to herself and gave herself entirely to God, but the Lord gave Himself to her at the same time. She saw Him yet more beautiful than she had ever imagined Him. Grace shed light upon the unfathomable depths of uncreated beauty, and experiencing this newfound light, she consigned to the shadows all that she had so far known and loved.

Her relationship with Our Lord was raised to the level of intimacy that is experienced in the married state. However, the goods that the Lord contributed to their common property were above all His suffering for the redemption of the world and His cross. As for Jenny, there no longer was any of the anxiety and fear known in the past, when she first came into contact with Dom Guéranger, or whenever she had a presentiment of trials to come. On this day, she felt secure in God's own strength. At the moment when she came to belong to Him as a spouse, everything became possible and the prospect of any suffering was seen as suffering borne by two, together.

The actual text of her vow has been preserved. The formulation was her own, but the wording was submitted to Dom Guéranger, who, no doubt, perfected it so as to specify with clarity to what it was she was committing and what would be the consequences thereof. The formula was read just before Communion, at the elevation of the Host, as is done by the Jesuits and many other religious orders:

"O Jesus, my Creator and my Savior, Who have deigned to reveal Yourself to my heart and inspired in it the desire to give myself to You, I, Cécile Jenny Bruyère, today, which is the day of my own birth, consecrate myself entirely to Your Divine Majesty, making at this moment, for love of You, a vow of chastity. I renounce any spouse other than You alone so as to fully possess You. It is You, O Jesus, Who have attracted me by Your unspeakable grace. Keep me in Your love and make me faithful forever."[10]

The final clause is discreetly reminiscent of the *Suscipe* pronounced at monastic professions—no doubt a suggestion of Dom Guéranger's. Mother Cécile Bruyère's spirituality will remain marked by this first vow. Its character becomes imprinted upon her, that is, an emphasis on virginity and the quality of spouse; the gift of self made out of love. The relationship of these two elements to the mystery of the Church was not yet apparent to her, but this notion will develop naturally over time, for the Church is Virgin and Spouse. Individual souls can only possess these attributes through the Church, which mediates an intimate participation in these Her unique prerogatives. Later, the rite of consecration of virgins will make these privileges evident, as a public sign that makes of the virgin a visible image of the Church before all the members of the mystical Body.

After Mass, Dom Guéranger received Jenny in his small parlor and gave her a ring which she placed on her finger. It was discreet enough not to be noticed, which seems to indicate that the young girl normally wore rings.

She returned to Coudreuse on that early autumn day and found her small room as before. Its window, opening to the southwest, revealed a vast horizon of meadowland. "And life resumed its ordinary course," writes Dom Delatte, "but henceforth, everything was new. The soul was attached to its center and forever."[11]

The Lord had promised her a portion of His suffering. The first signs of this were not slow in coming. A few days after her consecration, Jenny went to Mass at the church in Chantenay, which was cold and humid that morning. As a consequence, she caught a strong cold with a high fever that kept her in bed at first, and then confined her to her room through the winter. Her health, which already was not good, further weakened with this bout of illness.

---

[10] Original kept in the archives of the Abbey of Sainte-Cécile.
[11] Delatte, "Vie," chap. 1.

Would she ever have enough strength to enter Carmel, where life is so austere? She did wonder about that. For the moment, however, the need to stay inside kept her from Mass and frequent Communion, but it also protected her, during her sojourn in Paris, from the worldly social gatherings that she so wholeheartedly detested.

Following the secret proceedings of the twelfth of October, 1861, Dom Guéranger wrote Jenny: "Listen to the interior word, and keep yourself in true humility and complete detachment from yourself. . . . Need I tell you again how happy I am? How much I ask God for the grace of fidelity for you? You well know all that. Look for my prayer of October 12 in the history of your patron saint; you will find it on page 69. . . . I say it every day; do the same, for you can apply it to yourself as well:

"Domine Jesu Christe, Pastor bone, Seminator casti consilii, suscipe seminum fructus quos in Cæcilia seminasti." [12]

These same lines can be found at the back of the abbatial church of Sainte-Cécile, above the door: "Lord Jesus Christ, Good Shepherd, Sower of the vow of chastity, receive the fruit of the seeds you have sown in Cecilia."

---

[12] Letter dated October 17, 1861. Dom Guéranger alludes here to his book *Sainte-Cécile et la Société Romaine à les deux premiers siècles* (Saint Cecilia and Roman Society in the first two centuries).

Chapter 7

Waiting

IN 1888, THÉRÈSE MARTIN[1] obtained permission to enter Carmel at age fifteen. There had been no opposition to this from her father, but rather, from the ecclesiastical authorities. For Jenny Bruyère, however, things would go differently. Dom Guéranger would have had no hesitation in giving her permission to enter religious life immediately, knowing her mature character and the firmness of her vocation—a vocation awakened at the very dawn of reason. But between Monsieur Martin and Monsieur Bruyère there was a world of difference.

The possibility of his daughter's entering religious life—above all his eldest daughter—was a notion absolutely foreign to the master of Coudreuse. Were someone to broach the subject with him, he would have taken it as an ill-advised jest. His only thought was to marry his

---

[1] Marie Françoise Thérèse Martin (1873–1897), known also as St. Thérèse of Lisieux, was the child of holy parents, Blesseds Louis and Zélie Martin, whose five daughters became nuns: four Discalced Carmelites and one Visitandine. Thérèse lost her mother to cancer at age five, and was brought up by her two elder sisters, Pauline and Marie, who entered the Carmelite monastery at Lisieux. At age fifteen she requested entrance to Carmel, but, while her widower father and the nuns themselves were supportive, she was refused by the religious superior priest because of her young age. Her earnestness and determination eventually led to both the superior's and the bishop's acquiescence and she became a Carmelite with the name in religion of Thérèse of the Child Jesus and the Holy Face. She was imbued by her parents and sisters from her first years with a clear notion of the need for self-abnegation and total abandonment to the will of God for love of Him, and the value of little acts of sacrifice and charity for souls. In her simple and routine life in the monastery, she performed feats of charity, patience, and self-abandonment to a heroic degree throughout her short lifetime, propelled by a boundless love of God and an immense zeal for the salvation of souls, particularly in the missions. Her last year, at age twenty-four, was marked by immense physical and interior suffering. Her autobiography, *Story of a Soul*, written under obedience to her superiors, contains her doctrine of the "Little Way" of simplicity and zeal in little things for the love of God. It is a classic that has touched countless lives throughout the world, as have the many miracles of interior and exterior grace which she has wrought, the "shower of roses" that shortly before her death she had promised to send from heaven. St. Thérèse was canonized in 1925, made co-patroness of missions, with St. Francis Xavier, in 1927 and, with St. Joan of Arc, was declared co-patroness of France in 1944. In 1997 she was proclaimed a doctor of the Church.—Trans.

daughter within her proper milieu and find her a partner to suit himself, over and above suiting her.

The future as it lay before Jenny offered little attraction. She would have to wait five years before reaching the age of legal majority. That was an eternity! Until this remote date should arrive, she would have to hold her ground, discouraging with perseverance any proposals for marriage presented to her, and thus inevitably run into conflict with her father at each turn. The latter's character promised to make for some violent outbursts, causing pain to the entire household as well as to the two protagonists themselves.

Life, therefore, promised to be difficult for the young girl. She knew full well to what she had committed herself on that feast of the dedication of Saint-Pierre de Solesmes in 1861, in pronouncing a vow of virginity during Dom Guéranger's pontifical Mass.

On the other hand, Dom Guéranger knew the highly exacting character of Jenny. He had doubts about whether she would not be disappointed upon entering a monastery and discovering the concrete reality of community life. Given her character, would she be able to accommodate the imperfections of her sisters? Moreover, the superficial rigidity with which religious community rules were observed—at times too detailed—did not at all please the abbot of Solesmes. "I certainly would not want to steer you away from the fullness of the evangelical counsels, my child. But given your upbringing, perhaps you would develop less in the cloister, given the narrowness that reigns nearly everywhere, than in the situation in which you find yourself now."[2]

Whenever she spoke to him of her desire for the life of Carmel, he became pensive. Dom Guéranger rather had in mind for her a form of consecrated life in the world. However, he realized it was not his own ideas that mattered, but the inner urgings of her soul, the vocation that God Himself had inspired in her. Jenny recoiled at the idea of a life in the world, pulled between two poles—she would be forever constrained into a form of compromise so as not to seem uncivilized to others, while at the same time seeking to maintain the integrity of

---

[2] "Annals: Origins," p. 19.

her interior life and a spirit of prayer. She did not see how she could ever achieve this; it was just too much to ask of her.

Jenny spoke of Carmel because she was not aware of any other possibility. She would occasionally visit a Carmelite friend in Paris, at the rue de Messine close to Parc Monceau. Thus, she gradually became familiarized with monastic life and spirituality. But in the secret recesses of her heart, she dreamed of something similar to Solesmes, a religious life that would resemble that of Dom Guéranger and his monks. She spoke to no one of this, not even her mother, because she thought that Benedictine nuns were something of the past, and that the French Revolution had completely eradicated them, just as it had the monks. She was not even aware of the existence of the monastery of Benedictine nuns of The Temple, in Paris, located at the rue Monsieur since the Revolution of 1848.

In any event, there was no pressing need to make a choice about the course of her life. Her twenty-first birthday, at which point she would reach legal majority, was still far away, and it would not be possible to do anything before then. She would have to continue living as Monsieur Bruyère desired. On this point, Dom Guéranger thought it apropos to emphasize:

"As to your wardrobe, you must resign yourself to following the fashions in Paris, while distancing yourself ever more, in your innermost heart, from all the worldliness it implies. Our Lord will recognize you despite your garb and will not be confused. But this only provided that, following the example of your dear patroness, you keep watch over yourself, interiorly rejecting the external circumstances to which you must submit yourself because of your position. Let your mother have her way and do not cry anymore."[3]

Indeed, the Bruyère family frequented a vast social circle. Jenny's paternal uncle, Jacques Mallet—general inspector of bridges and roadways and soon-to-be senator (1866)—had close ties to the court of Napoleon III. The occasions to go out were frequent, invitations abounded and it was not always possible to avoid them.

Dom Guéranger's plea did not succeed in making a cheery girl out of Jenny: "You have understood perfectly, my dear child, where this

---

[3] Letter dated February 28, 1860.

icy reserve comes from. It is a vestige of the hardness of pride that has reigned in you for such a long time, and of which I have rarely seen you rid yourself. It is imperative that it collapse in ruins, and that you come to realize that graciousness is a form of humility. It is also a form of charity, and frankly, isn't it a pity that worldly people should have reason to say that pious souls are selfish and indifferent toward their neighbors? Saint Catherine of Siena and Saint Teresa were very warm and welcoming. You must give of yourself. Remain in the center of your heart, keeping company with Our Lord as Saint Mary Magdalen did, while at the same time coming out of yourself for the good and pleasure of others."[4]

Jenny tried her best, but did not do well. She regretted not being able to mold herself according to Dom Guéranger's counsels; she thought his severity was well justified, but she could not bring herself to obey him as she would have liked to. Something in her put up obstacles to this. In lamenting this "hardness of pride" in the young girl, perhaps the abbot did not sufficiently take into account her natural shyness and the part it might have played in her behavior. Later, Mother Cécile would recognize having been excessively "concentrated" and "reserved" during her youth. She had great difficulty in changing this natural disposition and, compounded with this personality trait, there was an instinctive reticence provoked by an environment apt to offend her modesty. Marie Guyart,[5] who enjoyed exceptional gifts of communication and sociability, nonetheless writes in her "Spiritual Relation" of 1633: "I suffered more than ever in the world when I heard words that offended God, especially words contrary to purity. It was a true interior martyrdom, making me tremble when I was in places or situations that I could not avoid. And, yet, the more I heard this type of conversation, the more my heart attached itself to God and protested before Him."[6] Jenny reacted in the same way.

"With regards to what goes on exteriorly, Father," writes Jenny, "I am making incredible efforts to be charming, which is not to say that

---

[4] Letter dated August 19, 1862.

[5] Marie Guyart (1599–1672), was an Ursuline nun from Tours sent to Quebec in 1639, better known as Marie de l'Incarnation.—Trans.

[6] "Spiritual Relation" of 1633, no. 54.

I actually succeed in it. I deck myself superbly; I dress my hair; I talk of dresses and chiffon as if I understood something about the subject; I play the piano to entertain our world; I sing with my best voice. If need be, I confect bonbons for the more epicure guests. Papa is elated and showers a thousand caresses upon me. He accepts everything I want, would like me to take all manner of precautions against my heart troubles, and, despite himself, sees me leave for Mass without uttering a single word because I've told him that Mass is good for me."[7] She also mentions her exploits as a master chef. One of her nuns later would write: "We know that our Mother Cécile had remarkable culinary talents, which her father's demands had contributed in developing; so much so that at one point she had every expectation that Dom Guéranger would appoint her the Sister Cook of the new foundation."[8]

Jenny likewise had a very beautiful voice that charmed her audience. Another nun recalls in her memoirs the impression Mother Cécile's voice made upon her when she first entered the monastery: "Our prioress herself took the part of first chantress and gave her daughters such great impetus in their singing; I was profoundly struck. ... The short responsory [of Ascension] as sung by her is unforgettable to anyone who has ever heard it. After forty years it still echoes within my heart."[9] However, for the moment this voice still echoed in the salons of Paris, so as to please Jenny's father.

At the beginning of 1862, Dom Guéranger took upon himself to translate the *Exercises* of Saint Gertrude. Foremost in his mind, when he engaged in this project, were Jenny and the use she would make of the saint's writings. He didn't realize that in this way he might be steering her toward the Benedictine life. "I work on it a little each day, and I hope that I will finish it in three months. Ask Our Lord to help me in this small labor of mine that is very dear to me and to which I give precedence over many other tasks. It makes up the best moments of my day."[10]

---

[7] Letter to Dom Guéranger dated July 22, 1862.
[8] Letter from Mother Eulalie Ripert, January 18, 1885.
[9] Memoirs of Mother Agathe de la Fourgère, p. 4.
[10] Letter dated January 10, 1862.

That first year following Jenny's consecration through her private vow was a time of growth in prayer. Her prayer life became simplified to the extreme and was marked more and more by graces of a mystical character: "For the moment, I am not able to apply my soul to any particular prayer subject," she wrote on August 17, 1862, "because as soon as I begin to pray, my heart turns to Our Lord with such an ardent love that any other thought is impossible to me, except thoughts that are directly related to this love, such as zeal for the salvation of souls. Even then, I am no longer mistress of myself, and it seems that I would babble a thousand words without coherence."

All contemplative souls who have written of their relationship with God, have gone through this stage in their spiritual life. There was nothing in what Jenny said that could cause any concern to Dom Guéranger. However, in order to better understand and guide her, he asked Jenny to describe her experiences in writing from this point on. These revelations of her conscience were strictly confidential. The young woman translated into human terms, to the best of her ability, what she perceived interiorly in particular circumstances, the illuminations God might have granted her. These accounts were intended exclusively for the abbot. She continued this after the death of Dom Guéranger, at first directing her accounts to his successor, Dom Couturier, and then to Dom Logerot[11] who became her confessor. Dom Paul Delatte and Father Louis-Étienne Rabussier, a Jesuit friend, eventually had her cease this practice as it was not without its risks. It was susceptible of being an occasion for indiscretion and placing too much weight on self-introspection. God bestows graces on souls in order to unite them more closely to Himself, not so that they may draw an inventory of their gifts.

October 12, 1862 would mark the first anniversary of her gift of self to God. One month before, on September 13, Dom Guéranger made an appraisal of this twelve-month cycle that was about to end. "What a year! It had its trials affecting your health, but who could

---

[11] Dom Athanase Logerot (1840–1908), monk of Solesmes, was secretary to Dom Guéranger and then master of novices. After the death of Dom Guéranger, he became Mother Cécile's confessor until November 1890, when he was sent to the monastery of Saint-Maur de Glanfeuil. Later he became prior at the monastery of Sainte-Anne de Kergonan, founded in Brittany in 1897.

complain about that or be surprised? The accidents of our life belong to Him who has become the Master of that same life. It is up to Him to dispose of them at His good pleasure. All is good that comes from Him, especially when we know that He reserves His greatest tenderness for those who suffer. Tomorrow will be the feast of the Exaltation of the Holy Cross. Ask the Master that you may love His cross ever more, and, at the same time, that He may deign to preserve your strength so that you can glorify Him in the cross, courageously and perseveringly. Recommend to Him this new year that will soon begin. Through His grace, it must be and it will be fuller, more devout, more immersed in humility and love than the year that has gone by."

As the renewal of her vow of chastity on October 12, 1862 drew near, Jenny had strong hopes that the abbot would agree to transform that vow which had initially been for a year into a commitment for life. In her heart, her vow was already for life, but Dom Guéranger had only accepted it for a limited period of time. "I do not hide from you, Father, that it is with great joy that I see one year already gone by, for I so long for the eternal bonds. I have a hidden anxiety, though, that wells up spontaneously within me. It drives me, with incredible ardor, to wish to make my vow perpetual. Upon reflection, this desire seems absurd, since, after all, in my heart I consider my vow to be perpetual already. But I am unable to quiet myself down. . . . I think about this constantly and despite myself."[12]

In fact, Dom Guéranger was only waiting for this request to be made of him in order to grant it: "I grant you what you desire. I grant it not by way of giving in to you, but rather, so as to obey something greater than you or I. Now it is up to you to do the rest, aiming always at the best. I was almost decided about it myself, but it was best that you request it of me, and request it in total submission."[13]

The words employed by the abbot of Solesmes are very strong. He had nurtured this decision; it was the fruit of prayer and a lengthy process of discernment. Jenny's desire was the expression of an

[12] Letter to Dom Guéranger dated October 8, 1862.
[13] Letter dated October 9, 1862.

obvious vocation, and to refuse to grant her request would be to oppose the actions of the Holy Spirit.

The promise was thus renewed on the feast of the dedication of the Abbey of Saint-Pierre in Solesmes,[14] in the same way that it was done the previous year. However, this time the commitment was permanent. A few days later, on October 18, Dom Guéranger wrote to Jenny: "Set forth with confidence upon this path, but with severity toward yourself. Converse in a way that all your words may be offered to Our Lord, even when you do not speak of things that concern Him, and thus be cheerful and do all you can to be gracious toward everyone. . . . Use your tongue, as well as all of your person, for the glory and love of Our Lord, with both that sweet liberty and that prudent reserve which are perfectly reconcilable when we keep our eyes and heart fixed upon Him Who sees you as His own good and Whom you look upon as your all."

The translation of the *Exercises* of Saint Gertrude would soon be ready. He makes mention of this when exhorting Jenny to deepen her faith in the power of divine love, which is the source of all inner peace: "I trust Him Who, since your earliest childhood, attracted you to Himself. If I tell you all these things it is because you are but a poor little creature who can stand only for as long as God sustains you. He will not abandon you first, you can be sure of that. As for you, you enjoy the word 'forever' too much to turn your head away. The proofs of your little book are on my desk. I hope to send it to you on the seventh to arrive on the twelfth [of December]."[15]

In fact, the abbot had already taken the proofs of the first pages to Jenny. In her memoirs of 1875 about Dom Guéranger, Mother Cécile relates that "in 1862, October 23, the Right Reverend came to Coudreuse and brought me the first pages of the translation of the *Exercises of Saint Gertrude*, which he used to call 'my little book.' I asked him if he had deliberately chosen this date, but he replied:

'Why, my daughter?'

---

[14] October 12, 1862, also the birthday of Jenny.—Trans.
[15] Letter dated November 28, 1862.

'It is because today is the anniversary of my baptism, Father, and you have brought me the *Exercises* which are precisely for the renewal of this great favor.'

'Oh! See, my child, it is always like that! Without my knowing how, Our Lord surrounds me with these most charming coincidences.'"[16]

But seventeen was already the marriageable age for young women of good families, and not a little did Monsieur Bruyère apply himself to securing a groom. The candidates streamed one after the other into his home, where they were guaranteed a warm reception provided they had the good fortune of possessing the qualities desired in an ideal son-in-law. Monsieur Bruyère gave little thought to Jenny's projects, of which he was unaware, or to her reserve, which he took for her natural shyness and the unsociability which had been hers since early childhood.

---

[16] "Souvenirs sur dom Guéranger,"p. 58.

Chapter 8

A Second Monastery in Solesmes?

In 1853 THE ABBEY OF SOLESMES founded the monastery of Saint-Martin de Ligugé, whose ranks Dom Guéranger continued to fill in the ensuing years with monks from Solesmes. However, these transfers still were not enough to provide sufficient space for the community in Solesmes. Using the meager resources at his disposal, Dom Guéranger had to enlarge the monastery in 1858.

The church, as well, needed to be expanded. In 1833, the architects charged with its restoration had deemed it vastly spacious for such a small number of monks. By now, it had become too small for the celebration of solemn liturgies. The community had to resort to having spare chairs by the choir stalls, moved about as needed. Always short of the means to feed his own monks, Dom Guéranger could not dispose of any funds to enlarge the church. Fortunately, however, the money was spontaneously offered to him by one of his companions from the days of his vicariate at the parish of the Missions Étrangères in Paris (1829–1830) who had been living at the monastery as a lay affiliate for three years. Father Ausoure was older than the abbot and had retired at the age of sixty after serving as curate of the wealthy parish of Saint-Philippe-du-Roule. He had forty thousand francs at his disposal, which he offered to Solesmes. Other monetary gifts began to arrive at Solesmes as well; notable among these was a donation from the "Holy Man of Tours," Léon Papin-Dupont,[1] accompanied by the words "I've heard that you have

---

[1] Venerable Léon Papin-Dupont (1797–1876) is known for promoting the devotion to the Holy Face of Jesus, first revealed in 1844 to Sr. Marie de Saint-Pierre, nun in the Carmel of Tours, and made universal for the Church by Pope Leo XIII in 1885. In his private living-room turned chapel, he had an oil lamp perpetually burning before an image of the Holy Face, a replica of Veronica's veil. The oil from this lamp had miraculous healing properties, which led Pope Pius IX to comment that Léon Dupont was perhaps the greatest miracle-worker in Church history. He is also responsible for beginning and promoting the practice of nightly adoration of the Blessed Sacrament in France, in tandem with Fr. Augustine of the Most Blessed Sacrament, Carmelite and convert from Judaism, formerly Hermann Cohen, prodigy pianist and protégé of Franz Liszt.—Trans.

undertaken the considerable project of expanding the holy refuge that is Solesmes, and in gratitude, it is my duty to contribute to the costs."[2]

At a chapter meeting, the decision was made to construct a new choir by lengthening the church, nearly doubling the size of the original. The choice of architect for the construction project, Monsieur David from Le Mans, was most fortuitous. His work in Solesmes is considered one of the architectural masterpieces of the middle of the nineteenth century. Basing his plans on the structure and design of the choir of the ancient Abbey of Saint-Serge in Angers,[3] he translated the general lines of his medieval model into the architectural language of the late fifteenth century, since the new choir was to be annexed to a structure that had been almost completely remodeled in the fifteenth and sixteenth centuries.[4]

Dom Guéranger took advantage of the construction work already underway to have some additional modifications done to the church. He had the arches along the nave opened and side chapels built for the altars upon which the priest monks individually celebrated their early morning Masses. The ancient chapel of Saint Martin was remodeled into a large sacristy, located at the angle formed by the old sanctuary and the southern arm of the transept. The small church that Jenny had known was transformed into a large church that has not been substantially modified since.

Ground was broken on Holy Saturday, April 4, 1863, the fifty-eighth birthday of Dom Guéranger. Ten days later, the cornerstone of the building extension was blessed and laid. The abbot himself supervised the construction project in the measure that his other occupations allowed. And while work progressed at Saint-Pierre, the friends of Solesmes were preparing a new foundation of monks in Marseilles.

Since the entrance into the monastery of Théophile Bérengier, a young postulant from Provence, Dom Guéranger had been in contact

---

[2] Letter dated December 20, 1863.

[3] Built in the eleventh century.—Trans.

[4] Monastic life was established in Solesmes in 1010 by a charter of Geoffroy de Sablé. The abbey church of Solesmes dates from the eleventh century and was rebuilt in the fifteenth century with only portions of the original church walls left intact.—Trans.

with his eldest sister, Madame Durand, wife of a merchant of the port of Marseilles. They came from a very large family that included two priests, three Visitandines, and two architects. Madame Durand had entrusted the care of her soul to the abbot, and he in turn had found in her a trusted confidant. She spent her summers in Solesmes, at a house facing the entrance of the abbey that she had purchased in 1853 from Monsieur Anjubault, an old officer of the imperial army. The Bérengier family was among those who ardently desired to have a foundation of Solesmes in the region of Provence.

In a letter to Madame Durand, Dom Guéranger spoke of the two projects—the foundation in Marseilles for the monks and the construction of the choir at Saint-Pierre: "You will remember that, in our conversations during your last stay in Solesmes, you found me more disposed toward making a foundation in Provence, and that I listened to your thoughts on the project. . . . Théophile must have told you that I am having a choir built in our church. A rather large sum was given for the work, which allowed us to accomplish the essential; the decoration, still missing, will be taken care of over time. But in the meantime, supervising this construction already is an overload for me."[5] A third project was about to arise—the foundation of Sainte-Cécile, which would find an echo among the friends of Madame Durand and the Bérengier family.

Might the *Exercises* of Saint Gertrude have served as catalyst for Jenny Bruyère's dreams of entering religious life? It seems that her reading and study of this book brought to the surface of her soul something that had been dormant therein for a very long time. In any event, she opened herself about it to Dom Guéranger on the day following the feast of Saint Gertrude, November 16, 1862: "Yesterday, when the Church celebrated the office of Saint Gertrude," she wrote, "I was unable to keep the thought away, all day and all night, that I will be part of the same spiritual family as she. And no matter how much I tried, I was unable to free myself from the idea. This astonished me because, despite the little inclination I have to become a Carmelite, it seems to me that this would be more in line with what you have told me—that if I were to enter a convent, it would be a

---

[5] Letter dated June 12, 1863.

Carmel. . . . What also astonishes me about this idea is that there are no Benedictine nuns in France, as far as I know. It is because I want all my thoughts to be submitted to you that I have told you about what might be but a figment of my imagination. What I do know with certainty is that I am ready, as you tell me, to do everything that Our Lord wants of me. . . ."

This premonition was obviously engraved deeply in her soul, as she repeatedly came back to the subject in her correspondence: "How many times I have sighed for a black veil and habit, Father!"[6] Madame Bruyère, who knew her daughter better than anyone else, also believed that Jenny would someday become a nun under the direction of Dom Guéranger. She spoke about this to him more than once. "I admire your castle in the air," he replied one day. "Let us wait and see. In any event, there is no harm in it. The good God will do whatever He wishes, and you have more time ahead of you than I do."[7]

One day, when she was speaking with him about the future of her daughter, Madame Bruyère asked Dom Guéranger if he would not consider founding a monastery of nuns close to Saint-Pierre. He answered that "he had never considered such a project, knowing by experience the amount of labor, cares, pain and suffering a foundation involves. His entire life had been spent in establishing just one monastery, and he did not think he had enough time, energy and years ahead of him to launch upon another such work."[8]

He knew what he was talking about. First there was Solesmes, the hopes and disappointments of the beginnings, the pontifical approval, the conflict with Bishop Bouvier.[9] Then there were the two attempts, at Saint-Germain in Paris and at Bièvres, that came to a catastrophic end. There was the tribulation caused by the Benedictine nuns of Andancette,[10] and there was the adventure of Acey and Dom

---

[6] Letter to Dom Guéranger dated December 25, 1862.

[7] Letter dated November 28, 1862.

[8] "Annals: Origins," p. 22.

[9] Jean-Baptiste Bouvier (1783–1854) Bishop of Le Mans from 1834 to 1854. He had objections to the pontifical status of the Abbey of Saint-Pierre de Solesmes.—Trans.

[10] A legal process over borrowed money, which Dom Guéranger lost.—Trans.

Dépillier.[11] The only foundation that was successful, thanks to Bishop Louis-Édouard Pie,[12] was Ligugé. Given his experience, the abbot of Solesmes could not find the courage to launch upon a new adventure at his own initiative.

Mother Cécile herself related a conversation she had at that time with Dom Guéranger, who had told her about Madame Bruyère's request. It is not possible to exactly reproduce the dialogue, but the gist of the exchange went like this:

"I do not know why I tell you this, my dear daughter, you who are a convinced Carmelite."

"A Carmelite? Yes, my Father, to be a Carmelite rather than remain in the world. But that is not by preference; if you establish a monastery of Benedictine nuns, I will be one of them because for a long time I've been thinking about the Order of Saint Benedict, but there are no longer any daughters of Saint Benedict in France."

"Why, yes! There are more than forty Benedictine monasteries."

"I didn't know that, Reverend Father, and I was thinking to myself that if this idea of a foundation comes from God, it will move ahead without my being involved in it; otherwise, I will be wasting your time in useless dreams."

"What a singular girl you are! But one thing is certain, and that is that I will not establish a monastery with you all by yourself!"[13]

Jenny was evidently not well informed about the revival of Benedictine life in France among women, starting at the beginning of the century. It had advanced more quickly than the restoration of the monks. It is true that the nuns did not begin at such a low ebb as did the monks. In its first months, the French Revolution was less radical against nuns; all women's communities were able to continue living within the walls of their convents until the abolition of the monarchy

---

[11] The author evokes the more salient difficulties encountered by Dom Guéranger since the re-establishment of Solesmes. (For Dom Dépillier, see chap. 3, p. 28, n. 4.—Trans.)

[12] Louis-Édouard Pie (1815–1880), named bishop of Poitiers in 1849, was elevated to the cardinalate in 1879 in recognition of his untiring defense of the prerogatives of the Holy See over the Church in France, and his contribution to the promulgation of the dogma of papal infallibility in the Vatican Council I; in both cases, the common causes shared by Cardinal Pie and Dom Guéranger made them close collaborators and friends. The ancient abbey of Ligugé lay within his jurisdiction.—Trans.

[13] "Annals: Origins," pp. 22–23.

in August 1792. Only then did the dispersals and direct persecution begin. Many died martyrs, but once the Reign of Terror softened to some degree, scattered Benedictine nuns came together again to observe their communal life as best they could under the circumstances.

The new climate permitted the reconstitution of a number of communities under the tolerance of the imperial government, which, in fact, actually encouraged women's institutes dedicated to education and the care of the sick. Verneuil-sur-Avre was one of the first monasteries to come back to life in 1795; Vergaville (now Eyres-Moncube) restarted in 1802, Sainte-Croix de Poitiers in 1807, Lisieux in 1808. The monasteries belonging to the Congregation of Benedictines of the Blessed Sacrament re-emerged in 1802; others, of the Congregation of Calvary, in 1809. For her part, Mother Thérèse de Bavoz, nun of Saint-Pierre de Lyon, assembled around her a number of former religious in Pradines, thus establishing in 1814 the beginnings of the Congregation of the Holy Heart of Mary, which later made several foundations. Jouarre, re-erected in 1821, became part of this congregation. This was roughly the situation when the musings of Jenny Bruyère led Dom Guéranger to ponder a possible foundation of Benedictine nuns in Solesmes.

He would soon discover that Jenny Bruyère and her mother were not the only ones entertaining such thoughts. In Sablé, there was the young Henriette Bouly, whose father had recently been made director of the mines (1859). She had once come to the abbot to ask for counsel regarding a possible marriage that seemed ill-advised; the engagement was eventually cancelled. She used to frequent the abbey church of Solesmes, and little by little she began to feel attracted to religious life. One day she inquired with the abbot whether there were not in France any contemplative Benedictine nuns leading a life similar to that of the monks of Solesmes.

There were also some candidates in Marseilles, members of the group led by Canon Coulin.[14] The "Great Catechism" was an

---

[14] Canon François-Xavier Coulin (1800–1887) was the founder of the "catechism of perseverance" in Marseilles. (The "catechism of perseverance," taught through conferences by Canon Coulin on dogma and Christian life and morals, was directed in part to men whose education in their Catholic faith had been faulty.—Trans.)

apostolic work begun in 1830 that had formed several generations of solid Christians in Marseilles. It had three hundred members, and counted its own chapel and facilities. The founder was beginning to feel the weight of the years and, under pressure from his directees and other friends, was now willing to entrust his work to Dom Guéranger, on condition that a foundation of Solesmes be made in Marseilles upon approval of the local bishop.

Within the Great Catechism, there was a core group formed by Father Coulin, which he named the "Seminary of the Blessed Sacrament," whose members wished to lead a consecrated life in the world. There were about thirty people in the group, and among the earlier members, nine had already entered religious life as soon as it had been possible for them.

Canon Coulin came to Solesmes in July 1863 to discuss with Dom Guéranger the details of the transfer of his apostolate to the monks and the foundation of a monastery in Marseilles. He was accompanied by three women members of the Catechism, who were captivated by Dom Guéranger and revealed to him their desire for religious life. The abbot then resolved to tell them, under the seal of secrecy, that perhaps someday soon he would decide to found a monastery of nuns in Solesmes.

In fact, he had confided this idea to his prior and confessor, Dom Couturier, so as to secure his opinion about it. Knowing that he was little given to enthusiasm, and overly ponderous and cautious, Dom Guéranger believed his prior would discourage any thoughts about a foundation for women. To his great surprise, Dom Couturier answered him quietly: "Why are you so afraid? Who knows if, instead of another burden, this isn't a consolation that God has in store for your latter years?"[15]

This opinion, so unexpected from a man that was eminently circumspect, brought an end to any hesitation on the part of the abbot. There would be a foundation, therefore, and the cornerstone upon which he knew he would be able to build was Jenny Bruyère, this young woman of seventeen, so ardent and so reserved at the same time, so firm in her desires and so strong, so generous and so

---

[15] "Annals: Origins," p. 23.

mature. Without further delay, he began to prepare her, applying himself to providing her with the particular formation needed for her future responsibilities. Of course, he told Jenny nothing about his plans to make her foundress and first superior of the new monastery.

As the occasions presented themselves, he gave her explanations about monastic observance. It seems that he started along these lines before Henriette Bouly made her vocation known to him (1863) and without waiting for the visit of the three young ladies from Marseilles (July 1863).

In order to prepare Jenny for her role as superior, the abbot insisted on the need for interior mortification and self-vigilance. As to exterior mortification, he had to moderate and temper the excessive ardor of the young woman, who did not have physical strength to spare.

Henriette Bouly had met Jenny. The two young women became friendly and guessed at each other's desires. It was not surprising that this should happen, as they saw each other frequently at the monastic offices in the abbatial church. But if they knew of each other's aspirations for religious life, they had not spoken yet of Benedictine life per se. Dom Guéranger was in no hurry and respected their respective secrets.

Thus, by the end of 1863, Dom Guéranger knew he could count on Jenny Bruyère, Henriette Bouly and Marie de Ruffo-Bonneval from Marseilles. Two other young women from Marseilles were also prospects: Amélie Brusson and Élise Meiffren. Each went along at her own pace, not knowing how committed the others were. In fact, Jenny Bruyère and Henriette Bouly did not know the group from Marseilles, at first. Marie de Ruffo-Bonneval belonged to an old family of Roman stock, related, it was said, to the ancient *gens Cæcilia*. In any case, she was of noble lineage and had inherited from her ancestors a tendency to be authoritarian, which would cause her a few troubles and at times be a burden to the community.

At Coudreuse and in Paris, Jenny continued to carry on with her life, seemingly as before, but marked by greater recollection. "The longer I live," she wrote to Dom Guéranger, "the more I feel that I belong to God, and in this sweet belonging there is an inexpressible calm that makes me understand this salutation of Our Lord: 'Peace be with you.' I no longer experience any disquiet, any eagerness to hasten the good as I did before; likewise, I am neither troubled nor astonished at evil. The only way I can explain this state of my soul is by comparison to a person who loves with great ardor, and cannot be distracted from the object of her affection by anything whatsoever that may happen. All joy outside of the happiness of this love is pale and colorless, and all suffering is too small a thing to lessen the delight of a pure and ardent love. My comparison is imperfect. Though nothing troubles me, I can discern the difficulties and obstacles more clearly than ever, because I no longer am swayed by passion. . . . Also, I have noticed that each time I practice some additional penance, my soul takes flight toward God in a more real and enduring way. And it is with calm and firmness that I now await the approach of the world [another suitor or simply relatives and friends?]. By the grace of God, I will show myself to be the true and faithful spouse of Jesus Christ through charity, sweetness, and humility; after all, it is not forbidden me to make this known through this silent but convincing language."[16]

The greatest concern regarding the future of the foundation was without doubt Jenny's poor health. Her suffering was overwhelming at times. But her soul had found a better balance between the interior life and her relations with others: "Interiorly, I am ever more attentive to Our Lord, while exteriorly, I am ever more for others. It is amazing to see how these two lives are compatible with each other, even though they are so different. In fact, I believe that they perfect one another."[17] This must have been reassuring to Dom Guéranger. If there is one life that is torn between the need for intimacy with God and the care for one's neighbor, it is the life of a religious superior, particularly in a cloistered monastery where an abbess is appointed for life. He experienced this himself.

Jenny continued writing letters to Dom Guéranger each week, as the meetings with him were too few and too short to allow for extended conversations. Confession occurred every two weeks at Saint-Pierre, provided nothing prevented Jenny from going; it was

---

[16] Letter to Dom Guéranger dated August 16, 1863.
[17] Letter to Dom Guéranger dated September 9, 1863.

short, five minutes at most, followed by a ten-minute visit at the parlor. This was the usual routine. The abbot could not give more of his time, having to mind all his other responsibilities and the construction in the church. Besides, the letters were an essential complement to Jenny's spiritual formation, in which she could expand more in detail about the graces God granted her and the events in her life:

"On Sunday, all during Mass and up to noontime, I had to make a great effort to be aware of what I did, what I said, and what I saw. I thought of nothing but Our Lord; it is as if I were the only one on earth, my mind unaware of the existence of other creatures. It even seemed that part of me wanted to detach itself and take flight to heaven. I heard a voice inside of me so sweet as to cause me to die, and yet my ears perceived no sound."[18]

These are clearly revealing words. Dom Guéranger did not base his assessment of Jenny on words alone, but especially on the fruits that these graces produced in her life. He had by now known Jenny for many years and had followed the development of her interior life. He was sure that he had made a good choice and that he would not be disappointed. The foundation he was about to undertake, despite himself, appeared to be an expression of the will of God.

---

[18] Ibid.

Chapter 9

The Pre-Novitiate

"FOR SOME TIME, FATHER, I have been feeling intensely drawn toward perfection. I would like my least actions to bear the stamp of divine love. . . . This desire for perfection fills my every moment; it is the object of all my prayers and all my efforts. I no longer desire to become better, as before, in order to be freed from the illnesses that afflict me or to satisfy a type of pride. I desire it for pure love of God. It is as if I desired it for someone else, such is the indifference I feel as to the means by which I am to attain perfection; I would go through every humiliation, every reproach, almost unconcernedly."[1] Dom Guéranger was happy to find in Jenny such resoluteness toward perfection in the love of God. He discerned in this a confirmation of her calling to a life of total consecration.

Up to this point, what was missing for Jenny was a friend of her own age. In Paris she had no companion; her lessons were all at home under the direction of Alix Royer de la Corbière, whom she loved very much, certainly, but who was her teacher nonetheless. In Solesmes she met Henriette Bouly, and a profound friendship was born: "What a soul and what a heart I have found in Henriette. She is of a candidness and simplicity that are utterly captivating. At least Our Lord will be served more worthily by her than by me; she will cover me with the mantle of her virtue."[2] But Henriette lived in Sablé, not in Chantenay.

Christmas in this year of 1863 brought Jenny a most profound spiritual experience. She related it to Dom Guéranger the following day: "At Midnight Mass, I had a most extraordinary experience. I was at the service and understood all its beauty; however, I was following it in Solesmes as well as in the church where I actually was at the moment. I understood the total union of the liturgy with the birth of Our Lord in Bethlehem, at which I seemed to be present. In short, I

---

[1] Letter to Dom Guéranger dated November 17, 1863.
[2] Ibid.

felt within me the manner in which saints have celebrated the feast in Heaven, praising the Son and the Mother. . . . I understood that all these marvels took place for me alone. . . .

"Toward the reading of the Gospel, I lost all awareness of what went on about me without ever losing sight of the service, and then, I am unable to explain what happened inside of me. What I know is that I desired to possess Our Lord with such ardor that it seemed my life was about to be cut short under such strain. . . ."[3]

This account, sent to Dom Guéranger by a girl who had just recently turned eighteen, bears the signs of authenticity: "Since then, I feel somewhat like an exile on earth, for I have caught a glimpse of my homeland. . . . It saddens me that I am so inadequate in putting my thoughts into words, my good Father, and if I hadn't promised to tell you all that goes on within me, I would not have told you about this, as it is so hard for me to say poorly what I feel so clearly."[4]

The abbot knew that these graces were not equivalent to sanctity; Jenny was far from attaining sanctity: "Inflexible as you are," he would tell her, "what a sad figure of a pious soul you would be if you were not obliged to follow someone else's will, and along paths that you assuredly would not have chosen yourself."[5]

Alix Royer de la Corbière, Jenny's tutor, left the Bruyère home to enter the Ursulines of Château-Gontier, where she made her profession on June 22, 1864, receiving the name Mother Saint Catherine of Siena. The distance separating the two provided the occasion for an intimate correspondence in which Jenny expressed herself more freely than in conversation. When asked about the persistence of her illnesses, which the former teacher had witnessed, the young woman responded:

"This state of affairs persists since the trial year that the Reverend Father had me undergo before the great day; the struggles were such that nature succumbed to them. . . . Usually I have palpitations of the heart, bouts of low fever and violent headaches, but these complaints intensify, without fail, from Wednesday noon until Friday around four o'clock. On this final day, I fall into such a state that it seems I

---

[3] Letter to Dom Guéranger dated December 26, 1863.
[4] Ibid.
[5] Letter dated February 20, 1864.

will be an invalid for the rest of my life. . . . It is remarkable that these symptoms are lessened when I have a number of social obligations, and in this case, they are always imperceptible. If, out of compassion or in the hopes that I will be healed, someone insists that I take some rest, I become worse. And if someone makes me take some medicine, I'm left with horrendous stomach aches. The good souls that are aware of this believe that I am wasting away from practicing mortification; however, it isn't that at all. Father Abbot has such great prudence in this regard that I cannot avoid complaining to him about it sometimes. . . ."[6] The discreet allusion to those particular weekdays indicates that Jenny considered these ailments to be a participation in the Passion of Christ: "The devil has certainly been given permission to torment me for the rest of my life. In fact, a year ago Father Abbot had to admit that the Lord wants me like this. . . ."[7] However, Jenny revealed this state of affairs only to Dom Guéranger and to her correspondent, who knew her from having lived with her family for many years, and who had inquired specifically about the matter. There is no trace of exhibitionism in what Jenny writes.

In Chantenay, Jenny had some good friends among the peasant girls, who had confided to her their desire for religious life. Marie Bignon lived in a small farm next to Coudreuse; her sister had epilepsy. Marie dreamed of entering the Sisters of Charity of Notre-Dame d'Évron, but her parents had no intention of letting her depart and leave them alone with the invalid girl. She placed all her hopes in Jenny, who spoke about it to Dom Guéranger. "Do what she asks of you regarding her parents," the abbot replied. "Instruct her as needed, but do not think that you are superior to her. The odds are that she is humbler than you."[8]

Thus, Jenny took advantage of the slow season, when work at the farm came to a standstill, to give lessons to Marie Bignon and prepare her for her future life as a religious teacher. But the young peasant's vocation gradually evolved under contact with Jenny. Marie spoke enthusiastically to all about the young lady of Coudreuse, and brought her friends to her: Jeannette Martin, Anna Frénay, Louise

---

[6] Letter dated September 16, 1865.
[7] Ibid.
[8] Letter dated November 15, 1861.

Deshayes. Two sisters also living in Chantenay and relatives of Jenny's tutor-turned-Ursuline nun, Noëmie and Berthe de la Corbière, would also join the group.

The assistant to the curate of Chantenay, Father Delaroche, decided to transform this small group that had sprung up spontaneously, into an actual confraternity. He asked Jenny to be its president, which she declined, alleging that she lived far away for nearly five months out of the year, that she was younger than the others and that in Coudreuse she often had to care for the responsibilities of her mother as mistress of the house. Besides, she felt no inclination to direct others.

Since Father Delaroche insisted, she told him that she would present the matter to her director, the abbot of Solesmes. The latter did not at all mind having the opportunity to observe the manner in which Jenny would acquit herself of the charge of directing others. Just as he expected, Jenny did marvelously. The young, and not so young, women loved her and had great trust in her; and she, on her part, was cheerful, understanding and affectionate. On Sunday evenings, when the group went to church for the last time before parting, the regulars at the café would quip: "Well! Behold the pious ladies going by!" and again "There goes the convent on the march, with mother abbess at the head!"[9] These permanent residents of the local pub were not at all prophets; they were simply using old French parlance—the leader of a band of youth was an "abbot" or an "abbess;" it had been so for ten centuries.

In the summer of 1864, an accident nearly destroyed the manor house in Coudreuse. It was the evening of August 26; Jenny had had the inspiration of placing the family and the house under the protection of the holy angels, reciting the Compline prayer: "Visit this place, O Lord, . . ."[10] At night, a fire started in the kitchen and went around the entire room, burning the shutters, the cupboards, and shattering the windows; it scorched the walls of the vestibule next to the kitchen, arrived at the portal of the staircase leading to the second

---

[9] "Annals: Origins," p. 47.
[10] "Visit this place, O Lord, and drive far from us all the snares of the enemy. Let Thy holy angels dwell herein to preserve us in peace, and let Thy blessings be always upon us, through Christ Our Lord. Amen."—Trans.

floor and attacked the floor boards above, and then died away on its own. The following day, news of the happening spread to the neighboring farms and into the town, and the people came on location to see the extent of the damage done by the fire that could have become a veritable disaster. Twenty years later, people still recalled the event: "Oh, that is not surprising. At Coudreuse nothing bad can happen; they have an angel that protects them!"

Dom Guéranger saw the project of the foundation of Sainte-Cécile defining itself, almost without his knowing how. He continued, therefore, preparing for the future: "I'm pleased that you like the Rule [of Saint Benedict]. But you will see how your comprehension of the Rule will grow with time. Think that thousands upon thousands of holy souls have lived it in the course of fourteen centuries, that Saint Gertrude found in it her treasure and nourishment. But note well the proper approach—the Rule is for whomsoever comes from outside to serve God: salvation first, and then perfection. Read also and meditate upon the *Life of Saint Benedict*,[11] which is the complement to the Rule; in knowing the man you will better penetrate his precepts."[12]

In June 1864, the abbot of Solesmes went to Marseilles by invitation of the ordinary, Bishop Patrice Cruice, joining the large number of French prelates who had been invited for the inauguration and consecration of the Basilica of Notre-Dame de la Garde.[13] He took advantage of this occasion to request the bishop's authorization for the foundation of the priory of Sainte-Madeleine, which Canon Coulin desired be made so that his Great Catechism[14] could be transferred to its care. There, he became acquainted with the young girls and women of the apostolate. Until then he only knew of them through what had been said by Madame Durand, sister of Father Bérengier, and by the three ladies who had come from Marseilles with the Canon to see him at Solesmes in 1863. "I will have so much

---

[11] Written by Pope St. Gregory the Great (*ca.* 540–604).—Trans.

[12] Letter dated June 11, 1864.

[13] Impressive neo-Byzantine structure built (1853–1864) upon the highest point of the city of Marseilles, on the site of a thirteenth-century chapel dedicated to Notre Dame de la Garde, patroness of Marseilles and of seafarers.—Trans.

[14] See chap. 8, p. 79, n. 14.—Trans.

to tell you when I return, about what I have learned and seen here with my own eyes!" he wrote to Jenny. "The graces that the Lord is showering upon us from heaven these years are innumerable and of the choicest kind. Similar situations; so many sisters, from all over! We are living at a time when no one any longer helps Our Lord; He is thus forced to take care of His affairs on His own, and He certainly knows His business well. May He be blessed from north to south, from east to west."[15] The two foundation projects—the foundation for monks in Marseilles, and the foundation for nuns in Solesmes—were beginning to take shape.

As the moment Jenny had been awaiting drew nearer and nearer, a quiet and peaceful joy swelled ever greater in her heart: "At times I am astonished to see myself so love the calm, regular, monotonous life; I was truly made for this type of life. At times I dream of this life in Solesmes, wearing another garb, with the hope that it will be forever," she wrote on August 1, 1864. It was clear as crystal. The last vestiges of hesitation on the part of Dom Guéranger were vanishing away.

"Midas, King Midas has the ears of an ass," sang the Phrygian reeds whenever the slightest breeze caressed them. All secrets end up by being revealed, whether they be entrusted to the king's barber[16] or whispered from mouth to ear by well-meaning souls. Upon her return to Coudreuse in May 1865, Jenny heard that a foundation of nuns was being prepared in Solesmes. Everyone was speaking about it, whereas she had thought that only she and Henriette Bouly shared knowledge of the project. She alerted Dom Guéranger that the secret had been let out.

The abbot came to Chantenay on May 30 for confirmations; Lise Bruyère was among the confirmands. But he had another matter in

---

[15] Letter dated June 11, 1864.

[16] Reference to Greek mythology. King Midas favored Pan in a music competition between the demi-god and Apollo. The latter, disgruntled, cast a spell on King Midas, making his ears grow exceedingly long. The king summoned his barber to fashion a wig that would hide the deformity, threatening death should the barber reveal his secret. The latter, however, could not contain himself and finally ran off to the fields where, into a hole in the ground, he shouted "Midas, King Midas has the ears of an ass." Reeds eventually grew over the hole, and whenever touched by a breeze, echoed the barber's cry for all to hear: "Midas, King Midas has the ears of an ass."—Trans.

mind. He wanted to see Bishop Fillion, a well-beloved friend, and arrange for him to observe Jenny before any action was taken. This happened at Coudreuse—Monsieur Bruyère, as a good master of the manor, had invited both the bishop and the abbot for dinner.

Bishop Charles-Jean Fillion[17] was of the clergy of Le Mans. He was born in Saint-Denis-d'Anjou, in Mayenne, not far from Solesmes. At first made bishop of Saint-Claude in the Franche-Comté, he was appointed to the see of Le Mans in 1862, to succeed Bishop Jean-Jacques Nanquette. For the people of the province of Maine, Bishop Fillion continued to be "Monsieur Charles," as he was called when he directed the seminary. He was one of the most faithful supporters of the abbot of Solesmes.

The bishop revealed his impressions to the abbot immediately following the meal: "My most Reverend Father, your dear daughter Cécile is consecrated to God, isn't that so? There is nothing to be concerned about. Don't you believe that God has some special designs upon this soul? It is a great consolation to me that this excellent family lives in my diocese and that you have introduced me to them."[18]

This was not yet the moment to speak to the bishop about the monastery project of Sainte-Cécile, but Dom Guéranger was happy that Bishop Fillion had discerned the spiritual mettle of the young woman. When the time would come to request his approval for the foundation, the bishop would know what could be expected from her.

Besides Jenny Bruyère and Henriette Bouly, as well as the candidates from Marseilles, Dom Guéranger would soon count upon Berthe de la Corbière of Chantenay, and Honorine Foubert, whom Jenny had met in Sablé at music and voice lessons with Monsieur Karren. Honorine wanted to be a Benedictine nun, and she was the one to speak about it first to the abbot. He let her know about the project, but without revealing the names of the other candidates.

The future monastery was silently being readied; in private conversations it was referred to as the "wooden house." But this

---

[17] Born in 1817, died in 1874.—Trans.
[18] "Annals: Origins," p. 49.

"wooden house" intrigued Monsieur Bruyère, who suspected something might be brewing. He wanted to clear things up for himself, and one November evening brought up the subject of cloistered nuns in conversation with his daughter, declaring quite clearly that they were perfectly useless. Jenny unsuspectingly took to their defense, and so he realized that there was danger looming in the very heart of his own family. For once, at least, he did not move to have the last word and impose his own point of view.

On December 30, 1865, Jenny gave an account of the graces received on Christmas in a letter to the abbot: "As to Bethlehem itself, I seemed to be watching the Most Holy Virgin and contemplating the Divine Infant. Without a word being uttered, or my hearing anything, it seemed that the all-lovable little Jesus made me understand that in order to love Him perfectly and to imitate Him, it was necessary for me to observe the three religious vows, and, at the same time, it seemed I understood how I should practice them. I was moved to offer the beginnings of the "wooden house" to Our Lord and it seemed that Our Lord was pleased by it, accepting it from me with a smile. . . . There is no visible image and no sound, but I have such a vivid impression, that I feel as if I were actually seeing and hearing."

After the feast of the Epiphany, Dom Guéranger had to leave for Marseilles to establish the monks' priory. On his way there, he stopped at Albi to visit the great fortified cathedral, the only one in France dedicated to Saint Cecilia, in order to entrust to that saint another foundation—the monastery of nuns already in the planning. On his way back, he stopped in Paris at the Bruyères. But in order to speak privately with Jenny, he arranged for a meeting at the Madeleine. The conversation took place in front of the church door: "Assuredly, my daughter, when your grandfather was building this colonnade, he could never have imagined what we would come to do here today, amidst this great city so oblivious to things supernatural and to the interests of eternity. Isn't it amusing to be here, you and I, intent on planning a monastic foundation?"[19]

Monsieur Huvé, the grandfather of Jenny and architect of the Madeleine, did not have the soul of a Pierre de Montreuil, the

---

[19] Ibid., p. 67.

architect of the monks of Saint-Germain-des-Prés, to whom the Sainte-Chapelle is attributed, nor of a Pierre de Craon, the master craftsman in Paul Claudel's play *L'Annonce fait à Marie (The Tidings Brought to Mary)*. He was not a builder of cathedrals. The idea that one of his granddaughters would some day become a religious foundress and abbess would have struck him as a mighty sad quip.

Chapter 10

The "Wooden House"

FOR THE RESTORATION OF Saint-Pierre de Solesmes in 1833, Dom Guéranger had begun with a church and the full array of buildings of an ancient monastery. For the foundation of Sainte-Cécile in 1866, he had nothing—neither land upon which to build, nor resources of any type. In his correspondence with Jenny, the future monastery was referred to as the "wooden house," as mentioned previously.

He had not yet asked the bishop for his authorization. Exhausted as he was, the abbot had to muster great confidence in order to launch upon this adventure. His youth of the days of the restoration of Solesmes had long waned away. But the will of God seemed quite obvious, and supernatural prudence required that he move ahead, setting all objections aside.

"I wish to take yet another burden upon myself; isn't that heroic of me?" he wrote to Amélie Brusson of the Great Catechism of Marseilles (who would not be able to enter Sainte-Cécile until 1887). "I desire to bring together these mischievous girls from the north and from the south, and thus voluntarily pull myself away from the quiet that I would need so as to be able to die in peace. . . . My last strength will be spent on you. Ten years ago, the thought of caring for doves was far from my mind; but they came tapping upon my window, and I do not have the heart not to open it to them."[1] His correspondent replied: "Yes, I understand your heroism, taking on this new burden of our desires and our plans amidst the many other cares that already have been weighing upon you for a long time. But since our aspirations cannot but come from Our Lord, I firmly hope that He will give you new strength and many years ahead to complete the work."[2]

There were still seven months before Jenny would attain her majority on October 12, 1866. She had already declined many a

---

[1] Letter dated March 21, 1866.
[2] Letter dated March 27, 1866.

marriage proposal that would have been very convenient for her father. Her critical spirit—which could immediately discern the weaknesses of the suitor and make those around her see them as well—had several times saved her from a tight spot. "She is too astute," confided Monsieur Bruyère to Dom Guérager one day. "She quickly detects the chink in the armor, is attracted to things of the intelligence, loves the artistic; she will suffer if she has an ordinary man for a husband. I know well this scrutinizing spirit, with a certain tendency to analyze in depth, which makes a person rarely satisfied because nothing can correspond to the ideal in mind. But perhaps there will come a time when, after having rejected every reasonable suitor, she will regret her refusals and will accept a life below that which is being offered her today."[3]

However, at the end of May 1866, a matchmaker, as they existed back then (a fearsome, nearly extinct species), presented her candidate at a gathering in La Grange. Monsieur Bruyère believed he had found the *rara avis* in whom his eldest daughter, despite her infallible intuition, would not be able to discover the flaws of character she had so easily detected in others. The introduction to the "perfect young man" went as planned. Back in Coudreuse, Monsieur Bruyère awaited word as to the intentions of the suitor, and then called his daughter and spoke to her about the proposal. "The young woman listened in silence at first, standing there before her father, much as a defendant before her judge. Then, very calmly, she explained to him that, until now she had always given to understand that she was firmly resolved not to get married, but since this went ignored, she would like to declare very frankly that she was strongly decided to be a religious."[4] Confronted with this formal refusal and startling revelation, the father exploded. There followed a scene of extreme fury that lasted for three hours. "My father was wild with rage," wrote Jenny. "He wanted to kill himself. We threw ourselves at his feet; he solemnly swore to me that on the day I would pronounce my vows, there would be one more damned soul in hell."[5] But in the end, emotional blackmail triumphed; Monsieur Bruyère asked only

---

[3] "Annals: Origins," p. 67.
[4] Ibid., p. 110.
[5] Letter to Dom Guéranger dated May 27, 1866.

for a delay. In a postscript to the same letter, Jenny added: "I beheld my father at my feet, begging me to give him only the respite of a delay, promising to allow me to go free a little later if I persisted in my decision, because then he would be convinced of it; alleging that he wouldn't know how to pray except at my side, that I had his salvation in my hands, that he did not, in any way, wish to place himself between God and me, but that I didn't know how much more time he had to live and that certainly the good God had placed this ardent desire in his heart to have me close to him so that he could be saved. . . ."[6]

Monsieur Bruyère was a passionate man, as well as tender. At the least thing he would fly into fits of rage. His violent tantrums were legendary. Mother Cécile loved him too much to dwell on this aspect of his character, but others spoke about it.

A particularly painful crisis occurred on June 3 and 4. Jenny could not leave Coudreuse. She wrote a long letter to Dom Guéranger on the fourth, a type of will and testament; it is unknown who took that letter to Solesmes. Following another scene, in which her father imposed an ultimatum demanding a response by the next morning, she wrote a second letter, also dated June 4. She asked Marie Bignon, the young woman from the neighboring farm, to take the letter to Dom Guéranger, with hopes that Marie would bring back a response from the abbot with her. But, unfortunately, he was not in Solesmes then, but in Précigné, and Marie returned on foot to Chantenay without bearing a message for Jenny. On the fifth, Lise, in her turn, left very early in the morning for Solesmes, saw Dom Guéranger there and brought with her his reply, at long last. She arrived in Coudreuse before eleven o'clock.

The confrontation left Jenny profoundly stricken, and she knew there would be more such episodes. She wondered whether her heart, already weak, wouldn't give way at some point: "My good Father, we must expect anything. If Our Lord permits that I die in this conflict, that my heart suddenly rupture, my last thought, my last word will be an act of love of God. I forgive all those who have injured me and I so strongly desire their salvation that I would

---

[6] Ibid.

undergo death itself in order to obtain it for them. Also, my good Father, I must for once tell you what is in my heart; I am not one to be complimenting others, nor am I given to eloquence, but in truth and gratitude I must say that I owe you the life of my soul and its welfare. I deplore and regret all the difficulties I have caused you, and will still cause you, and I will pray each day that Our Lord bless you and protect you until the day when, in His mercy, He will give you rest. Would that the deep, devoted and lasting affection I have for you could be a source for you of abundant blessings!"[7]

If the letter read like a final will, the closing codicil left room for hope: "My martyrdom will last four and a half months, if God does not end it before then by either calling me to Himself or through a miracle." She had not made any promises to her father and was intent on claiming her liberty on the very day she attained majority, either to join the others for the foundation of Sainte-Cécile or to await that moment while working to earn a living, far from her family. Her father had asked her to commit to staying with him until she reached her twenty-fifth year, and she left the decision of whether or not to cede to his wishes to Dom Guéranger.

The abbot read Jenny's letters in the evening of June 4 upon his return from Précigné, and spent the night in prayer. In the morning, before Matins, he awoke two of his monks to ask them for their view, one of whom was his prior, already familiar with the situation. He then penned his response and entrusted it to Lise who had just arrived at the monastery.

If Jenny was to commit to anything, it should be to stay until she was twenty-one, without specifying anything further: "My dear child, do what you find best, but without haste, if possible. Once freedom is lost, it cannot be regained. If you say yes, limit yourself to saying that you do not intend to depart on the very day of your twenty-first birthday, that you will not refuse to stay long enough to assuage his concerns; that, in fact, he had been ready to allow you to leave with a husband; that you retain your complete liberty even while you consent to stay, and that you will not suffer being limited in what regards religious practice; that otherwise you will leave upon

---

[7] Letter to Dom Guéranger dated June 4, 1866.

reaching majority, as is your right. Do not speak at all of a specific number of years."[8]

Dom Guéranger's counsel was the fruit of careful reflection. On the one hand, he wanted to avoid a drama; on the other hand, he did not want Jenny to undermine her own liberty and, out of tenderness, make a commitment to which she would be firmly held. He recognized that Monsieur Bruyère was not a man to easily lay down his arms, but he emphasized how profoundly illogical his attitude was—he would readily become separated from his daughter for an advantageous marriage, but could not be separated from her were she to give herself to God. Double standards indeed!

The situation had the potential of adversely impacting Dom Guéranger and his community. Monsieur Bruyère had challenged him and threatened to petition the Emperor for the dispersion of Solesmes, should anyone touch his daughter. And he perhaps had the means to succeed in this, given his relationships at the imperial court and the delicate position of religious orders in those days due to the tension created by the Roman Question.[9] The previous year, the abbot had written to Madame Durand: "The good and Catholic society of Marseilles has no inkling of the danger that threatens all religious orders since the declarations made to the Senate by those two governmental figures, Rouland and Bonjean.[10] All understand that from hence the government is determined to stunt the growth of the Church."[11]

---

[8] Letter dated June 5, 1866.

[9] See chap. 5, pp. 50–51.

[10] Gustave Rouland (1806–1878) held several high ranking positions in the Second Empire. As Minister of Public Education and Religious Cult (1856–1863) he issued a circular letter to the bishops of France in 1860 about the Gallican policies of the Empire toward the Holy See. Louis Bernard Bonjean (1804–1871) likewise held high posts, ministerial and juridical, in the governments of both Louis-Philippe d'Orléans and Louis-Napoléon Bonaparte. In the Senate, he was the most vocal advocate of Gallicanism; his anti-papacy discourse to the Senate on March 15, 1865 is of note (which Dom Guéranger most likely has in mind here). Bonjean also consistently inveighed against religious orders, particularly the Jesuits, for their fidelity to Rome. With the fall of the Second Empire in 1871, he was imprisoned by the Commune and executed in May 24, 1871 alongside the Archbishop of Paris, Georges Darboy. Having reconciled himself to the Church while in prison, he received the last rites from a priestly fellow-prisoner, a Jesuit.—Trans.

[11] Letter dated May 18, 1865.

Confrontations continued erupting at the Bruyères: "During the summer," wrote Jenny's mother, "we made a trip to Normandy, but the least thing would provoke a scene."[12]

With or without Jenny—but preferably with her—the foundation of Sainte-Cécile would take place in the fall. She was not the only interested party. Others awaited the moment with equal impatience, and it seemed that, with the participation of the Marseilles contingent, the future of the monastery was assured. Marie de Ruffo-Bonneval, one of the older candidates in the group (she was thirty-three) had recently lost her mother. She was not yet free of responsibilities since she had charge of her invalid sister, but she could dispose of her estate, with which perhaps a property could be bought and construction begun. Dom Guéranger asked her explicitly on May 26: "Would you be able to be the foundress in what concerns the temporal order? Everything is in place. For the provisional establishment we will need fifty to sixty thousand francs. Would your personal assets allow you to make this loan?" The reply was conditional—Canon Coulin's approval would be necessary. However, since the latter's knowledge of the project was limited, he did not give his approval.

The walls of Coudreuse were not enough to contain Monsieur Bruyère's outbursts. Everyone in Chantenay knew of the drama and it was the subject of conversation in the neighboring farms. Thus the peasant friends of Jenny came to know about the foundation, which left her free to speak about it with them and invite those who wanted to join the founding group as the first lay sisters of the new monastery.

The most urgent affair at hand was to communicate with Bishop Fillion in Le Mans and alert him of the volatile situation brewing within the Bruyère family, before he should hear of it through the public forum. The foundation depended primarily on him, for no religious house can be erected without the permission of the local ordinary, and he had complete jurisdiction over the monasteries of women religious in his diocese. The abbot of Solesmes planned to adopt a particular juridical status for Sainte-Cécile that was no longer

---

[12] "Récit de madame Bruyère," copy, p. 11.

in use in France except in the case of Trappist and Carthusian nuns. Under this arrangement, jurisdiction over the monastery was divided between the bishop and the religious superior.

Dom Guéranger went to Le Mans on June 30 to present his plan. Thankfully, Bishop Fillion had already been won over ahead of time. He had complete confidence in his friend and accepted the solution proposed to him regarding jurisdiction over the monastery. He also decided to present himself officially as the party principally responsible for the foundation, so as to diffuse the storm clouds that were gathering over Saint-Pierre de Solesmes.

As to the material aspects of the foundation, at the beginning of the summer the abbot still lacked the needed resources. There were no prospects of funds to come from the families of the candidates from the Sablé region. If there were nothing to be had from Marseilles, the situation would remain at an impasse. Thus, Dom Guéranger decided to address himself directly to Canon Coulin and reveal to him all the details of the project. Now that the bishop of Le Mans was aware of it and had given it his full approval, there would be no imprudence in doing so. The letter is very revealing of what the abbot thought of Jenny Bruyère, whom he had known for a very long time and whose development he had closely followed. The text is priceless and worth citing at length. Either Dom Guéranger was terribly mistaken, or he saw things as they truly were before God. After all, he was not penning a hagiography here, but simply exposing a problem to a friend:

"Among the young women in our part of the country whom divine grace has engaged for our future monastery, there is one I have been directing for ten years and whom Our Lord has covered with rare favors. Her soul is a sanctuary of perfection and her life entirely that of a saint. Her father has no religion and is a despot; her mother, a holy woman and tender mother, offered this child to God at birth. She witnessed with joy her daughter consecrate her virginity to Our Lord at the age of sixteen, and later, did not flinch when the young spouse of Christ told her of her intention to enter Carmel upon attaining majority.

"I had no thoughts yet of making a foundation for Benedictine nuns. But an occurrence set me along that path, and Cécile (her name as a consecrated virgin) declared that this was the desire of her heart, that she had never dared to reveal it to me, and that she had only wished to be a Carmelite because she thought I had no plans of founding a monastery for the daughters of St. Benedict. This was about three years ago.

"We are calmly waiting for her majority to be reached on October 12. Four or five marriage proposals have been made and Cécile has declined them one by one. Last May, the devil mounted his most formidable attack thus far. An officious lady in our area proposed to find a husband for the poor child; she created illusions in the father's mind, brought the young man to him and managed the introductions. Things were already at such a stage that Cécile found it necessary to go beyond simply repeating that she did not wish to be married. She revealed that her decided intention was to enter religious life; and so as not to implicate me, she mentioned, more or less vaguely, the word 'Carmelite.'

"The father, who was already well advanced in his negotiations, was thrown into a fit of extreme furor by this news. The child, her mother and her younger sister have been suffering cruelly ever since. Naturally, the father made me responsible for everything, and the friendly relationship that once united us has given way to violent indignation, accompanied by threats against me.

"Under these circumstances (which I had not thought appropriate to relate to you, Reverend Father, at the time), feeling the need for support, I came here yesterday to see the bishop, who has been an intimate friend since his youth. In any event, I would not be able to establish a community of religious sisters without his cooperation. I told him everything, and he realized perfectly well that my making arrangements for the foundation would bring a storm of attacks upon me, and that his duty as bishop and friend was to cover for me. He decided to take full responsibility for everything before the public. My young daughters will write to him and he will reply that he approves their desire to be daughters of St. Benedict, and that he places them under my direction. . . . He decided that, while not revealing the names of the candidates from our part of the country, he will present the work as intended for the ladies of Marseilles who desire to embrace our Rule, in the wake of our recent foundation in that city.

"But here is the burning issue, Reverend Father, that I must recommend to your zeal for the future nuns. Cécile's mother had hoped that her daughter's dowry, which would be substantial, could be used to meet the costs of the foundation. We were counting on a docile reaction from her father at the moment of her majority. The good relationship I enjoyed with him would facilitate all arrangements; he would likely even feel flattered to be able to cooperate with an establishment in which his daughter would be one of its first ornaments. This unfortunate failed marriage has launched him into a terrible rage against me, the effects of which the poor child suffers every day. He will give her neither a penny, nor his consent. . . .

"Therefore, everything might have come to an indefinite halt if the idea had not occurred to me to propose, Reverend Father, that you consider whether Marie de Ruffo, heiress to her mother, could not be the foundress of the future monastery. . . . I thus leave everything to your wisdom, and I go to sleep now trusting in God and in you, having nothing else to say. Your answer will determine everything."[13]

That is to say, Dom Guéranger let Canon Coulin know, in no uncertain terms, that from here on everything depended on him. Instead of replying to the letter, Canon Coulin took the train from Marseilles with Amélie Brusson, arriving in Solesmes on July 8. Marie de Ruffo-Bonneval and Noëlie, her invalid sister, followed suit the next day. However, the funds immediately available to Marie had been considerably curtailed. Her young brother, a stockbroker, had recently lost all the capital that had been set aside for Dom Guéranger in the financial collapse triggered by the victory of Prussia over Austria in Sadowa.[14] Nonetheless, this was only a temporary hindrance.

Dom Guéranger did not let himself be disconcerted by this new setback and decided it was too late to desist. God would provide. A field located on higher terrain, at the edge of the village in the

---

[13] Letter dated July 1, 1866.
[14] July 3, 1866.—Trans.

direction of Sablé, was purchased on July 16, 1866, with a sum found by the abbot; for legal purposes it was placed under the name of Marie de Ruffo-Bonneval. Two other lots, contiguous to the first, were acquired on the twenty-second. Marie and her sister decided not to return to Marseilles; they took up residence in the former Anjubault residence facing the abbey, which Madame Durand placed at their disposal.

Chapter 11

"Sainte-Cécile-la-Petite": Little Sainte-Cécile

WHEN DOM GUÉRANGER SPOKE of the "wooden house" to his prospective candidates to monastic life, he was speaking in earnest, as he actually did envision building a temporary monastery of wooden lodgings. However, one of his directees, Paule de Rougé, chatelaine of Bois-Dauphin in Précigné (in religion, Sister Marie de la Réparation, d. 1896) had done the same thing when she founded near her chateau the community of the Little Sisters of Jesus and the orphanage in Vairie.[1] Aware of his plans, she strongly discouraged the abbot from incurring the expense of erecting buildings that would be costly but would not last because they would eventually be replaced by permanent construction. The example of Vairie had shown her that, in trying to save money, funds were often unnecessarily wasted.

Sainte-Cécile, therefore, would be a true traditional monastery. However, building a monastery would take time and the small community needed lodgings in the interim. Madame Durand would have gladly offered use of her home in Solesmes for this purpose; the confabulations about the foundation had mostly taken place within its walls. But the house was too small to meet all the requirements of a monastery in formation and it was encircled on all sides by neighbors who had a view of it and its gardens. Dom Guéranger had something else in mind. Some time before, Monsieur Huré, friend of Solesmes and a headmaster in Paris, had built a spacious vacation home for his large family of fifteen children in Solesmes, where his eldest son was a monk. The house stood close to the outer limits of the village, on the road to Sablé.

Monsieur Huré was at the monastery for the feast of the Assumption during this period. After the festive meal, Dom Guéranger came to converse with his guests, and then led his friend

---

[1] Vairie ("Vérie" on today's maps) is close to Précigné, a village south of Sablé, located five miles from Solesmes.

to the great arbor, where he confided his plans to him. He asked Monsieur Huré if he would accept to rent his house for the initial stage of the Sainte-Cécile foundation, while the new monastery buildings were being constructed. His friend concurred wholeheartedly, placing his house at the disposal of the nuns when they would come together in the fall, refusing to receive any money in return.

Build a monastery? How and with what? Dom Guéranger had intended to ask Dom Fonteinne, the cellarer of Solesmes, to take on the task of master builder of the new monastery. However, Marie de Ruffo-Bonneval would hear none of that. She had been involved in different construction projects in Marseilles and knew that, in matters of dealing with contractors, the best strategy was to secure the services of an architect. She had only limited confidence in Dom Fonteinne and his know-how, and demanded that an architect be recruited, which was wise if they were to build for generations to come.

Thus, Dom Guéranger began his search. It would be better not to engage an architect from Le Mans so as to avoid the possibility of the public's becoming aware of the details of the project from its very first drafts. Monsieur Bruyère had contacts in Le Mans. This forthwith excluded Monsieur David, who had recently completed the difficult construction of the choir of the abbatial church at Saint-Pierre de Solesmes. The abbot chose the architect of the diocese of Angers, Louis Duvêtre,[2] who made his first visit to Solesmes on July 28, 1866.

Except for those few who were privy to the secret, nothing had been said about the project to the monks at Saint-Pierre. But in order to complete the area needed for the cloister of the future nuns, it would be necessary for the monks to cede a field that belonged to them. For this, the consent of the monastic chapter was required, and the abbot thus took the opportunity to inform the entire community about the upcoming foundation of nuns. This occurred on the day of the Transfiguration, August 6.

---

[2] Louis Duvêtre, architect, was born in 1816 in southern France, in the Rhône-Alpes region. He forged a successful career in the northwestern area of Maine-Loire, leaving his considerable estate to the city of Angers upon his death in 1881. —Trans.

After this, knowledge about the foundation spread very quickly, despite the secrecy of capitular decisions. Therefore, on the following day, Bishop Fillion came to Solesmes to show to all that the "Marseillaise" foundation was being established under his paternal authority. He received Marie de Ruffo-Bonneval and afterwards went with Dom Guéranger to visit the property where the monastery of Sainte-Cécile would be erected.

Meanwhile, Henriette Bouly prepared her own family for her approaching departure. The reaction on the part of her father was nearly as lively as what had transpired in Coudreuse. "The papas are not very pleased when their daughters refuse to marry," wrote Dom Guéranger to Dom Bastide, abbot of Ligugé. "Pray hard for me and for your future sisters."[3]

As to Marie de Ruffo-Bonneval—who was already a mature woman, a *superadulta*, as Saint Paul would say—the news that she would not be returning to Marseilles provoked a tempestuous commotion in the heart of the Great Cathechism and within circles of Catholic women of the town. Noise is easily amplified under the grand Marseillaise sun, at the feet of Notre-Dame de la Garde. The abbot of Solesmes, it was said, would be taking away ten young women of the Great Catechism without even informing their families, good heavens!

"Canon Coulin was quite disturbed by all this chatter, which was going too far and putting him in a difficult position. . . . He wrote about it to Dom Guéranger, whose patience was being tried to the utmost by these developments and who attached no importance whatsoever to any of the petty gossip," commented Mother Cécile Bruyère in her "Notes" written at the request of Bishop Pie beginning in 1877.[4]

The storms in the Old Port are rarely catastrophic and serenity soon returns. It was not a matter of emptying out Marseilles, nor of deporting its entire female population to the banks of the Sarthe. Marie de Ruffo-Bonneval reemerged in Marseilles and was able to reassure everyone. It had been necessary for her to make this trip in

---

[3] Letter dated August 24, 1866, cited in the "Notes on the life of Dom Guéranger" requested by Bishop Pie, which Mother Cécile Bruyère began to compile in 1877, p. 4905.
[4] Ibid., p. 4916.

order to settle certain affairs, choose an attorney, and negotiate a loan on some real estate she had not been able to sell. She ran into all manner of difficulties, which very nearly discouraged her.

At Solesmes, the laborers had begun their work upon the slopes of the hill and the foundations of the new buildings were already surfacing above the ground, in the midst of the field. Dom Guéranger had wished that the cornerstone of Sainte-Cécile be blessed by the bishop on October 12. But the prelate was not free on that day and opted for the eighth instead. Jenny did not attend the ceremony, thinking it best not to unnecessarily awaken the volcano that for now lay dormant. The monks assisted at the blessing, which took place in the presence of Marie de Ruffo-Bonneval, Henriette Bouly, and two young women of Chantenay: Jeannette Martin and Anna Frénay.

There were still preparations to be made. Marie de Ruffo-Bonneval attended to these in the measure that the care of her sister Noëlie allowed. The date for entrance into Sainte-Cécile-la-Petite was set for November 16, 1866, the vigil of the feast of St. Gertrude in the Benedictine calendar of those days. And to facilitate the entry of Marie de Ruffo-Bonneval, who could not be separated from her sister, Dom Guéranger decided, with the concurrence of Bishop Fillion, that the invalid would be taken care of by the new postulants.

Jenny Bruyère would be reaching her majority on October 12. On the seventh, she wrote the bishop to officially request that she be accepted into the new religious house about to be established, since all was done under his authority. This measure was intended to protect Dom Guéranger vis-à-vis her father. Bishop Fillion replied: "I will be happy to count you among the generous souls whom God has chosen for this foundation. You will find in the Rule of Saint Benedict everything that the Rule of Carmel has to offer, and perhaps something more in agreement with your aspirations and your aptitudes. Granted that you are willing to abandon everything in order to obey the voice of God, here you will still give your family the consolation of knowing that you are very close to them and that they will be able to continue contact with you, which will be very precious to them. And it will be no small advantage to you to live under the same wise and enlightened direction that has guided your first steps in the Christian life, and that henceforth will aid you in advancing in the perfection of religious life. It is on the feast of Saint Gertrude, on November 15 [sic], that our dear daughters will be gathering in Solesmes."[5]

Dom Guéranger thought it would be best for Jenny to leave her family on the day of her twenty-first birthday, and lodge with the Visitation sisters of Le Mans while waiting for all to be readied at Solesmes. She rejected the idea, not wanting to seem to be needlessly defying her father; but she was not rewarded for this gesture. Her father resumed his violent outbursts and threats, attacking not only Dom Guéranger, but the bishop as well. "At the beginning of November," wrote Madame Bruyère in her recollections on Jenny, "she announced that she would be departing for the new convent in Solesmes. [Her father] recommended his behavior, treating her more severely than ever. He would turn his back to her at table, and, one evening, toward midnight, he went to her room to throttle her. The poor child put up no resistance, raising her two arms . . . At this sight her father was appeased, or at least, he let her go."[6]

Nevertheless, on Tuesday, November 13, after renewed scenes, Monsieur Bruyère at long last consented to his daughter's departure. It was decided that the family would go to the Huvés in La Grange, while Madame de la Corbière would accompany Jenny to Solesmes. Before leaving her, Monsieur Bruyère embraced his daughter, saying that this was in reality the only time that she had caused him any grief, but he added: "I know well that you are obeying a call that you believe to be God's voice."

Marie de Ruffo-Bonneval and Élise Meiffren awaited Jenny at Monsieur Huré's summer house, the temporary "Sainte-Cécile-la-Petite." Dom Guéranger was alerted of her arrival and came to bless the future novices. Together, they recited a *Te Deum*. Jenny, who henceforth would be called Cécile, had sung the same chant of thanksgiving with her mother, in the latter's room, before leaving Coudreuse.

On the following day, it was Henriette Bouly's turn to leave her family and Sablé, after a painful parting from her father: "The

---

[5] Letter dated October 8, 1866.
[6] "Récit de madame Bruyère," copy, p. 11.

fourteenth was also passed in preparations," one reads in the Annals of Sainte-Cécile, "but the pitch of joy was heightened with the definitive arrival of Mademoiselle Henriette Bouly, who came accompanied by her excellent mother and her sister, Madame Dufougeray. Monsieur Bouly as well, showed himself reasonable at the eleventh hour, and agreed to say his farewells to his daughter. Here too God's blessings were palpable and consoling."[7]

November 15 marked the arrival of the young women of Chantenay: Jeannette Martin, Anna Frénay, and a third candidate who was asked to leave after a few weeks. Honorine Foubert would be joining the small group as soon as she was free of her duties as music teacher. Her mother had attended catechism classes alongside the young Prosper Guéranger.

Sainte-Cécile-la-Petite had its oratory, chapter room, work room, refectory, parlor and its cells; with some good will, a place had been found for everything. On November 16, at the abbatial church and in the presence of the postulants, Dom Guéranger consecrated the altar stone that would be used at their chapel. He had explained the ceremony to them beforehand: "On the morning of the sixteenth, the small community went to the abbatial church, where, under our eyes transpired the incomparable rite of dedication of an altar," read the Annals. "What lofty a lesson for these souls who also had left everything to be consecrated in honor of the august and tranquil Trinity! How profound this first impression was for them, who had come from afar to encircle the altar of the Living God and sing His praises during all their lives, *die ac nocte!*"[8]

Following dinner, the first moments of the afternoon of the sixteenth were employed in receiving final visits and attending to last arrangements. Dom Guéranger would be coming at half past one as representative of the bishop, to officially inaugurate monastic life at Sainte-Cécile. The celebration would be intimate. The foundation had already elicited enough storms, and, besides, there was no room inside the chapel for guests, once a place had been set aside for the sanctuary and the choir of the future nuns.

---

[7] "Annals: Origins," p. 251.
[8] Ibid., pp. 252–253. ("Day and night," reads the Latin.—Trans.)

The abbot arrived. He first gathered the choir sisters, who had already put on the postulant habit including a small bonnet. The conference took place in the room above the oratory, on the second floor. Dom Guéranger gave each her name in religion: Marie de Ruffo-Bonneval (thirty-three) became Sister Gertrude, Elisabeth Meiffren (thirty-six), Sister Scholastica, Jenny Bruyère (twenty-one) was Sister Cécile, and Henriette Bouly (twenty-eight), Sister Agnes. Thus Cécile was the youngest.

The abbot, grave and recollected, read them four pages of text he had composed to serve as the program for their monastic life. Then he continued: "And now, my dearest daughters, we need to convene your small meeting and distribute the different offices. Each of you must be ready for all that obedience might impose on you, without having any desire or choice of your own in the matter. We must, first of all, name a superior to whom you will submit yourselves with love; and she who is to be appointed shall exercise her function with humility, without thinking that it is due to any superiority whatsoever that she has been placed over her sisters. God owes no explanation as to why He decides on those He chooses to direct others, and, moreover, this charge is not at all an honor that is granted, but an act of love that is solicited. When Our Lord, Prince of Shepherds, chose Saint Peter to be the head of His Church, He did not say merely 'Peter, do you love me,' but 'Do you love me more than these?' And it was at Simon's affirmative response that the Lord placed the burden upon his shoulders as a mark of trust. Thus, in virtue of the power that has been given us over your souls, we have resolved to assign the government of this house to Sister Cécile Bruyère, who from now on you will consider your superior."[9]

He had said nothing of this beforehand to Jenny; he had given her no inkling that her role, in beginning her monastic life, would be to direct her elders. For there were two groups: the group from Marseilles, more mature in age, and that of Chantenay, younger, made up of Sister Cécile and the lay sisters, Jeannette Martin (Sister Apolline), twenty-seven and Anna Frénay (Sister Colombe), eighteen.

---

[9] "Annals: First Year, 1866–1867," pp. 2–3.

The age of Sister Agnès Bouly, of Sablé, was midway between the two groups.

Sister Cécile had nary a moment, at that instant, to dwell on the problem of her nomination. Dom Guéranger went on to distribute the other charges: Sister Gertrude de Ruffo-Bonneval was naturally made cellarer,[10] as the others could have guessed, since the abbot had not made her superior. To Sister Agnes Bouly, who already knew the lay sisters, was entrusted their direction, along with the office of sacristan. Sister Scholastica Meiffren was the kitchener[11] and infirmarian.

There followed Vespers, presided without difficulty by the young superior, whose voice immediately assured the dignity of the Office. Dom Guéranger then consecrated the chalice to be used at the sisters' oratory. In the course of the ceremony, Sister Cécile tipped over a porcelain vase filled with a bouquet of roses: "My first act of authority!"

Dom Guéranger returned for Vigils in the evening, after Compline, and here the fledgling conventual cart got stuck in the mud. Sister Cécile could not manage the parts that pertained to the superior, and the abbot exclaimed with his usual spontaneity: "She'll never get through the Office!" On that night, they limited themselves to the first nocturn of Saint Gertrude.[12]

It need not be said that Sister Cécile would have preferred the first moments of her new charge to have gone differently. After all the emotions of the day, she must not have slept very much. The following morning, on November 17, Dom Guéranger came to celebrate Mass, assisted by Dom Logerot, who was from Sablé. He

---

[10] Monastic office of bursar, which includes care for all the material goods of the monastery as well as supervision of material work done by its members.—Trans.

[11] Religious in charge of the kitchen, refectory and meals, responsible for food supplies and their storage, working under the supervision of the cellarer.—Trans.

[12] "Vigils" in the monastic office corresponds to Matins, the first "hour" in the Roman rite office. A nocturn, of which there are two or three in the monastic office, depending on the rank of the feast, consists of six psalms with antiphons followed by a variable number (according to season) of lessons—which are taken from Scripture and the writings of the Church Fathers or, more recently, from conciliar documents—each followed by a responsory. On Sundays and feast days there is a third nocturn consisting of three canticles from the Old Testament, in addition to the singing of the *Te Deum* and the reading of the Gospel of the day.—Trans.

proceeded to install the Blessed Sacrament and establish the enclosure. Sainte-Cécile had begun, ever so modestly.

Part II

The Young Superior
1866–1875

Chapter 12

Dom Guéranger, Master of Novices

THE DOORS OF SAINTE-CÉCILE-LA-PETITE now opened to the mysteries of monastic life, a life of solitude in the presence of God. They closed upon a world deeply in turmoil with which the community would eventually have to reckon, whether they liked it or not. Monasteries do not exist out of time and cannot escape the circumstances within which they are born and develop.

The map of Europe was no longer the same as had been determined by the Treaty of Vienna in 1815, which had been drawn in the hopes of assuring durable peace. Borders were quickly being redefined, foreboding a number of conflicts to come; entire countries were taken apart, giving rise to new geo-political states. This process had begun with the gradual weakening of the Ottoman dominion over the Balkans and the move toward independence by the different ethnic groups that occupied that peninsula. Then the principalities of Italy were absorbed, one by one, into the Kingdom of Sardinia. The unification of the German kingdoms and palatinates had gained momentum, but Bismarck did not think that unification with the southern states would easily come about. A common war against France, he surmised, would bring these states to unite themselves to Prussia in the subsequent euphoria of victory. In this same year of 1866, he had already eliminated Austria as a political power in a matter of seven weeks, demonstrating in the battle of Sadowa that the Prussian army was the most organized in Europe.

The Austro-Prussian war compelled Napoleon III to recall the task force he had deployed in Mexico, thus setting stage for the demise of the fragile rule of Emperor Maximilian. French imperial policy regarding the new situation in Germany was slow to define itself given the opposing views that surfaced within the government body. Napoleon III himself harbored certain sympathies toward the kingdoms of Italy and Prussia, which inhibited his intervention and irritated public opinion. In addition, the deplorable state of his health kept him from assuming as active a role as he would have liked to have in these affairs.

If the international situation in the fall of 1866 was troubling and already looming darkly with threats, the political scene in France was no less menacing. Republican opposition was growing and being affirmed everywhere. Signs of this were already evident at the local level in large cities; however, an electoral offensive was being mounted at the national level as well. Concurrently, the labor movement was organizing itself against the incumbent government. In 1867 the French branch of the International[1] would be created, only to be dissolved after it staged a protest in favor of the socialists in Italy.

At Sainte-Cécile, the postulants gave little thought to the political climate, but the general context in which they were living is relevant to understanding the events that would directly affect monastic life in France and, thus, the development of their new foundation.

In her extensive "Notes" about Dom Guéranger, Mother Cécile Bruyère describes how he himself took charge of the formation of the first nuns:

"From that point on, Dom Guéranger added the charge of 'novice mistress' of his daughters to his already overwhelming schedule. A new and remarkable dimension of his personality thus emerged. Generally, he gave the postulants a spiritual conference each day and initiated them into the recitation of the Breviary, teaching them—in minutest detail and with admirable patience—how to pronounce the Latin well, to sing the Gregorian chant, and to understand the rubrics. Then he instructed the sisters on how to live from the Divine Office, and gave the salient traits of the saint of each day, sketching in broad outline the historical context in which the saint had lived. His penetrating commentaries on the Holy Rule were of a captivating charm. He knew how to communicate at the level of his audience

---

[1] The International Workmen's Association, sometimes called the First International, was an international socialist organization that aimed at uniting a variety of different left-wing political groups and trade union organizations following Marxist concepts of the working class and class struggle. It was founded in London on September 28, 1864. It folded in 1876, but reemerged as the "Second International" and then the "Third International" in the course of the late nineteenth and early twentieth centuries.—Trans.

with such great wisdom, such consummate prudence, that the sisters made steady progress, day by day, without fatigue or difficulty and without even realizing how much knowledge they still lacked, which would have frightened them mightily had they been aware of it. On the contrary, thanks to the discernment and discretion of the Master, each postulant progressed along her way with no preoccupation other than that of not missing any of the lessons he gave them.

"As on Wednesdays Dom Guéranger did not have recreation with his monks—something from which he ordinarily never excused himself—he would come after dinner to the parlor of Sainte-Cécile-la-Petite, but again, with the intent of instructing his daughters. He would bring them pictures from the abbey's library and take them on a tour of the catacombs, with Bosio and de Rossi.[2] Or, he would show them reproductions of the best schools of art, the life of Saint Benedict at San Miniato in Florence,[3] or, still, the floor plans of ancient monasteries [perhaps the illustrations in the *Monasticon gallicanum*?[4]]. He had a marvelous ability to awaken minds, drawing interest and stirring the intelligence in such a way that afterwards the nuns' readings and private studies took on an entirely new character; minds were activated and began their work. He knew how to teach through conversation, never in monologue, showing the relationship of things to each other, asking questions to make sure he was being understood, and giving a novel turn to saying the most banal of things, so that they were deeply etched in the memory of his listeners. . . ."[5]

---

[2] Antonio Bosio (c. 1575–1629), born in Malta, was the first systematic explorer of subterranean Rome (the "Columbus of the Catacombs"), and as such, the precursor of "Christian archaeology." His findings compiled in *Roma Sotterranea*, were published posthumously in 1632. He was the inspiration for the work of Giovanni Battista de Rossi (1822–1894), an Italian archaeologist, famous for his rediscovery of early Christian catacombs, including the Catacombs of Callixtus in 1849.—Trans.

[3] San Miniato al Monte is a basilica in Florence, considered the finest Romanesque structure in Tuscany and one of the most beautiful churches in all of Italy. The sacristy is decorated with a great fresco cycle on the life of St. Benedict by Spinello Aretino (1387).—Trans.

[4] The *Monasticon gallicanum* (Paris, 1871) is a collection of 168 plates of topographical illustrations of Benedictine monasteries of the Congregation of Saint Maur, compiled by the antiquarian Achille Peigne-Delacourt (1797–1881), and published by Leopold Delisle (1826–1910).—Trans.

[5] "Notes pour la vie de dom Guéranger" (Notes for the Life of Dom Guéranger), p. 4980.

Sister Cécile, who by lineage and nature was sensitive to all forms of art, benefitted the most from these lively and concrete lessons employing images.

"He never set down a custom or observance for us without first explaining its reasons. He himself determined the readings done in the refectory and those customarily done during manual work time, as well as the sisters' private reading, always requiring an account of these from each. He also supervised the studies each one of us could pursue, and exhorted us to use every spare moment and to profit from everything for our own development and instruction. . . ."[6]

Most astonishing, perhaps, is the fact that the monks at Saint-Pierre did not feel frustrated, or at least not too frustrated, since, as Dom Guéranger lacked the gift of ubiquity, his conferences at Saint-Pierre became less frequent in the measure that those at Sainte-Cécile multiplied. Touching on this situation, the first publishers of the letters of Louis Veuillot took care to include a very amusing piece written during a sojourn at Solesmes. In the letter, Veuillot complains to his sister that Dom Guéranger's attention was absorbed by Sainte-Cécile, and that the *Année liturgique*[7] would have to be finished by itself, as best it may. It was no longer a matter of Madame Swetchine,[8] but of a young girl with whom he had fallen in love at first sight.[9]

"That which most captured the attention of Dom Guéranger and to which he dedicated himself with the greatest care," continued Mother Cécile, "was the celebration of the Divine Office. When he first authorized the singing of the martyrology at Prime,[10] he himself

---

[6] Ibid., p. 4982.

[7] The *Année liturgique* (*The Liturgical Year*) is a monumental commentary on the liturgical year by Dom Guéranger, which he undertook to write and publish in several volumes. The first volumes were very well received and readers clamored for the remaining issues; however, Dom Guéranger died before he could finish the work. The *Année liturgique* was read by the Martin family; thus it was these books by Dom Guéranger that first introduced St. Therese of the Child Jesus to the liturgy of the Church.

[8] Sophie Swetchine (1782–1857) was a notable Russian convert of the nineteenth century who first came to know Dom Guéranger in 1833. She kept up an extensive correspondence with him during the first years of the Solesmes restoration and frequently received him in Paris.

[9] Letter from Louis Veuillot to his sister, dated October 14, 1867. (Uncharacteristically, the author does not quote directly from the letter, but paraphrases Veuillot's facetious remark, of a humor that may seem inappropriate to some.—Trans.)

[10] The office of Prime, said after Lauds, is one of the Little Hours of the Divine Office. It was immediately followed by the recitation of the martyrology, that is, the announcement of the

trained the acolyte for the first five or six times; the hebdomadarian[11] also had her rehearsals; he also would come often for Vigils, which on several occasions he himself presided. In this case, he would place himself inside the oratory against the communion rail that separated the oratory itself from the choir of the postulants. After the office, he had them sit down and each sister was corrected in her turn. The least misplaced accent, double letters overlooked, everything, in a word, was revised and corrected on the spot, in order to avoid our developing bad habits. The zeal, animation, and minute attention with which Dom Guéranger proceeded would seem to indicate that all this work was a great delight to him. . . ."[12]

Sister Cécile wanted to be a perfect novice, but Dom Guéranger wished that she be a perfect superior as well. It was not an easy task. She had some training in this area as she had often substituted for her ailing mother as mistress of the house, both in Paris and in Coudreuse. However, this experience was obviously not enough.

On the vigil of the feast of Saint Cecilia, Dom Guéranger announced at the evening conference that he would have to be absent the following day. He would be leaving after Benediction for Le Mans, where he had been invited to receive the profession of vows of a religious, thus he would not be able to give the usual conference: "It will be Sister Superior who will give it."

Sister Cécile thought he was in jest, but in trying to ascertain the truth, found that the abbot was speaking in all seriousness: "It is a good thing for you to become accustomed to giving the conference, since there will be times when I will not be here, having to occupy myself with other matters; and though I customarily will reserve my time, as far as possible, to come preside at this exercise, there will be occasions when this charge will fall upon you."[13]

---

saints of the following day, and the reading of the pertinent section of the Holy Rule. Prime was eliminated from the Roman liturgy in the liturgical reform of 1970. However, in the revised monastic office of 1977, one of the four possible schemas, Schema A, has retained it. —Trans.

[11] The hebdomadarian is the religious appointed to lead the canonical hours for the week. The word is derived from the Greek for seven, "hepta," and "hebdomas," a group of seven things, such as seven days in a week. —Trans.

[12] "Notes," pp. 4986–87.

[13] "Annals: First Year," p. 16.

Obedience did not come about easily in this case. Sister Cécile still was—or still thought herself to be—very timid. Hearing her own voice resounding alone in the silence put her in a panic. It had already cost her tremendously to be able to recite a prayer out loud or even to make a reading in front of her elders. A conference was something altogether different! On the evening of Saint Cecilia's feast, things went fairly well since she knew her subject and had fixed her attention on the postulants of Chantenay, who were her longtime friends (the lay sisters were ordinarily present at conferences on feast days). However, Dom Guéranger had to prolong his absence through the following day, November 23, and this time around the prioress stopped short after the first few sentences.

Soon afterwards, Dom Guéranger asked her about her impressions as a young religious superior: "Still, you are a strange girl; you haven't said a word to me since I've placed you at the head of the house, and you have taken it as a given. One would think this is entirely natural to you."[14]

Instantly, she unleashed a torrent of words upon him, in which all she had held in her heart came pouring out: her difficulties, her incapacity, her repugnance. The cup was flowing over. The abbot reassured her—he had entrusted her with the charge because he could not do otherwise, having judged in all conscience that this was the will of God.

Outside of the monastery, criticism about Dom Guéranger's choice was obviously not lacking, but he had his reasons to have acted in this way and had shared these with Bishop Fillion.

"My dearest daughter in the Lord," the bishop wrote her during the first few days, "my blessing has preceded you to Solesmes, it has welcomed you upon your entering our dear house of Sainte-Cécile, it will accompany you in the charge that Our Lord has imposed upon you and that He will aid you in fulfilling, for His glory and the good of your sisters. . . . I cannot say how happy I am to see rise in the shadows of the abbey, a convent of Benedictine nuns who will draw the true spirit of Saint Benedict from the experience and the lights of the Very Reverend Father Abbot, a spirit to be passed on for

---

[14] Ibid., p. 18.

generations to come. What we are missing in our days is not action, not the type of charity dispensed in exterior works, but that charity which consumes itself in sacrifice and prayer. Souls who, like the censer closed at its base facing the earth, are open toward heaven, continually raising the fragrance of their vows and their homage: *quasi thus ardens in igne* (like incense burning in fire). Blessed be God for having wished to choose some of these souls to bring them together upon the soil of my diocese, like a magnet that will attract many others still. It is one of the most consoling joys of my episcopate. Amidst the difficulties and cares inherent to my office, so beyond my strength, I delight in thinking of my dear family of Solesmes, and count on their support before God."[15]

Bishop Fillion fully understood the nature of contemplative life, and his support for it was unwavering. He offered words of encouragement and spiritual counsels. This was a reassurance for the future of the house. He trusted Dom Guéranger.

Shortly after Christmas, however, the abbot became gravely ill. A young guest from Laval had brought the smallpox virus with him, and died of it at the monastery's guest quarters. Dom Michelot, the infirmarian, had nursed the young man and succumbed to the virus in his turn. It was a time of great apprehension for all; the prior, Dom Couturier, also contracted the disease. Of a sudden, the young postulants at Sainte-Cécile were, therefore, left entirely on their own. Consistent with her customary attitude of silence and discretion, Sister Cécile kept from disturbing the ailing abbot, refraining even from writing to him. In his feverish state, he became anxious at the lack of communication and sent a very severe letter to the young superior. Subsequently, this letter was entirely forgotten by Dom Guéranger, but Sister Cécile had been deeply affected by it, suffering greatly for a number of weeks.

Once convalescent, Dom Guéranger returned to Sainte-Cécile on January 15, 1867, with a mask concealing the pockmarks on his face. The visits resumed, at a slower rhythm at first, gradually returning to their former frequency. When the situation became normal again, Sister Cécile judged it proper to ask for a clarification regarding the

---

[15] Letter dated November 25, 1866.

letter he had written her and presented it to him. He was aghast, and immediately destroyed it.

Honorine Foubert, one year older than Sister Cécile, had been unable to free herself at the time of the foundation, being delayed for several more weeks at Mamers where she taught music. She was able to join the community on February 8, 1867, bringing the total number of choir postulants to five. She was given the name Sister Mechtilde and the function of chantress. Shortly afterwards, on March 13, the postulants obtained permission from Dom Guéranger to call Sister Cécile by the title "Mother."

Now that the group of foundresses was complete, Dom Guéranger began his commentaries on the Rule of Saint Benedict; notes were taken and edited by Sister Mechtilde. The last monastic observance to be implemented was the chapter of faults.[16]

It will be recalled that in order to avoid delaying the entrance of Marie de Ruffo-Bonneval, under whose name transactions regarding the property had been made, the abbot had agreed to have her invalid sister Noëlie taken care of by the postulants, within the cloister. Noëlie passed away after Mass on Holy Thursday (then celebrated in the morning), on April 18, 1867, at the age of fifty-five. This was the first bereavement experienced at Sainte-Cécile.

Meanwhile, in Westphalia, Princess Catherine of Hohenzollern[17]— restorer and benefactress of the Abbey of Beuron—followed with great interest the foundation of Sainte-Cécile: "This happy beginning inspires only one prayer in me, a lively and ardent prayer," she wrote to Dom Guéranger. "You know my prayer, my Father, and God can answer it! I await your decision with confidence...."[18] She had

---

[16] A regularly held meeting of a religious community in which members accuse themselves of their faults against the Rule and observances, whereupon a penance is prescribed by the superior. It is usually begun by an exhortation concerning a particular point of the Rule or observance. —Trans.

[17] As a widow, Princess Catherine von Hohenzollern (1817–1893) had inherited the property of a former Augustinian monastery in Beuron, south Germany, and using her funds, re-founded Beuron as a Benedictine monastery under the brothers Dom Maurus and Dom Placidus Wolter. From its very inception, the life of the monks at Beuron, and especially their liturgical life, was profoundly influenced by the Abbey of Solesmes and Dom Prosper Guéranger. It is now a Benedictine archabbey. —Trans.

[18] "Annals: First Year," p. 87. As Dom Guéranger supported Beuron Abbey with his counsels, it was entirely natural that he should be in contact with its benefactress.

already attempted religious life in 1854, at the Dames of the Sacred Heart in Kientzheim, Alsace.

The abbot responded that her place was by the monks at Beuron, and that she would be more useful to them there than at Solesmes, thus sparing the young novice-superior at Sainte-Cécile a most uncomfortable situation. However, he did not decline the princess's offer when she proposed to use of her influence to assist him in the erection of the permanent buildings of the monastery of Sainte-Cécile. Dom Guéranger had considered taking some time to go to Rome in June on the occasion of the celebration of the eighteen-hundredth anniversary of the martyrdoms of Saints Peter and Paul. But Bishop Pie of Poitiers dissuaded him from the idea. The trip seemed premature to him, and there would be little chance of obtaining a quick solution amidst the celebrations, shortly before the Roman holidays.

Chapter 13

The Monastery upon the Heights

BECAUSE OF THE CIRCUMSTANCES attendant on the foundation of the Abbey of Saint-Pierre, Dom Guéranger had brought together his first companions at Solesmes without their having previously benefitted from any monastic formation. Since the Revolution, there were no monasteries of Benedictine monks in France. The young prior was able to acquire some notion of the daily life, usages and traditions of an active monastery during a brief stay with the Trappists of Port-du-Salut. Beyond that, he had to have recourse to books, and books alone, to glean information on monastic life. The ceremonial of the monks of the Congregation of Saint-Maur had a particularly prominent role in this regard.

The nuns, on the other hand, enjoyed a more favorable situation since several of their ancient monasteries had survived the Revolution. After the dispersion of 1792, some religious were able to re-group following the Terror and were tolerated under the Consulate and the Empire. Continuity with the past had thus been preserved and their monastic customs and usages kept alive.

Dom Guéranger had his own particular plans for the foundation of Sainte-Cécile, and the postulants themselves wished their lives to be as close as possible to that of Saint-Pierre. Nonetheless, it was felt that a sojourn in a long-standing monastery of nuns would still be the best way of conveying to an entirely new community such as Sainte-Cécile, what daily life in a fully established monastery entailed. This was also the opinion of Bishop Fillion. Therefore, they concluded that Sister Cécile was to spend some time at a monastery of the Benedictine Order. When this was proposed to the community, the postulants protested. They did not want to be separated from their young superior, even if only for a short amount of time. The abbot then designated Sister Gertrude de Ruffo-Bonneval to take her place. He thought of sending her to the Abbey of Pradines or to Saint-Jean d'Angély, which he knew personally. Bishop Fillion, however, argued for Jouarre Abbey[1] where there were nuns from Le Mans. It was a brief stay of only ten days, during which the postulant took note of everything. When she returned, Dom Guéranger wished Sister Cécile to welcome her ahead of her arrival, so the young superior preceded Sister Gertrude to Le Mans, where she was received at the monastery of Visitation nuns closely linked to the history of Solesmes.[2]

Upon the hill behind Sainte-Cécile-la-Petite, the structure of the definitive monastery was quickly being raised. Dom Guéranger intended to have the sisters begin their regular novitiate, now donning the habit, on the feast of the Assumption in 1867. The erection of the buildings proceeded with admirable speed and skill, given that the plans were complex and required great knowledge of the art of construction both on the part of the architect as well as of the construction workers.

By 1866, the neo-Gothic style had already been firmly established in the provinces, while making little headway in Paris where the neoclassical still reigned, championed by the École des Beaux-Arts. In the area of Anjou, where René Hodé was active, the neo-Gothic had appeared early on and with success.[3] There where Dom Guéranger had sought the architect for Sainte-Cécile, the neo-Gothic was rooted in the particular traditions of the region, reviving its ancient forms of construction, most notably the "western Gothic" or Plantagenet style. Angevin traits are discernible in the church of the new monastery in the broad width of its nave, its modest height, and the rounded vaults in the form of domes. However, as to the conventual buildings, the architect gave free rein to his creativity, bringing about a synthesis that accommodated the needs of life in the nineteenth century while using certain decorative elements from the neo-Gothic architectural vocabulary.

---

[1] Jouarre Abbey was founded ca. 630 in northwestern France (Seinne-et-Marne department) by the Abbess Theodochilde.—Trans.

[2] Dom Guéranger was a frequent and well-beloved preacher at the Visitation monastery in Le Mans beginning in the 1830s. The nuns accompanied closely with their interest and prayers the very beginnings of the establishment of Saint-Pierre de Solesmes.—Trans.

[3] The architect René Hodé (1811–1874), active in the Anjou region, was the primary responsible for the revival of the Gothic style in the eighteenth century, thus "neo-Gothic." His work flourished particularly in the 1840s.

The architect had been actively doing his best to advance the construction, but, as far as he was concerned, Dom Guéranger's conversation about occupying the monastery by mid-August defied reality. Nonetheless, the abbot held firmly to his stance and encouraged the postulants in this hope.

The day of the establishment of Sainte-Cécile-la-Petite is considered the actual date of the foundation of the monastery. However, in reality this was but its preparation, an essay at monastic life. Canonically, the inauguration of the novitiate had greater import. Thus, in the first days of August, Dom Guéranger went to Le Mans to settle the procedures regarding the erection of the monastery with the bishop. However, Bishop Fillion determined that he should preside at the ceremony, being the abbot of Solesmes: "The ceremony is yours: it entails the entrance of the first postulants into the Benedictine family. It falls upon you, then, the father of this great family, to receive them. To myself I will reserve the pleasure simply of coming to bless these your children before they leave the Huré home."[4] Granted that memorable words of the past cannot be exactly reproduced, this was, nonetheless, the sense of what the bishop said.

In effect, the architect made it clear that the monastery was not ready; it still lacked half its doors and windows. However, Dom Guéranger was adamant. The future nuns would use the areas that were inhabitable while work would continue in other parts of the construction. Opposition to these plans was great outside of the confines of the community. Bishop Fillion was informed of the situation and came to Solesmes on August 6 and 7; but in the end, this was only to give his permission for the abbot to move forward with his plans. The sisters moved in on the thirteenth and fourteenth, as best they could, and thus began their monastic life at "Sainte-Cécile-la Grande," big Sainte-Cécile. The episcopal ordinance of erection of the monastery is dated August 12, 1867.

All the furniture was moved out of the Huré house beginning on the morning of August 12, and piled into the two large rooms that were available at the new monastery. Then the postulants hastened to settle in to the best of their ability. On the fourteenth, in the

---

[4] Delatte, "Vie," chap. 3.

provisional oratory, Dom Guéranger presided at the ceremony of the clothing with habit while the majority of guests stood in the vestibule and adjoining corridors. The fifty construction workers also wished to watch the ceremony, which they did from nearby windows or perched on their ladders.

To complete the community, Berthe de la Corbière joined the novices on the same day as the clothing ceremony, receiving the name Sister Marie. Célinie Gomer also entered as a lay sister in 1867, as did Jeanne Deschamps, as an extern sister, and Louise Deshayes, as oblate. All these reinforcements came from the parish of Chantenay and the confraternity that Jenny Bruyère had led in Coudreuse. Other postulants hailed from further away. Thus, Marie Marcus came from Alsace where she had finished her studies at Molsheim, with the Canonesses Regular. Sister Odile, as she was named, was the second sister to enter Sainte-Cécile to be younger than the superior.

At the end of 1867, Monsieur Bruyère agreed to see his daughter again, now wearing the religious habit. He came with his wife while Lise remained at La Grange with the Huvés. He visited the monastery, and as an architect, admired the construction already in its advanced stages: "If the birds are in a cage, the cage is quite pretty," he is said to have remarked.[5]

As soon as the choir was finished—smaller than the present-day choir—it served as the oratory, instead of the chapter room as before. Dom Guéranger blessed it, prefiguring in this way the dedication of the church. He likewise blessed the monastery building before establishing the enclosure. The conventual Mass was sung for the first time on the feast of Saint Gertrude, November 17, the anniversary of the inauguration of the postulancy at Sainte-Cécile-la-Petite.

The abbot observed the way in which Sister Cécile governed her house. He said nothing and never complimented her; but one knew how to interpret his silence. When he said nothing, that meant that all was well, and that sufficed. Sister Cécile was used to receiving few signs of appreciation from her spiritual father.

At Sainte-Cécile she no longer had any time for herself, belonging entirely to her sisters. The temptations to impatience were numerous,

---

[5] "Annals: First Year," p. 202.

and at times she let escape some expression of irritation. But on these occasions, she would immediately chastise herself with great severity; Dom Guéranger had difficulty restraining her ardor in this regard.

Some notes have survived, addressed to the abbot, that witness to great physical suffering during this time: "I had a dreadful fever with frequent shortness of breath, even though I was almost sitting upright on our bed.[6] Moreover, a thirst so odd, the likes of which torment I have never endured before. I thought of the *"Sitio"* of the Cross."[7] "The pangs in my heart are so sharp, I can barely move my left arm because of the pain. . . ."[8] And at another time: "I suffer in my whole body, as if I had red-hot iron inside of me, and I feel as if my head were pressed in a vise."[9]

The first weeks of 1868 were passed in this way, in close communion with the sufferings of the Lord. Sister Cécile saw in these, however, a certain form of liberation: "The sufferings of the body make me sense what a soul must experience when it is delivered from the bondage that keeps it captive and enchained. I find in this a well-being of sorts, though it does not in the least assuage the physical suffering."[10]

Dom Guéranger had given up finding any medical explanation for these afflictions. He limited himself to simply observing them and taking the human precautions called for by prudence. On May 4, 1868, he wrote to a correspondent of his: "Our little Mother is suffering at this moment. Her soul finds little latitude to take flight in her poor body, which is often faint and weak. I hope this crisis does not last long; but then, it will be only to await the next bout. None of this causes any concern to those who know her. I have been quite terrified in the past, but not anymore, having seen that Our Lord— who has the right to do what He wills with us—always ends up by returning her to us just as we would like her to be. I've had a good

---

[6] Religious customarily express their vow of poverty in speech by using the plural form of possessive pronouns, denoting that they individually possess nothing of their own: thus, "our bed."—Trans.

[7] Letter to Dom Guéranger dated January 9, 1868. (*"Sitio"* refers to Christ's words upon the Cross: "I thirst."—Trans.)

[8] Letter to Dom Guéranger dated January 10, 1868.

[9] Letter to Dom Guéranger dated January 13, 1868.

[10] Delatte, "Vie," chap. 3.

number of years to steel myself against any worry, since even when she was in the world the Master was wont to deal with her in this way, without ever consulting her or anyone else. May He be praised in all that He does."[11]

What Sister Cécile was experiencing was nothing new. Throughout many years she had suffered these conditions. The abbot, from whom she kept no secret, had had all the leisure to discern the nature of the bouts she periodically endured. As he expressed in his letter, they no longer disturbed him because he had witnessed the fruits they produced in and about her.

During all his life, Dom Guéranger had fought against the *a priori* denial of the supernatural, and yet he was not one to be credulous. Many a time in the course of his life he had had to unmask delusions and bring souls back to a more proper appreciation of the fundamentals of the spiritual life, which they believed themselves to have well surpassed. Neither did Dom Couturier or Dom Delatte let themselves be easily deceived. The latter, in the manuscript of his conferences on "The Spiritual Life," has some strong statements about false mystics. However, all three abbots recognized in Mother Cécile Bruyère the authentic signs of the action of God. They were not the only ones to ascertain this; other great spiritual lights who came into contact with her arrived at the same conclusion.

But Dom Guéranger watched over the well-being and health of the young superior and, since he could not be continually by her, he delegated his powers to Sister Gertrude de Ruffo-Bonneval, who was given the mission to force Sister Cécile to take some rest when she deemed it necessary. He was obeyed, perhaps with exaggerated strictness and authority. This guardianship weighed upon the patient, who would have preferred to have greater liberty over herself. However, as Dom Delatte writes: "It was proper to exert a gentle, and at times imperious, pressure to force the twenty-two year old superior to rest and to take certain precautions. She was much too accustomed to carrying on without having the strength for it,

---

[11] Letter to Mademoiselle de Gobineau dated May 4, 1868.

compelled as she was to spend herself and bear the weight of the house on her own during the absences of Dom Guéranger."[12]

Indeed, it must be remembered that none of the novices had the sense of the long term in the monastic life, and therefore of the necessity of a gradual introduction to its practices. Dom Guéranger was the only one among them with thirty-five years of religious life behind him, which had taught him much about how to treat "brother ass."[13] He who wants to travel far must take care of his mount!

Even at a time when machines and motors did not reign supreme, the bustle of the construction at such close quarters—where workers gave very low priority to silence—did not make for an atmosphere of recollection. The cloister was not yet finished, and it would not be so until Palm Sunday in 1868. The nuns could follow the progress of the work from some of the windows giving onto the activities, longing for the day when this distraction would be removed from their lives.

Postulants continued presenting themselves at Sainte-Cécile's doors. There was the sister of Honorine Foubert from Sablé, Elisabeth, who was named Sister Lucie. And just as he had invited Marie de Ruffo-Bonneval to enter while she still had the care of her invalid sister, Dom Guéranger also received Caroline de Gobineau, a mature woman already suffering from poor health. She was remarkably cultured and her correspondence with her brother, the Count Arthur de Gobineau, has been published. He is today universally known for his questionable role in the development of European thought.[14] She became Sister Benedict and suffered "with heroic patience" for the intention of "ransoming her loved ones."[15]

---

[12] Delatte, "Vie" chap. 3.

[13] "Brother ass" is how St. Francis of Assisi famously referred to his body.—Trans.

[14] Count Joseph Arthur de Gobineau (1816–1882) was a diplomat, novelist and man of letters who contributed to the development of the racialist theory of the Aryan master race. When he was fourteen, his mother, a Creole from Haiti, eloped to Switzerland with another man, taking her son with her. There he developed an interest for Orientalism. He later entered the diplomatic corps of the Second Empire, and was stationed in Persia and Brazil, among other countries.—Trans.

[15] Letter from Mother Cécile to the Countess de la Tour dated February 19, 1884. The most interesting correspondence between the brother and sister de Gobineau was published in two volumes by A.B. Duff (Mercure de France, Paris: 1958). In her letter of May 27, 1868, Caroline informs her brother of her discovery of the monastery of Sainte-Cécile. "There, I re-encountered my childhood memories, the chant of the religious so solemn and touching, that

Dom Guéranger dedicated the greatest care to the new monastery, watching over the recruitment of new vocations. In February 1868, he travelled to Marseilles to attend to matters concerning the priory of monks at Sainte-Madeleine, and took the opportunity, as well, to examine the vocation of possible postulants for Sainte-Cécile.

Among those who frequented the temporary chapel of the novices (the future chapter room) was Prince Walerian Kalinka.[16] He was in Solesmes at the time, assisting Dom Guépin[17] with his book on the life of Saint Josaphat of Polock (1580–1623), Uniate bishop killed by adversaries of the reconciliation of the Orthodox with Rome.[18] His presence attracted other young men of the Polish nobility to Solesmes. One of these, Anton Kolikowski, who led a highly loose life, was so impressed by what he saw at Sainte-Cécile that he converted. He commissioned a painting of Our Lady for the monastic church, which was still under construction, on condition that the nuns pray for his country and for himself. Thus, in April 1868, a replica of the icon of Our Lady of Czestochowa arrived at the monastery. Dom Guéranger decided that it would be placed in the sanctuary of the chapel, on the wall that ran alongside the cloister. He came to bless it on April 3, feast of the Compassion of the Most Blessed Virgin. Later the icon would be transferred to its definitive location above the altar in the chapel of Our Lady, which faces the nuns' choir.

Dom Guéranger at this time was working diligently on the composition of the constitutions, aiming at having them finished in time for the first profession of the novices. For the formulation of the constitutions of Saint-Pierre in 1837, he had relied heavily upon the *Déclarations sur la Règle* (Declarations on the Rule) of the

---

monastic poverty of ancient times combined in perfect harmony with the meeting of their needs, a charming cloister, and finally, it must be said, a superior full of warmth and intelligence who received me as one of her own daughters."

[16] Prince Walerian Kalinka (1826–1886), Polish priest and historian born near Krakow, he founded the Polish branch of the Resurrectionist fathers. —Trans.

[17] Dom Alphonse Guépin (1836–1917), monk of Solesmes. In 1894 he would be sent to Spain to make a foundation in Silos, becoming also its abbot. His correspondence—which attests to his gift for writing— is a valuable source of information for the history of Solesmes at this time, as will be seen further on.

[18] The title of the published book is *Saint Josaphat, archevêque de Polock, martyr de l'unité catholique et l'Église grecque unie en Pologne* (Poitiers: Henri Oudin, 1874). —Trans.

Congregation of Saint Maur, so that the constitutions of Solesmes were an adaptation of this source. But the constitutions of Sainte-Cécile naturally required that texts regulating the lives of nuns be consulted. For this he used three sources: the constitutions of Val-de-Grâce, promulgated in the seventeenth century by Marguerite d'Arbouze, the constitutions written by Mother Thérèse de Bavoz at the beginning of the nineteenth century for Pradines and the Congregation of the Holy Heart of Mary,[19] and the constitutions recently created for Benedictine nuns in Italy, written in great part by Dom Leopoldo Zelli, abbot of the Abbey of Saint Paul Outside the Walls, whom he knew personally.

The first collaborator in this laborious enterprise was Sister Cécile. The abbot then would submit the texts to the other novices, in the measure that they were written, to obtain their remarks and observations and subsequently correct or adapt them accordingly. Nevertheless, the authorship undoubtedly remains Dom Guéranger's.

At the beginning of August 1868, two weeks prior to the date fixed for the first profession ceremony, he brought the text of the constitutions to Bishop Fillion for his approval. The latter approved it without hesitation, accepting the principle of a type of co-jurisdiction shared with the abbot of Solesmes, which would later become a source of difficulty with Bishop d'Outremont (1875–1884).[20]

The Council of Trent had conferred upon diocesan bishops vast juridical powers over communities of nuns, including those which were immediately dependent on the Holy See, for which function they were given the permanent status of apostolic delegates. The legislation for nuns subject to male religious superiors, however, did not change, in principle. Nevertheless, during the seventeenth and eighteenth centuries, bishops often had to take the place of weak religious superiors, or, in some cases, the nuns themselves asked to be placed under their jurisdiction (the case of Port-Royal is well-known[21]). In the course of this development of juridical practice,

---

[19] See chap. 8, p. 79.—Trans.

[20] Hector-Albert Chaulet d'Outremont (1825–1884), Bishop Fillion's successor in Le Mans.

[21] Reference to the seventeenth-century Cistercian nuns of Port-Royal des Champs who, under the influence of Jean Duvergier de Hauranne, abbot of Saint-Cyran, adopted and

common law eventually removed all monasteries of nuns from the influence of the men religious of their respective orders, with only a very few exceptions. The foundation of Sainte-Cécile marks the first stage in the reversal of this process. But the law itself would not be changed until the pontificate of Pius XII. A new function—that of religious assistant—would be created and made universal, even for those monasteries that remained under the jurisdiction of the bishops. Once again, Dom Guéranger had anticipated future institutional developments.

promoted Jansenism, a rigoristic heresy that, among other things, required near perfection for the reception of the sacrament of the Holy Eucharist. —Trans.

Chapter 14

"Prepare Your Lamps"

I keep myself pure for Thee, and with alighted lamp in hand,
I go forth, my Spouse, to meet Thee.
From the heights of heaven, O virgins,
a voice that awakens the dead has sounded:
'Go forth together to meet the Spouse,
in your white robes, lamps in hand,
toward the East.
Arise before the King passes the threshold.[1]

METHODIUS OF OLYMPUS, WHO died a martyr about 311 at Chalcis, wrote a play modeled upon Plato's *Banquet* to celebrate Christian virginity. In it, ten virgins, each in her turn, pronounce a eulogy in praise of chastity consecrated to the Lord. The last virgin, Saint Thecla, the disciple of St. Paul, sings a passionate hymn of twenty-four stanzas, the first of which is cited above.

Since early childhood, Jenny Bruyère had been strongly attracted to the ideal of consecrated virginity, without yet knowing exactly what this meant. Her mother relates that, when small, she would make a scene if someone took her by surprise when being given a bath or when she was being dressed. There is nothing astonishing about this, since the sense of modesty develops very early in children, if they are taught it.

At age five or six, she very much admired wedding processions; watching them was one of her favorite diversions, just as boys of that age are excited about military parades. And when she was asked if she would like to be married later in life, she would answer: "Yes, if I am not obliged to take a husband. . . ."[2]

Jenny was completely taken by the story of St. Genevieve when she was first told about it. She dreamed of imitating her and being discovered by a bishop who would consecrate her to God, as St.

---

[1] From Chapter 2 of the Eleventh Discourse in St. Methodius's *The Banquet of the Ten Virgins.*—Trans.
[2] "Récit de madame Bruyère," p. 22.

Germain d'Auxerre had done for St. Genevieve. Puvis de Chavannes's[3] fresco did not yet adorn the Church of St. Genevieve, which the Third Republic turned into the Pantheon in 1885. But Jenny was able to admire in the church of St. Vincent de Paul—modeled on Roman basilicas, with its lateral tribunes—the famous procession of saints with its choir of virgins painted by Hippolyte Flandrin[4] from 1849 to 1853.

Dom Guéranger, who was not one to shy away from creating precedents, had taken it to heart to revive an ancient tradition during the ceremony of profession scheduled for August 15, 1868 at Sainte-Cécile. He would combine the rite of monastic profession with the rite of consecration of virgins, just as it was described in the Roman Pontifical.[5] He wished thus to revive an ancient tradition that had been in usage in the Church since the fourth century (he believed it to be even earlier), but that had fallen into disuse, nearly universally, in the fifteenth century.

Since the revival effected by Dom Guéranger, the number of communities among the ancient monastic orders that have embraced the rite of consecration of virgins has not ceased to grow. In 1950, the apostolic constitution *Sponsa Christi* positively encouraged nuns to adopt this solemn rite, "one of the most beautiful monuments of the ancient liturgy." Later, the liturgical reform resulting from Vatican II once again extended the rite of consecration of virgins to women living outside monasteries, under the supervision of their bishops. Thus, in the matter of consecration of virgins, the example of Solesmes was followed, just as it was in the practice of having nuns assisted by male religious of their respective orders. The two options adopted by Dom Guéranger, revolutionary in his time, gained wide

---

[3] Pierre-Cécile Puvis de Chavannes (1824–1898), symbolist painter famous for his murals, some of which are found in the Sorbonne, the Pantheon, as well as the Boston Public Library in the United States. He also produced a number of works on religious themes.—Trans.

[4] Jean-Hyppolyte Flandrin (1809–1864), recipient of the Prix de Rome, spent five years in Rome studying painting. His successful career centered mostly on religious themes commissioned by churches in Paris and in other major cities of France.—Trans.

[5] The Roman Pontifical (or *Pontificale Romanum*) is the liturgical book that contains the rites performed by bishops. At this time it would have been the Pontifical of Benedict XIV (1740–1758); however, the rite for the consecration of virgins that would have been published there had not been modified since 1595.—Trans.

acceptance and eventually became the common law, sanctioned and encouraged by the Holy See.

As before, it would again be necessary to persuade the bishop of the idea. Just as he had agreed to share jurisdiction over Sainte-Cécile with the abbot of Solesmes, whose ideas and person he highly respected, Bishop Fillion brought up no difficulty with regard to combining the ceremony of profession with that of the consecration of virgins. If the church possesses and proposes rites in her liturgical books, it is not so that these rites may be preserved for archaeologists and historians. The liturgy is a living reality and, if it is not living, the fault lies with those who neglect it.

The first five choir nuns and the first two lay sisters of Sainte-Cécile would, therefore, make their profession on the day of the Assumption, in the church of the monastery. A great many guests were due to come and Sister Cécile had strongly hoped that her father would agree to attend. But he did not yet have the courage: "Finally, my well-beloved daughter, my dearest Jenny," he wrote her, "incapable as I feel of expressing any sentiment other than tenderness for you, I tell you: do what you must, I will always love you. May God, who is Master of our hearts, have mercy on us. Your father, who embraces you in tears."[6]

He had come a long way since the distressing scenes that had transpired before her departure from Coudreuse. However, she would still have to wait for the conversion which she so longed for and for which she had prayed so diligently since her childhood.

The proceedings of August 15 were an event for the entire Solesmes family. At one point there had been thought of holding the ceremony at the Abbey of Saint-Pierre, but Bishop Fillion did not dare to permit it. Thus, all the monks came to Sainte-Cécile with Dom Guéranger on that day, and accompanied the seven newly professed from the beginning until the end of the ceremony: they came in conventual order to fetch them at the door of the enclosure, led them in procession to the church, responded to their *Suscipe*[7] and, at last,

---

[6] Letter dated July 13, 1868.

[7] The *Suscipe* is the verse from Psalm 118 which, as prescribed by St. Benedict, monks recite on the day when they formally enter monastic life through their profession. They chant it three times: "*Suscipe me, Domine, secundum eloquium tuum et vivam; et non confundas me ab*

after Mass, they accompanied them back, chanting the *Te Deum* with them. The congregation was made up mostly of the families of the nuns. Dom Guépin, describing the ceremony to an absent monk, wrote "It was sublime! The union of these two monasteries, which God has brought together in support of each other, will never be more strongly expressed."[8]

Many years later, in a conference to her nuns, Mother Cécile explained all that she understood the word "consecration" to entail: "The true consecration of a soul consists in faith, hope and charity having reached their zenith. A consecrated soul is one in which God finds all His pleasure as He does in His only Son. The truly consecrated soul resembles the true worshipers whom the heavenly Father seeks and of whom Our Lord spoke to the Samaritan woman.[9] The soul adores God because all things are in perfect balance within it, harmony has become perfect. These are those whom the Word desires to find upon earth to present to His Father in union with Himself. He awaits them as the fruit of the mysteries of the Incarnation and Redemption. . . ."[10]

And in a letter of 1872: "We sing already in heavenly joy: *Ecce quod concupivi, iam video; quod speravi, iam teneo. Illi sum juncta in coelis quem in terris posita [tota devotione dilexi].* (Behold, that which I desired, I now see; that which I hoped for, I now have. I am united in heaven to Him Whom on earth I loved with all my soul.)[11] After this, what further is there for us to desire and to long for? What are to us the obstacles, trials, sufferings, and thousand miseries of time? *"Iam"* (now); we no longer live in time, and it would seem that we cannot be touched but by joy alone. What are to us all that which seems to be affliction to others, if not simply the proof of our love and our fidelity? What happiness to be able to *give testimony* of our love!

---

exspectatione mea" (Receive me, O Lord, according to Your word, and I shall live; and let me not be confounded in my hope. Ps. 118[119]:116). The verse is repeated by the entire community at each of the three occurrences.

[8] Letter from Dom Guépin to Dom E. Viaud, dated August 25, 1868.

[9] John 4:23–24.—Trans.

[10] Conference of October 12, 1897.

[11] Antiphon from the Office of St. Agnes, also sung at the consecration of virgins.—Trans.

Martyrs testified by their blood; we testify by the divine fire. In both instances, always the color red, always the witness. . . ."[12]

The regular election of the prioress was held the day after the profession. Dom Guéranger presided over the vote, assisted by two monks. His prior, Dom Couturier, was there, grave as usual. "My good Father Prior," whispered the abbot, "liven up a little![13] You are not at a funeral. Do not look so disconcerted, Father Prior; it is not you who are being elected."[14]

Bishop Fillion was notified of the result of the election—of which there had been little doubt—and was given an account of the ceremony of profession. "Just as much as you, I also lived those moments at Solesmes, during the profession of our dear daughters and the election of the mother prioress," he wrote. "Nothing surprises me about the details you have given me, so touching and so full of interest. However, I cannot help but admire the attention of Our Lord in bringing upon His spouses the blessings of His Vicar, at the very moment that they were consecrated to Him."[15] Indeed, Pius IX had sent his apostolic blessing for the ceremony.

During the novitiate, Sister Cécile had considered herself a novice among other novices, even while being at the head of the monastery, and Dom Guéranger had dealt with her more or less as such. After the elections, however, she was surprised to see him change his attitude and address her as he would the real superior of a real monastery. He continued as the counselor, but he was no longer the master of novices and determined that the monastery of Sainte-Cécile would no longer be kept under tutelage.

"'I no longer can substitute for you,' were substantially his words, spoken with that tone of resolute kindness that would suffer no reply. 'I did so while it was necessary, my dear child. Now, I want to see you act. You may do so under my eyes, if you so wish, for as long as the Lord leaves me in this world. You will draw strength and experience from this, but understand well that the intention of the

---

[12] Letter to Mme. Gertrude d'Aurillac Dubois, dated August 22, 1872.
[13] An ancient expression of the Sarthe area, "s'affloner" [the verb used by Dom Guéranger—Trans.] means to have spirit, to be enthused.
[14] "Annals: Second Year," p. 128.
[15] Ibid., p. 132.

Church is that you govern. Therefore, you will appoint those who are to fill the several monastic offices, after having chosen them yourself. I agree to your submitting a list of names to me, and we can discuss it together, but the initiative of choosing the appointees will be yours.'"[16]

How far from those scenarios in women's religious life of the nineteenth century where the power of men is often depicted as oppressive and absolute! Mother Cécile accepted this particular form of obedience, but she was still only twenty-three and had no more experience in religious life than her sisters. In a note dated January 22, 1869 she signed: "Sister Cécile, obediently prioress,"[17] as in other religious orders, according to seventeenth-century tradition, they would sign: "unworthy prioress."

However, the relatively frequent absences of the abbot made her feel each time as if she had been left in a vacuum: "At first, when you go away leaving me alone, I very much resemble these little children whose mother lets go of their hands in order to make them take a few steps on their own. I am frightened, and the house seems immense to me. Thanks be to God, these first moments do not last long; I quickly turn to Our Lord, stifling all my other worries, and I attach myself to Him so energetically that I am able to move forward, one day at a time. It seems to me that there is more courage in making an act of self-abandonment into the hands of Our Lord in this way than to look at the burden and measure it to my shoulders. As objective as I am, I cannot without danger keep pondering things in my brain. Besides, Our Lord, Who has given me this charge, knows well what I am capable of carrying; the remainder belongs to Him by right, so why would I be troubled? Thus, I am full of joy; my Father, go ahead, you can leave!"[18]

Saint-Pierre was not far away, nor was Dom Guéranger. He would remain with them for six more years, a brief period in a human life. Mother Cécile would not yet be thirty on the day when he would die. In the interim, the new monastery and its young prioress benefitted from his instruction and his solicitude. Memories preserved by the

---

[16] Ibid., p. 139.
[17] "Soeur Cécile, prieure de bonne volonté."
[18] Letter to Dom Guéranger dated April 10, 1869.

first nuns and novices show how close and fatherly he was to them. The letters of Mother Pudentienne Marsille to her mother at the time of her novitiate in 1871 abundantly attest to this: "Truly, we are downright spoiled children and God will be severe with us if we do not multiply the talents entrusted to us. My dear Mama, I wish that you could attend one of our conferences to have an idea of the fatherly kindness with which the Father Abbot treats us. After having said the *Veni Sancte* (Come, Holy Spirit)[19] he sits himself down on his straw armchair and begins always with these words: 'Well, my dear children, what would you like to ask me this evening?' Then each one of us submits her questions, and we see this man—so wise, so enlightened that the bishops consult him as a guide and judge— respond to all the questions asked of him with the simplicity of a child. He never gives the impression that he finds our questions too naïve; sometimes, however, he bursts into laughter and says: 'Oh, little daughters, my little daughters, how sweet you are!' And then, with his usual mildness he gives his explanation, asks if we have understood him, and after having thus satisfied all the queries posed—regardless of whether by choir or lay sisters—he takes up the subject of his conference."[20]

Even as prioress, Mother Cécile still profited by the rich teachings of the abbot. She was not abandoned to herself; the spiritual direction that had faithfully accompanied her since the time of her first communion was still at hand. To better know what God was accomplishing in her, the abbot ordered her to set aside her natural reserve and give him an account of her interior life. He often had to insist, as Mother Cécile would have readily taken refuge behind the pretext that any attempt at expressing herself was useless because of the difficulty of rendering into words what was, in effect, an unutterable reality.

She had an intense longing for the beatific vision. Dom Guéranger thought, with reason, that it was still a bit early for her entry into eternity. Before that could happen, she still had to serve the Lord and fulfill the task He had entrusted to her. "Isn't 'doing His will' (*eius* –

---

[19] Verse, response and prayer invoking the aid of the Holy Spirit.—Trans.
[20] Letter dated December 17, 1871.

His) the only compensation for the drudgery of this exile? I should tell you, my Reverend Father, that this is my present disposition. I am weary of life! It isn't at all dryness or discouragement that I feel; and still, I suffer, and this pain is very sharp. I would like to see Our Lord and no longer remain in the miserable conditions of this life. Despite all, I linger on. I seek a counterbalance in work, prayer, in devotion to others, but I cannot fill the immense void that is in me. Nothing can distract me from this pain, nothing has the power to relieve me. . . . Am I not sufficiently rich by belonging to Him and by being able to grow each day in His love? *Domine non sum dignus* (Lord, I am not worthy). Reason tells me so, but my heart, despite everything, still goes further and forgets in a way the distance that exists between He Who is, and she who is not."[21]

A few days later she explains anew: "The sentiment of weariness that I described to you the other day keeps growing and is quickly reaching agonizing levels. Our Lord removes Himself more and more from my soul, leaving there only a vehement desire to see Him. . . . Added to this quest—painful because it is fruitless—and to this darkness, is a poignant realization of my infirmities. I am nothing but misery, imperfection, nothingness, I am horrified at myself! O my Father, how I suffer. . . . My suffering is akin to that which the souls in purgatory must feel."[22]

Dom Guéranger's absences necessitated that Mother Cécile commit to writing what were essentially accounts of her prayer life. These vary according to the state of her soul and one should not read into them more than what the prioress intended to reveal: a particular experience within a given situation. She often did not even read her notes, which were directly filed in the personal archives of the abbot, and she eventually forgot about them. They reflect the echoes of a very intense and profound inner life:

"It seems to me more useful to explain to you what I ordinarily understand by 'being close to Our Lord.' Thus you will have this information in mind for the present instance, and for all others henceforth. This state which I described to you comes upon me

---

[21] Letter to Dom Guéranger dated April 16, 1869.
[22] Letter to Dom Guéranger dated April 18, 1869.

unexpectedly, without anything having occasioned it or prepared the way for it, and in the most diverse circumstances. Sometimes it is during the office or at prayer, or during work, when reading, when speaking to a sister, even at the parlor. Likewise, no effort can prolong it once it has come to an end. And nothing exterior is the cause of its interruption, just as nothing exterior brought it about. All of a sudden my soul feels something like a thrill of joy. Then everything seems beautiful and radiant to me because I find the Lord in all and that His love renders a festive air to everything, like the delights of springtime.[23] Exterior things become transparent to me . . . in an entirely spiritual manner that I cannot explain. I only know that everything brings me to God, that it is impossible to be distracted because that which is ordinarily a distraction becomes for me the means of union with Our Lord. It is sometimes a type of inebriation. . . . At other times this visit of Our Lord brings about in me a singular state of recollection, as if my soul entered within itself. In this case, exterior things tire me and I must make an effort to occupy myself with whatever it may be."[24]

---

[23] "Puis tout me semble beau, heureux, parce que j'y trouve le Seigneur, et que son amour met tout en fête comme un printemps délicieux."—Trans.

[24] Letter to Dom Guéranger dated March 18, 1869.

Chapter 15

Abbess

SINCE HIS FIRST VISIT TO Sainte-Cécile on November 13, 1867, Monsieur Bruyère had mellowed; he no longer displayed the same hostility when someone spoke about the vocation of his daughter in his presence. However, the road back to God still stretched long ahead, and Mother Cécile was in haste to see him soon set upon it for good. In the spring of 1869, he had an attack of hemiplegia in Paris. Contrary to all expectations, he showed no resentment. His patience and calm hinted at an interior process that bode of an approaching transformation:

"[I believe] that my father's mind is occupied with thoughts stronger than the desire for the recovery of his health. He feels stricken to death, he feels himself in God's hands, he thinks of his daughter, compares, examines; and aided by grace, what effect will these long and difficult hours of inactivity not have? As for myself, I pray with ardent confidence," wrote Mother Cécile.[1]

Madame Bruyère's reports confirmed the intuition of her daughter. The family returned to Coudreuse, but the proximity to Solesmes was illusory. Visits from Coudreuse to Solesmes became veritable expeditions. Mother Cécile thus vividly experienced the measure of sacrifice that she had accepted in placing a monastic cloister between her and her family. Great was her suffering and she had need of every encouragement from Dom Guéranger: it was a good thing that she was undergoing this trial before any of her sisters, since, as prioress she would have to support them when they should go through similar afflictions.

The novitiate at the monastery continued steadily growing, counting more sisters than all other groups within the young community. However, this growth was no sudden surge, so that it was possible to care for the formation of each novice individually. The task, nevertheless, proved arduous: "I live in a continual bustle,"

---

[1] Letter to Dom Guéranger dated April 24, 1869.

the young prioress wrote to her mother, "giving of my all, as much as possible, I believe, not losing any time, and still not achieving anything. What will I do when we are sixty?"[2] This was not yet the case, however. On October 12, 1869, three nuns made their profession: Mother[3] Odile Marcus, Mother Lucie Foubert and Mother Eulalie Ripert. One of these, Mother Lucie, was gravely ill and died six months afterwards, on March 13, 1870.

If Mother Cécile still had but a limited experience of community life, in the domain of the spiritual life she was no longer a novice. Her heart spoke easily when it was a matter of the truths of the faith. There are still some notes preserved from this period, which served her as framework for a series of conferences on the Creed she gave to her nuns. Certain passages are of great lyrical beauty:

"O Church of God, sprung forth from the sacred side of the Spouse asleep upon the Cross, founded on Christ, the corner stone, you are my love and my life! You are my mother, mother without stain or blemish, mother of incomparable beauty, strength, and splendor! You are truly holy, you who are united to the Author of all holiness; you are universal, you who extend across all the earth and belong to the Master of heaven and of earth; you are truly apostolic! In your bosom are found the true, the beautiful, the good—every good thing that the earth brings forth comes directly or indirectly from you."

The themes that will inform her profound thought are already present in these lines in which she shows herself to be a faithful disciple of Dom Guéranger. In Mother Cécile and her daughters, love of the Church and devotion to the mystery of the Church are consistently present.

Besides her charge of the community and the novitiate, other cares were added to Mother Cécile's responsibilities. Sainte-Cécile was justly considered the work of Dom Guéranger; no one, or barely anyone, knew the prioress, who had not yet emerged from her anonymity. Because of Dom Guéranger, however, Sainte-Cécile was

---

[2] Letter dated June 23, 1869.
[3] At that time choir nuns went by the title "Mother," while lay sisters and externs went by the title "Sister." This distinction in nomenclature is no longer made, but is retained in the translation.—Trans.

perceived as a model of monastic life, even after only two or three years of existence. For the moment, requests were coming only from the ancient monasteries that were already more or less open to the influence of Dom Guéranger, such as Sainte-Croix of Poitiers in France, and in England, the Abbey of Stanbrook, whose chaplain, Dom Laurence Shepherd, expected much from the new foundation. A monk of the English Benedictine Congregation, he was an admirer of everything that issued from the Abbey of Solesmes and the translator of *L'Année liturgique* (*The Liturgical Year*).

In this same year, 1869, the prayers of the nuns were united to those of the entire Church, in preparation for the Council.[4] It had been expected that Dom Guéranger would go to Rome, as all had been done to have him present, but he did not feel he had the strength to make the trip and then to handle the fatigue of having to participate in commissions and plenary assemblies. He believed that a written contribution would be more important than his presence, and he needed time to compose his *La Monarchie pontifical*[5] (The pontifical monarchy).

Louis Veuillot announced the publication of the book to the readers of *L'Univers* on February 18, 1870, excusing himself for his belated report: "I have not yet spoken to you of the book by Dom Guéranger in rebuttal of Bishop Maret, referencing other Gallican heads[6] as well. Quite simply, we did not yet have it. It has finally arrived. I can tell you that you will devour it; it is admirable. Verily, in this country of good judges, this work by our illustrious friend and patron has only found admirers. Praises resound for its vast and certain knowledge, its good sense, its brevity, its clarity. . . . In my

---

[4] First Vatican Council.

[5] Dom Guéranger published *La Monarchie pontifical* in spring 1870, with the intent of clarifying the theological, patristic and historical arguments impacting the definition of the proposed dogma of papal infallibility for the fathers of Vatican Council I in the course of their ardent preparatory discussions.

[6] Under this term ["Gallican heads"], Louis Veuillot includes several religious personalities such as Bishop Felix Dupanloup [bishop of Orléans] and Father Joseph Gratry—opposed, like Bishop Maret, to the definition of the dogma at issue—whose assertions were criticized by Dom Guéranger, not in *La Monarchie pontificale*, but in pamphlets published shortly afterwards.

opinion, Dom Guéranger's polemics perfectly embody the theory of the art [of polemics]—strength without effort."[7]

In this way, the abbot found indulgence for not having made his appearance at the conciliary *aula*. He was present there in the form of a dissertation in historical theology that, in three hundred pages, refuted several objections to the dogma, and helped many bishops to discern more clearly the truth of a subject that still presented numerous difficulties.

Mother Cécile could only rejoice at the approval given the book by Pius IX: "I have already read the [papal] brief," she wrote (it appeared in the second edition of the book), "and I am happy. Defender of the Bride that he is, it seemed I was hearing the compliments of the Bridegroom. His congratulatory words are even more precious because they are at the same time an affirmation of the truth. I am not ambitious for you, my good Father, which would be vanity, but I admit that I am not insensitive to seeing you enveloped with the glory of the doctors. I am happy for the gifts that God has given you, and glorify Him in them as if they were my own; in effect, they are indeed mine since you are my father and more a father than can be imagined."[8]

Another joy that came to her that spring was the engagement of her sister. Lise, unlike her elder sister, had never shown any inclination for the religious life; quite the contrary. She loved to be in the company of young men and took visible pleasure in being courted. And her choice was excellent. Léopold Eynaud was a maritime engineer; he belonged to a new generation that had benefited from a true Christian education. The marriage took place on June 21, 1870. The new household promised to be calmer than that in which Mother Cécile had grown up. It was Dom Guéranger who blessed the marriage in Chantenay, and he was happy for the opportunity to re-establish friendly relations with Monsieur Bruyère.

Mother Cécile felt more assured now in her role as prioress than she had in the beginning. She was gifted with all the qualities needed to govern a community, but she had not been aware of this when

---

[7] *Rome pendant le Concile* (Rome during the Council), *Complete Works*, T. XII, pp. 210–211.
[8] Letter to Dom Guéranger dated March 23, 1870.

Dom Guéranger first chose her from among her companions. She discovered in herself a maternal grace that emerged when she came into contact with souls. Previously, she had received certain lights in this regard, but she had interpreted them as related to a hidden motherhood toward souls, not discerning clearly that God had destined her for a real motherhood. She had been prepared for her future role in silence.

It was a joy for her to be able to understand her daughters and to feel loved and trusted by them. This was the best initiation into spiritual direction, something in which she would excel during her mature years. However, vestiges from her childhood were still manifest in her tendency to pass severe judgments in her innermost heart, to measure others in the scale that she had always applied to herself, and to be astonished at irrationality and laxity, which she had never allowed in herself.

Gradually she felt less and less repulsed by her charge, barring some occasional impatience at seeing herself a prisoner of the thousand little problems of her daughters. What helped her in her task was the gift of recollection with which she had been favored very early in life. When the time for the Divine Office or for personal prayer would arrive, writes Dom Delatte: "all other thoughts vanished or became to her like the distant murmur of running waters to which one gets so accustomed that awareness of it is lost."[9] The comparison reflects local reality, as the Abbey of Saint-Pierre sits above a dam that lies between two marble workshops, and during summer the incessant noise of the waters flows in through the open windows that face the river. It invades everything and drowns out other familiar sounds that won't re-emerge until that time of the year when the floodgates of the locks are open, so that the waters no longer pass over the dam to precipitate below in a roar.[10] But the din of the great waters recedes to a far corner of one's consciousness

---

[9] Delatte, "Vie" chap. 4.

[10] This annual event is designated by a specific term which the author includes in this poetical description, the "écourues." The floodgates of dams along a river are left open for a period of time, in order to lower the level of the river so as to allow for maintenance, repairs, etc., along its banks. While the "écourues" season was a universal practice in France in former times, it is now restricted precisely to the area of Le Mans and Sablé.—Trans.

when an absorbing occupation holds the attention captive. Thus it was with Mother Cécile.

She had attained a form of interior peace that, while not eschewing blows and sufferings, allowed her to place herself above the life of the senses, far away from the fluctuations affecting the surface. Dom Guéranger spoke of the "prayer of union," which frightened her and put her ill at ease: "Could I ever have imagined that you would even allude to such a thing in reference to a poor girl such as myself? These words make me afraid, they can never apply to me; in short, I do not want them to be." [11]

What she read about the mystics troubled her. She believed that their vocation was not for her: "You may try as you might to dress me in fine gowns," she would tell God when she lay awake at night, "I will never be a grand lady. I will embarrass You with my blunders and coarse manners. Please allow me to stay in Your country house. There I will care for your lambs, I will remove the manure, I will sweat blood and water if you wish: *Non recuso laborem* [the "I do not refuse the work" pronounced by Saint Martin on his deathbed]. [12] Have the likes of a Teresa, a Catherine of Siena dwell in your palaces; that is quite simple: they are noble, they are beautiful. But me, I am a peasant and I am ugly. While I was not aware of what You were doing in me, I went along blindly and in simplicity, seeing nothing but You. But now that I am told these things, I pray You, do not entertain these divine fantasies. In heaven, all that will be very well and without inconveniences. Here below, I have always been afraid of all these things and I have dreaded them more than all sufferings imaginable." [13]

Dom Guéranger saw things more simply. God is master of His gifts, and since He shepherds souls, the only proper response on their part is to allow themselves to be taken along the ways that He Himself has chosen for them. It is useless to try to substitute oneself for Him. That would be akin to insulting Him. If He says "go," we

---

[11] Letter to Dom Guéranger dated June 9, 1870.

[12] St. Martin of Tours (316-400), is to have said upon his deathbed, at the promptings of his disciples who did not wish to see him leave them: "Lord, if Thy people still need me, I do not refuse the labor. May Thy will be done." —Trans.

[13] Letter to Dom Guéranger dated June 9, 1870.

must go; if He says "come," we must come. We must obey God, obey His inspirations, after having gone through the necessary discernment process so as to eliminate any danger of illusion. In life there is but one thing to do—to want what God wants and to say "Yes." All else comes from the devil!

On July 19, 1870 a dispatch received at Solesmes announced the definition of the dogma of papal infallibility, which had occurred the previous day at the Council. *"Te Deum laudamus!"* wrote Louis Veuillot from Rome. "It is done. Except for two dissenting voices, now in submission, the dogma was passed in unanimity. By abstaining, the opponents of the dogma allowed for a unanimous vote. They had already done much through their opposition (there were sixty-six absentees). . . . I heard the *Veni Creator*, the *Te Deum*, the acclamations of the council and of the people. I do not wish to describe anything. . . . A dreadful storm surrounded Saint Peter's, enveloping the basilica in almost complete darkness. The dogma was proclaimed amidst lighting and thunder. In the crowd, some thought of Gallicanism and said: 'It is a funeral!' Others thought of things to come and said: 'We are on Sinai.'"[14]

Another event would deeply move the two communities when they learned of it, with the exception of the abbot, who was privy to the secret. Some days after the telegram from Rome had come, a letter from Bishop Fillion arrived at Solesmes:

"My Very Reverend Father, you must be surprised at my long silence, and I must confess that it has cost me much. But I was awaiting my audience each day, which had first been requested on June 20. Finally, I was admitted yesterday into the Holy Father's presence. I found him in good health and wonderful disposition, neither much surprised nor affected by the sixty-eight *non placet*.[15] After having spoken about your past works and those which you propose to engage in, I put forth the question of the abbess. The Pope told me: '*Sarebbe mettere il carro avanti i bovi*' (It would be putting the cart before the oxen.) First the monastery must be elevated to the status of an abbey.' I responded: 'That matters little, as long as the

---

[14] *Rome pendant le Concile*, pp. 537–538.

[15] This expression refers to the stance of sixty-eight prelates opposed to the dogma of papal infallibility (66 absentees and 2 abstentions). [*non placet*, it does not please.—Trans.]

cart still moves forward. If by Your Holiness's grace we are given an abbess, the Congregation of Bishops and Regulars perforce will have to grant us an abbey.' He took the petition and put his spectacles on, saying 'But this is a whole sermon! Leave it here with me and I will read it later, at my leisure.' 'If your Holiness will allow me, I will read it to you, it will not take long.' When I finished, Pius IX took his pen and wrote: '*Pro gratia speciali, in exemplum non adducenda, petitam facultatem concedimus.*' (We grant the permission requested, by special grace that will not be adduced as a precedent.) His conversation, his manner, made me understand that it was to you that he was granting this truly exceptional favor.

"Now, my Right Reverend Father, it falls to you to prepare Mother Cécile for this great blow. Just as much as her daughters will rejoice, so much will she be afflicted. I will bring you the rescript."[16]

This happened on July 14, on the feast of Saint Bonaventure, that is, exactly thirty-three years after the elevation of Dom Guéranger to the abbatial dignity. This coincidence was interpreted as a sign of Divine Providence. From then on the date became an integral part of the history of Solesmes. "We already held Saint Bonaventure, the great seraphic doctor, in high esteem," wrote a monk, "but now he has the right to more zealous homage on our part. It is from him that we have our two abbatial crosiers, the abbess's and the abbot's."[17]

Dom Guéranger kept the contents of the letter to himself and awaited the bishop's return from Rome. Bishop Fillion came to Sainte-Cécile on August 9 with the rescript. We have an account of the scene as it transpired when the matter was revealed to the community. It took place in the workroom, since the chapter room was again being used as a chapel because of construction being done in the church. Dom Guéranger purposely arrived late so as to leave to the bishop all the joy of announcing the great news:

---

[16] Letter to Dom Guéranger dated July 15, 1870. (Rescript is "a response of the pope or a sacred congregation, in writing, to a question or petition of an individual. A rescript usually affects only the person to whom it is addressed although at times it can have the force of a general law." The Maryknoll Catholic Dictionary, Albert J. Nevins, ed. (New York: Dimension Books, 1965), p. 490.—Trans.)

[17] Letter from Dom Guépin dated July 17, 1871.

"So, Monseigneur, are our daughters happy with what you have reported to them?"

"Oh, no, my Right Reverend Father, I did not want to tell them anything in your absence."

Then, he continued before the highly intrigued nuns:

"Well, my daughters, the pope, happy with all that your Father Abbot did during the Council, desired to reward him, and searching for what would most touch his heart, he found nothing better than to gratify his daughters."

After a few seconds of silence:

"He has allowed me to bless an abbess for you!"[18]

There followed a few words of clarification, and then he read out to the community the rescript that he had brought back with him from Rome—Mother Cécile had been appointed abbess at the age of twenty-four. The joy was uncontainable; Madame Prioress alone seemed aghast.

The situation was quite paradoxical: she was the abbess of a monastery that was still only a simple priory! But the rest would follow . . . the oxen behind the cart.

---

[18] "Annals: continuation," August 8, 1870.

Chapter 16

1870 – "L'Année Terrible"[1]

NOW IT WAS A MATTER of setting the date for the abbatial blessing; however, the Franco-Prussian War (1870-1871) would delay the event.

France was at war, and on August 9, 1870, news of the first reversals arrived in Maine province by telegraph: the defeat of Napoleon III and Lebœuf at Sarrebrück and Spicheren on August 6, in the Sarre region; the defeat of Mac-Mahon at Wissembourg and Froeschwiller on August 4 and 6, in Alsace.

The declaration of war against Prussia came as a surprise to many, given that on June 30 Prime Minister Émile Ollivier[2] had stated to the Chamber that in no other period in history had the peace of Europe been more assured. But the candidacy of Prince Hohenzollern to the throne of Spain was put forth, and this alarmed Napoleon III's government, as well as public opinion, beyond what was reasonable. From our vantage point, this anxiety seems an anachronism. After all, the nineteenth century, with its constitutional monarchies, had little in common with the times of Charles V, or the end of Louis XIV's reign, which had witnessed the long and terrible War of Spanish Succession. However, the rhetoric of French diplomacy abruptly came into play in a manner that was offensive to Prussia, and the tone of hostility quickly mounted on both sides of the frontier. The press both in France and Germany played a disastrous role in the entire affair, pouring oil upon fire and kindling the arguments in favor of war. The Emperor and Ollivier were overwhelmed by the events, admitting themselves to be helpless before the power of public opinion.[3]

---

[1] "The Terrible Year"—the title of a series of poems written by Victor Hugo (pub. 1872), which deal with the Franco-Prussian War.—Trans.

[2] Olivier Émile Ollivier (1825–1913), Prime Minister of the Third Republic, the thirtieth Prime Minister of France.—Trans.

[3] The chronology of events is as follows: Prince Leopold von Hohenzollern-Sigmaringen (1835–1905) announces his candidacy to the vacant throne of Spain on June 21, 1870; on July 6 the French Minister of Foreign Affairs, the Duke de Gramont, declares that France is opposed

This presumptuous and exacerbated nationalism of the public was above all a product of Paris and its journalists. The provinces followed behind only very reluctantly, dragging their feet. For the people of the countryside, in particular, the war was a calamity. It was difficult for them to conceive of having to be cannon fodder yet once again; the massacres of the first Empire were still engraved in their memories. In the regions of Champagne, Franche-Comté, Bretagne, the *Te Deum*—which the Emperor had ordered the clergy to sing in all churches—became a portent of mourning. Sung with a French accent in parody, "Te Deum" turned into "Tue des hommes," meaning, "kill the men":

> *Te Deum*
> Il faut des hommes,
> *Laudamus te,*
> C'est pour les tuer.[4]

The clergy, therefore, was not popular with the people when they read from the pulpit the pastoral letters required by the government ordering that a *Te Deum* be sung for some victory won in a far distant land. In general, the peasantry was vehemently anti-military. In the Vendée region they sang:

> I m'emmenions dans un grand champ
> Qu'i z'appellaient champ d'bataille.
> I s'étripaient, i s'éplumaient.
> C'était pis qu'd'l'volaille.
> Ma foué, la peur m'a prit,
> J'ai pris mon sac et m'ensauvit . . .[5]

---

to the candidacy; on July 12, Prince Leopold von Hohenzollern withdraws his candidacy; on July 13 the French Ambassador, Count Vincent de Benedetti, delivers to King Wilhelm of Prussia, in the city of Ems, a formal communiqué requesting that he confirm his support of and adherence to the withdrawal. Wilhelm communicates the desired confirmation in a message hand-delivered by an aide-de-camp, who tells the ambassador that "His Majesty considers the affair closed." The Prussian Chancellor, Otto von Bismarck, issues a widely circulated account of the proceedings emphasizing the fact that the "king refused to receive the ambassador again." This is immediately taken up as a provocative gesture by the French press, which foments sentiments that grow to an incandescent scale, eventually leading France to declare war on Prussia on July 19.—Trans.

[4] *Te Deum* (Thee, O God) / They need men / *Laudamus te* (We praise Thee) / To have them killed.—Trans.

After the first setbacks of 1870, rumors began spreading through the land that it was the priests and religious who had brought the Prussians in and were the cause of the calamity. The delusion was just as absurd as that which circulated in May and June of 1940, whereby fifth column agents purportedly went about disguised as priests and religious. What was the origin of this rumor which took hold in the winter of 1870-1871? Perhaps the clergy had abused the terrifying rhetoric they employed in their sermons, threatening chastisements and the judgments of God. When the tragedies began to occur, the people took the priests to be responsible for them.

Be that as it may, it would be a while before the matter of the abbatial blessing and the consecration of the monastic church at Sainte-Cécile could be given any thought. This was not the time for festivities, even if liturgical. With news of the two disasters in Sedan and Metz, it became evident to the greater number of career officers in the French army that the best solution to the conflict would be the prompt execution of an armistice. The founders of the Third Republic, however, did not see things in this way. Ignorant of the problems posed by modern warfare and still spellbound by the memory of Valmy,[6] they believed that an improvised army would be able to prevail over the invader. Thus, with the impending siege of Paris, they sent a governmental delegation to Tours, later joined by Léon Gambetta,[7] with the objective of organizing the resistance and

---

[5] In Vendéen dialect, this reads: "They sent me to a great field / which they called the battle field. / They gutted, they tore (out the feathers), / It went worse for them than with fowls. / My heavens! Fear took hold of me, / I grabbed my bag and ran away to safety." Many decades previously, the Vendéens had famously resisted the imposition of the anti-clerical and anti-royalist tenets of the French Revolution, in response to which the central government issued orders to its military forces to kill all living things in the Vendée, men, women, children and beasts, orders that were carried out to the level of a genocide.—Trans.

[6] The "Battle of Valmy," fought on September 20, 1792 in northern France, brought about a decisive victory for the French Revolution in the War of the First Coalition (1793–1797). The French defeated the highly trained Prussian and Austrian contingents of the military coalition made up of multiple European powers that had come together to contain revolutionary France. This victory spurred the National Convention, on the following day, September 21, to declare the abolition of the monarchy, executing King Louis XVI four months later, on January 21, 1793.—Trans.

[7] Léon Gambetta (1838-1882), one of the agents of the establishment of the Third Republic, was Minister of the Interior during the Franco-Prussian war, and credited with organizing the resistance to the German invaders.—Trans.

creating a new army that would force the enemy to raise the blockade of the capital city. The war threatened to continue without any definitive results and to leave the country even more vulnerable to the invader. For Gambetta, this was a revival of the days of the "conventionnels en mission."[8]

Dom Guéranger and Bishop Fillion considered whether it would not be wise, in these circumstances, to disperse the nuns, having them take refuge in private homes. Mother Cécile was perturbed by the idea. She spoke of her concern to Sister Apolline (Jeanette Martin, of Chantenay), who, at age thirty-one, was in the infirmary near death. The latter only laughed: "You, my Mother, leaving Sainte-Cécile because of those heretical villains? Oh, no! That will not be. Do not worry, my Mother. Monseigneur the Bishop and the Right Reverend Father Abbot will soon see that we run no danger, and we will stay put here where we are."[9]

The combat zone moved to closer quarters when the Army of the Loire, commanded by Chanzy,[10] retreated to Le Mans in the middle of December. At first, a no-man's land was established to the east of Le Mans, between the valleys of the Huisne and the Loir rivers until hostilities resumed at Nogent-le Rotrou and at Vendôme. Then came the bloody battle of Le Mans on January 11, 1871. Chanzy lost 25,000 men, killed or taken prisoner, while another 50,000 availed themselves of the confusion to desert the army. But the Bavarians (who were not "heretical villains," but Catholics, unlike the Prussians) were exhausted and unable to take advantage of their victory.

At this juncture, Dom Guéranger was away from Solesmes on a begging expedition for his monastery, always in financial straits. On

---

[8] The "conventionnels de mission" were members of the National Convention (1792–1795) who were deployed in the provinces to carry on propaganda for the Revolution (thus "mission"), as well as to control the local governments. The National Convention was the constitutional and legislative assembly of the French revolutionary government, holding executive power in the first years of the First Republic. — Trans.

[9] Mother Cécile Bruyère, "Biographie de sœur Apolline Martin, " p. 153.

[10] General Antoine Eugène Alfred Chanzy (1823–83), commander of the XVI Corps of the Army of the Loire in the Franco-Prussian War. As "Gambetta was the soul, Chanzy was the strong right arm of French resistance to the invader." He later held political and diplomatic posts. (Quote from http://www.1911encyclopedia.org) — Trans.

January 14, he was able to return to the abbey by carriage from Angers, taking roundabout ways, wondering whether it would be French or German troops that he would find when he arrived in the village. Again, there was discussion about sending the nuns back to their families: "I do not know what obedience will have me do," wrote Mother Cécile to her mother, "but what is certain is that, if I were the one to make the decision, I would remain firmly at my post. ... We are all unperturbed, resolute and filled with confidence in Divine Providence. We belong to God, Who can do all. We must not be religious in habit only; we must feel what we are, and our conduct must reflect that."[11]

Before and after the battle, many soldiers passed through Solesmes, both French and Bavarian, requiring shelter and food. By an error of the enemy's military command, who thought that the village of Solesmes was more significant than it in fact was, between 1,600 and 1,800 men had to be lodged there on January 23. The following day twenty-five uhlans[12] fell in an ambush carried out by franc-tireurs[13] in the territory of Souvigné. The German officer in charge of the Sablé sector called for a reprisal and, confusing Solesmes with Souvigné, gave orders that Solesmes be set to flame. The mayor of Sablé interfered and, after much negotiation, was able to convince him of his mistake. In the end, both villages escaped destruction. On that night, because of a piece of miscommunication that came from Saint-Pierre, the nuns remained in prayer until two o'clock in the morning, reciting the psalter in choir.[14]

The village of Solesmes was located sufficiently far away, to the southeast of the immediate zone of military operations. The retreat and pursuit took place on the direct routes leading west from Le Mans to Laval. Thus the inhabitants of Solesmes did not have much to suffer, but they experienced their share of strong emotions.

After extensive negotiations, the head of government authorized the signing of the armistice, on January 25, 1871, a few days after the

---

[11] Letter dated January 15, 1871.

[12] Members of German light cavalry regiments with lances as their main weapon.—Trans.

[13] Irregular military formations deployed by France during the early stages of the Franco-Prussian War, precursors of guerilla warfare.—Trans.

[14] "Annals: continuation," January 1871, p. 54.

apparitions of Our Lady in Pontmain.[15] The general relief did not last long, however, as alarming news soon arrived: the occupation by troops of the new German Empire, which had been proclaimed in the very halls of the palace of Versailles, and the two tragic months of the Commune, the bloodiest of all the Parisian revolutions (20,000 dead), with a second siege of Paris, this time by the French army.[16]

Nonetheless, life went back to normal soon enough. Dom Guéranger's weakened state, however, already hinted at the approaching time when the monastery of Sainte-Cécile and its abbess would be left to themselves. In the meantime, the abbot continued giving the new monastery everything it could receive, and the young community felt compelled to store away everything that it could take in. But at sixty-five, the condition of his heart no longer allowed Dom Guéranger to go on foot from Saint-Pierre to Sainte-Cécile as he did before. So he asked that the abbey's donkey be harnessed to the small monastery cart normally used for transporting provisions; a chair was placed inside it, and he would cross the village in this vehicle, conducted by a young boy who took the donkey by its bridle. This was a far cry from the scene painted by rumors in Rome of his solemn entry into his monastery in 1837—the legend of the state carriage drawn by four white horses. Cinderella's pumpkin pulled by four rats was closer to reality. Still, the monks of Saint-Pierre deemed the

---

[15] For weeks the five hundred villagers of Pontmain, in the diocese of Laval, had not heard from their thirty-eight young men sent to war. They had lost hope and confidence in their own prayers. They were especially despondent as German troops stood before the gates of Laval on January 17, 1871, and perplexed at the earthquake that shook the area at noon. That same night, two young brothers helping their father in their barn spotted a beautiful lady hovering above a neighbor's house. As villagers gathered, attracted by the commotion, a few other children of the hamlet also saw the vision. The Virgin Mary was silent, but a banner that unfolded below her feet displayed the words: "But pray my children, God will soon grant your request. My Son has allowed Himself to be moved by compassion." Two days later the French government opened negotiations to surrender. The beautiful details and significance of this event are worth examining.—Trans.

[16] (a) One of the provisions of the Treaty of Frankfurt (May 10, 1871), which ended the war, was that German troops would remain on French soil until the indemnity of 5 billion gold francs had been fully paid, which occurred on September 23, 1873. (b) King Wilhelm I of Prussia was crowned Emperor of Germany on January 18, in the famous Hall of Mirrors in Versailles. (c) On March 17 Parisians revolted against the National Assembly and established a short-lived revolutionary government, overthrown by the French army on May 28 of the same year.—Trans.

provisions cart a bit lacking in decorum, so they purchased a mini-gig with two seats: one for their abbot, and the other for the budding carriage driver. The cart was returned to its vegetables.

"This is quite a find, this conveyance and the small donkey," confided Dom Guéranger to the nuns. "To think that without it I would not be able to come here to be with you! As long as this sumptuous rig finds favor with St. Bernard[17] and that he doesn't take up again his tirades against the grandeur of the abbots of Cluny . . ."[18]

By June 1871, calm had almost completely returned to France. Paris had been retaken by the troops of Versailles during the bloody week between May 21 and 28, when the Commune massacred its hostages, among whom were Archbishop Darboy[19] and a number of priests and religious. The majority of Catholics ardently desired a return to the monarchy, with Count de Chambord[20] crowned as king,

---

[17] Dom Guéranger is here alluding to St. Bernard's *Apologia*, written c. 1127 in the form of a defense of his own order of Cistercians, but in fact an indictment of the laxity that had crept into the Benedictine monastery of Cluny, especially in the areas of food and clothing. St. Bernard of Clairvaux (1090–1153) was born near Dijon in Burgundy of the nobility. Brilliant, affable and attractive, after the death of his mother, to whom he was very attached, he decided to enter the monastery of Cîteaux, which had been established as a reform of the Benedictines in 1098. This effort to return to the original austerities of the order—which became known as the Cistercian reform—had been in danger of collapsing for lack of vocations, when, in 1112, St. Bernard arrived with thirty friends and relatives, including four of his brothers, all influenced by his convincing words on the sublimity of the religious life. In 1115 he was sent to the diocese of Langres in Champagne to establish the first daughter-house of Cîteaux, which was later renamed Clairvaux and itself became the motherhouse of sixty-eight foundations. A tower of learning, eloquence, wisdom and sanctity, and a prolific writer, his reputation lead him to become advisor to princes and popes, and a sought out arbiter to settle disputes throughout Europe. The enterprises he was called upon to undertake were as diverse as preaching the Second Crusade, stopping a series of pogroms in the Rhinelands, and disputing Abelard's errors at the University of Paris, eventually obtaining his condemnation and retirement. St. Bernard had great devotion to the Blessed Virgin Mary and to the Infant Jesus, and is credited with adding the words "*o clemens, o pia, o dulcis Virgo Maria*" to the Salve Regina antiphon. One of the greatest men of the Middle Ages, St. Bernard is known as the Mellifluous Doctor; he was canonized in 1174, declared a Doctor of the Church in 1830, and is considered the last of the Fathers of the Church.—Trans.
[18] Delatte, "Vie," chap. 4.
[19] George Darboy (1813–1871), Archbishop of Paris from 1863 to his execution in 1871.
[20] Henry V of France and Navarre (Henri Charles Ferdinand Marie d'Artois de France, 1820–1883), Duke of Bordeaux and Count of Chambord (his preferred title), was the posthumous son of Charles Ferdinand, Duke of Berry (assassinated before his son's birth), the younger son of Charles X of France. With the abdication of Charles X on August 2, 1830, followed twenty minutes later by the abdication of his eldest son, Louis-Antoine of France, Henry was

and discussions with the pretender to the throne commenced. By now Dom Guéranger had long abandoned his Bonapartist sympathies, which dated from his childhood years surrounded by the imperial legend.

At the beginning of June, Bishop Fillion came to Sablé for confirmations. He took the occasion to visit Saint-Pierre and Sainte-Cécile and set the dates for the abbatial blessing of Mother Cécile and the consecration of the nuns' monastic church. Dom Guéranger and all others concerned hoped that the dedication of the church could occur on the anniversary date of the dedication of the Abbey of Saint-Pierre. Bishop Fillion complied and reserved October 12 on his agenda, mentioning that the abbatial blessing of the prioress could take place the following day, on the 13. When he proposed the date at the parlor at Sainte-Cécile, he was met with general disappointment. Surprised, he asked the reason for this reaction. The nuns replied that the date was just too far away; it had already been eleven months since the nomination was decreed. Bishop Fillion once again consulted his calendar. One of the sisters suggested the fourteenth of July, the anniversary of the historic audience with Pius IX, and Bishop Fillion happened to be free on that day; so the ceremony was set for July 14. In those days, no one remembered the taking of the Bastille, simply another day of conflict among the many troubled days of the French Revolution. July 14 would not become a national holiday until the hundredth anniversary of the event in 1889.

"Abbess at such a young age! Can this be truly reasonable?" it was said when news broke out of the upcoming event. Weren't Bishop Fillion and Dom Guéranger being a bit precipitous? The bishop, above all, who had dared to present such a request to Pius IX and who was the party principally responsible for this step! When the concession was first granted by the pope, few people had been made privy to the secret. It was only when preparations for the ceremony of the abbatial blessing commenced that the fact became public knowledge.

---

immediately proclaimed king of France and Navarre. However, in seven days the National Assembly decreed that the throne pass to his regent, Louis-Philippe, Duke of Orléans.— Trans.

Mother Cécile had been governing Sainte-Cécile for five years. She found greater ease in carrying out her responsibilities now, but occasionally the former aversion would resurface: "You must understand," the abbot wrote her one day, "that this distaste for your charge that arises when difficulties overtake you, has no other cause than the weakness of human nature, which, in the end, tires of the severe self-restraint; and that the devil finds the opportunity to give you a hard time, stirring up that old underlying base of independence that made you commit so many faults during your childhood."[21] "Do not forget for one minute that the Lord's rights over you are absolute. You must be willing to be prioress and even abbess. This constant and courageous will is proof of the true love that you owe the divine Emmanuel for all his advances."[22]

These are strong words. In effect, the abbot or abbess loses that remnant of personal autonomy that monks or nuns still have in their exercise of obedience. Quite literally, they no longer belong to themselves, not for an instant. Mother Cécile saw in the abbatial blessing, this definitive consecration of herself to the service of her sisters, the ultimate sacrifice of a liberty for which she would never again be able to hope.

She explained herself years later, in 1884: "I dreaded the irrevocability of the abbatial blessing: *Abbas semper Abbas* (an abbot is an abbot forever) goes the axiom. I dreaded the honors attached to the title. I strongly felt that all the self-effacement that I had striven for would now be impossible for me to attain. I understood well that I could not present myself for the imposition of hands with any reservations whatsoever in my heart toward this charge, for which I had a horror since my childhood."[23]

"So, you have not thought for a moment of the honor bestowed on you?" Dom Guéranger asked her a few days before the scheduled date.

"Oh, my Father! You know that I am terribly pragmatic. The sacrifice of myself seemed to be so great that it seemed extraordinary

---

[21] Letter dated January 4, 1871.
[22] Letter dated January 7, 1871.
[23] Letter to Dom Delatte, July 16, 1884.

to me that I could think of nothing else; I understood nothing of what was being said around me."[24]

"My poor child, you are absurd! The surrender of yourself is only one side of the question. You never see anything like others do! I understand that you would not have thought of the worldly honor, but that you did not consider with profound sentiments of humility the honor that Our Lord was bestowing on you by placing souls under your charge! There is nothing greater, nothing more admirable. You should be protesting that you are completely unworthy of such a favor, you, a poor little sinner who has received so much and have given so little. The rest is good but not enough."[25]

There was another aspect of her elevation to the abbacy that Dom Guéranger most certainly impressed upon her, mindful as he was of the importance of the liturgy. The abbatial blessing is a mainstay, a permanent entitlement to receiving from God the graces necessary for the government of a community. While not a sacrament proper, it is analogous to one, providing support at every moment. The abbatial blessing makes of an abbot the vicar of the love of Christ for his monks.

Mother Cécile was convinced of this and consciously abandoned herself to the profound change that the abbatial blessing would bring about in her, as revealed in the letter cited above. "It pleased Our Lord that this abbatial blessing would change my being entirely, and He allowed my soul to fathom under an intense light the detachment to which it has been called. Until then I had felt that the love of God could enable me to undertake anything. I now felt that the second commandment was like the first, and that I should be for my neighbor what I was for Our Lord, through Him and because of Him. I felt that I was to give of my time, my thoughts, in short, all of my life, to souls, to the Church, and that the abbatial blessing would sanction this complete holocaust to the honor of God."[26]

---

[24] "Oh ! mon père, vous savez que je suis terriblement positive, je trouvais le sacrifice de moi-même si grand que je trouvais extraordinaire de rien voir autre chose, je ne comprenais rien à ce qu'on disait autour de moi."

[25] "Souvenirs sur dom Guéranger," p. 53.

[26] Letter to Dom Delatte dated July 16, 1884.

She asked if she could make a retreat to prepare herself for the holocaust, but Dom Guéranger would not hear of it, "saying that I did not have the time, that this was good for others but all I needed was to care for my daughters as usual, and that Our Lord thought it best this way."[27] In truth, when July 14 arrived, she was ready, as, "starting on the eve of the fourteenth, my Spouse deigned to establish me in a profound peace. . . . I no longer felt any disquiet and I deeply abandoned myself into the hands of Our Lord. I still remember to what degree I abandoned myself totally into His arms so that He might do with me whatever He willed, thinking of nothing else but of seeing things as He does, while not letting myself lose anything that He was preparing for me."[28]

"Attending celebrations such as this abbatial blessing makes us feel that God has set His feet on this small corner of the world that we call Solesmes, we feel that God loves it . . . ," wrote Dom Guépin[29] a few days after the ceremony, in a long account addressed to the abbot of Ligugé who had been unable to come. This episode was, in effect, a great moment in the history of Solesmes. It was the first abbatial blessing witnessed by that monastic family. "I was thirty again!" exclaimed a radiant Dom Guéranger. He had prepared the details of the ceremony with meticulous care, even demonstrating to Mother Cécile how she should walk "with crosier in hand, with dignity and holding herself upright." Monsieur Bruyère—though paralyzed, shrunken and aged by his illness—was no less enthusiastic about it all. Then again, on that day, there was no one who was not.

It is not possible to include here the details of the function as it unfolded according to the pontifical rite then in use. However, two moments of the event merit being evoked as they aptly reflect the extraordinary atmosphere that enveloped it.

"The most touching part of this beautiful function was the enthronement of the abbess," continued Dom Guépin, echoing the sentiments of all who had been present. This may be surprising

---

[27] Letter to Mother Marie de la Croix, October 10, 1899.

[28] Ibid.

[29] Happily, Dom Guépin was moved to share this ceremony with monks of Solesmes who had left for a new foundation. His circular letter of July 17, 1871 is the only source of information for this unprecedented event.

because in itself, this rite, which comes at the very end after the *Ite missa est*, has nothing particularly touching about it. The bishop simply conducts the abbess to the abbatial throne, indicating by this gesture that she has been legitimately installed, in the name of the Church, to govern her monastery. But Bishop Fillion, perhaps without intending to, made this moment the most memorable of the entire event. At the signal of the master of ceremonies, he descended from the altar, proceeded toward the young abbess, took her by the hand and, to the astonishment of all, conducted her not to the throne that had been prepared for her, but to his own pontifical throne, that is, the same throne used by Father Abbot for solemn ceremonies. He made her ascend its steps and—awesome wonder—had her sit upon it. The young abbess was dead pale; 'she became green,' said someone who had been near her.

Whatever her exterior reaction might have been at the moment, we know her interior reaction through a letter written thirteen years later: "The bishop took my right hand and made me sit. No other idea crossed my mind than to let it be done to me. It was an acquiescence of adoration to the sovereign will, as if a mysterious and profound *Magnificat* were being chanted in the most intimate center of my being."[30] For a few instances the ceremony seemed suspended in time and every soul rejoiced at seeing the daughter seated upon the throne of her father, wrapped in "an indefinable beauty."

The exit of Mother Cécile was no less moving. Let us again allow Dom Guépin to describe this quasi-triumphal march to the strains of the *Te Deum* sung by the nuns "with enthusiasm enough to bring down the walls."

"She reverenced the bishop, the altar, the abbot, and with a pace at once firm and modest, left the church to reenter the monastery, bearing her crosier in hand with rare facility. The greater part of those attending the ceremony joined her cortege, while the bishop, abbot and clergy remained in choir. During the Mass, Dom David[31] had not wasted any time, working away to create a carpet of flowers extending from the door of the church to the door of the monastery.

---

[30] Letter to Dom Delatte dated July 16, 1884.
[31] Dom Louis David (1812–1876) was the monk in charge of all artistic work at Saint-Pierre. He would later spend many years in Italy studying the art of that country.

No one inside the church had expected this surprise; Madame Bruyère's eyes welled up in tears. . . . The large crowd lined up in the courtyard. The abbess walked alone on the beautiful carpet made of petals gathered from all the gardens of the village. No one had begrudged his flowers. They had been brought even from Chantenay; without knowing it, the abbess treaded upon roses and lilies from the gardens of Coudreuse, witness of her childhood games. . . . 'How beautiful she is, how saintly she is,' some friends murmured to each other. Yes, beautiful she was indeed. . . . Saintly, yes, she must be, for if she were not, she could not have been so beautiful, and her humility and childlike candor would have revealed something of an effort, some disturbance, some anxiety in face of all the honor being paid her. But it was all natural and true. . . . When the abbess arrived at the vestibule, the doors of the enclosure opened of themselves . . . and the abbess vanished away in a single movement of wings. She seemed to say: 'It is over; here I am at last.' *Haec requies mea in saeculum saeculi* (here is my repose forever and ever)."

At a later date, she described how she had lived those poignant moments: "When I left the monastery, at the very moment I put my feet out the door, Our Lord took pity on my weakness and drew me to Himself by a grace of ecstasy. I was no longer aware of the people, nor of the function, nor of anything exterior. All of that seemed to me a dream, whereas what went on interiorly was the reality."[32]

From henceforward, Mother Cécile was fully the first abbess of Sainte-Cécile; the irrevocableness of the abbatial blessing had been accomplished in her. "Who knows if, instead of another burden, this isn't a consolation that God has in store for your latter years?" Dom Couturier's intuition so assuredly stated nine years earlier to the founder of Sainte-Cécile,[33] revealed itself to be remarkably prophetic.

---

[32] Letter to Dom Delatte dated July 16, 1884.
[33] See chap. 8, p. 80.

1 – Louis Bruyère (1758–1831)

2 – Jean-Jacques-Marie Huvé (1783–1852)

3. La Madeleine

4. Léopard Bruyère (1810–1872)

5. Félicie Bruyère (1823–1872)

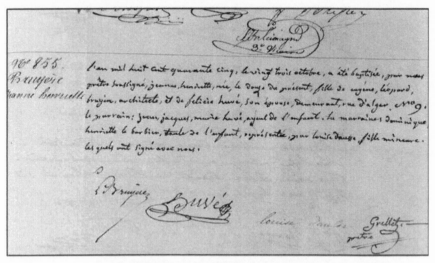

6. Act of Baptism of Jenny, no. 8-55-1845

8. Church of Saint-Roch

7. Neighborhood of the Church of Saint-Roch

9. Baptismal font

10. Lise and Jenny Bruyère with their nanny

11. Jenny Bruyère in 1850

12. Félix Huvé (1816–1887)

13. The manor of Coudreuse in 1845

14. "La Grange" in Port-de-Juigné

15. Members of the women's choir of the parish of Chantenay

16. Lise and Jenny Bruyère (in 1861)

17. Bishop Charles Fillion (1817–1874)

18. Dom Prosper Guéranger (1805–1875)

19. Dom Charles Couturier
(1817–1890)

20. Canon François-Xavier
Coulin (1800–1887)

21. The Abbey of Saint-Pierre of Solesmes in 1875

22. Sainte-Cécile-la-Petite in Solesmes

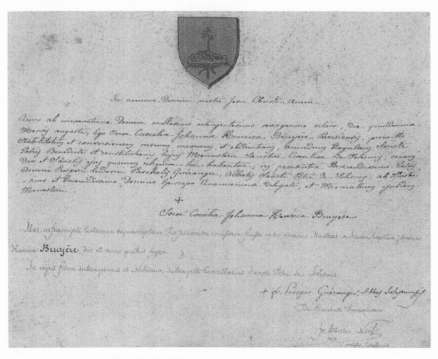

23. Charter of profession of Mother Cécile Bruyère

24. The monastery of Sainte-Cécile of Solesmes in 1871

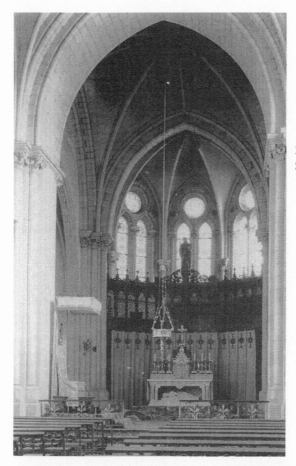

25. The original sanctuary at Sainte-Cécile of Solesmes

26. The replica of Maderno's effigy of Saint Cecilia

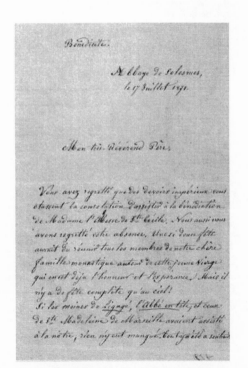

27. Rescript of Pius IX dated July 14, 1870

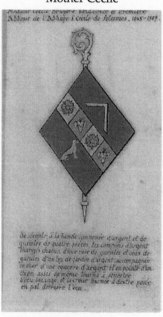

28. Heraldic emblem of
Mother Cécile

29. Dom Guépin letter on abbatial benediction

1. Louis Bruyère (1758–1831), grandfather of Jenny Bruyère, city planner for Le Mans and Paris. Bust sculpted by himself and later sketched by his great-grandson, Léo Eynaud.

2. Jean-Jacques-Marie Huvé (1783–1852), maternal grandfather and godfather of Jenny Bruyère, architect of La Madeleine, at first alongside Vignon and alone after 1828. By E.J. Delécluze.

3. La Madeleine, sketch dating from the mid-nineteenth century.

4. Léopard Bruyère (1810–1872), father of Jenny.

5. Félicie Bruyère (1823–1872), mother of Jenny.

6. Jenny Bruyère's baptismal record, in the parish register of the Church of Saint-Roch in Paris.

7. Neighborhood of the Church of Saint-Roch, taken from the map of Paris by Louis Bretez, known as Turgot Map, published in 1739. The church is at the center of the image. To the right, in the foreground, is the rue d'Alger where Jenny Bruyère was born.

8. Façade of the Church of Saint-Roch in Paris, the parish of the Bruyère family. Photograph taken in 1997.

9. Baptismal font at the Church of Saint-Roch where Jenny was baptized on October 23, 1845.

10. The Bruyère Children, Jenny Bruyère, aged six, and her sister Lise (1848–1879), aged two, with their nanny. Sketched by Léopard Bruyère in 1851 after a daguerreotype.

11. Jenny Bruyère around age five. "I don't know what will break this child." ("Enfance et jeunesse par elle même," p. 15.)

12. Félix Huvé (1816–1887), one of Madame Bruyère's brothers. It was he that informed his brother-in-law about the sale of the Coudreuse manor during the summer of 1853, thus bringing him to the area of the Sarthe.

13. The Manor of Coudreuse. Sketch by Léopard Bruyère in 1854, at the time he was renovating the old homestead.

14. "La Grange" in 1997. The house was built by Adrien Huvé (1819–1873), brother of Madame Bruyère, and enlarged at a later date. Jenny often stayed there, where she spent the night of October 11, 1861, prior to pronouncing her vow of virginity on the following day during the Mass celebrating the dedication of the abbey of Saint-Pierre.

15. The Little Confraternity of Chantenay of which Jenny was the president. In the front row at left is Lise Bruyère; Jenny is fourth from the left; behind Jenny, with an open book is Berthe de la Corbière, future choir nun of Sainte-Cécile. Several other members of the group will become lay sisters at the monastery.

16. Jenny Bruyère with Lise at the time when she made her vow of virginity (1861).

17. Bishop Charles Fillion (1817–1874), bishop of Le Mans beginning in 1862. He received with joy the project of the foundation of Sainte-Cécile and proved to be extremely solicitous and kind to the young community, supporting it with all his authority.

18. Dom Prosper Guéranger (1805–1875), first abbot of Saint-Pierre of Solesmes. Photograph taken on September 10, 1860, during the time he was directing Jenny Bruyère, unwittingly preparing her for a monastic vocation.

19. Dom Charles Couturier (1817–1890), prior of Dom Guéranger. He encouraged Dom Guéranger to set out on the project of founding Sainte-Cécile, and succeeded him as second abbot of Saint-Pierre in 1875.

20. Canon François-Xavier Coulin (1800–1887), founder of the Grand Catechism in Marseilles, an apostolate that counted among its members several future nuns of the abbey of Sainte-Cécile.

21. The abbey of Saint-Pierre of Solesmes as Jenny knew it. She made her vow of virginity here on October 12, 1861, her sixteenth birthday.

22. "Sainte-Cécile-la-Petite" is the house indicated by a cross. It was here that Dom Guéranger established monastic life for the first nuns of Sainte-Cécile, on November 16, 1866. They left these lodgings for their permanent monastery on the eve of their clothing ceremony, August 13, 1867. In the background, at left, is the parish church of Solesmes next to the abbey of Saint-Pierre.

23. Charter of profession of Mother Cécile (August 15, 1868). It is the first charter of profession of the abbey of Sainte-Cécile. On the document appears the signature of Dom Guéranger, in whose hands Mother Cécile made her profession.

24. Monastery of Sainte-Cécile of Solesmes. The buildings appear as they were originally, the last touch having been the cross above the belfry, affixed on September 26, 1870.

25. The sanctuary of the abbatial church of Sainte-Cécile, just as it was during Mother Cécile's time and just as it remained until its renovation in 1974.

26. Recumbent effigy of Saint Cecilia. A replica of the celebrated Roman statue by Maderno, which Dom Guéranger placed below the high altar of the abbatial church.

27. Rescript of Pius IX. The last of three pages comprising the petition presented by Bishop Charles Fillion to Pius IX on July 14, 1870 requesting the dignity of the abbatial rank for Mother Cécile. Below the text, Pius IX wrote before his signature: "*De speciali gratia et in exemplum non adducenda, petitam facultatem concedimus.*" (By special grace, we grant the permission requested, which will not be adduced as a precedent.)

28. Copy of the letter of Dom Guépin describing the abbatial blessing of July 14, 1871. This copy was made by Mother Gertrude de Ruffo-Bonneval for the archives of Sainte-Cécile. Presently, it is the only testimony of the ceremony that has been preserved. The lengthy account by Dom Guépin (28 pages) received the approval of Dom Guéranger and Mother Cécile before being sent to the monks of the Congregation who could not be present at the ceremony.

29. Heraldic Emblem of Mother Cécile Bruyère. Vert [green] a bend compony of four, Argent [white] and Gules [red], charged alternately with single roses and lilies counterchanged. Between in chief a square and in base a Talbot sejent, contourné Argent. *Note: the arms are displayed on a lozenge (diamond shape shield) surmounting a crosier in pale turned to the dexter.* [Description courtesy of James-Charles Noonan, Jr.— Trans.]

Chapter 17

Dedication and Spiritual Maturity

THE BELLS OF SAINT-PIERRE are heard twenty-five times a day, adding the calls for meals and the chapter meeting to the many times they sound for prayer. At the parish, the bell tolls for the *Angelus* three times daily, for baptisms, marriages, funerals, and, on Sundays, for High Mass and Vespers. For centuries the two bell towers, a few dozen yards apart, have carried on a fine rapport exchanging their peals back and forth—the great belfry of the monks, covered by its grey-slated dome, and the small parish steeple, topped by a narrow pointed roof.

The spire of the monastery of Sainte-Cécile, newly arrived in the neighborhood, did its best to match Saint-Pierre's, so that the villagers of Solesmes lived under the constant peal of bells. "Here the bells toll the whole blessed day long," a guest once remarked. At the first rays of dawn they began their play, and again in the evening, they would launch into a beautiful carilloning cascade.

The construction of the nuns' church had been completed, including its decoration at which Brother Joseph Bourigaud—a student of the painter Émile Lafon[1]—had worked from the time of his entry into the novitiate of Solesmes. He would later become the abbot of Ligugé. However, the new church had not yet been consecrated, for the haste of the nuns had pressed Bishop Fillion to bless the abbess even before consecrating the church.

Monsieur Bruyère's hostility toward him had disappeared of a sudden; he no longer begrudged the bishop's having taken his daughter away from him. On the day of the abbatial blessing, after the event, he made a point of coming up to Bishop Fillion: "Monseigneur," he said, "I owe you my apologies and my thanks on this day, and I wanted to present them to you without further delay."[2] No doubt, fatherly pride played a role in this reversal. For

---

[1] Jacques-Émile Lafon (1817–1886), born in Périgueux, was a successful painter of religious art. He was a friend of Louis Veuillot.—Trans.

[2] Letter written by Dom Guépin dated July 17, 1871.

the master of Coudreuse, it was not a small thing to be the father of an abbess. But this was not the sole sentiment prompting him. He regretted having poorly employed his life and having so much with which to reproach himself. God was not far. His daughter's prayers would soon be heeded.

A writer and artist friend of Lacordaire and the first Dominicans,[3] Étienne Cartier (1813–1887), who had recently become a permanent guest at Saint-Pierre, discovered in Rome a replica of the celebrated sculpture by Maderno found in the church of Saint Cecilia in Trastevere.[4] Cardinal Pitra[5] wished to make of it a personal gift to the nuns, so the statue was sent to Sainte-Cécile to be placed below the high altar. "Madame has arrived," Mother Cécile notified Dom Guéranger on August 4, 1871. "Madame is in the parlor. Madame, the great Mistress of the place, our Queen and our Patroness. See how courteous she is, how affable; she knows that Monsieur Cartier is nearly a son of Saint Dominic, so she most graciously arranged to arrive on the feast of that great saint."[6]

The long awaited date, October 12, at last arrived. Bishop Fillion, who took his liberties with liturgical rules, after having himself performed the magnificent liturgy of the consecration of the church, insisted that the abbot celebrate the Mass of dedication, despite the fact that the two rites are indissolubly linked. Dom Guéranger let it be. That evening, the abbot had a warm conversation with the nuns,

---

[3] Jean-Baptiste-Henri Dominique Lacordaire (1802–1861), while in the beginning of what promised to be a brilliant career in law in Paris, converted back to his faith and became one of the most effective defenders of the Church in France and one of the great apologists of the nineteenth-century. For some time a collaborator of Lamennais, he was a friend of Dom Guéranger's and, similarly, became a Dominican in Italy, subsequently re-introducing the Dominicans into France in 1843 following their eradication during the French Revolution. Thus the author's reference to the "first Dominicans."—Trans.

[4] The celebrated statue of St. Cecilia by Stefano Maderno (1610), modeled on her own incorrupt body as it was found when exhumed in 1599.—Trans.

[5] Cardinal Jean-Baptiste Pitra (1812–1889) was at first a monk of Solesmes, then prior of the ill-fated foundation in Paris. A renowned patrologist, he was called to Rome as an expert and was made a cardinal by Pius IX in 1863. He always kept a profound attachment to his monastic family and to Dom Guéranger in particular.

[6] Letter to Dom Guéranger dated August 4, 1871. [The reform of the liturgical calendar following the second Vatican Council moved the feast of Saint Dominic from August 4 to August 8. The previous calendar is still used in celebrations according to the Extraordinary Form of the Roman Rite.—Trans.]

recalling the birthday of their Mother Abbess on the same day in 1845, and concluded: "I will forever hold a debt of immense gratitude to Monseigneur of Le Mans[7] who gave me the consolation of singing the first Mass celebrated at this consecrated altar. The young nuns will remember this, and tell those who will come afterwards that Father Abbot was very happy on that day."[8] He had not hesitated to mobilize all of Saint-Pierre to heighten the magnificence of the ceremony, which took place before an estimated six hundred people. There was even an article in *L'Univers* describing the event.

England was represented at the ceremony in the person of Dom Laurence Shepherd, who customarily came every year to spend some time at Saint-Pierre and visit Dom Guéranger. This time he was accompanied by two nuns of Stanbrook Abbey whom he wished to have initiated into the life of Solesmes. During his visit of 1869 he had persuaded Dom Guéranger to let him have a copy of the "Declarations on the Rule," composed for the monastery of Sainte-Cécile. He subsequently translated the work into English, after having discussed it with the abbess of Stanbrook and explained it to the nuns of the abbey. As a consequence, the nuns of Stanbrook sent a petition to the president of the English Congregation, Dom Burchall, signed by the entire chapter (except three members), asking permission to adopt the Declarations. The permission was granted on an experimental basis, so that since Easter 1869 the nuns of Stanbrook had been living according to the Declarations on the Rule observed at Sainte-Cécile. Subsequently, in the fall of 1871 the abbot president authorized Dom Shepherd to bring two nuns with him to Solesmes in order for them to study on location the practice of the Declarations. These were the nuns that accompanied him to the consecration, the young French prioress and novice mistress, Mother Gertrude d'Aurillac Dubois, and Mother Mechtilde Knight, a newly professed nun.

Their stay at Sainte-Cécile extended from October 6, 1871 to July 15, 1872. Upon their return to Stanbrook, in 1872, the elderly abbess, Mother Scholastica Gregson, submitted her resignation, and on

---

[7] Bishop Fillion.—Trans.
[8] "Annals: continuation," October 12, 1871.

September 16, Mother Gertrude was elected to succeed her, under special dispensation since she was only thirty years of age. In his joy, Dom Shepherd wrote to Dom Bérengier[9] on October 9, 1872: "Now monastic life will flourish here. *Deo gratias!* And we owe all this, after God, to the well-beloved and venerable Father Abbot. If I had not known Solesmes, what hope would we have here? Wonderful are the ways of God!"

The presence of two foreign nuns at Sainte-Cécile meant additional work for Mother Cécile. Thankfully, her English was adequate enough for her to communicate with Mother Mechtilde Knight; she had learned it with ease many years before.

Around this time, Father Schliebusch (1827–1904), a friend of Dom Guéranger and Solesmes, agreed at last to come visit the monastery of Sainte-Cécile. The "good Father Schliebusch," as he was called, was a holy man, as original in his own way as St. Philip Neri. He was the pastor of Saint-Christophe in Kerentrech, at the doors of Lorient.[10] A friend of Dom Guéranger for many years, he had great admiration for the abbot. On coming to Sainte-Cécile de Solesmes, it was love at first sight. He was struck by Mother Cécile—"This is Dom Guéranger in women's clothing!" he is to have said. His friendship would endure through all trials. A quarter of a century later, he would be the person to contribute most to the two foundations made in Kergonan.[11] For the moment, he was happy to send novices to Solesmes.

The parents of Mother Cécile were not elderly; her mother was still fifty and her father was only fifteen years older. But their health had never been good. At age sixty, Monsieur Bruyère, it will be recalled, had suffered a hemiplegia attack from which he never recovered. Dom Guéranger, whose state of health was little better, would visit them at Coudreuse in the name of their daughter whenever he had the opportunity.

---

[9] Dom Théophile Bérengier (1827–1897), monk of Solesmes, as secretary of Dom Guéranger, was well placed to enter into contact with Dom Shepherd. In 1870, he was sent to the foundation in his native Marseilles.

[10] In south Brittany, northwest of Nantes.—Trans.

[11] In Brittany.—Trans.

On December 27, 1871, Madame Bruyère was so ill that the curate of Chantenay did not waste time in giving her viaticum and administering extreme unction. Dom Guéranger, in whom she had placed all her trust since he had become her spiritual director, came to Coudreuse on the morning of the twenty-eighth: "The absence of Cécile does not cause me pain," she told him. "I sense her close to me; since she is where Our Lord has always wanted her to be, my greatest sorrow would be to see her here."[12]

The abbot told her that her work was not yet finished, that she still had to remain by her husband and accompany him in his final return to God: "My good Father," she replied, "I do not refuse the work if Our Lord judges it still necessary, even though I feel a great need to see Him and nothing here below satisfies me any longer. And besides, my Father, isn't my task here below already completed? Cécile belongs entirely to God, and in her I have rendered back to the Lord the treasure he entrusted to me. Lise is in a Christian marriage and will be a good mother to her family. My husband and my brother are not yet Christians, but they are on the way and I believe that all that I could do for them here on earth has already been done. Now I need to be closer to the Lord in order to obtain the final grace for them."[13]

She died on January 2, 1872, surrounded by her family. Monsieur Bruyère asked that she be buried within the enclosure of Sainte-Cécile in the cemetery reserved for the nuns. This death was a portent of the upcoming conversion that she and her daughters had so greatly desired.

As soon as Dom Guéranger heard news of the death, he came to Mother Cécile's family in Coudreuse. On that day he noted in his diary: "Monsieur Bruyère took hold of my cross, which he had seen his wife kiss whenever she took leave of me, and he fervently kissed it himself, in tears. He told me that he wanted to go rejoin his wife in heaven and that he had resolved to reconcile himself to God."[14]

"Marvel with me at the mercies of our sweet little King, Father," wrote Mother Cécile to Father Schliebusch a few days afterwards.

---

[12] "Souvenirs sur dom Guéranger, " p. 60.
[13] Ibid.
[14] "Chronique de dom Guéranger," p. 132 (in the copy kept at Sainte-Cécile).

"Barely an hour after my saintly mother had departed, a smile still on her lips, my father was on his knees at her feet, promising to fulfill his Christian duties so as not to be separated from her."[15]

Monsieur Bruyère would die less than two months later, on February 12, 1872, at the home of the Eynauds in Cherbourg. On January 22, he returned to the practice of the faith of his childhood. "This was a morning of great celebration; heaven let us have a glimpse of its beauty," wrote Lise to Mother Cécile. "Our good father received Holy Communion this morning with touching piety and a child's simplicity. Ah, how beautiful it was, my dear, if only you had seen it! Last evening, in telling me to prepare everything, he charged me with writing to you, something I do with great delight. This morning, when the ceremony was finished, he told me: 'See, I am now like your mother, but I do not deserve it.' In short, a touching humility and an admirable resignation in his sufferings. He asked us to hang Mama's crucifix in his room, so that he can look at it when he is in pain."[16]

Thanks to permission given by Bishop Fillion, his body was laid to rest next to his wife in the cemetery at Sainte-Cécile; Mother Cécile thus could visit them every day. The last visible ties to her childhood were vanishing. At twenty-six, she was now the eldest of the family. It was a painful parting. But now Mother Cécile could belong entirely to Sainte-Cécile without any other immediate concern.

The young abbess's particular charism was spiritual motherhood. She had felt a type of maternal solicitude even with regard to the soul of her father. In this way, God had given her to comprehend her role of intercession and assistance to souls.

A trip of Dom Guéranger's to Saint-Omer in 1871, on July 31 and August 1, gave occasion to a new instance of spiritual motherhood for the young abbess, this time toward Thérèse Bernard, a sixteen-year old from Lille. She was an orphan entrusted to her grandmother, Madame Dambricourt, who lived in Hallines not far from the city. Thérèse felt attracted to Carmel and sought spiritual direction from Father Henri Graux, director of the school of Saint-Bertin. He was the

---

[15] Letter dated January 11, 1872.
[16] Letter dated January 22, 1872.

brother of two Solesmes monks and had a great desire to join the community himself.

Father Henri had complete trust in Dom Guéranger, and consulted him about the young girl, whose rich nature was in great need of spiritual cultivation. The abbot recommended that he stress sweetness, humility, goodness, and indulgence, which Thérèse still lacked. And he counseled her to seek contact with Mother Cécile, as she herself had had to overcome the same type of difficulties.

Following this exchange between her director and the abbot, Thérèse wrote to Mother Cécile for the first time on October 26, 1872. The young abbess's response brought great joy to the adolescent, who had ardently been seeking a maternal heart capable of fully understanding her. She decided to come to Solesmes for the profession of one of Father Henri Graux's brothers, on December 9, 1872. The first meeting at the parlor was an event with immense impact on the young girl. The idea of entering Carmel was definitively set aside, while her desire for the religious life crystallized—Sainte-Cécile became for her the only place on earth that mattered.

A regular correspondence ensued between Mother Cécile and the young woman, with the abbess writing a letter every two weeks: "It is true that I have other daughters. But each daughter is herself, and not one of them is you. I miss you, therefore, as a dear unique daughter." [17] "Nothing can distract mothers from their tender care." [18] Two months after the December 1872 visit to Solesmes, the abbess of Sainte-Cécile, with the agreement of Father Henri Graux, gave Thérèse permission to pronounce a private vow of virginity for one year. In doing this, she had her own experience in mind, recalling the directives she herself had received from Dom Guéranger. Later, this commitment would become a definitive gift of self. Thérèse Bernard had to defer her entrance to Sainte-Cécile to the day she attained legal majority, another similarity between her and Mother Cécile.

Thus, already at this time, the first letter of Thérèse Bernard and the first visit from Father Schliebusch were preparing the ground for

[17] Letter dated July 26, 1874.
[18] Letter dated April 7, 1875.

the two foundations to come—in Artois and in Brittany. The future was taking shape, while God's plans remained concealed.

For the moment, there was no inkling about these prospects. The abbess applied herself to her work, giving herself entirely to the formation of the young women who arrived in great numbers at the monastery. But her interior life was made more of suffering than of joy.

A ray of the infinite purity of God often touched her soul, making her poignantly aware of her unworthiness and the need for redemption, a redemption for which she wanted to carry her share, as a Simon of Cyrene. "Yes, my Spouse, I will go with You, first because I love You, and then because I have placed an unbearable burden upon Your shoulders. You will support me, You will carry me, because I would die at the sight of the Divine Justice of Your Father if You were not there to give me courage and life. But given that You let Yourself be treated according to how I myself should be treated, then at least, for love of me, do not keep what is bitter to Yourself alone, but let me relieve You as much as is within my capacity. Can it be just that You should take upon Yourself all that is pain and suffering, while you leave to me only of the fruit of Your Love? To realize that I have drawn upon You the blows of Divine Justice, is this not the source of the most unbelievable suffering?!"[19]

She also experienced the same sentiments that had prompted Saint Peter to exclaim by the banks of the Sea of Galilee, after the miracle of the fish: "Depart from me, O Lord, for I am a sinful man!" (Lk 5:8). "Yesterday, just as in the last days, I was plunged into the abyss of my profound misery, having no other light than that which revealed to me the hideousness of my soul. During the entire night I was violently torn between a sort of terror at the thought of approaching Our Lord in Holy Communion, and an extreme desire to receive Him. Nonetheless, I felt that the terror was out of love, for it was prompted by a fear of imposing myself—I, unworthy as I am—upon Sovereign Holiness. Oh, what incomparable agony to see ourselves as we are, to sense that there is no life outside of God, and yet, to experience an impulse to distance ourselves from this Divine Center because we feel

[19] Sunday, March 17, 1872.

ourselves to be too unworthy! There is no need for Divine Justice to act—the soul applies justice to itself, causing suffering that is beyond description. I believe that this state could be the equivalent of the pains of Purgatory."[20]

This work of purification—effected by fear of intrusively entering into the center of the furnace of God's love, combined with an irresistible attraction toward this living fire—will be one of the traits of the spiritual experience of Mother Cécile. Echoes of this appear more than once in the writings of Dom Delatte, to whom she entrusted her soul in 1890.

There was no dearth of trials provoked by exterior circumstances either. The first years of the monastery's life were marked by several bereavements. The sisters were not dying of old age, for the nuns in the community were still all young, but some were in haste to depart to the next world: Sister Apolline Martin and Sister Lucie Foubert did not wait long to go.

The monastery had been well built, for the nuns needed a roof over their heads and a church worthy of the Lord where they could come to pray in choir seven times a day and once each night. But there were no resources left to ensure that the daily needs of the quickly-growing community were met. The practice of poverty was an unavoidable necessity; the beginnings of Sainte-Cécile were not easy. "Anything that was not strictly necessary and indispensable had to be foregone," wrote Dom Delatte. "Frugality reigned supreme in the refectory of the nuns."[21] Mother Cécile kept to herself the worries that would surface at regular intervals during the first decade of the monastery's existence. Saint-Pierre did not have the wherewithal with which to help the nuns; Dom Guéranger had to beg for his own monastery until the last limits of his strength. Help came above all from Étienne Cartier, the guest resident at Saint-Pierre who, because of his affluent circumstances, could temporarily pull the monastery out of its difficulties.

Sainte-Cécile would be provided the means to dispense alms some years later. Then, the monastery would give with joy and generosity.

---

[20] Letter to Dom Guéranger dated February 25, 1873.
[21] Delatte, "Vie," chap. 5.

Chapter 18

Final Years of Dom Guéranger

WHEN, AT THE REQUEST OF Rose Rondelou Huvé, Dom Guéranger had accepted to prepare Jenny Bruyère for her first communion—which she had been unable to participate in at her parish in Paris, Saint-Eugène—he could not have guessed at the depth of the soul that had been entrusted to him. He encountered a young timid girl, reserved in the extreme, who thought only of loyally relating to him her sins and defects, without telling him anything else. Little by little, he came to know her. At first contact, he realized that he had before him a very gifted, though difficult, child; he detected her exceptional intelligence and the richness of her heart. However, in order to penetrate the interior life of the young girl, he had had to question her, to require written accounts from her and then to ask for further details.

When the time came to choose who would be the superior of the monastery of nuns that he was making ready to establish, he had no hesitation. Despite her young age, Jenny, now Sister Cécile Bruyère, was the only one to have combined in her all the indispensable and requisite qualities, and to possess the necessary spiritual maturity for the role. But she was as yet so little fashioned for community life and the direction of other souls that Dom Guéranger wondered whether she would succeed in carrying out her charge.

It did not take long for him to see that he had not been mistaken. She had the qualities of a leader. Her spirit—clear, just, gifted with extraordinary insight and a capacity for instant comprehension—was able to discern the best course to take in any given situation. She had a gift for choosing her collaborators, directing them and employing them to the best of their capacity. Authority came naturally to her. But above all, her mystical life shone about her person, exerting a sanctifying influence on her sisters.

Some of the friends of Dom Guéranger were tempted to consider the foundation of Sainte-Cécile as an obstacle to the activities which, according to their view, he should be carrying out on a broader scale,

174

as he had done in the past. Louis Veuillot was one of these. So was Bishop Pie who, in the beginning, had cautioned Dom Guéranger against spreading his efforts too thin. He would have preferred that the abbot of Solesmes pursue his writing of *The Liturgical Year* and finally compose a "Life of St. Benedict," instead of forming young women in religious life.

Bishop Édouard Pie (1815–1880), a great admirer of Dom Guéranger, had given him hospitality when the latter came on pilgrimage to Notre-Dame de Chartres, at a time when he himself was still the vicar of the cathedral. Named bishop of Poitiers in 1849, he soon applied himself to the restoration of Ligugé, the first monastery of the Gauls.[1] He would be raised to the cardinalate in 1879.

As bishop, he also occupied himself with the nuns of Sainte-Croix;[2] thus a visit to Sainte-Cécile was called for. He came there in the beginning of May 1873, on the occasion of a trip to Laval for the consecration of Bishop Alexandre-Léopold Sebaux, elevated to the see of Angoulême. While Dom Guéranger was delighted to extend to him the honors of the new monastery, Mother Cécile showed less enthusiasm at the prospect of this visit, which scared her: "I would like to be ill tomorrow, to be consigned to the sick bed, consigned to silence."[3]

Bishop Pie scrutinized the monastery in detail, and then declared to the community gathered in the chapter room that, upon examination, Sainte-Cécile revealed itself the most beautiful of the foundations of Dom Guéranger, the one which he preferred above the

---

[1] A monastic community was first established in Ligugé by St. Martin in 361, before he was appointed Bishop of Tours. It was St. Hilary, Bishop of Poitiers, who extended the invitation and donated the land to him. The abbey suffered several vicissitudes throughout its long history from Norman raids, English invasion, Huguenot attacks, and finally dissolution of the community by the French Revolution and sale of the property into private hands in 1793. In 1852 the property was bought by Bishop Louis-Édouard Pie, of Poitiers, with the purpose of having monastic life restored to the historic abbey by Dom Guéranger. —Trans.

[2] The Abbey of Sainte-Croix, in the diocese of Poitiers, was founded in 552 by St. Radegonde, at first following the rule of Saint Caesarius (468-542), Bishop of Arles—which he had written for the community of nuns established by his sister (*Regula ad virgines*)—but soon adopting the Rule of Saint Benedict; it was thus the oldest community of Benedictine nuns in France.—Trans.

[3] Delatte, "Vie," chap. 5.

others because it had benefited from his mature years and his long experience. A few days later, Bishop Fillion confirmed this assessment by letter: "Monseigneur, the bishop of Poitiers, came back charmed by Sainte-Cécile, charmed by its material edifice and by its spiritual edifice."[4]

These were the beginnings of the relationship between Sainte-Cécile, the latest-born monastery of Benedictine nuns in France, and Sainte-Croix de Poitiers, the most ancient. During that summer, it was proposed to the chapter of Sainte-Croix that the community adopt the "Declarations" in usage at Sainte-Cécile and approved by Bishop Fillion. Mother Cécile would not of herself go after additional work, but she did not shy away when asked for counsel:

"Can you believe that I have just these days received a letter from the superior of Sainte-Croix of Poitiers who wishes to reform her house and thinks that I can help her? I know what these things mean: work for me. I see that with Stanbrook. And still, how can I refuse when the sanctification of souls, the good of the Order, and the glory of God depend on the care we put into such labor?"[5]

There were other ancient monasteries seeking help from Sainte-Cécile. A letter from Mother Bénédicte de Gobineau to her brother mentions the Benedictine nuns of the Blessed Sacrament: "Our Mother and Mother Prioress . . . are busier than usual having here three Benedictine nuns from Rouen who have come to study the constitutions of Sainte-Cécile so as to reform their own monastery accordingly. This is already the fourth community that comes to us to learn true Benedictine observance; and there are others to come."[6]

The state of Dom Guéranger's health was becoming a cause of concern. Mother Cécile noticed that his resistance was waning month by month. The prospect of a future without his presence, his teachings and his counsels seemed a fearsome thought. The days ahead loomed difficult, if not impossible, should he depart from them.

As to Dom Guéranger, the material difficulties affecting Saint-Pierre were a source of torment for him; he would have liked to leave

---

[4] Ibid.
[5] Ibid.
[6] Letter to her brother dated September 26, 1875.

no debt behind him. By force of circumstances, since the Paris catastrophe of 1845[7]—the year Jenny Bruyère was born—he had had to continually be preoccupied with paying debts. The cellarer at Solesmes, Dom Fonteinne, already had his hands full dealing with the monastery of Saint-Pierre alone, and refused to let himself become involved in the debts contracted by the ill-fated foundation of the priory of Saint-Germain in Paris (1845). Thus, Dom Guéranger had carried this weight himself all his life without ever liquidating the debt, while he drew new loans to meet financial deadlines that could not wait. This forced him to make numerous trips, alternating between the roles of collector and beggar. He would not be able to continue in this way for much longer, given his growing weakness.

Mother Cécile was aware of this situation, at first through allusions made in her presence, and then by bits of information confided to her in conversation with Dom Guéranger. During the first weeks of 1874, in the hopes of freeing himself from several financial obligations, the abbot traveled to Le Mans, Tours and Blois. However, in the aftermath of war and after the indemnities paid to Germany, the level of generosity was not the same as it had been during the prosperous years of the Second Empire. Dom Guéranger began to feel overwhelmed with discouragement.

"Oh, how your letter filled me with sorrow!" responded Mother Cécile. "You cannot imagine what moral suffering I went through this week because of this. To realize how weary you are, far away, burdened with so much worry; I can assure you, this is too much for the heart of a daughter. I take all your cares upon myself, and it seems to me that if I had been more faithful to God and more resolutely virtuous, my Spouse would not be able to refuse what I ask of Him for you. . . . It is true, my dearly beloved Father, that I am only a child, but I cannot be satisfied with praying alone; I would like to act, and at times I have such an intense desire to act that I wonder whether this could come only from my imagination. What often keeps me from talking about it is the fear of being indiscreet and of upsetting you by involving myself in things that do not concern me. I

---

[7] In 1845, Dom Guéranger was obliged to close a monastery that he had just recently founded in Paris, becoming liable for the substantial debt of the house, which would, in time, even threaten the future of Solesmes.

would be very sad if I kept you, by venturing into this area more than you would want me to, if I kept you, as I say, from pouring your heart into mine. But why is it that I tell you all these things?"[8]

Why? Because she had discerned a way of coming to Dom Guéranger's aid and because Dom Couturier, knowing that the abbot's days were numbered, had asked her to take some action. She spoke to him about it sometime afterwards, seizing an opportunity when he was being a bit more loquacious about the thorny matter:

"My Father," she said, "couldn't I help you a little with your affairs, know your debts, the payment due dates, the interest rates, all these details that uselessly weary you? I would not be acting as a person, but simply as your pen, and then as your talking agenda."

"That is very difficult, my child!" Then, after a pause: "We could, perhaps, try."

"Would you like to, Father, right away?"[9]

Thus it was that she launched upon the work. The abbot started itemizing debts and due dates, which she wrote down black on white. During the following days he brought his files to the parlor, and little by little his accounting was put in order. Always pressured by payment dates and other urgent work, Dom Guéranger had never taken the time to detail the facts of the situation. With the help of Mother Cécile, one now knew where matters stood, and at his death there would be no disagreeable surprises.

It is in great part due to this secretarial work that Mother Cécile carried out at the parlor's grille, annotating information supplied by Dom Guéranger, that three months after the abbot's death, Bishop Pie was able to present the situation in clear terms to Parisian friends of the abbey. At the home of the Viscountess des Cars[10] in Paris, he outlined the precise financial status of the Abbey of Saint-Pierre, proposing ways of remedying the situation. There was no secret about the matter any longer; the text of his talk was published in 1879, in the ninth volume of *Œuvres de Monseigneur l'évêque de Poitiers*:

---

[8] Letter to Dom Guéranger dated February 21, 1874.

[9] "Notes," pp. 8401–8402.

[10] The Viscountess des Cars, president of an association of Catholic ladies in Paris, offered to help Bishop Pie in regularizing the finances of Saint-Pierre de Solesmes.

"Substantial amounts have already been paid, thanks to intelligent employment of monastery resources and, above all, to donations made by generous benefactors. Thanks to this liberality—inspired by God Himself in strong Christians, to benefit a work that is His and that He will preserve because it is grafted directly upon the Gospel—the situation is already much improved. Two hundred and fifty thousand francs would render Solesmes entirely free of debt. ... What is to be done, then? Firstly, we are seeking to substitute interest-free loans for interest-bearing loans. This is how we have gone about it, particularly in Poitou. We have told some people: 'Lend us three thousand francs without interest during ten years. The knowledge gained each year will allow us to roughly calculate our projected resources. In the space of ten years we will be able to count on a sum above the amount of our debt; at the end of this period we will be in a position to reimburse you; by letting us keep the interest of your money each year, you will have helped us live, and we will come out of our predicament without being reduced to begging.'"[11]

The above-quoted text is not a digression in the life of the abbess. Rather, it demonstrates how useful the clarification of accounts done at the parlor of Sainte-Cécile had been. Granted, Mother Cécile was not the only person to have worked on the matter. In Ligugé, there was Dom Bastide; in Solesmes, Dom Guépin and Dom Massiou dealt with transfer of the title deed of the abbey's property (property deeds of religious establishments were still under the name of individuals because of French law) and transfer of the copyrights owned by Dom Guéranger, so that the succession would be assured. But Mother Cécile was the first to frankly broach the subject with the abbot, thus helping him resolve to take the necessary steps and leave a perfectly healthy situation behind.

Dom Delatte described it thus in his "Vie de dom Guéranger" (Life of Dom Guéranger): "The Cape of Storms had been rounded:[12] contracted loans, old debts, backed-up interest, everything was listed.

---

[11] *Oeuvres de Monseigneur l'évêque de Poitiers* (Works by the Bishop of Poitiers) (Paris: Librairie Oudin Frères, 1879) Tome 9, pp. 114–115.

[12] "Cape of Storms" was the original name of the Cape of Good Hope, given by Bartolomeu Dias, the Portuguese navigator and first European to round the dangerous cape in South Africa in 1488, a feat that signaled the opening of navigational routes to the Indies.—Trans.

Even if no payments were made against the principal, at least the liabilities to be paid off were now known."[13] The finances of Solesmes were actually nothing to be despaired of, which the address given by Bishop Pie demonstrated, and in a few years they were stabilized. The intervention of the abbess had been providential, opening the way for others to act.

But this was only a passing instance of action taken by the young abbess to the benefit of the monastery next door, where she had received so much. She had a presentiment of something to come that would be more profound, more lasting, more spiritual. She was given a grace of illumination regarding this on February 10, 1874, the feast of St. Scholastica, when some of the monks of Solesmes were present at the chapel of Our Lady facing the nuns' choir, to participate in the ceremony of profession of Sister Domitille Teissier. However, she waited until February 21 to submit this experience in writing to Dom Guéranger:

"On the day of Sister Domitille's profession, I had a singularly unique impression which I had not thought of telling you about, but which returned to me very strongly this week by pressure of the concern I have been feeling for you. At the moment when the *two choirs* responded to the *Suscipe* of our new spouse of Christ, I was lifted out of myself, and without any movement of words, without any form, but through a powerful impression from the Beloved, He gave me the responsibility and charge of the family that was occupying the chapel of the Holy Virgin. So effective was this impression that in my heart I can no longer perceive any distinction between those who made up the *two* choirs. The affection I feel, the solicitude for their material as well as moral good is the same. At first this seemed a remarkable thing to me, but now I am used to it, and I speak to Our Lord equally about one and the other, unable to distinguish between them."[14]

Dom Guéranger reflected upon this unique illumination and prayed. He did nothing to give it a comforting interpretation, and kept himself from reassuring Mother Cécile and from telling her that

---

[13] 1984 edition, p. 879.
[14] Letter to Dom Guéranger dated February 21, 1874.

this solicitude should remain something interior, without being exteriorly translated into concrete action.

Some days later, in the evening of March 11, the abbot of Solesmes came to Sainte-Cécile. He had just celebrated First Vespers of the feast of Saint Gregory the Great at Saint-Pierre:

"I found him in a remarkably recollected state," wrote Mother Cécile, "and I was highly impressed by this. Immediately, in that solemn tone that indicated he was being moved by lofty thoughts, he said to me: 'My daughter, on this day of Saint Gregory, I come on the part of Our Lord. Following what has transpired in these last days, He has clearly manifested His will to me, and He urges me to bless you in His name as charged with a new flock. Are you ready to receive this new burden?' Despite my emotion, an overwhelmingly powerful feeling took hold of me in such a way that I answered him affirmatively. I went down on my knees and he blessed me in a tone of voice and with an expression that I will never forget. Something great had been effected in me by the hands of this Patriarch. I understood then what the blessing of the Old Law was and why the patriarchs attached so much importance to it. When I was raised to my feet, after a moment of silence, he added: 'My daughter, you are now twice a mother, and this day is one of the most important and most consoling of my life. Our Lord has given me a great grace and I begin to understand why He brought you to me, and why He has done so much in you. Oh, my little Mother, my Cécile, I will die in peace; do not forget what you are and what the Spouse has done today through my hands. Everything is in your hands; work, my daughter, and know that I charge you with what pertains to both the material and the moral. Be mother and totally mother.'" [15]

This act of Dom Guéranger was confirmation of the interior light she had received on the feast of Saint Scholastica and that had remained with her during the ensuing days. One month later, the abbot had come to entrust to Mother Cécile, in the name of the Lord, a maternal mission toward Saint-Pierre similar to that which she already exercised over her daughters at Sainte-Cécile. She had accepted it without giving much thought, at first, to what it would

---

[15] "Souvenirs sur dom Guéranger," pp. 40–42.

entail. Later, she confessed to Dom Guéranger that this mission seemed very heavy to her: "It is my repose and my peace, my child, to feel that I can tell you anything," he told her. "Doesn't it mean anything to you, to be the assurance of your old father? I have worked hard; it is now your turn, and with this I will depart to Our Lord in tranquility."[16]

But Mother Cécile would exercise this maternal role at the price of the blood of her heart.

---

[16] "Notes," p. 8403.

Chapter 19

The Two Founders Depart

WELL BEFORE TURNING THIRTY, Catherine of Siena had become the head of a group of disciples who dealt with her on intimate terms and did not hesitate to call her "dulcissima Mamma." She herself found joy in referring to the group that had gathered around her as her "bella brigata."[1] It was composed at first of "mantellate,"[2] Dominican tertiaries, about twenty women, who were joined in time by others, mostly men, both religious and lay, young and old. Catherine had the heart and soul of a mother for these her numerous spiritual children: "Until death, amidst tears, I want to continue bringing disciples into the world," she wrote in one of her letters.[3] Parting from them was always painful for her, and she would call them back to her "just as a mother calls her child to press it against her breast."[4]

St. Catherine of Siena died at age thirty-three. Many of the people she had directed were older than she, including her three secretaries, Dominican theologians, one of whom was the celebrated Blessed Raymond of Capua. There were also great humanists, scholars and people of all walks of life among them.

Dom Guéranger knew this. He was not one to be alarmed by the weight of responsibility that he had placed upon the shoulders of Mother Cécile. The Holy Spirit could very well operate in the nineteenth century what He had done in Tuscany during the fourteenth. There was no romanticism in this notion. However, this century, the bourgeois and conformist century par excellence, would

---

[1] "Dulcissima Mamma," most sweet Mother; "la bella brigata," the jolly band.—Trans.

[2] "Mantellate" (plural of "mantelatta") refers to the habit worn by these lay tertiaries.—Trans.

[3] See letter T126 in *The Letters of Catherine of Siena, Volume II*, trans. Suzanne Noffke, O.P. (Tempe, AZ: Arizona Center for Medieval and Renaissance Studies, 2001), p. 436. The author here paraphrases from the passage: "He and the others were given birth with plenty of tears and sweat, and I will continue to give them birth until I die, as God grants me grace in this sweet time of solitude that gentle First Truth has given to me and to this poor little family." —Trans.

[4] The image of a child at its mother's breast is a recurring motif in St. Catherine's writings.—Trans.

undoubtedly be less prepared than medieval Italy to witness a young religious fulfilling such a role.

The foundation of Sainte-Cécile had only been possible thanks to the ordinary of the diocese, Bishop Charles Fillion. Twelve years younger than Dom Guéranger, he was fifty-seven in 1874, and one could expect him to remain at the head of the diocese for a long time still. However, in June 1874 his health suffered a sudden collapse. On the twenty-sixth, Dom Guéranger wrote to Bishop Pie: "Our good bishop has all but left us. The outcome is not yet sure. We pray much, but there is no human hope. If God calls him, you know how important the question of his succession will be for Solesmes. . . ."

He died on July 28. Bishop Pie gave the funeral oration at the thirty days' Mass on August 27, 1874. Mother Cécile, who knew Bishop Fillion well and was sure that she could rely on him, was strongly affected by the blow. But this only led her to abandon herself yet more completely to God: "Our Lord is always there," she wrote on July 29. "He does not die, He does not sleep, and He knows well why He has struck us. Job of the old covenant loved God to the point where he could say: *Si bona suscepimus de manu Dei, mala autem quare non sustineamus?* (If we have received good things at the hand of God, why should we not receive evil?[5]) I who have felt the trembling hands of this good prelate upon my head, depositing there all the powers of the Holy Spirit . . . for me, my well-beloved Father, this is an acute sorrow of the type that endures. It intensifies all our other worries. But with God's help, these will pass, I am firmly confident, while the sorrow will not."[6]

Thanks to the influence of Bishop Pie, to whom Dom Guéranger appealed, the new bishop of Le Mans was chosen from among the friends of Solesmes. This was Bishop Hector Chaulet d'Outremont, a close friend of the Holy Man of Tours, Monsieur Papin-Dupont.[7] He had been the bishop of Agen since 1871 and had just completed his forty-ninth birthday.

Bishop Chaulet d'Outremont was a convert. He had not received a truly Christian education, but discovered the faith of a sudden during

---

[5] Job 2:10.—Trans.
[6] Letter to Dom Guéranger dated July 29, 1874.
[7] See chap. 8, p. 74, n. 1.—Trans.

his philosophical studies. His family was not well disposed toward his plans for the priesthood. However, he had to thwart them in their hopes for his worldly advancement and, in 1853, presented them with his decision to become a priest. Monsieur Papin-Dupont had helped the young man to take this step.

Thus, Dom Guéranger was reassured in what concerned the succession of Bishop Fillion. But for Mother Cécile, it could never be the same as with him who had seen the project first emerge, had founded the monastery, had doted over it during its first years, who had himself requested of Pius IX the title of abbess for the young prioress. A page had been turned. Shortly before dying, Bishop Fillion asked his brother to send to Sainte-Cécile certain mementos of his affection.

But the state of Dom Guéranger's health, as well, was more and more a cause of concern, and the doctors in Le Mans gave little hope. The hour was approaching when he too would have to leave his daughters. He did not excuse himself from giving the last retreat, while agreeing to limit himself to a single conference per day, leaving it to the abbess to complete his teaching with practical applications. "When the good God calls me to Himself," he told a nun three years before his death, "I will die in peace because I know in whose hands I am leaving you. She will hold all my thoughts; whenever she speaks, you will be able to say: 'That is what our father abbot would want!' She has always been so docile. To tell you quite frankly, I don't believe she ever once resisted grace. May Our Lord bless her for all the consolation she has given me."[8]

The last vestiges of strength abandoned Dom Guéranger on Christmas 1874, during the course of the night. In his "Règlement du noviciat" (Rule for the novitiate), he had taught his young monks not to fear the "holy fatigue" they might feel during the solemn celebration of the liturgy on certain days; he did not say that the true monk did not feel fatigued. He could still come to Sainte-Cécile. He celebrated Mass there for the last time on Saturday, January 16, 1875. On the twenty-third, he was again at Sainte-Cécile for confessions, and on the twenty-seventh, he gave his last conference, which had to

---

[8] "Annals: continuation," September 1874, p. 165.

be shortened because of his great weakness. He told Mother Cécile, who was anxious about him: "It is I who am unhappy with you; so be convinced that it is your health that is important now. You must not become ill; rather, you must be doubly on your feet."[9]

"His voice was a bit tremulous and halting, and Father Abbot rose abruptly," wrote Mother Cécile, "without waiting for the arrival of his vehicle to be announced, as he usually did; he blessed the abbess and walked toward the parlor door. But, be it because he did not want to leave her with the impression of this apparent rudeness, be it because he was moved by an altogether different sentiment, he came back and before departing he blessed her once again, saying in his most affectionate tone: 'A Dieu, my daughter!' and then he left."[10]

He did not rise from bed on the following day, and the last phase of his life began. It would be short—only two days. News of his state kept arriving at Sainte-Cécile at every hour, and the nuns prayed. Mother Cécile left personal memoirs of her sentiments during the agony of the father abbot, which warrant being transcribed here:

"[On Friday, the twenty-ninth,] a little before eleven o'clock [in the evening], I was suddenly awakened by so strong and so sweet a fragrance of incense that it seemed a censer was burning under my nose. It remained in the air during a few minutes after I had awakened. I savored the perfume with bitter sorrow, as past experience, and words I had heard from my Father Abbot in a similar circumstance, sufficiently indicated to me what this manifestation meant. Nonetheless, I continued struggling with my Spouse to keep hold of this life so dear to me, and I struggled with desperate determination, while still remaining in peace and continuing my care for our dear infirm one. I wanted his soul to be so beautiful as not to be missing anything, to be without trouble and without pain, and I avidly imbibed, so to speak, all the anxieties and worries of all kinds that could have assailed him. Before they should reach him, I took them upon myself with incredible suffering. Oh, how many times I died during those hours! I did not think I would be able to continue until the end, and, nonetheless, I was ready to take on whatever there

---

[9] "Notes," p. 8646."
[10] Ibid.

was to be had. My soul also worked within the souls of all his children in an inexpressible manner. It was as if to arrange loose pieces of wood of all types so that they could be fit together and that the work par excellence of my father, the restoration of monastic life, could receive the holy unction of pain and sorrow as a splendid consecration that would be its strength and its greatness.

"Saturday morning, when I received Holy Communion, I did what my Father had done so often for me. He would always tell me: 'During the last fifteen years, my daughter, not for a single time have I celebrated Holy Mass without you and without having you partake of my chalice.' And since I did not receive my Lord except by his express order, often renewed, he had a great part in this solemn moment of my life. But this Saturday! I told my Spouse that I was receiving Him in viaticum and that He should visit my father, enveloping him in divine sweetness. And as soon as I made this request, the sensible presence of my Lord left me and I saw it penetrate the soul of my father in a mysterious way.

"The entire morning unfolded in this laborious and painful struggle that I've described. . . . Toward one o'clock, I went to place myself before the Blessed Sacrament, and I found my father there entirely. But all of that was without any consolation; all was anguish, agony, death. My own sorrow was only a drop compared to all the other sorrows that I was carrying. I saw all things as from the threshold of eternity and as if I were responsible for the existence of my father. A little before three o'clock, I cannot say at what exact minute, my Spouse said to me: 'I will not take your father from you; I wish that you freely give him to Me.' A lightning bolt would have struck me less powerfully. Then I began telling the Lord that He was cruel, that, in any case, there was no hope, that his last hour was imminent, that I couldn't do anything anymore, etc., etc., in short, I was trying to escape. But my Beloved continued his pursuit: 'Still, you love Me,' He said, 'so I do not want to do anything that you yourself do not want; I am waiting on you.' I bent over in excruciating anguish and this lasted a good quarter of an hour. At last, I was afraid of displeasing my Spouse and I recollected myself a moment, to be as He wished me to be. He continued: 'Give him to Me, but standing upright, as my mother offered Me on Calvary.' I felt then that my soul rose to offer a sacrifice. Nonetheless, I still hesitated to say the final solemn word. Then my father spoke to me: 'My daughter, haven't I often told you that I would not die except when you so desired? You didn't understand me then and this distressed you; still, you hear the Master, and me; I am waiting on you.' On hearing this voice that had always been obeyed, I turned myself toward Our Lord and told him: 'I freely give him to You.' And immediately I placed myself on my knees in spirit before my father. . . . I felt myself being blessed, and then I heard: 'Adieu, my Cécile, à Dieu, my daughter." [11]

It was the struggle between Jacob and the angel. The Lord always asks souls for their freely given consent to that which He has decided for them, and this consent is rarely obtained without struggle. Mother Cécile, in her prayer, experienced this great truth in dramatic fashion. What is remarkable in her case, is how intensely she was aware of it, and how precisely the interior events corresponded to the exterior events. At the moment when, at last, she said her "yes" without reserve and without second thoughts about not contesting God, Dom Guéranger ended his existence on earth and breathed his last. She knew it because the prior, Dom Couturier, sent her news immediately—it takes six minutes to walk from Saint-Pierre to Sainte-Cécile—and shortly the death knell sounded from the belfry of the abbey nearby.

Instances of telepathy are relatively frequent, particularly among people who are linked by strong ties of affection. However, Mother Cécile's description goes well beyond even this. Not only did she live the rhythm of the final moments of Dom Guéranger, which were transpiring several hundred yards away, but she was invited to give her active assent—she, herself, present to God him who had been her spiritual father.

The abbot had died toward half past three in the afternoon. After Vespers, the nuns came to Mother Cécile to share their sorrow. The evening conference occurred as usual. Then, on the following day, the nuns prepared the pontifical vestments with which the body of the

---

[11] Letter to Dom Couturier dated February 1, 1875.

abbot would be laid in his coffin, and which he would take with him to his tomb.

The body was brought to Sainte-Cécile on the evening of February 3 and laid in the church. The nuns, surrounding it, sang the Office of the Dead and recited the psalter during the intervals between the hours of the Divine Office until the time of the funeral ceremony celebrated at Saint-Pierre on the following day. Bishop d'Outremont came for the transfer of the body, and then it was time for the farewell. Not entirely, however, since Dom Guéranger had bequeathed his heart to Sainte-Cécile. It would be put to rest in the sanctuary, below a marble plaque fixed in place by four copper nails, engraved with an inscription.[12]

According to the wishes of the abbot, the panegyric to be delivered at the Mass of thirty days was entrusted to Bishop Pie—he, better than anyone, would know what should be said. In order to prepare it, the bishop asked Mother Cécile to supply him with some notes. The same was done the following year by Bishop Freppel, of Angers, for the anniversary Mass. In their discourse, both retained long passages as they had been written by the abbess of Sainte-Cécile.

Thus, without delay, she was called to distribute day after day what she had received from the abbot, bearing her own stamp, to all those who came to her: her daughters first of all, but also Dom Couturier, the faithful man, successor of Dom Guéranger. Because of his great timidity, he had need of reassurance and confirmation upon the course he applied himself to maintain, come wind, come rain.

---

[12] The inscription reads: RMVS IN XP PATER / D PROSPER LVDOVICUS PASCHALIS / GVERANGER / ABBAS SOLESMENSIS / DILECTISSIMIS AD S CAECILIAM FILIABVS / COR SVVM LEGAVIT / HIC DEPOSITVM / IN PACE. (The Very Reverend Father in Christ / Dom Prosper Louis Paschal / Guéranger / Abbot of Solesmes / to his well-beloved daughters at Sainte-Cécile / bequeathed his heart / which is placed here / in peace.—Trans.)

Part III

Heiress to the Founder
1875–1890

Chapter 20

Solesmes without Dom Guéranger

DOM GUÉRANGER DEPARTED AT a crucial moment in the history of France. The year of his death was a watershed, marking the end of an era. Starting with the first elections in 1870, the people of the provinces—opposed to any prolongation of the war and fearful of the consequences of social upheavals in the capital—elected to the Chamber a majority comprised of prominent figures with conservative tendencies. With the return to normal life, the political climate changed quickly. It was precisely in 1875 that a new order of things was established.

The divided majority worked as it could to restore the monarchy; however, as they could not agree, the process came to a complete stalemate. The electorate drew a simple conclusion from this: given that the restoration of the monarchy—be it Bourbon, Orléans or Bonapartist—did not seem possible, the only solution was to vote for moderate republicans. Since the country had a republican constitution, they might as well turn to the partisans of the republic.

The tragedy was that the republicans, even those labeled as "moderate," were viscerally opposed to the Church and believed that the triumph of the republic was equivalent to the triumph of the "immortal principles" of 1789, too often interpreted in the mindset of the men of 1793.[1] Any criticism of the system was considered a "blasphemy against the Nation," as had been declared at the trial of Louis XVI.

During the years since the Consulate and the Empire, religion had been more or less permitted by the elite, as an indispensable factor for the morality of the people; but for the people alone, as there was no danger of its being accorded the least credibility among enlightened society. With her action duly controlled, the Church was a lesser evil, since she contributed to public order. However, she had been overly

---

[1] "1789," a reference to the tenets of the French Revolution; "1793," the atrocities of the Reign of Terror.—Trans.

successful in the course of the nineteenth century, going beyond the limits to which it had been intended she be confined. Her ascendancy over society was deemed excessive and nefarious. It was time to put an end to this by changing the legislature. The hour had come to take control of the education of all strata of society, not only of the elites, as the universities had applied themselves to do since their reorganization under the Empire.

Secularization, as it emerged in France at this time, took the form of a type of religion intended to replace Catholicism. The avowed program was to form civil society, to legislate and govern, not only independently of the Church, but against her. The only authority the secular state would be anchored upon was reason and science, faith in humanity.

The program did not yet surface in its complete form in 1875, but a change of mentality was already evident, marked by the well-known affirmation: "The republic will be secular or it will not be at all." The coming years promised to be troubled, and the republican government, which the monarchists had created in 1871 while awaiting the reinstatement of the monarchy, was proving to be a passing thing. The constitution of 1875 was not what hard-core republicans, who considered themselves in the line of "the great ancestors," would have liked it to be, but it was a sufficient base to secure a majority for them in the Assembly. The "opportunists," headed by Gambetta,[2] joined forces with the majority, with the firm intent of amending the system so as to have it conform to the ideals of the "radical republicans."

It would take four years for the republicans to gain control of the new republic, but the first decisive victory was won at the elections of 1876. The new Chamber of Deputies emerged with 340 republicans against 155 monarchists or bonapartists. The proportion was two to one, and soon a round of partial elections raised the number of republicans to 363. For the moment, the majority in the Senate remained monarchist, but only until the next election. In the interim, governing the country was like squaring a circle, and President Mac-

---

[2] See chap. 16, p. 154, n. 7.

Mahon,[3] following upon a conflict with the deputies, decided to dissolve the Chamber. But despite the efforts of the administration, the leftist margin was still considerable with 320 deputies. Moreover, the clergy was compromised after the electoral campaign for having openly supported the defeated candidates.

This is not the place for a thorough review of the political history of France as background for the particular history of the two communities in Solesmes. However, its consequences will so directly impact them that our understanding of events would be inevitably impaired if we had not provided this brief summary.

A monastery cannot remain without an abbot. The death of Dom Guéranger deprived Saint-Pierre of its abbot, and a new one was needed without delay. In fact, the choice of a successor to the first abbot of Solesmes was simple: Dom Charles Couturier, the prior for fifteen years and master of novices for nineteen, seemed the obvious choice for this charge. Dom Léon Bastide, abbot of Ligugé, presided at the election of Thursday, February 11. In the first round of votes, the forty-seven chapter members, minus one vote, unanimously elected Dom Couturier as second abbot of Solesmes. He was confirmed by Rome on March 5 and installed on the thirteenth. The history of Solesmes continued in peace, at least internally.

With the death of Dom Guéranger, Mother Cécile no longer had the sole spiritual director she had known since her childhood, from the time of her first communion. She would subsequently find good counselors, confessors, but her father abbot would never truly be replaced. At Saint-Pierre, she entrusted herself principally to Dom Couturier, the new abbot, and also to Dom Logerot, the new master of novices. But the latter had such veneration for her that he rather considered himself her disciple. His tendency was to communicate this veneration to all the novices of whom he had charge, without

---

[3] Patrice de Mac-Mahon, (1808–1893)—whose family fled from Ireland to France during the reign of James II—was President of the French Republic from 1873 to 1879. A highly respected military officer whose career unfolded in Algiers, the Crimean War, the Italian wars of unification, and the Franco-Prussian War, he was created Duke of Magenta and Marshal of France as a result of different military victories. He was a conservative but not a monarchist—in his own words, loyal to the "integrity of the sovereign power of the Assembly."—Trans.

thinking that certain of them, having come already formed and with their own prejudices, would not necessarily agree with his views.

In actuality, during the years between 1875 and 1880, the direct influence of Mother Cécile over the monks and the novices of Saint-Pierre was limited, for the good reason that they lived in their own enclosure, behind their walls, and that access to the church and parlor at Sainte-Cécile was limited to the necessities of their ministerial care for the nuns. Eventually, the brutal expulsion of the monks from their monastery in 1880 and 1882 and their taking lodging in the village would increase the frequency of contact between them and Mother Cécile. In addition, these years coincided with a growing fatigue on the part of Dom Couturier, and a certain deficiency in government when overarching principles were not in question. Dom Delatte would re-establish firmer control of the community in 1890, and Mother Cécile would then be happy to refer the monks back to him. Thus, the number of years in which the abbess was called to respond to specific spiritual needs is limited to a period from 1882 to 1890, that is, a total of eight years. Before 1882, she was not directly sought, except by Dom Couturier himself and by Dom Logerot. After 1890, and even before then, Dom Delatte, who had complete trust in Mother Cécile, would curtail the too-numerous contacts she had with individual monks.

Such a clarification is germane. At the time of the denunciations made in Rome—which prompted an apostolic visitation in 1893—there was talk of a veritable governance of the two monasteries by Mother Cécile, which is obviously erroneous. The generalization made about her influence on Saint-Pierre was exaggerated both in time and space. Mother Cécile exercised her maternal charism toward the community of Saint-Pierre, but within well-circumscribed limits. Her maternal solicitude expressed itself above all through prayer. She gave advice when sought by the abbot and the master of novices, and occasionally she met with some of the young monks referred to her. But there was no desire on her part to spontaneously intervene. Her nature, as well as her personal inclinations and her own grace were contrary to this. Her concerns were of another kind:

"My Lord, my King and my Spouse, those you have given me as sons, *non ex sanguinibus, neque ex voluntate carnis, neque ex voluntate viri, sed ex Deo nati sunt* (born not of blood, nor of the will of the flesh, nor of the will of man, but of God. Jn 1:13), I have engendered them in Your love; You have given them to me to replace my fathers (cf. Ps 44:17). This life that they have received is not a natural life; it is the life that is in You, the life that is You, of which the universal Vivifier and Sanctifier is the principle. I beseech You, then, and it is my desire as spouse and mother, that this ineffable life which You have given them, superabound in them and that it grow unto holiness. . . . Therefore, Lord, cast Your glance over all the members of this my family; look at them with this glance that purifies and transforms, touch them with this divine finger that renders fertile the sterile soil, consume them with this fire which You came to set upon the earth, with such great desire that it be enkindled.

"Alas, what shall I do if You refuse me Your help? Then, I will dare to reproach You for having given them to me. . . . Complete Your work in them all, You Who have created them, redeemed them, and chosen them. That they may follow You not in languor and dejection, but with firm steps and in the holy ardor of love! That they may run toward the odor of the fragrance that emanates from You; from You, their head, their king, their brother, and their friend! Finally, my Lord, You, the sovereign and prince of my heart, if Your divine justice requires compensation, recognize my rights as a mother and deign to reckon with me rather than them. Give them of the mysterious milk of infants, the honey in the comb, the wine prepared with aromatic spices. To me, if need be, give vinegar and myrrh. Do I not have You always as my portion, and can I fear anything that You may send me? Deign, then, to cover them with your gifts and unite the feebleness of my humble request to the victorious strength of that permanent supplication that You present without ceasing to the Father. Amen! Amen!"[4]

There is nothing here that resembles a desire for power, a desire to impose one's personal influence at long last recognized and appreciated. There is no basis for allegations that Mother Cécile was one of those women who love to exert power over men, happy to obtain her ends by manipulating people.

---

[4] Letter to Dom Couturier, November 30, 1875.

The diocese of Le Mans came close to losing Bishop d'Outremont even before his installation. The ordinary of Tours, Archbishop Fruchaud, died of a cerebral congestion on September 9, 1874, and d'Outremont's name had been proposed as a successor. However, the Ministry of Religions discarded his candidacy, as there was concern that he might become too involved with the legitimists[5] of the Touraine region. Thus Le Mans was spared from having to face the uncertainties of a new choice that would be crucial for the future of the two monasteries during this time of transition.

In the wake of Dom Guéranger's demise, at the time of the Ascension a few months later, another of Mother Cécile's first companions departed for the eternal abode—a sister who had come from Chantenay, Marie Bignon. For the abbess this was the friend of sixteen years, , it will be recalled, her neighbor in Coudreuse who had expressed a desire to study under her direction in order to someday become a Sister of Charity of Notre-Dame d'Évron. She had entered Sainte-Cécile shortly after its foundation. Seeing her leave this earth so sweetly, Dom Couturier commented: "One does not die here as elsewhere, and everything I see here is like nothing that I have seen until now."[6]

The same year that Dom Guéranger died, Cardinal Pitra[7] finally made the trip from Rome to Solesmes. Father Ambroise Ledru[8] claimed that his elevation to the cardinalate had chilled relations between him and the abbot of Solesmes, who purportedly had coveted the dignity for himself. According to Ledru, this was why the cardinal, a former monk of Solesmes, had not wanted to show himself again at the monastery on the banks of the Sarthe while Dom Guéranger was still alive. But there is nothing that confirms this hypothesis. Cardinal Pitra had met Dom Guéranger in Marseilles, but did not want to come to Solesmes because this would put him in the

---

[5] The "Legitimists" wanted the return of a Bourbon to the throne, that is, the Count of Chambord.—Trans.

[6] Mother Cécile Bruyère, "Biographie de sœur Augustine Bignon," p. 56.

[7] See chap. 17, p. 166, n. 5. Cardinal Pitra was a monk of Solesmes who had been called to serve in Rome, thus his predicament related to protocol as explained in this paragraph.—Trans.

[8] Ambroise Ledru (d. 1935), priest of Le Mans, historian who took an antagonistic position toward the monastery of Solesmes in 1893 (see chap. 31, p. 313).

position of having precedence in protocol over his own abbot. Under Dom Couturier, there was no longer any hindrance to his visit, except the distance. He arrived in Solesmes on July 10, 1875 for the feast of Saint Benedict.[9]

He was curious to see the priory of Sainte-Cécile and meet its young abbess. His first stop, upon arriving in Sablé, was the nuns' monastery, even before coming to Saint-Pierre. He was received there with great festivity—the main courtyard was decorated and decked with banners, and the all bells pealed at once. "I am your brother," he exclaimed, "and despite the splendor of the reception, nothing is different in Solesmes these days; it is only that now there is one more monk here."[10]

In the course of the following days he came often to hold long conversations with Mother Cécile, as his sojourn in Solesmes lasted more than a month. A profound friendship grew between the two. He spoke to the community about Rome: "With such kindness and warmth," wrote Mother Eulalie Ripert to her parents, "he spoke to us for nearly an hour about the Holy Father and Rome. He described to us, with the minutest details, the daily routine of the Holy Father, and then he took us on a tour of the principal basilicas of Rome, all punctuated by anecdotes and details full of interest."[11]

On the day before the feast of the Assumption, which signaled his approaching departure, he visited the cemetery of the nuns, and he expressed the desire to be laid to rest there at his death. In point of fact, he was interred in the cemetery at San Lorenzo in Agro Verano, in the vault of the Sacred Congregation for the Propagation of the Faith, from whence he was later transferred to the Abbey of Saint Jerome in Rome, amidst other monks of Solesmes. Then, after the closure of the abbey that had completed the critical edition of the Vulgate of Saint Jerome, he was taken to Saint-Pierre of Solesmes, and laid in the chapel of Saint Scholastica.

---

[9] The author refers here to the solemnity of St. Benedict, i.e., July 11, which marks the *translatio* (translation or transfer) of St. Benedict's relics from Monte Cassino to Fleury. The feast of his *transitus* (passing) is celebrated on March 21 — Trans.

[10] Delatte, "Vie," chap. 5.

[11] Letter dated August 16, 1875.

Before leaving Saint-Pierre, the cardinal sent a farewell note to Mother Cécile: "Madame Abbess, my last day, my last night in Solesmes advances; in a few hours I will have to distance myself from here and the isolation will resume. . . . See my weakness. Help me, as you have already done in such an unexpected way; help me to carry my poor soul in both hands; above all, pray my good angels to keep me in their hands, to raise me and guard me along so many somber ways, where the very silence that envelops me, terrifies me."[12] Cardinal Pitra never became accustomed to the moral solitude that had been his lot since the pope had called him to Rome. He forever missed the community life which he had, in fact, so little known.

In the fall, Mother Cécile agreed to open a small "alumnat"[13] at Sainte-Cécile, at the request of families of the nuns. There was already something analogous for about half a dozen or more boys at the priory of Sainte-Madeleine in Marseilles. But they did not lodge at the monastery; they would arrive in the morning from their family home and return there in the evening. Dom Guéranger had always been opposed to having his monks become supernumerary teachers. He had determined clearly what the orientation of Solesmes should be in this regard. They should not be like the last generation of monks of Saint-Maur, who had seen in teaching a guarantee of survival for the monastic order in a society where the value of contemplative life was entirely unrecognized.

Nonetheless, in the Declarations of Sainte-Cécile, he had made provision for the possibility of "bringing up a few children in the monastery, but always in very restricted numbers" (in the thirtieth chapter of the Rule). The "alumnat" at Sainte-Cécile had only two members in the beginning, one aged nine and the other seven. These were two young daughters of Monsieur de Marquié,[14] Germaine and Jeanne, who arrived on October 2, 1875. The group never comprised more than five children at a time, and the total number altogether did

---

[12] Letter written the night of August 15 to 16, 1875.

[13] *Alumnat*, from the Latin *alo, alere*, nurture, bring up. In the Benedictine Order this term is applied to the schools run by their monks or nuns.

[14] Monsieur de Marquié, spiritual son of Dom Guéranger, became a widower upon the birth of his third daughter, Thérèse, in 1870.

not surpass fifteen. Half of these eventually became Benedictine nuns; two others entered the Daughters of Charity of St. Vincent de Paul.

At long last the abbess of Sainte-Cécile, according to the desire expressed by Dom Guéranger, made her oft-deferred visit to the abbey of Jouarre, in order to work there on the Customary[15] of Sainte-Cécile. "Imagine an abbey rich in magnificent memories, and presided by an abbess who knows them all," she wrote to Dom Couturier. "Madame Abbess reminds me very much of the Right Reverend d'Aiguebelle (Dom Marie-Gabriel) while being much more dignified and a little less jovial than he. . . . She is good and motherly beyond anything that can be expressed, but perfectly dignified and an abbess from head to toe. Her manner is noble and simple. The grand nun, the true deaconess, conscious of what she is, with a humility so forthright and so true that it reminds me of the humility of my father abbot in heaven."[16]

The last expression, so tenderly possessive, reveals the soul of Mother Cécile. For all the monks and nuns of Saint-Pierre and Sainte-Cécile, Dom Guéranger had become "father abbot in heaven," but for the abbess, he was by right particularly her own.

---

[15] Book prescribing the daily and seasonal rituals and customs of a particular monastic community.—Trans.

[16] Letter dated December 11, 1875.

Chapter 21

The Congregation of France

WHY WAS DOM GUÉRANGER so adamant that Mother Cécile enter into personal contact with the abbey of Jouarre? As with Saint-Pierre in 1832-1833, the monastery of Sainte-Cécile was a new creation while at the same time being the restoration of an ancient form of religious life. Dom Guéranger's intent had been to reconnect with a distant past, known to him most especially through the study of written sources.

In 1837, at Saint Paul Outside-the-Walls in Rome and at Subiaco, Dom Guéranger had encountered the continuity of tradition, admittedly in a form that he deemed imperfect and that did not satisfy his thirst for authentic monasticism, but nonetheless, he had found the heritage of a living past. Later, he had the same experience in Monte Cassino and at monasteries of the English Congregation, most notably at Belmont. He was strongly convinced that nothing could replace direct contact with a monastery possessing a long tradition.

Jouarre was another instance of monastic restoration, a slightly later one than Saint-Pierre as the nuns only reoccupied the ancient monastic buildings in 1837. But they had come from Pradines, where Mother de Bavoz, in the wake of the Revolution, had regrouped old religious of different monasteries. At Jouarre itself, some nuns had been able to maintain themselves and to purchase back their abbatial home in 1821, living long enough to see their monastery reborn.

The Customary of Sainte-Cécile—at which Mother Cécile worked intensely with the abbess of Jouarre, Mother Athanase Gilquin—is, therefore, a legacy of the grand French abbeys of the seventeenth century, but in revised form and divested of what pertained only to the particular usages of that century, the "grand siècle."

"I have had long meetings with Madame Abbess, who is full of learning and the spirit of God," wrote Mother Cécile. "She is truly a powerful personality, one of those grand abbesses of royal lineage. You would not believe what sound and precise ideas she has about the spiritual life, what firmness and what sweetness. She told me that she has sought nothing outside the Holy Rule with regards to their spirituality; that therein is everything needed for the nuns. She said that it is impossible to have any scruples if souls are always conducted in the truth. The results are marvelous, and the more I come to know each nun with the insight that Our Lord has given me, the greater is my admiration. You can be sure that Jouarre is unique in France and perhaps in the world. What this great abbess most mercilessly chastises is the *sans-gêne*[1]—she says there can be no progress towards holiness with that."[2]

Mother Cécile returned to Solesmes for the festivities of Christmas 1875. January 30, 1876 marked the first anniversary of the death of Dom Guéranger, and she relived in her heart the events of the previous year. Some months later, on March 16, 1876, Bishop Charles Freppel[3] delivered the second panegyric on the abbot of Solesmes. He had been in Angers for only six years and thus, was among the more recent friends of Solesmes. His grand exposé about the dignity of the monastic order, illustrated by the figure of Dom Guéranger, owed even more to Mother Cécile than had the panegyric written by Bishop Pie in 1875. "Isn't it a bit you, Madame, whom we have heard?!" he exclaimed at the parlor of Sainte-Cécile that afternoon, in the presence of other bishops, when the abbess had thought it appropriate to thank him publicly for the address he had just delivered.[4]

The Abbey of Saint-Pierre established by Dom Guéranger, was still only a project of a monastery, as he himself used to say—not in what concerned monastic principles, but in their realization. The ancient priory of Solesmes was erected as an abbey in 1837 with the mission of restoring the Benedictine Order in France, but the first few foundations made by Dom Guéranger had failed. Finally, with the help of Bishop Pie, he was able to restore Liguge, for which he obtained the status of an abbey. Marseilles was a priory whose

---

[1] No one expression in English does justice to this French word, which means casualness to the point of lack of decorum, an excessive familiarity, a lack of deportment and consideration.—Trans.

[2] Letter dated December 15, 1875.

[3] Charles-Émile Freppel (1827–1891), bishop of Angers from 1870 to his death.—Trans.

[4] Delatte, "Vie," chap. 5.

development was proving to be difficult. Sainte-Cécile had episcopal approbation only. There was still a considerable amount to be done in order for the Congregation to become firmly rooted and expand.

In 1837, the government of the infant Congregation had been organized in a provisional and embryonic manner. The first General Chapter was only held after the death of Dom Guéranger and was dedicated to completing the constitutions of the Congregation. Dom Couturier worked to settle organizational problems concerning government, which had been left unresolved in 1837. His was the delicate task of clarifying and completing Dom Guéranger's work in total fidelity to his thought.

The first matters that needed to be determined were the structure of the Congregation, procedures for the general chapter, the status of each monastery, the relationship of Solesmian monasteries with other congregations of the Benedictine Order, as well as the nature of the abbacy. This was the aim of different General Chapters—the one held in 1876, then those of 1878 and 1883. The presence of Mother Cécile at the monastery nearby was an assurance to Dom Couturier. He could consult with her on the original intentions of Dom Guéranger, as he did with the other witnesses to the teachings of the deceased abbot.

One thing is clear. Dom Guéranger desired that each of his monasteries be a true family, a point which Mother Cécile could decidedly confirm by her own witness. At the General Chapter of 1878, Dom Couturier insisted upon this aspect, which was particularly dear to him, as his choice of coat of arms and motto indicates. His coat of arms includes a beehive; and his motto, "*Consortia tecta*," is taken from a passage in Virgil,[5] the tenor of which is as follows: "Only the bees practice the communal life of children, *sharing the same roof* in their dwelling, and they busy themselves under the sway of the great eternal laws." The beehive was a symbol that Dom Bourigaud[6] had used in his decoration of Sainte-Cécile, placed on the reredos behind the high altar, at the feet of Saint Ambrose.

---

[5] Virgil, *Georgics*, 4.154.
[6] Monk and artist who as a novice had been charged with decorating the newly constructed church. See chap. 17—Trans.

Efforts of Dom Guépin, aided by Cardinal Pitra in Rome, resulted in a pontifical decree of July 26, 1879, which accorded to each monastery of the Congregation the right to a superior for life and the faculty of possessing its own novitiate. Each of the families comprising the Congregation of France could receive professed members, who would commit to stability in the monastery of their profession.[7]

The monastery of Sainte-Cécile corresponded to the family ideal of Dom Guéranger. The bishop of Le Mans had approved its "Declarations on the Rule" on August 12, 1868. The document, however, lacked explicit approval by the pope, which Bishop Fillion and Dom Guéranger believed would be easily obtained since Pius IX had already agreed to grant an abbess to the young monastery. The immediate canonical situation of Sainte-Cécile, however, was unusual. Cardinal Pitra had obtained formal approval, both for Sainte-Cécile and Stanbrook, of the "Cérémonial de vêture et de profession" (Ceremonial for the clothing and the profession of vows) composed by Dom Guéranger. This set a precedent in the liturgical domain, but was not enough to authenticate the "Declarations," nor to convert the priory of Sainte-Cécile into a regular abbey. The cardinal—familiar now with the customs and practices of Roman Congregations—did not think the opportune moment had yet come to present the "Declarations" for approval. There was a risk of the document being returned by Rome with significant modifications that would have altered the work of Dom Guéranger. The episcopal approval given by Bishop Fillion would have to suffice for the time being.

However, the "Declarations" had already been circulated to other Benedictine houses at their own request. Dom Beda Hessen, of the Congregation of Beuron, found himself in a situation similar to Dom Laurence Shepherd's at Stanbrook. He was restoring the ancient Abbey of Nonnberg, near Salzburg, and had requested a copy of the document from Mother Cécile on August 18, 1877.

---

[7] St. Benedict, in his Rule, prescribed three vows: stability, *conversatio morum* (often translated as "conversion of life") and obedience, and this has remained the Benedictine practice to this day.—Trans.

Mother Cécile concluded that the time had come to print the text of the "Declarations," as the nuns could not continue indefinitely making copies by hand without the risk of introducing variants and omitting segments of phrases. Thus, she entrusted to Dom Couturier's care the task of requesting an imprimatur from Bishop d'Outremont. The abbot went to Le Mans on August 19 and left the text of the "Declarations"—along with a copy of Bishop Fillion's ordinance of approval—at the episcopal offices in order to obtain permission to print the document.

On October 10, 1877, Bishop d'Outremont let Dom Couturier know that he wanted to meet with him in person. On the following day, the abbot presented himself at the episcopal offices in Le Mans, whereupon Bishop d'Outremont handed him the "Declarations" saying that he could not approve it—the fact that the nuns depended both on the bishop and the religious superior seemed to him to be contrary to the juridical practice then in force in the Church. The observation was correct, for Sainte-Cécile had adopted usage that pre-dated the Council of Trent and had been preserved in only a few religious families. A dispensation from the common law had been explicitly requested in the petition of 1870,[8] in which the abbatial dignity had been requested for a superior who would govern "following the example of monasteries of Trappistine nuns of France, where the authority of the bishop remains secured and entire, but a link to the Order is kept through which the spirit of the particular monastic institute and regular observance will be more surely preserved."

It was evident that the bishop had submitted the text to a canonist of his diocese who had given it an unfavorable evaluation, adding to his assessment some other grievances which the bishop repeated to Dom Couturier: when Dom Guéranger had written the "Declarations" he was already an elderly man in decline; Mother Cécile's influence had become invasive and should not have gone beyond the walls of her monastery; there was too much interchange going on between the two monasteries; the practice instituted by

---

[8] Reference to the document submitted in person to Pope Pius IX by Bishop Fillion, requesting abbatial status for Mother Cécile. See chap. 15.—Trans.

Dom Guéranger of Mass sung in two choirs on the occasion of professions, the nuns alternating with a group of monks, was inadmissible. Already the accusations that would provoke the apostolic visitation of 1893 began to emerge. Nonetheless, Bishop d'Outremont chose not to change anything, and continued, on a provisional basis, to allow the abbot to hold the position of ecclesiastical superior of Sainte-Cécile until a definitive solution could be reached.

Dom Couturier returned to Solesmes very depressed. Mother Cécile took the matter seriously, but not as a tragedy. To what point were the injurious remarks of the bishop an expression of his own thought or that of his assistant? No doubt, they reflected the opinions of both, as the subsequent attitude of Bishop d'Outremont clearly showed that he did not intend to follow the line of his predecessor in making an exception in favor of Sainte-Cécile. The monastery should be governed like the other houses of nuns in his diocese—the Carmelites and the Visitandines.

Mother Cécile wrote to the bishop on October 13, 1877, to remind him of the terms of the pontifical concession, but she did not receive any response from him. Dom Couturier did the same, with no better result.

Bishop Pie, who was duly consulted, insisted that the brewing conflict not degenerate any further, as had happened with Dom Guéranger and Bishop Bouvier[9] in 1837–1845. Still, Mother Cécile thought it prudent to present another petition to the pope, in order to obtain a confirmation of the apostolic concession of July 14, 1870, substantiated now by the practice of seven years. In fact, she had already taken her precautions. On the same day she wrote to the bishop (October 13, 1877), she addressed another letter to Cardinal Pitra: "It is not good news that brings me so soon to Your Eminence. On the contrary, it has pleased Our Lord to mark the beginning of my

[9] When Dom Guéranger returned from Rome in 1837 with the title of Abbot of Solesmes, the bishop of Le Mans, Bishop Bouvier, not knowing the rights of religious orders, refused to accept the practical consequences of the privilege of exemption, which places members of these orders directly under the papacy. Dom Guéranger had to refer the matter to Rome. Thus began the dispute between the abbot and the bishop, which lasted the entire duration of Bishop Bouvier's tenure.

thirty-third year with the seal of His Cross. Your Eminence knows that Monseigneur, the bishop of Le Mans, has shown, until this day, perfect courtesy and paternal kindness toward this little Cecilian monastery. However, on account of an imprimatur that we requested for our "Declarations," the prelate now wishes to sever the cherished links that keep us united to the Congregation of France and to the Order; and this decidedly not because of any arbitrariness, but in the name of the common law."

The matter was resolved shortly after the election of Leo XIII in 1878. During Cardinal Pitra's first audience with him, on March 6, 1878, he spoke to the pope about Sainte-Cécile, with a view of providing him with some basic understanding of the issue that he intended to openly discuss with him at the time of another audience, on March 13. At this second meeting, the canonical discussion was intense, as the cardinal reported in his letter to the abbess written on the same day: "The meeting lasted more than an hour, without any respite." In conclusion, the pope stated that he would willingly grant a brief[10] clarifying the ambiguous points of the petition, but that, beforehand, he wished to have in hand a solid and substantial memorandum expounding in detail the relevant historical tradition and formulating the arguments in favor of the provisions made by Dom Guéranger and Bishop Fillion.

Mother Cécile was not caught unprepared—she had worked on such a document since the preceding summer with the aid of the canonists at Saint-Pierre. She submitted the memorandum to Bishop Pie for his critique. In Rome, the prefect of the Congregation of Bishops and Regulars, Cardinal Ferrieri, confirmed the rights granted in the rescript of 1870. However, this was only a provisional guarantee; it did not touch the fundamentals of the problem. The Congregation did not want to create a juridical precedent that might put into question the common practice of the Church—in place since the Council of Trent—and that could give rise to a series of similar requests: "We cannot grant what Cardinal Pitra asks because the Franciscans, Dominicans, and Carmelites would all come to ask us for

---

[10] A brief is a "papal document less formal than a bull. It is signed by the secretary for briefs and stamped with the pope's ring, i.e., the Ring of the Fisherman." *The Maryknoll Catholic Dictionary*, Albert J. Nevins, ed. (New York: Dimension Books, 1965), p. 86.—Trans.

the same thing. But the bishop of Le Mans, who has just left here, has told me that he would like to continue what his predecessor established and wants to make no changes to the current state of things." These were the words of Cardinal Ferrieri to Dom Guépin in a later audience.

Since 1870, the monastery had had an abbess, but it did not hold the title of an abbey. The situation was irregular, at the very minimum. Under the episcopacy of Bishop Guillaume Labouré (1885-1893), successor of Bishop d'Outremont and future cardinal of Rennes, Mother Cécile would apply herself to putting all things in order reaffirming, once again, the status of Sainte-Cécile under the double authority of the bishop of Le Mans and the abbot of Solesmes.

Bishop Pie was more interested in the project of a biography of Dom Guéranger than in the production of a canonical memorandum. He insistently demanded that Mother Cécile launch upon this work: "I give you the task of starting, without further delay, a life of the Right Reverend Father Dom Guéranger, drawing from personal documents as well as your own memories. To begin, you shall make a list of chapters dividing the overall subject, and you shall never let two weeks go by without having completed one of those chapters. You shall say nothing of this to anyone except the abbot; and if he deems it good, he will send your work to me when opportune."[11]

It seems that there was a fundamental disagreement between Mother Cécile and Bishop Pie regarding the basic concept of the work. The bishop was not asking for an exhaustive biography but rather, for a relatively brief work, written quickly, that could be set before the public in short order. A list of chapters would be drawn and each section would be written up in two or three weeks. By following this scheme, the first collection of memoirs on Dom Guéranger would be available to the French readership in one year or a little more. It would be a portrait, rather than a complete biography.

However, perhaps erroneously, Mother Cécile did not feel she had the capacity to complete this project: "I do not know how to write, Monseigneur, and the subject would require true talent. I have little physical strength and little time, which is easily consumed by the

---

[11] Letter dated October 29, 1877.

pressing duties of my charge. The Dom Guéranger whom I knew, venerated, and loved most tenderly is well-nigh a different person than he whom everyone believes to know, so much so that it would seem I had written about a figment of my own imagination."[12]

She added that she would gladly agree to provide Bishop Pie with the materials if he himself would undertake to write the work. The bishop did not say no, so thus began the compilation of the immense documentation that, much later, would serve Dom Delatte for his own biography. "I have more than 120 pages about our father abbot," wrote Mother Cécile to the bishop some time afterwards. "I put all my heart into this work, all my time and all my memories. As soon as I arrive at the beginnings of Solesmes, I will send the notes to Your Excellency so that you may tell me if I can continue in the same vein. But I can already discern, with much gladness, that you will not be able to finish this work, Monseigneur, without coming to Solesmes! The thought alone fills me with joy."[13]

Had Bishop Pie not died prematurely two years later, he would probably have pressed Mother Cécile further and it is possible that even with her incomplete notes, he would have written a first biography himself. However, in retrospect, it is somewhat unsettling to think of the oratorical tone that the bishop of Poitiers would inevitably have employed in his book. His published works are all either of this type, or funeral orations; not exactly what one expects in a biography.

Mother Cécile consulted all the personal archives of Dom Guéranger and Dom Couturier asked the correspondents of the abbot to provide the letters they had received from him. This voluminous material was organized in an immense collection of documents, in which each element was annotated, placed in its chronological context, and illustrated with press cuttings or with citations taken from contemporary publications. To this material, the abbess added everything she knew herself, especially about the last ten years of his life (1865-1875). The outcome was an impressive compilation of 9,224 manuscript pages, 8¾ inches by 11¾ inches each, that wasn't finished

---

[12] Letter to Bishop Pie dated November 5, 1877.
[13] Letter dated May 31, 1878.

until January 30, 1900. The work had taken twenty-two years to be completed. One wonders how Mother Cécile was able to manage all her tasks.

The health of Madame Bruyère's two daughters was evidently as delicate as her own, for Lise went through a dangerous pregnancy at the end of 1878: "My poor sister's health is always a cause of great concern to me," wrote Mother Cécile. "But I believe in the love of the Divine Spouse, and rest in the certainty that He will do nothing that is not for the good of all." [14]

The young woman was only thirty. Her poor health had become yet worse after a tragic event that occurred at the family home. Mother Bénédicte de Gobineau described it to her brother: "The cause of the desperate state into which this poor young woman has fallen is a frightful accident that happened to her young little boy, aged two. While playing near the fish pond in Coudreuse, he fell into the water and was unconscious when taken out. For more than two hours, Madame Eynaud held him in her arms and it was only by vigorously rubbing his body that she brought him back to life. She had already been very ill for a year, so that the violent emotion caused by the incident brought her close to death." [15]

Monsieur Eynaud took his wife to Pau. [16] The doctors thought that the climate there would be better for her than at Cherbourg where she had spent the first years of her marriage. On a trip to Marseilles with Dom Cabrol, [17] Dom Couturier made a detour in order to visit her. "My poor little sister is neither alive nor dead," wrote Mother Cécile to Father Schliebusch. "It is impossible not to discern a most particular divine intent in this inexplicable prolongation. ... Her disposition is consoling and truly admirable. Holy communion brings her so much peace and joy that she feels she is nearly cured right after receiving It. One thing alone causes me grief, a grief which I can only offer to my Spouse. She suffers from not having me with her, and she says so, most sweetly and with resignation. Pray Our Lord that I may

[14] Letter to Cardinal Pitra dated March 23, 1879.
[15] Letter to her brother dated October 1, 1878.
[16] City on the northern edge of the Pyrenees, about 60 miles from the Atlantic Ocean.—Trans.
[17] Dom Fernand Cabrol (1855-1937), monk of Solesmes where he was prior to Dom Delatte in 1890. He was abbot of Farnborough in England at the time of his death (see chap. 31).

feel her sorrow in double measure, and that she no longer think of it. It is just that the poor thing, my good Father, has always loved me tenderly and has considered me more of a mother to her than a sister. She thinks that all good things would come to her if I were with her. In her, this is as much a thought inspired by faith as it is a sentiment of human affection. In short, Father, pray much for them." [18]

Lise Eynaud died in Pau on June 2, 1879. For Mother Cécile, it was the last page of the book of her youthful years that had been turned. She confided her sentiments to Dom Couturier, as she had previously done with Dom Guéranger: "I fathomed the total solitude that enveloped me concerning my childhood memories, the innumerable difficulties that will follow for my brother-in-law, his shattered life at thirty-eight years of age, his children left orphans. All of this was grasped with such intensity, such breadth and in such detail; nothing could allay it. But at the same time, bending nature to absolute submission, and loyally offering myself to God, there was grace. At the same time, my soul . . . trusted in the Lord my Spouse, in this trial. It did not wish to see, nor reason, nor turn inward upon itself. I cannot quite analyze this movement of faith that blossomed into the blindest of trust, into the total submission of all my being to the Most High and Most Sublime Majesty." [19]

---

[18] Letter dated May 18, 1879.
[19] Letter to Dom Couturier dated June 10, 1879.

Chapter 22

Evicted from Saint-Pierre

EFFORTS BY THE CONSERVATIVES TO regain a majority in parliament in 1877 were fruitless, despite the pressures of the government and the clergy's intervention from the pulpit. During the electoral campaign, even before the second victory of the republicans, Gambetta had declared: "Clericalism—that is our enemy!" This cry was not just an expression of his reaction to the maneuvers of the right. It traced out a course of action; it synthesized and stamped Gambetta's activities since the fall of the empire and the proclamation of the Third Republic on September 4, 1870. In his republic there was no room for the Church; it was either one or the other.

The English historian Geoffrey Best has compared two mindsets, that of de Carrier, member of the National Convention[1] sent on mission to Nantes in 1793, who said "We will change France into a cemetery before we allow its regeneration to fail," with that of the Nazi youth of 1933, who chanted: "What does it matter if we destroy the world? Once it is ours, we will rebuild it!" In both cases there was a desire to "regenerate." The goal of the republicans of 1877 was likewise the regeneration of France; they intended to introduce a "moral order" in their own manner.

In the same collection of essays,[2] another English historian, Norman Hampson, notes that, while to claim that the French revolutionaries invented "democracy" is an abuse of language, the Terror most certainly did invent something—belief that a few enlightened individuals can regenerate humanity. This belief, he says, has had a long and disgraceful posterity and is re-encountered in modern totalitarianism. Thus, one must recognize in the men of 1877—partisans of secularization at any price—the heirs of this tradition created in 1793.

---

[1] See chap. 16, p. 155, n. 8.—Trans.

[2] Geoffrey Best, *The Permanent Revolution: The French Revolution and Its Legacy, 1879–1989.* (London: Fontana Press, 1988).

In any event, their goal was not to innovate, but to apply the laws passed during the years of the Revolution—this time without the spilling of blood—which they considered still valid and in place, since they had never been abrogated. The offensive against religious communities was a direct consequence of the legislation of 1790. Religious and communal life was and remained illegal. Thus, the French Republic entered into a phase of active purification and elimination of the religious resurgence that had been tolerated by preceding governments since the Restoration of 1814-1815.

Communities of men were the first to be targeted, but the time would come when women religious would also be affected. The decrees of March 29, 1880, signed by Jules Ferry and countersigned by the Minister of the Interior and of Religions, Charles Lepère, gave the Jesuits three months to dissolve their communities and evacuate their establishments in France, and required that all non-authorized congregations or communities take action to have their statutes approved by the state within the same three-month period. Should they fail to comply, the revolutionary laws, still in force, would be applied.

Religious were invited to "abandon the Jesuits" and, each congregation for itself, to seek some precarious protection through formal authorization from the government. Dom Guéranger, a strong advocate of the ideal of Church liberty formulated by Lamennais in his youth, had always refused any such demand from the government, claiming the liberty of conscience for all citizens recognized in the Charter of 1830 and by the several constitutions that were subsequently drawn up for the country. Saint-Pierre de Solesmes, along with all other non-authorized congregations, made common cause with the Jesuits, abstaining from taking the least measure in response to the government's demand.

There was little doubt about the consequences of such a stance. From June to October 1880, the Abbey of Saint-Pierre and other men's communities lived under the expectation of being evicted. Dom Couturier moved to prepare a possible place of refuge abroad and sent three of his monks to explore prospects in the neighboring countries: Dom Guépin went to Spain, Dom L'Huillier to England, and Dom du Coëtlosquet to central Europe. In Bavaria, Prince

Loëwenstein offered buildings and the church in Neustadt, which would accommodate about fifteen monks, as well as his castle of Zebau in Bohemia for another group. . . . But hopes were that refuge would be found at closer quarters to the abbey.

The monks were finally expelled from Saint-Pierre on November 6, 1880, amidst the deployment of a considerable number of troops and units of the police on the one side, and manifestations of support for the monks on the other. Étienne Cartier[3] wrote an account, in epic style, of those eventful days and Dom Louis Soltner recounted the history of the expulsion in 1981-1982, on occasion of its hundredth anniversary.[4]

It was during the months following the issue of the decree of expulsion, that Cardinal Pie—elevated to the cardinalate the year before—died suddenly in Angoulême, on the night of May 17, 1880. He was still young, being only 65. With his death, Mother Cécile lost the person whom she had counted on to write the life of Dom Guéranger.

"In this death, I saw the salvation of the Church in France, because a victim was necessary for this work to be accomplished, a choice victim by whose agency all the sound portions of the Church felt touched. I was conscious that the great bishop had felt he was dying . . . and that, rallying all his strength in an acquiescence of great merit to the divine will, he offered himself up, thus marking with this final and supreme seal his most noble career of pontiff and doctor. I thus saw the victory of good over evil obtained and assured by this sacrifice of the Church Militant. At the same time, it was shown to me that her most noble champions often have been taken away at the very moment when everything seems to depend on them and they appear to be indispensable."[5]

These lines were not written for the public eye, not even a restricted public, but for Dom Couturier alone. They demonstrate how the abbess—even amidst the profound distress caused by the death of a man whom she considered one of the pillars of the Church in France—did her best to discern the significance of this sudden loss

---

[3] See chap. 17, p. 166.—Trans.

[4] See conferences published in *Lettre aux amis de Solesmes*, no. 28 (1981–4) and no. 32 (1982–4).

[5] Letter dated May 19, 1880.

in the plan of God. The death of Cardinal Pie, at a time when his firmness would have been most necessary to support the religious who were fighting for their survival in France, was incomprehensible to her except by reference to the custom that God has of dispensing with the best human instruments and acting on His own when it comes to insoluble situations.

Indeed, the bishops as a whole were not quite willing to stand by the religious, since the secular clergy and the Concordat were not in question. Bishop Freppel was nearly alone in the struggle to support them. Cardinal Pie would have used all his influence in such a situation, for he clearly perceived that, beyond the Jesuits and the non-authorized religious congregations, it was the entire Church that was being targeted, and thought that all the bishops should have reacted more energetically. But there had been plenty of reassuring words from the government. Jules Ferry solemnly stated on June 28, 1879: "There is no intention in the mind of any member of the government, not the vaguest intention, even remotely so, to engage in—and I do not say persecution—but even simply an attack against Catholicism. To attack Catholicism, to enter into war against the belief of the greater number of our co-citizens, this would be the ultimate and the most criminal of follies! You say that Catholicism is being persecuted? The Republic would be insane if it harbored even the mere thought of fighting against Catholicism!"[6] Ironically, a few months later the facts would give the lie to so solemn and definitive an affirmation.

Mother Cécile was the last person to believe that the future could be guaranteed by failing in solidarity with the immediate victims of the government. "To distance ourselves from the Jesuits would be an infamy; and this action demanded of us [i.e., the declaration of disavowal of the Jesuits, upon which the government would desist pursuing measures against other religious communities] is of a baseness without description which will be a scandal to all lay Catholics—civil authorities and others—who confront everything, draw upon themselves all manner of wrath, and sacrifice the very bread of their wives and children at times, in order to defend us. They

---

[6] Official journal, June 28, 1879, p. 5726.

will not understand anything of this cowardly abandonment, and their broken souls will no longer know in whom to place their trust and esteem."[7]

One year after Jules Ferry's reassuring declaration, the evictions of religious communities from their homes by military action began. The monks of Solesmes were forced to seek refuge in small groups at the great houses of the area, placed at their disposal by friends. Thus, a constellation of provisional priories emerged around the abbey, where only the "property owner" monks were still allowed to dwell. Dom Couturier took up quarters in the house owned by Madame Durand, across from the gates of the abbey, which became "Saint Charles House," in honor of his patron saint. Other monks lodged throughout the town.

Life at Saint-Pierre continued in this way for eight months, a type of underground existence subtly carried out, until the moment when the "property owner" monks believed themselves authorized to receive their exiled brothers at their home on a permanent basis. On June 29, 1881, on the feast of Saint Peter, the entire community of monks was again reunited within the walls of their abbey— discreetly, without using the bells, but effectively reunited.

However, members of the Masonic lodge of Sablé, true to their anticlericalism, complained of this to the government. Thus, in the morning of March 22, 1882, the police undertook to expel the monks yet a second time—a less spectacular eviction than the first one, but much more effective. None of the monks was allowed to live within the abbey buildings, the property was officially sealed off and a corps of police officers placed at its gates in order to prevent any new attempts at an "invasion."

The monks camped out in the village around their own walls, in the firm hope that this surreal situation would quickly come to an end. However, this time around, the administration was as obstinate as the monks: "The Benedictines believe they are giving us a lot of trouble by remaining as they do in Solesmes," said the prefect to Monsieur de Léobardy, an assistant to the mayor. "Little does it

---

[7] Letter to Cardinal Pitra dated August 30, 1880.

matter to us! We will not cease guarding the abbey any more than they will cease staying in Solesmes."

On July 20, 1884, on pretext of inspecting the detachment of guards stationed at the monastery, General Thomassin, army commander in Le Mans, came to Saint-Pierre. He visited the church, prayed there, admired the statuary and, upon leaving, commented to his aid: "How absurd! How absurd!" It is no wonder that this period produced a Courteline.[8]

As a true daughter of Dom Guéranger, Mother Cécile judged that the moment had arrived for her to discreetly intervene in the public debates going on at the time. She did so several times, signing only with her initials. The first time was in the April 1, 1882 issue of *L'Univers*, in which she defended the abbot of Solesmes in his refusal to obey unjust laws and disband his monks. The time had come, she said, for each one to fulfill his duties as a Christian, even if this meant facing the entire world.

Some weeks later, a paper entitled "Lettre relative à la loi de laïcisation des écoles" (Letter on the law of secularization of schools) was presented, commented on and vigorously applauded at the general assembly of the Cercles Catholique d'Ouvriers.[9] Presented by the Count Albert de Mun, its authorship was attributed to a Belgian bishop. In reality, this letter—which according to the commentator of *L'Univers*, displayed the "imprint of a personality of great strength bearing indisputable authority"—had also been composed by Mother Cécile: "Will I entrust all my money to a shady character, on the strange pretext that I will keep an eye on all his actions? Were I to do so, I would become the laughingstock of others, and no one would feel sorry for me if I ended up by losing my money. What difference is there in confiding my child to hands that I do not trust? An immense difference, as far as I am concerned, for the primary subject in question is a hundredfold dearer to me than all my goods.

---

[8] Georges Victor Marcel Moinaux (1858-1929), born in Tours, was brought up in Paris where he became a novelist and leading dramatist known for his satirical style, writing his plays under the pen-name "Courteline."—Trans.

[9] The Cercles Catholiques d'Ouvriers (Catholic Circles of Workers) was founded in 1871 by Count Albert de Mun, as a social and political movement to bring to bear Catholic interests upon the public forum.—Trans.

Moreover, the risk is doubled, since, besides the loss I might suffer, my child would be in danger. How low have we fallen that such simple truths do not jump out at all of us!"

It was with this second eviction of March 1882 that, by dint of circumstances, the life of the two monastic communities of Saint-Pierre and Sainte-Cécile, became more closely linked. On weekdays, the monks could celebrate the office and their conventual Mass in the parish church. However, on Sundays and feast days, the church naturally had to be left to its parishioners. Thus, the monks would go to the nuns' monastery instead. At first, from March to December 1882, the community of Saint-Pierre fit their offices between those of the nuns, but when Christmas came, it became impossible to schedule all the offices in this way. It was then that Dom Couturier decided that, to simplify matters, the office would be chanted simultaneously by the two communities, who would alternate the chanting like the two sides of one same choir. Ancient monastic history does not lack precedents to this: the double monasteries of Ireland, the Abbey of Fontevrault in France, the Abbey of Sempringham in England, as well as the Brigittines of Sweden . . .[10]

The beauty of this solemn celebration in two choirs, which took place on Sundays and feast days, was admired without reservation by guests of the monastery: "When the Benedictine monks receive their church back," wrote the chronicler of *L'Univers* on July 17, 1887, "such quasi-divine melodies will without doubt become a concert most rare. We should bless God for having arranged for us to experience this echo from paradise."

---

[10] A brief and informative article on the double abbeys of the Middle Ages can be found at www.newadvent.org under the subject "Order and Abbey of Fontevrault." —Trans.

Chapter 23

The Contemplative Charism of Solesmes

THE YOUNG CANON OF Le Mans, Prosper Guéranger, was only twenty-six in 1831 when he suddenly realized that God was calling him to work for the restoration of monastic life in the ancient priory of Solesmes, which he frequently visited from his early childhood on. He knew about monks through reading about them and through their own writings, but he had no experience of their actual life.

The two models of the practice of the Rule of Saint Benedict available to him were the Congregation of Saint-Maur and the Trappist reform. His preference lay with the monks of Saint-Maur. Nonetheless, he wanted to have a direct understanding of the Trappist reform of the Cistercians, brought about by the Abbot de Rancé,[1] and thus spent time in retreat at the Abbey of Notre-Dame de Port-du-Salut, near Laval. Both models emphasized separation from the world and solitude; the Trappists, in addition, insisted upon penitence and manual labor.

The century of "Enlightenment" had understood little of the life of contemplation and prayer. Monks were commonly perceived as parasites, idle people useless to society. To justify their existence, the monks (who preferred to be called "solitaries") had to bring to evidence the "services" that they had rendered to society in the past and could continue doing so in the future. The Trappists were thus presented as experts in the clearing of land for cultivation and as

---

[1] Jean-Armand le Bouthillier de Rancé (1626–1700), born of a wealthy and ambitious Parisian family, and having Cardinal Richelieu as his godfather, was made canon of Notre-Dame-de-Paris at age eleven, as well as abbot of La Trappe and of several other abbeys. He was ordained a priest in 1651 by his uncle, the Archbishop of Tours, and appointed first chaplain of the Duke of Orléans. Gifted with a brilliant mind, and immersed in wealth and worldliness, he led a scandalous life until he was brought to reflect upon the vanities of life by the deaths of the beautiful Duchess of Montbazon in 1657 and the Duke of Orléans in 1660. He subsequently disposed of all his possessions, excepting the Cistercian Abbey of La Trappe, entered religious life in his own abbey, and became its regular abbot in 1663, proceeding to renew monastic life at La Trappe, thus giving birth to the Trappist reform of the Cistercians.—Trans.

agriculturists without equal, the Maurist Benedictines, as paleographers and scholars.

Prior to the radical suppression of monastic life unilaterally decided upon by the Constituent Assembly of 1789, there was already a tendency in France to transform the Benedictine Order into a teaching institution. This inclination, which arose both internally and through exterior pressure, and affected the three Benedictine Congregations of Saint-Maur, Saint-Vanne and Cluny, became particularly pronounced after the suppression of the Jesuits in 1773. From 1770 until the French Revolution, civil authorities made numerous requests to the Benedictines to take charge of schools in their towns, citing the example of the two model establishments of Sorèze and Pontlevoy.[2]

One of the first important endeavors to reintroduce Benedictine life in France was by Dom Charles Verneuil, former prior of Saint-Denys, who bought the ancient monastery of Saint-Vincent de Senlis in 1816 to establish there a school for children of the Knights of Saint-Louis.[3]

In restoring the priory of Solesmes, Father Guéranger had no intention of following this example. He would later discourage proposals from certain of his monks who believed that by opening a school the safety and future of the monastery would be guaranteed. His model of Benedictine life was the Congregation of Saint-Maur: a life of prayer, solitude and intellectual work at the service of the Church.

---

[2] The Benedictine Abbey of Sorèze was founded by Pepin I (nephew of Charlemagne) in 754. Over the centuries it went through the vicissitudes commonly affecting such ancient monasteries—destruction by Vikings and then by the Huguenots, etc. At length it was rebuilt by Dom Barthélémy de Robin, monk of Compiègne, to whom Louis XIII donated the property and abbatial ruins in 1636. In 1682, a seminary was founded at its premises by the abbot Dom Jacques de Hoddy, thus establishing the precedent for Benedictine schools. The Abbey of Pontlevoy, in the Loire valley, was founded in 1034 by a crusader, Gueldin de Chaumont, in fulfillment of a pledge. It housed one of the greatest libraries of the Middle Ages, destroyed by fire in 1264. In 1631 it was entrusted to the Benedictines of Saint-Maur who created therein a school in 1644. Both schools were made royal military academies by Louis XVI in 1776.—Trans.

[3] The Royal and Military Order of Saint Louis was founded by King Louis XIV in April 1693 for military officers who were admitted based on merit, regardless of ancestry. Eliminated during the Revolution, it was reestablished during the Bourbon Restoration from 1814 to 1830.—Trans.

Dom Claude Martin,[4] in his *Pratique de la Règle de saint Benoît* (Practice of the Rule of Saint Benedict), wrote in 1674: "The particular aim specific to the Rule and Order of Saint Benedict is none other than contemplation, as all the means employed therein are practices of the contemplative life, such as withdrawal from the world, silence, psalmody, prayer, meditation, reading, fasting, manual labor and other such practices. . . . A Benedictine's entire thrust and attention should be to attain to the perfection of charity, as is true of all religious, but the religious of the Order of Saint Benedict must proceed along the way of contemplation, which is their own specific and particular end."[5]

But it took time for Dom Guéranger to fully realize the requirements of this charism. At first he thought it was compatible with other subordinate goals, in particular a marked specialization in scholarship and studies, without detriment to the quest for God alone. He was not opposed, either, to occasional ministerial activities, such as deploying some of his monks in the missions, both within France and abroad. Events and the lack of laborers for the tasks he envisioned led him to understand that Solesmes should be solely a "school in the service of the Lord," according to the expression in the prologue of the Rule.

The contemplative charism of Saint-Pierre that may be noted at the time of the abbacy of Dom Couturier was not an innovation. True, it had been less pronounced in the beginnings of Solesmes, when Dom Guéranger, in founding the monastery, had in the back of his mind an image of the intense intellectual activity that developed around de Lamennais at La Chênaie.[6] He had envisioned a broad undertaking in this area, to remedy in part what was lacking in the formation of the clergy of France. All these wonderful projects gradually vanished one after another, as if, through the very circumstances themselves, the Lord wanted to show him another

---

[4] Claude Martin (1619–1696) was a Benedictine of the Congregation of Saint-Maur, prior of several houses of his congregation, and twice assistant to its General Superior. He was the son of Blessed Marie of the Incarnation, mystic, who established the Ursuline Order in New France (Canada). — Trans.

[5] *Pratique de la Règle de saint Benoît*, (Paris, 1674), p. 20.

[6] See chap. 1, p. 7, n. 13. — Trans.

way. At first, his monastic ideal was Maurist, not as practiced by the great majority of Maurist monks, but as one might have imagined it in view of the numerous works accumulated over the course of one hundred and fifty years of existence, produced by a constellation of indefatigable laborers. The monks of Solesmes, however, were not many and, for the greater part, were ill-prepared for this particular type of scholastic activity.

Again in the "Rule for the Novitiate," which he wrote when he entrusted the formation of the novices to Dom Couturier, Dom Guéranger incites them to pray that God send to Solesmes men "powerful in deeds and words," in order to realize the goal expressed in the Constitutions of 1837, ratified by the Holy See.

With the passing of the years, he came to understand more and more clearly that monastic life was sufficient unto itself in its quest for God alone through prayer and contemplation. "It is by the Rule of Saint Benedict that we will become Benedictines," he would say. Dom Couturier, his successor at the helm of the community, man of fidelity par excellence, had absorbed the thinking of Dom Guéranger in its mature stage and always insisted upon this essential work of the monk. He was powerfully aided in this by Mother Cécile. The very nature of a monastery of nuns, with its enclosure and its life with no other end than the quest for God, predisposed her to better comprehend the importance of contemplation in monastic life.

Dom Charles Couturier was little inclined to putting himself forward. He felt crushed by the charge that had been given him. "He was a saint," wrote Albert Houtin about him. "In his most profound humility, he considered it a duty to continually guide himself by the principles and examples of his predecessor. When confronted with serious affairs in which the solutions were not clear to him, he would always consult the abbess, whom he considered to be the heiress of their common father."[7]

Dom Couturier willingly allowed those monks who wished to do so, to take counsel with Mother Cécile. Two monks in particular were more diligent in this: Dom Lucien Fromage, who had been charged

---

[7] Albert Houtin, *Une grande mystique. Madame Bruyère, abbesse de Solesmes (1845–1909)* (Paris: Alcan, 1930), p. 12.

with finishing *The Liturgical Year* of Dom Guéranger and who submitted each page of his work to the abbess for her review so as to ensure that he kept faithfully to the first author's intentions, and Dom Athanase Logerot, who became novice master in 1879. It is through the latter that she was led to have influence over the novitiate of Saint-Pierre, particularly during the period of forced residence in the village, beginning in 1882. "She wanted to form monks, true monks, who would not be editors of cartularies, or compilers of chronicles, but mystics who would regenerate the Church,"[8] wrote a contemporary. In other words, true contemplatives.

This is what she consistently inculcated in them when they came to ask for her advice and inquire into the thought of Dom Guéranger. In this respect, she was very valuable to Dom Couturier. She expressed her thoughts on the apostolic role of the contemplative life, in very clear and succinct terms, in her *The Spiritual Life and Prayer According to Holy Scripture and Monastic Tradition*, a work that will be examined further in a later chapter. "The soul that has attained consummate union is an exact miniature of the Church, One, Holy, Catholic and Apostolic. The more she [the soul] identifies herself with her mother, the more surely does she reach the Heart of Him who has done everything in this world for His collective bride, and who, in the carrying out of His designs, has but one type."[9] The contemplative soul, united to God, is therefore a mother of souls, as is the Church. Contemplation is inevitably fruitful for the salvation of the world.

"What is contemplation if not an interior movement of the soul who places herself before God, as much as it is possible to do so? It is the first work that will be asked of a soul when she enters religious life. . . . This deep sentiment of the soul, who says to herself: 'God is there!,' is vital and essential, I say, to advancement in the spiritual life. Once the soul is thus recollected, let her then act, let her operate, fine: it will always be within God that she does so. The more frequently this movement toward God is renewed and the more it develops and grows, the more the soul advances and the easier the practice of virtue becomes. . . . From the starting point to the summit,

---

[8] Ibid., p. 14.
[9] Bruyère, *The Spiritual Life and Prayer*, p. 391.

it is always the same—the point of culmination, does it not consist of this habitual and continuous movement of the soul towards God? She can be said to have arrived when she can say: 'I find God within myself every time I descend therein, and I never find my own self there, nor anything else.' All methods are good provided that one arrives there."[10]

Young monks who had received a letter or a short note from Mother Cécile on the occasion of their profession or ordination, or upon other circumstances, carefully kept these usually brief messages, several of which have fortunately been preserved. We randomly cite a few of them here.

To Dom Logerot, still a young monk, she speaks of the unfathomable riches of the liturgy: "Oh! mark well, my brother, come to know profoundly the liturgical prayers and all that makes up the public prayer of the Church, and no one will be able to remonstrate with you in matters of doctrine. . . . With this, priests and saints can be formed, and I reckon that if this were the basis of education in theological schools, it would bring about the development of souls. Poetry, music, and the arts would play their part, as much as the intelligence and the heart, and instead of producing either 'nullities' or 'specialists,' we would see the emergence of 'men,' that is, intelligent creatures, complete and able."[11]

The same recommendation was given to the young Father Cécilien Fabre: "My dear little brother, run well after the fragrance of the perfumes that our great King has left behind Him in His Church,[12] by which I mean, always profit by the Holy Scriptures and the sacred liturgy."[13]

In the following year, the same monk received these lines: "I ask you, my dear son, guard well your heart, and, standing before Our Lord, in a heart to heart with Him, always look upon the miseries of your soul and love them in so far as they show you who you are. Self-

---

[10] Conference given on September 13, 1888.
[11] Letter dated May 27, 1875.
[12] Language and imagery that Mother Cécile often evokes, taken from Scripture (Cant. 1: 2-3) and used as one of the antiphons of the office of the Blessed Virgin Mary: "We run to the odor of thy ointments; the young maidens have loved thee exceedingly."—Trans.
[13] Letter dated July 4, 1879.

knowledge is as necessary to your sanctification as knowledge of God."[14]

Upon presenting his "petition," the customary request for admission into religious profession, Brother André Mocquereau received some words of encouragement from Mother Cécile, referring to the sacrifices that awaited him: "Follow Abraham in faith, and whatever it is God may ask of you, say *adsum*! (here I am). So that, in the present situation, I would not have said 'I accept a difficult life,' but: 'I acquiesce to what you ask of me without knowing what it may be.' . . . Courage! Attack your self-love under whatever form it may present itself to you."[15]

And a few weeks later, at his profession: "What marvels! Behold what grace!—to immerse yourself ever further into the ocean of sovereign sanctity, without ceasing; to fasten yourself to it so profoundly through your sacred commitment. You are like a ship that has cast its anchor in clear, deep, tranquil waters."[16]

On the day of his profession, Dom Fernand Cabrol received a letter that he never forgot: "I was with you this morning, my dear father, blessing God with all my soul for the inestimable favors with which He was enriching yours. Assuredly you will not yet comprehend all the grandeur of this life that goes on blossoming and expanding into eternity, but its base rests solidly upon Christ, Who is its foundation and its crown. The intimate peace that you feel is a guarantee from the Lord; it is an actual and complete assurance that He is pleased with you. How sublime it is that God can be pleased with us! Nonetheless, thus it is when the creature generously gives away that which it is and what it has. . . . Who is He that has captured you with so much love, not bearing that you should distance yourself from Him? Grand *Viator* (traveler) that you are, He could not suffer you to separate yourself from Him, and He wishes you to stay there until the day when it will no longer be only He Who seizes you, but you yourself who will be the *comprehensor* (who will seize God)."[17]

---

[14] Letter dated May 16, 1880.
[15] Letter dated February 23, 1876.
[16] Letter dated March 14, 1876.
[17] Letter dated September 29, 1877, the feast of Saint Michael.

And on Christmas of the following year, she dwells on the name of the archangel Saint Michael, which Father Cabrol had taken as his motto: "The *'Quis ut Deus?'* (Who is like God?) is a vibrant form of this gratitude that adores, that is imbued with filial fear and that consecrates itself in love. Fully enjoy the gifts of the present, which are a deposit toward many other gifts, but it may well be that the trial will arise. Do not fear it; only remember the days of joy. This was the secret of our august Queen: *'Conservabat hæc omnia in corde suo'* (She kept all these things in her heart).[18] This is the one key to fidelity. To remember God's gifts to us is to do justice toward Him and it is a force against our enemies and against ourselves. The devil is forgetful, like all those who are ungrateful."[19]

Mother Cécile was deeply convinced that what God expected from Solesmes, above all, were the fruits of sanctity, much more than works for the Church, whatever their benefit might be; this was her conviction. "[Truly contemplative souls] are the hidden spring, the moving principle of everything that is for the glory of God, for the kingdom of His Son, and for the perfect fulfillment of His Divine Will. Vain would it be to multiply active works and contrivances, yea, and even deeds of sacrifice; all will be fruitless if the Church Militant have not her saints to uphold her."[20]

The insistence of Mother Cécile upon a return to the essentials, to the soul of Benedictine life, could not uniformly please those who were slow in following the evolution of the thought of Dom Guéranger and were still fascinated by the idea of engaging in works for the good of the Church. The palpable tension between pure contemplation and the intellectual apostolate, felt in Solesmes itself and in the Congregation as a whole at the time of the abbacy of Dom Delatte, already existed in the years immediately following the death of Dom Guéranger.

The Abbess of Sainte-Cécile did not hesitate to evoke, time and again, the need to be on one's guard against pure erudition apart from the spiritual life: "There is no true science other than the ever more profound plumbing into the things of God, and these things

---

[18] Lk 2:51.—Trans.
[19] Letter dated December 25, 1878.
[20] Bruyère, *The Spiritual Life and Prayer*, p. 346.

cannot be fathomed by a certain inquiry of the mind only, but by a soul sufficiently pure as to be capable of receiving them."[21]

Dom Logerot asked much of the abbess, both for himself and for the little band of novices that had been entrusted to him by Dom Couturier. An excellent monk himself, he had a tendency to overestimate the discretion and capacity of his young novices to understand. Others like him, with the same excellent intentions, have committed the same indiscretions. Thus it was that a number of writings, of a confidential nature, mistakenly fell into the public domain. It is these circumstances that are at the root of the misinterpretations that surfaced regarding the type of "contemplation" that Mother Cécile advocated at Solesmes.

---

[21] Conference given on June 3, 1895.

Chapter 24

The Reverend Olis-Henri Delatte

FATHER DELATTE, OF THE DIOCESE of Cambrai, knew two monks of Solesmes: Dom Aimé Graux and Dom Houllier, both of whom had taught at the minor seminary of Arras. In the summer of 1874, he wrote Dom Graux about his intention to come make a retreat at Solesmes. He received no reply at the time, since by then the monk had been sent to Sainte-Madeleine in Marseilles.

What he had in mind, however, was more than making a simple retreat. He actually was contemplating the possibility of entering religious life, and only the prudence of his spiritual director had delayed the decision: "At first I did not believe I should encourage his desires," wrote the latter to Dom Guéranger, "because I did not think he was sufficiently pious. But since he received the grace of the priesthood, that is, two years ago, he has shown the same passion for prayer and solitude that I knew him to have for his studies. Therefore, I no longer hesitate to send him to you."[1]

Father Delatte's stay in Solesmes in the beginning of October 1874, did not bring him to any decision. The novice master, Dom Couturier, had attended to the young priest, but true communication between the two never really was established. As to the two conversations he had with Dom Guéranger, these were not any more clarifying. The expectations of the young priest were still imbued with too many elements that were foreign to the essence of a monastic vocation. Father Delatte was bored to death and left convinced that Solesmes was not for him.

He returned, however, to accompany one of his directees, Rosine Cordonnier—the future Sister Walburga—who wished to discern her vocation at Sainte-Cécile. This time it was with Mother Cécile that he conversed, and he was conquered: "It goes without saying that Saint Cecilia has become somewhat my patroness," he wrote shortly

---

[1] Dom Augustin Savaton, *Dom Paul Delatte, abbé de Solesmes* (Solesmes: Éditions de Solesmes, 1975), p. 47.

thereafter, "that Solesmes is nearly a homeland to me, and that I do not let one day pass, when I come to Our Lord at Holy Mass, without beseeching Him to continue confirming and increasing that which He Himself has restored almost miraculously by the hands of one of His greatest servants. Perhaps the Lord will give some of this superabundant benediction to him who will be praying for you."[2]

That "perhaps" concealed a promise. Father Olis-Henri Delatte came back in 1880 for the Easter Triduum, and then on other occasions, each time a little more convinced. In July 1883 he brought another postulant to Sainte-Cécile, Sister Aldegonde Cordonnier, the younger sister of Rosine. On taking his leave of Mother Cécile he asked her: "Do you believe Dom Guéranger would still accept me were he alive?" Her response was unequivocal. The decision was finally made upon another visit to Solesmes, a few weeks later: "The young priest of whom I spoke to you," wrote the abbess to Father Rabussier,[3] "returned to Solesmes for the Assumption, and here he was inundated with such graces that even I was touched by them. He left yesterday to take care of his affairs and will come back as soon as he is able. I entrust him to your prayers, because this is a vocation that seems to me to be of great importance to Saint Benedict. I have never seen such broad thoughts, as we like them, with a more profound comprehension and love of Holy Church, a more complete understanding of the miseries and needs of our times, all combined with the suppleness and simplicity of a child."[4]

Father Delatte obtained the permission of his bishop and entered Saint-Pierre in September. He received the habit on the vigil of the feast of Saint Michael. Mother Cécile wrote to the abbess of Stanbrook: "For me, the clothing itself of Brother Delatte on the evening of the twenty-eighth was an event. Later on we shall see what a marvelous gift from God this soul is; for the moment, it is necessary that this remain the secret of the King. But I cannot hide from my dear daughter that I believe that Dom Guéranger's heir has been found. There can be no one more humble, more simple, more

---

[2] Letter written at the end of 1879.
[3] See chap. 7, p. 70.
[4] Letter dated August 21, 1883.

supernatural and more intelligent. And now Our Lord is acting with royal generosity toward him."[5]

She could now discern that the hour approached when the added burden that Saint-Pierre had become to her would no longer weigh upon her shoulders in the same way. In the abbey next door, there was now the promise of someone who, at the proper time, would succeed the aging Dom Couturier. However, this would not be in the immediate future, since the young priest—a professor at the Catholic University of Lille, and three years the junior of Mother Cécile— needed time to finish his monastic formation. There would be two years until his profession, which took place on March 21, 1885, then two more years in the novitiate following his profession, and yet another year before pronouncing his solemn vows, on April 1, 1888. But at least the future seemed assured.

Indeed, at the end of those five years, in 1888, on the very evening of the funeral of Dom Gardereau, prior of Saint-Pierre, Father Abbot Dom Couturier appointed the recently solemnly professed monk as the new prior: "I well know that he is the choice of the community," he said at the chapter, "but above all, he is my own choice."[6] The death of Dom Gardereau was sudden and unexpected; there had been no delay in choosing a new prior. Maneuvering on the part of the abbess, as Albert Houtin[7] charged her with, can hardly have been possible.

The choice of a new prior was made two days before Pentecost. In a letter to him written on the feast day, Mother Cécile expressed herself in terms resembling the words of St. John the Baptist to his disciples—"He must increase while I must decrease." "In the measure that God's plan for us moves from potential to act, a sense of contentment settles within me which I cannot describe, because everything is falling into place and is becoming ordered according to the interior order and the divine will stamped in my soul. . . . A word, however, about myself, for our lives are so united that my words were true when I said that 'you are the reason for my being.' Do not

---

[5] Letter dated October 2, 1883.

[6] Savaton, *Dom Paul Delatte*, p. 117.

[7] Details on this matter and Albert Houtin's role will be extensively dealt with in chapter 31.—Trans.

be disturbed, as it has nothing to do with you or with me, but with the plan of God. Yesterday, Sunday, I was reflecting on the Magnificat; I begin to understand it now. Our Lady recited it very often, ever in a new way as her Son grew, as His kingdom extended itself, and as His divine work unfolded in solemn grandeur. She then effaced herself more and more from the eyes of men, immersing herself ever more deeply into God. There she worked for Him, functioned for Him, lived only for Him. I also thought of my St. John the Baptist. *Qui post me . . . Oportet illum crescere, me autem minui* (He who comes after me . . . He must increase while I must decrease).[8] He would die without a head, having desired no other head than Christ. If you only knew what peace and tranquility has come to me by your having attained your majority,[9] your having entered upon public life at the time appointed by the Father. It is not at all that I will separate myself from anything, that I will no longer be interested in anything; rather, I will be able to hide myself more and more *in abscondito faciei Dei* (in the secret of God's face, Ps 30:21)[10] where I will remain buried for as long as you need me. Yes, this will be the measure of my earthly existence, and not any particular work or accomplishment, for my own work is you; everything else is for this work. As I will be relieved of certain exterior concerns—not in regard to outward labor, but to a certain direction—I will be able to freely realize what Our Lady continuously teaches me: *in omnibus requiem quæsivi et in hæreditate Domini morabor . . .* (and in all these I sought rest, and I shall abide in the inheritance of the Lord. Sir 24:11). Yes, I will labor, but I will not need to be concerned about looking for this labor; you will assign me my task, as extensive as you may wish it to be, but the assignment will come from you. What I have done as a daughter [for

---

[8] Mt 3:11 . . . Jn 3:30.—Trans.

[9] By "majority" here is meant Dom Delatte's having made his solemn profession, that is, having attained his "majority" in religious life.—Trans.

[10] The author uses the Vulgate numbering of psalms, which is based on the Greek Septuagint. In the Hebrew text, followed by the majority of translations today, most of the psalms are numbered one ahead of the Greek text. Thus, this citation would be Psalm 31, verse 20. All scriptural quotations by Mother Cécile are naturally from the Vulgate, the official edition of the Bible for the Latin Church since the Council of Trent. For purposes of the translation of the scriptural quotations in this book, we have used the published English translations closest to the quoted Latin, at times the Douay-Rheims and at times the Revised Standard Version.—Trans.

Dom Guéranger], I will do as a mother [for you], and I feel that I will be a hundred times more useful, firstly to you, and then to others, in bearing all my strength and my activity in God. He has made me for this, *above all*, and if indeed it was necessary for a time that I live in another way, this painful transition, accepted under obedience, by necessity had to come to an end. The end has arrived. I must thank my divine Spouse for having sufficiently sustained me so that I was able to traverse this frightful desert without committing more mistakes and, moreover, without causing others to blunder even more. No, you cannot comprehend the song that my soul sings at this deliverance; the monastic family has recovered its stability and its order; it has recovered its head; and I retake the spindle, which does not keep my hands from engaging in serious enterprises, but they are now sustained by your priestly soul and your authority as the heir. . . ."[11]

This letter is very important. It shows that Mother Cécile, who had been given a maternal mission by Dom Guéranger a few months before his death, discerned the conclusion of this mission in the nomination of the new prior. No one could ignore the fact that Dom Couturier had reached the extreme limits of his strength. It would not be long before he would pass away, but now he would be able to die in tranquility. Also evident in this letter is a curious presentiment of the future, for Mother Cécile would be emulating John the Baptist to the utmost. The effacement of which she spoke would go very far: not only a withdrawal from the affairs of Saint-Pierre, in which she had been reluctantly involved, but later, a physical decline that would follow shortly after her attaining to full maturity.

The abbacy of Dom Couturier lasted fifteen years, from 1875 to 1890. The second abbot of Solesmes had accepted the charge only very reluctantly, after pleading with the monks not to choose him. He had acquitted himself of his task under very difficult circumstances: the phase following the death of the founder, and then the period of the evictions, which was still underway. During these long years, he had relied upon Mother Cécile, thus obeying the intention and the mind of Dom Guéranger. The abbess discerned the end of these times

---

[11] Letter to Dom Delatte, on Pentecost, May 20, 1888.

with relief, paying homage to the fidelity of the first successor of the founder:

"Our Father Abbot held the crosier in very difficult times, for succeeding Dom Guéranger was a staggering enterprise . . . We owe him immense and personal gratitude for having made it possible for us to perform the role that God had given us and that Dom Guéranger had assigned to us. [Plural form is evidently used here in place of the singular.] Placing himself above all gossip and all criticism in order to defend the land that God entrusted to our Father Abbot in heaven [referring to the community of Solesmes still living in the village, grouped around the buildings of the abbey, which continued to be sealed off]. In short, this jealous care in guarding the *leges paternas* (the laws of the fathers) in everything and through everything. Simple as Mattathias and, like him, zealous for Tradition, immune to all seduction of vainglory or ambition, humble with a truthfulness most rare; having faithfully preserved what was deposited in his care."[12]

But Dom Delatte was only the prior, and would be so for two and a half years. What Mother Cécile's correspondence refers to was still at the time only prospects and expectations. In the interim, she would have to continue as before, and still support Dom Couturier for some time, whose strength was declining.

The spiritual life of Mother Cécile had deepened yet further prior to the entrance of Brother Delatte to Solesmes. On occasion of a preached retreat at Saint-Pierre in May 1880, she came to know the Jesuit Father Rabussier, who would play a primary role in the spiritual journey of Dom Jean-Baptiste Chautard, the abbot of Sept-Fons, author of *L'Ame de tout apostolat* (*The Soul of the Apostolate*),[13] which would exert such influence in the years between 1920 and 1950.

Father Louis-Étienne Rabussier was born in the vicinity of Paris in 1831, and died in Poitiers in December 1897, after having founded the

---

[12] Letter dated May 22, 1888, Tuesday after Pentecost.

[13] *L'Ame de tout apostolat* (Paris: P. Téqui & E. Vitte, 1917), with a profuse number of editions through the 1970s. The first English edition, *The Soul of the Apostolate*, translated by Fr. J.A. Moran appeared in 1926; TAN Books published a 1946 translation by the Trappists of the Abbey of Gethsemani in 1977.—Trans.

congregation of the Sœurs de la Sainte-Famille du Sacré-Cœur (Sisters of the Holy Family of the Sacred Heart), which he left in its beginning stages. The diocesan process for his beatification was opened in 1950. He helped Mother Cécile to moderate her ardor and better discern the attitude that she should bring to her contemplative prayer, while confirming her in her path. Thus he introduced her to a more peaceable, tranquil and simpler sphere:

"It is difficult for me to describe the sense of plenitude, of tranquil self-possession and redoubling of the supernatural life that I feel within me since I've tried to follow the counsels given to me by the *Vir Dei* (man of God). Words fail me to describe the peaceful and persevering activity that unfolds within me. The thousand difficulties that once hampered me, certain anxieties that pursued me, now are burnt to ashes and annihilated at the simplest movement of my soul towards its center again. I find, in fact, that this movement of the soul is gradually becoming habitual and automatic, resembling the pointer of a compass that always turns to the pole, and this movement is all its strength, all its action, all its life."[14]

Since the death of Dom Guéranger, Mother Cécile had been lacking true spiritual direction. Dom Logerot much admired the work of God in her, but behaved more like a disciple toward her than a director of conscience. Dom Couturier was already too much consumed with the affairs of his own community, and in his very great humility, considered himself insufficiently enlightened to aid the abbess in her spiritual progress. Father Schliebusch was a great friend; quite an original character, very saintly, but more of a friend than a counselor. With Father Rabussier, Mother Cécile felt confident and appeased.

Just as Dom Delatte would do, Father Rabussier discouraged the long accounts she habitually wrote of particular graces received. Dom Guéranger had asked these of her so as to better judge them himself, because at the time she had considerable difficulty in speaking and opening herself to him during their very brief meetings. He continued in this vein because, even during the beginnings of Sainte-Cécile, Mother Cécile was more prone to listening than to expressing herself.

---

[14] Letter to Dom Logerot, dated January 16, 1883.

Later, things changed and Mother Cécile spoke more easily about the experiences of her interior life.

Dom Logerot, her confessor, did not wish to change anything, since the custom was already well established. However, with the discernment stage once passed, these written accounts of her prayer, besides taking up precious time, could become harmful and might take away from her soul something of its spontaneity by necessitating that she dwell again on something already experienced.

It seems that Dom Logerot failed to see eye to eye with Father Rabussier, and his questions to Mother Cécile became more and more insistent. "My Father," wrote Mother Cécile at this time, "following your wishes, I am writing you to summarize somewhat the things that have been transpiring as of late, even though it seems to me that I have neither the leisure nor the desire for it at all. It is quite true, the very great repugnance I have for speaking is steadily growing. . . . It seems to me, as far as I can judge, that this is not due to character, such as the seriousness and reserve that are natural to me; rather, it seems to me that this tendency corresponds to the nature of what God is operating in me. What leads me to think in this way is that the repugnance I feel for talking isn't general, as was the case when it used to come from my character; it does not hamper my service to others and it only affects but one specific point. . . . The soul willingly would enclose itself alone with the Lord, asking only that others leave it be in this intimate sanctuary, without minding about what it becomes there, what it does there, for the soul barely knows itself, because it can only vaguely discern the simplicity of its union with the Spouse. The soul's distaste for spreading itself abroad has, therefore, several causes: firstly, it barely perceives the *quomodo* (the how) of its union with God. I say that the soul barely perceives it, not because there is any doubt about it, but I mean that the intellect cannot discern nor analyze this *quomodo* which is beyond it. Secondly, the intellect feels an understandable repugnance for attempting to translate into words what it perceives only indistinctly (though it possesses a certitude much superior to what its own perception can provide). For, if the intellect already has great difficulty in putting into words that which it can perceive supernaturally, how much more will it suffer and feel impotent at the thought of explaining something it can grasp only imperfectly? Thirdly: the third cause of the repugnance the soul feels for opening itself is the certainty that it cannot be understood except by special intervention of the same divine Spirit that operates in it. Indeed, should the intellect find the secret of how to render an account of this truth without distorting it, even then the soul feels that its language will not be able to communicate the thought except to those who have the spirit of this language, that is, those who have the experience."[15]

"My magnetic pole," she wrote during the same period, "is my well-beloved Lord Who deigns to reside in the depths of my being. And by dint of this one movement toward Him, the soul operates with such extraordinary activity and power that she herself is astonished. Or rather, . . . it is as if a bride were continuously moving toward the most intimate quarters of her abode where she finds her Spouse in the closest of intimacies, and she does not consent to undertake anything, command anything, and direct anything in her house which she does not undertake, command and direct from this her place of choice, having no desire to do anything on her own."[16]

When Dom Delatte began to direct Mother Cécile in 1890, he would only encourage further this great interior simplicity and this silence. His own nature tended toward this, and this trait would become more pronounced in him with the passing of the years.

---

[15] Letter to Dom Logerot, dated February 27, 1883.
[16] Letter to Dom Logerot, dated January 16, 1883.

Chapter 25

On Prayer

BISHOP D'OUTREMONT, THOUGH very courteous, had not hidden his dissatisfaction at the time Dom Couturier brought the "Declarations" to the diocesan offices of Le Mans in order to obtain his imprimatur. The monastery of Sainte-Cécile, he stated, represented a diminishment in religious life. The bishop was echoing a notion that had gained wide acceptance—the nuns at Sainte-Cécile "did not pray"; they were dedicated to the solemn celebration of the liturgy and the hours of the Divine Office, but they did not engage in prayer proper! Dom Guéranger would have shuddered at such an assertion, which, however, became commonplace half a century after his death. One must wonder whether the little book by Jacques Maritain, *Liturgie et contemplation (Liturgy and contemplation)*,[1] while reacting against the notion of a liturgy without interior prayer, does not still retain something of this perceived opposition between the solemn celebration of the Office and contemplative prayer per se, considering them antithetical.

The nuns of Sainte-Cécile were not given to methodic meditation as it had been established in the sixteenth and seventeenth centuries, unlike nearly all the "well-regulated" houses of their days, where the points for mental prayer were read in community each evening, to be the subject of a long period of methodic meditation in the very early hours of the following day. The meditation was carried out more or less rigidly or more or less flexibly according to the spiritual tradition of each monastery or to the personal counsels of the spiritual directors of its nuns.

It was a mistake to conceive of "mental prayer" only upon this one model and to condemn without right of appeal the form of prayer that Dom Guéranger had endeavored all his life to promote. Still in

---

[1] It was published in 1959 by Desclee De Brouwer (Paris). An English translation by Joseph W. Evans appeared in 1960 (New York: P.J. Kennedy & Sons).—Trans.

1930, Pierre Pourrat, the superior of the novitiate of Saint-Sulpice,[2] in his book *La Spiritualité chrétienne (Christian Spirituality)* criticized the approach taken by the abbot of Solesmes and Mother Cécile:

"So the attitude to be taken toward methods of prayer is chiefly negative: not to criticize them, but not to use them. As Abbess Bruyère sees it, monastic spirituality is characterized by absence of method. History does not support so absolute a statement. Should it be objected that to take away 'the safeguarding help of methods' is to 'leave the soul to proceed haphazardly and to pray at random,' the abbess answers:

'In the sacred liturgy the Church's children have all their mother's learning: it is the most perfect way of prayer, the most traditional, the best ordered, the simplest, and the one that gives the strongest impulse to the freedom of the Holy Spirit.'

"Later on, other writers spoke in the same sense; some of them gave an impression that they wanted to substitute a vague meditation on liturgical texts for the methodical prayer that had been in common use in the Church for so long."[3]

This reaction demonstrates how novel the practice of the monks and nuns of Solesmes was perceived to be, whereas, in reality, theirs was the more ancient and universal tradition. It is understandable that in 1880 and in 1893 the majority of spiritual masters of the time were not at all prepared to recognize Dom Guéranger's teachings on prayer. There was still a long way ahead before this would happen.

Toward the end of the Middle Ages, when ardent Christians aspired to a reform that would bring new vitality to souls, it was deemed that they should be instilled with solid convictions and, by means of study and personal reflection, should discover of themselves the practical resolutions leading to behavior that is in

---

[2] The famed Seminary of Saint-Sulpice was founded in Paris in 1642 by Fr. Jean-Jacques Olier (1608-1657) to provide more thorough and spiritual education of clerics than was commonly available. Besides being taught philosophy and theology, chant and liturgy, seminarians at Saint-Sulpice were guided in the practice of mental prayer and in developing Christian virtues. The church to which the seminary was attached is a well-known tourist attraction in Paris, second in size only to the cathedral of Notre-Dame.—Trans.

[3] Pierre Pourrat, *Christian Spirituality*, trans. Donald Attwater (Westminster, MD: Newman Press, 1955), p. 501.—Trans.

harmony with the teachings of the Gospels and the spiritual masters.[4] Meditation, thus, became a favored practice. The methods, properly speaking, of mental prayer emerged in the milieu of the *"devotio moderna"* in the Low Countries of the late fifteenth century. Prior to this, there had been attempts to systematize prayer according to the well-known principles of scholastic thinking, always ready to order and classify according to well-defined categories. But no one had yet thought of creating a logical system to be applied to all forms of meditation, that is to say, a method of mental prayer. Writings on prayer flourished beginning in 1483—the *Scala meditatoria* of Jean Wessel Gansfort,[5] a friend of Thomas à Kempis,[6] and the *Rosetum* or

---

[4] What is being described here refers to a movement closely related to the activities of Geert Groote (1340–1384). Born in Deventer, in the diocese of Utrecht, he pursued a brilliant academic career in Aachen, the University of Paris, and in Cologne, being appointed to canonries in Utrecht and Aachen in his mid-twenties. For ten years he led a life of vain worldliness, until a serious illness and the remonstrances of a Carthusian prior, Henry de Calcar of the monastery of Munnikhuizenhe, led him to reform his life. He spent three years in retreat at this monastery, following which he was ordained a deacon in 1379, and became an itinerant preacher in the diocese of Utrecht with a mandate from his bishop. His preaching was centered on a call to renounce sin and decadence, particularly among the clergy, and a return to a life of simple devotion to Jesus Christ. With a group of followers, both lay and clerical, he founded the Brethren of the Common Life, whose first aim was cultivation of the interior life. This lay association enjoyed papal approval and was protected by Eugene IV, Pius II, and Sixtus IV. Toward the end of Groote's life, some of the clerics attached to him asked that he form them into a religious community with vows. This community, following the rule of canons regular of St. Augustine, was established shortly before his death in 1384. In 1387 land was secured for a monastery in Windesheim, which, along with Deventer, became a flourishing center of the activities of the Brethren.

As a former scholar and professor, one of Groote's primary concerns was addressing the lack of basic education in the Catholic faith, not only among the laity, but the clergy as well. Thus, the main activity of the Brethren was educational, for which they founded schools and centers of intellectual life throughout the Low Countries and Germany, where teaching was offered "for the love of God alone." They disseminated their writings at first through the work of their own scriptoria, and later by print shops of their own.

The principal aim of the education provided by the Brethren was to foster a life of greater union with God through interior prayer, beginning from knowledge of the Scriptures and other fundamental texts. Their practice of mental prayer, according to certain methodology, was called *"devotio moderna."* The most well-known example of the *devotio moderna* and the ethos of the Brethren is Thomas à Kempis's *Imitation of Christ*, a classic cherished by many saints, including St. Ignatius of Loyola and St. Thérèse of Lisieux, who knew it by heart. A matter of interest is that Martin Luther studied at one of the schools of the Brethren in Magdeburg.—Trans.

[5] 1419–1489, born in Groningen, The Netherlands.—Trans.

[6] Thomas Hemerken (ca. 1380–1471) born in Kempen; see note 4 above.—Trans.

"Rosary of spiritual exercises and holy methods" by Jean Mombaer[7] (1494) were a watershed. But these two works still reflected medieval tradition, whereby, through reasoning, the subject of meditation is analyzed and reflected upon, ever more deeply, which leads to affective prayer, which, in its turn, tends to union with God in contemplation.

In the Renaissance, which brought major changes in people's mentality, spiritual masters were lead to promote a form of prayer adapted to the needs of those deeply involved in apostolic action — priests, religious and laity. St. Ignatius of Loyola conceived of a particularly effective method of spiritual formation. While not a prayer manual per se, his *Spiritual Exercises* presents a series of meditations aimed at total conversion and renewal of life; the method of meditation he proposes borrows from Mombaer and Gansfort. Thus was born the method of prayer of modern times that became the indispensible means of spiritual growth according to the mind of the clergy trained by the Counter-Reformation.

It is necessary to grasp this context in order to realize to what extent Dom Guéranger's approach must have seemed revolutionary and to understand what Bishop d'Outremont meant by a "diminishment in religious life," a type of regression, in reference to Sainte-Cécile.

The abbot of Solesmes had dealt with many a young woman who certainly loved the liturgy and had been formed by *The Liturgical Year*, who, at the same time, had also received another orientation with regard to prayer. During his conferences, Dom Guéranger imparted his own teaching on the different forms of prayer, on meditation and on contemplation. Following his method and in fidelity to his doctrine, Mother Cécile had continued in this vein.

Just as Dom Guéranger had outlined his thoughts on monastic life in his "Rules for the Novitiate," in the first months of 1885 Mother Cécile began writing a small treatise entitled *De l'oraison d'après la Sainte Écriture et la tradition monastique* (Prayer According to Holy Scripture and Monastic Tradition). The book was intended for use by the nuns of Sainte-Cécile alone; in this Mother Cécile imitated Dom

---

[7] Circa 1460–1501, born in Brussels. — Trans.

Guéranger, who had written his "Rules for the Novitiate" expressly for the novices of the Abbey of Saint-Pierre. However, after his death, the text was published under the title *Notions sur la vie religieuse* (*On the Religious Life*[8]) with a view of reaching a wider public. Similarly, the title of the abbess's book would eventually expand to *La Vie spirituelle et l'oraison d'après la Sainte Écriture et la tradition monastique* (*The Spiritual Life and Prayer According to Holy Scripture and Monastic Tradition*), reflecting the fact that she went beyond the subject of prayer proper to speak of the totality of the spiritual life, of which the normal outcome is contemplation through a life of personal prayer called mental prayer.

"I told you that I finally gave in to the requests of my daughters and produced a small treatise for their use on prayer according to monastic principles," wrote Mother Cécile to the abbess of Stanbrook. . . . "I had just finished it when, after a silence of two months, Father Rabussier wrote me saying: 'I believe that you would do well to write something on prayer from the point of view of scripture and the liturgy!'"[9]

In short, her intent was to write the book that Dom Guéranger himself would have written on the subject, had he had the leisure and the desire. She is truly the book's author, for, if the underlying notions are his, Mother Cécile made them perfectly her own and developed them in her own personal way.

Mother Aldegonde Cordonnier writes in her Chronicles, on March 13, 1886: "Madame Abbess asked that we say the prayer to the Holy Spirit this Compline for her intention. This intention is very much our own and it is very dear to us. Our Mother will be making the final review of the pages she has written on prayer, and then she will submit them to the print shop here. The number of copies will be relatively restricted, according to our Mother's desire, who maintains absolutely that these pages are to remain within our monastic family."

Dom Couturier had established a modest print shop, whose activity was growing and would soon develop into a veritable

---

[8] Dom Prosper Guéranger, *On the Religious Life* (Farnborough: Saint Michael's Abbey Press, 2006).—Trans.

[9] Letter to Mother Gertrude d'Aurillac Dubois, dated April 26, 1885.

enterprise; there was also a press at Sainte-Cécile. Thus it seemed more convenient to print the work *pro manuscripto*.[10] The only other way of reproducing texts at the time was by lithography, which was little suitable for a more extended work. The book was printed in 1886.

"The following pages . . . were not originally intended for public circulation. They were drawn up by the author with a view to one single religious family, to serve them both as a guide in the study of the numerous works on the subject of prayer bequeathed to us by Christian tradition, and as a clue in the maze of religious literature, which issues daily from the press, but in which truths and principles as old as the world are not always sufficiently explained. As misapprehensions on such subjects are the source of serious mistakes, it was thought well to help souls by stating clearly the main points of doctrine which throw light on the spiritual life."[11] These lines, written for the second edition—which enlarged on the original by the addition of new material to a total of four chapters—aptly define what Mother Cécile proposed to do with her book: to provide her nuns with a comprehensive treatise, following the teachings of Dom Guéranger.

Once the work was printed, some copies were circulated beyond the immediate circle of Solesmes, to friends of the community, and it began to become known in other monasteries. Given these circumstances, it was impossible to gauge how far its dissemination would actually go. In addition, Dom Couturier thought it appropriate to contribute a sort of approval to the first edition:

"It has come to pass throughout the centuries of Christian history that many, even among the greatest saints, have impressed the particular character of their own sanctity upon this science [of prayer]. This has caused difficulty at times because of the resulting infinite variety of teachings on prayer. For you, who are daughters of the holy patriarch of monks, who are guided and only wish to be guided by the traditional practice of the Church, it was a matter of drawing the true science of prayer from this somewhat confused

---

[10] A limited edition that is not-for-sale, a provisional edition.—Trans.
[11] Bruyère, *The Spiritual Life and Prayer*, p. vii.

variety of systems. It is true that Dom Guéranger left us a key to this difficult task in his *The Liturgical Year*, where he provides, often enough, both its principles and its model. But he never wrote anything that would resemble a comprehensive and systematic teaching on the subject. It would pertain to her who among all of us is the heir of his spirit and whom you have the good fortune of having for mother, to interpret and set down the teachings of our father Dom Guéranger, so that the true understanding of prayer may always be preserved intact among us."[12]

Dom Couturier would be hard-pressed to produce a stronger endorsement. While addressing himself solely to the nuns of Sainte-Cécile, he recognizes that the book applies to all the children of Dom Guéranger and is entirely in accord with his thinking. Mother Cécile herself is presented as the principal heir of his spirit.

Borrowed and passed on far and wide, the book was translated into German by a friend and nun, and presented to theologians beyond the Rhine, such as Dr. Paul Haffner, Bishop of Mainz, and Dr. Paul Keppler, who would be made bishop of Rottenburg. It was thus that the work was published in German in 1896, no longer as a provisional edition *pro manuscripto*, but as an official one, with a letter by the Bishop of Mainz:

"The present treatise on prayer was first of all printed privately in the French language, and was intended exclusively for the instruction of the daughters of St. Benedict. All souls, however, who are aiming at perfection may derive profit and edification from its pages. The spirit of the venerable Abbot Guéranger breathes through the whole work. What this distinguished man thought on the all-important subject of prayer, what he expressed in his conferences, and what he wrote in many parts of his classical work, *The Liturgical Year*, is found here systematically arranged. Some of the chapters are real masterpieces; therefore we joyfully welcome the translation of this book into German [and we most earnestly encourage its circulation.]"[13]

---

[12] Cécile Bruyère, *De l'oraison d'après la Sainte Écriture et la tradition monastique* (Solesmes, 1886), p. iii.
[13] Bruyère, *The Spiritual Life and Prayer*, p. viii.

Cardinal Manning[14] equally admired the book without reserve and encouraged its translation into English. Dom Germain Cozien, fourth abbot of Solesmes, recalled with delight that when he left the French College in Rome to teach at the major seminary at his diocese of Quimper, having completed his doctorate in theology, he asked his spiritual director, Father Fraisse, to recommend some material for spiritual reading. The first book to appear on the latter's list was the treatise by Mother Cécile, with a note: "It is a book written by a woman; it is said that the author is a Benedictine abbess. I do not know if you will like it, but it is solid, doctrinal, sure. Get it."[15] After a few years, the treatise would eventually bring him to Solesmes.

When the German version of the book appeared, Dr. Keppler published a review in which he expressed but one reservation: "The Fathers [of the Church] are thoroughly known by the author, who consults them with intelligence and discernment. It is only the author's trust in Dionysius that is unwarranted. According to the author, 'the incomparable Areopagite,' received his instruction directly from the Apostles."[16]

Indeed, like many mystics in the West starting in the ninth century, and above all with the Dionysian renaissance of the twelfth and thirteenth centuries, Mother Cécile read Dionysius with passion. The importance she attached to his writings was all the greater as she believed him to be a direct disciple of St. Paul, thus belonging to the

---

[14] Cardinal Henry Edward Manning (1808–1892), made Archbishop of Westminster in 1865, converted from Anglicanism in 1851, having been a member of its clergy. As a matter of interest regarding Cardinal Manning's role in the English translation of this work, which was done by the Benedictines of Stanbrook, the following appears in the Preface of the 1899 French edition: "Before the German translation appeared, a French copy of L'Oraison having come, in 1890, under the notice of Cardinal Manning, he warmly encouraged an English translation of the work, and this eminent prince of the church condescended to peruse the pages, and annotate them himself. Moreover, it was his wish that the translation should come before the public with a preface by himself; the first lines of it were already written when death hindered the completion of his work." (The Spiritual Life and Prayer, p. x).—Trans.

[15] Dom Germain Cozien, July 5, 1951, address for his priestly jubilee.

[16] Pseudo-Dionysius the Areopagite, is the anonymous theologian and philosopher of the late fifth to early sixth centuries whose Corpus Areopagiticum (before 532) was pseudonymously ascribed to Dionysius the Areopagite, the Athenian convert of St. Paul mentioned in Acts 17:34. Among his surviving works, considered the first writings in mystical theology, are Divine Names, Mystical Theology, and Celestial Hierarchy. He is believed to have been a Syrian monk.—Trans.

very origins of the Church. As such, he purportedly rendered the thought of St. Paul into theological and spiritual discourse, and thanks to him, the Church's mystical tradition could be traced to the apostles. It is probable that she would have given less attention to Dionysius if she had known that his works dated from the end of the patristic period.

In effect, the author, who goes by the pseudonym of Dionysius, had the ambition of culling the identity of the Christian spirit from its source, the preaching of the apostles, while showing that this met the deepest aspirations of the human soul who searches for true wisdom. Mother Cécile's aim resonated with his. According to him, union with God is attained through the preaching of the Gospel and the celebration of the sacraments, especially the Eucharist, for the principle of our unity rests in Christ, a unity that exists from the very inception of life in Christ and that tends to grow.

A synthesis between contemplation and liturgy is perhaps the most striking aspect of Pseudo-Dionysius, even more so than the apophatic[17] character of his mystical theology. Thus it is perfectly understandable that Mother Cécile should find nourishment in his writings since, good disciple and heiress of Dom Guéranger that she was, her mystical experience was founded on the liturgy and on participation in the sacraments.

Already in the very opening pages of her book, in the chapter entitled "Some General Principles," Mother Cécile considers the spiritual life from a perspective that has now become familiar, but which was far from being so at the end of the nineteenth century. She puts forth the principle of the general call to holiness; religious do not form a category apart in this regard: "The secrets of the spiritual life are not reserved exclusively for a few chosen souls, as people too often believe . . . All men are created by God; all are called to save their souls; all are regenerated by the same means."[18]

The earthly life of all Christians is a "novitiate for eternity," according to the beautiful expression of Dom Guéranger. Each soul must prepare itself for eternity by a life of close union with God.

---

[17] Pseudo-Dionysius insists on the fact that one cannot speak adequately of God using human language. God is ineffable, unspeakable; human language is insufficient.

[18] Bruyère, *The Spiritual Life and Prayer*, p.1.

Consequently, the spiritual life and prayer are a normal part of life: "We may not choose our own ways of reaching supernatural perfection. To pray or not to pray is no matter of choice; on the contrary, there is nothing more important than prayer."[19]

Another fundamental truth that Mother Cécile insists upon from the first pages of her book, is that man is created for happiness, and is always inevitably seeking it. Her own experience convinced her of the necessity of the cross: "God forbid that we should seem to lose sight of another great law—the law of reparation and expiation."[20] However, she condemns the love of suffering popularized by romanticism. ("Songs of despair are the finest of songs . . ." said Alfred de Musset.[21]) "But it is useless and even dangerous, as all illusions are, to seek suffering for suffering's sake. . . . Instead of glorying in such suffering far better would it be to get rid of it as quickly as possible, for it breeds sadness, while at the same time it puffs the soul up by fostering presumption, vain boasting of virtue and of special designs in its regard on the part of God."[22]

Another principle that Mother Cécile had at heart was the necessity of deepening one's faith, of making an effort to come to know what God has revealed of Himself, as opposed to one's remaining at the level of a child's faith or holding to a simple moralism: "In view of this it is important to observe how much more effectually the study of dogmatic theology transforms the soul than does the study of moral theology."[23] "It is absolute presumption to expect to obtain, by immediate light from God, that knowledge which we can and ought to acquire . . ."[24] While theology detached from a life of prayer is an aberration, a life of prayer detached from doctrine is just as aberrant.

It is, therefore, from this general perspective that Mother Cécile treats at first of the spiritual life, insisting on its fundamental source:

---

[19] Ibid., p. 7.

[20] Ibid., p. 5.

[21] Alfred de Musset (1810–1857), poet and playwright. The quoted line is from his poem "La Nuit de Mai" (A May Night). A published translation by Walter H. Pollock has it "The finest songs are children of despair."—Trans.

[22] Bruyère, The Spiritual Life and Prayer, p. 6.

[23] Ibid., p. 8.

[24] Ibid., p. 9.

the sacraments and the liturgy (chapters 1–6). Then she dwells on preparation for prayer (chapter 7) and comments on the "Our Father," the "treatise on prayer given us by Our Lord Jesus Christ" (chapter 8). After this, she deals with the question of methods of mental prayer (chapter 9), and outlines the doctrine of the relationship between the Divine Office and mental prayer, so dear to Dom Guéranger and all his spiritual heirs (chapter 10):

"Now private or mental prayer, though lower in dignity, has this advantage over social prayer, that it can be uninterrupted; it can be offered to God at all times and in all places, in sickness and in health, by day and by night. There can however be no advantage in making a jealous parallel between these two forms of Catholic prayer, or in making them stand alone in a kind of rivalry; we fail to see how they can either harm or exclude each other."[25]

"It is needless therefore to make contrasts between liturgical prayer regulated by the Church, and mental prayer as it takes its free and varied course; the former cannot be perfect without the latter, and the latter gains its strength from the former and leans securely upon it. The Church does not cripple the soul nor weaken her tendency to God. She fixes and regulates the forms of official prayer, and then leaves souls at liberty in their personal intimacy with God; she excludes nothing here below that can prepare the way for divine union . . ."[26]

"Plainly, therefore, mental prayer, as we understand it nowadays, is the indispensable preparation for worthily celebrating the Divine Office and for rendering to God the homage of perfect praise. . . . Thus, by a double current, which consists in praying mentally the better to celebrate the Divine Office, and seeking in the Divine Office the food of mental prayer, the soul gently, quietly, and almost without effort arrives at true contemplation."[27]

Mother Cécile then discourses on the subject of meditation, on the nuns' need for mental prayer, and on the obstacles put up by demons, whom the angels apply themselves to repel (chapters 11–13). The subsequent chapters are dedicated to the "three ages of the interior

[25] Ibid., p. 139.
[26] Ibid., p. 141.
[27] Ibid., pp. 143-144.

life," purification, contemplation, union (chapters 14–16), to which
she adds the charisms, such as they were understood in ancient times
(chapter 17). She dwells at length on the unitive life, its particular
trials and its grandeur (chapters 18–20). Then she passes on to the two
great models of the spiritual life: the Blessed Virgin Mary (chapter 21)
and the Church (chapter 22).

Dom Cozien, the fourth abbot of Solesmes, especially liked the last
chapter: "There is but One Liturgy." This chapter explains how by
means of the Word becoming flesh, rational creatures called to a
supernatural state become associated with His liturgical work: ". . . all
are priests, although in different degrees, and all are called to
concelebrate with the supreme Pontiff."[28] This vocabulary,
consecrated by the Second Vatican Council, has become familiar now,
though it was much less used in the preceding century. The liturgy
described in Revelation is at one and the same time the liturgy of
Heaven and the liturgy of the Church on its march toward the
heavenly city: "But during the days of her pilgrimage our Pontiff
would not abandon His bride; and by a wonderful way, and with a
wisdom all divine, He found the means of identifying the Sacrifice of
earth with that of heaven, since there is but one priesthood, that of
Jesus Christ, but one Victim, namely, the Lamb conquering yet
slain."[29]

Mother Cécile's treatise is a powerful work, admired by all who
have read it. It is true that its style does not have the same appealing
spontaneity of her letters and conferences; however, the book is
nonetheless very classical, a thing remarkable enough considering the
times in which it was written.

The book takes man from the moment of his creation—as he
leaves God's hands, which fashioned him out of nothing—and
accompanies him to the ultimate end to which he is called. "To learn
the pathway thither, to discern the obstacles which can either arrest
or turn aside, to obtain light as to the repugnances and opposing
forces within our very selves, is a study the most reasonable, the most
wise and the most necessary that can be undertaken."[30] This passage,

---

[28] Ibid., p. 409.
[29] Ibid., p. 413.
[30] Ibid., p. 1.

which does not appear in the original version of the text, was added by Mother Cécile in its second edition.

It is a watershed book that contributed to bring Catholics to the Bible and to the Church Fathers for their prayer, at a time when people drew on other less traditional sources for their devotions, and when devotions dating from the Tridentine reforms, without intending to, often cast a screen between souls and the Scriptures as they were read by the Fathers.

"You would do better to obtain a copy of *The Spiritual Life and Prayer According to Holy Scripture and Monastic Tradition* by Madame Abbess of Sainte-Cécile of Solesmes," wrote Maurice Barrès.[31] "You will find therein admirable insights presented by an admirable woman of our times, thus expounded in terms at your level of understanding, which will set you upon the path of a Pascal."[32]

Ernest Psichari[33] had the book as his constant companion after his conversion, reading it assiduously especially during the 1913–1914 winter, when he was beginning to write his *Le voyage du centurion* (The voyage of the centurion). And in *La Cathédrale*, Joris-Karl Huysmans[34] also spoke of Mother Cécile's book, placing the

---

[31] Maurice Barrès (1862–1923), French novelist, journalist and politician.—Trans.

[32] *Mes Cahiers, année 1909, Cahier Pascal* (Paris: G. Dupré, 1963), p. 443.

[33] Ernest Psichari (1883–1914), an officer in the French army. Son of a philologist, he wrote a modest number of books reflecting preoccupation with sociological matters. His intention to enter the Dominican order after his conversion was cut short by his premature death in World War I.—Trans.

[34] Joris Karl Huysmans (1848–1907), French novelist and civil servant born in Paris of a Dutch father and French mother. His is one of the extraordinary stories of conversion of late nineteenth-century France. A leading literary figure, his style over time proceeded from naturalism, to realism, to the decadent genre he helped create, a trajectory that reflected his own life of increasing depravity and baseness. Paradoxically, it was through his eventual involvement in the occult and Satanism and the realization of the hopelessness of his life that he began the gradual return to the Catholic faith of his childhood. A sojourn at the Abbey of La Trappe—following the schedule and discipline of the monks with the deliberate aim of purging himself of his carnal desires—congealed the course of his new-found life. Solesmes played a significant role in his full conversion, whereby he eventually became a Benedictine oblate attached to the Abbey of Ligugé. He corresponded with Mother Cécile Bruyère, and had great admiration for the nuns of Sainte-Cécile, whose singing he described in *La cathédrale*. He died of cancer of the mouth, refusing to take any painkillers.

Already upon the first stirrings toward his conversion, his literary output turned to the Catholic faith and his own experience of it. The depraved autobiographical character of his former novels, Durtal, turns to the faith in a trilogy which traces Huysmans's own conversion, as well as gives occasion to lengthy discourses on sacred art, architecture, music,

following words on Father Plomb's lips (the future Dom de Sainte-Beuve): "In short, it is the synthesis of her doctrine, the essence of her lessons, and it is above all intended for those among her daughters who cannot benefit from her direct instructions and conferences because they live far from Solesmes, in other abbeys founded by her."

That was not quite the case with regard to the first version of 1886, as at the time no other monasteries had yet issued from Sainte-Cécile, except indirectly. However, this would begin to happen from 1889, when the abbey by the Sarthe river sent out its first contingent[35] to Notre-Dame de Wisques.

---

and liturgy—*En route* (1895), *La cathédrale* (1898) (*The Cathedral*) and *L'oblat* (1903) (*The Oblate*). Among his "Catholic" works are *Sainte Lydwine de Schiedam* (1899), a starkly descriptive biography of the early fifteenth-century Dutch mystic, and *Les Foules de Lourdes* (1905) (*The Crowds of Lourdes*).

No citation is given by the author for this quote. An English translation of the book was done by Clara Bell in 1898 which is now in the public domain and is available in several reprint editions.—Trans.

[35] The author uses the term "essaim," a swarm of bees that leaves its original hive to form another one. This significant analogy is lost in translation.—Trans.

Chapter 26

The Growing Influence of Sainte-Cécile

DOM GUÉRANGER BELIEVED THAT nuns belonging to orders with both male and female branches had everything to gain from placing themselves under the direction of the religious superior of their orders.[1] Dom Beda Hessen's request for a copy of the "Declarations on the Rule" for the Benedictine nuns of Nonnberg in Austria was another instance of the importance in which Dom Guéranger's vision was held. But it would still take three-quarters of a century for Rome to fully adopt and encourage this viewpoint, which, while coming from tradition, was novel nonetheless to the jurisprudence current at the time. Too many monasteries suffered from being directed by those who knew almost nothing about religious life in general and about the specific spirituality of each religious family in particular. For many bishops, Benedictine, Cistercian, Carmelite, and Visitandine nuns were interchangeable and more or less the same.

Independently of the mode of government that it propounded, the "Declarations on the Rule" written for Sainte-Cécile, as well as the monastery itself and its abbess, aroused great interest in the monastic world, both in France and abroad. This was largely due to Dom Guéranger's personality. In regard to Stanbrook, Sainte-Cécile's influence is easily explained by the fact that the "Solesmian" orientation of the English monastery was brought about by a disciple and friend of the abbot, the Englishman Dom Laurence Shepherd. The same dynamic came into play in the case of Sainte-Croix de Poitiers, through the intervention of Bishop Pie.

Other monasteries, be they ancient abbeys or recent foundations, also turned to Sainte-Cécile: Saint-Nicolas in Verneuil, Saint-Gabriel in Prague, Maredret, Dourgne, Eibingen.[2] While this expanding

---

[1] As opposed to being under the canonical and spiritual direction of their local ordinaries.—Trans.

[2] The Abbey of St. Nicholas in Verneuil, Normandy, founded in 1627, which adopted the Rule only in 1888; the Abbey of St. Gabriel in Prague, founded in 1889; the Abbey of Saints John and Scholastica in Maredret, Belgium, founded in 1891; the Abbey of St. Scholastica in

influence of Sainte-Cécile extends over years, it seems appropriate to trace these developments collectively, as opposed to inserting them chronologically as they occurred in the course of Mother Cécile's life, thus giving a picture of the whole.

Mother Gertrude d'Aurillac Dubois [of Stanbrook] had first come to Solesmes in 1871, before her election as abbess. She returned some years later for an extended rest at Sainte-Cécile:

"Our Lord has arranged things for her in such a manner that, though she was a bit better, her daughters and the abbey's superiors came to the conclusion that there was only one way of saving her life: to send her to Sainte-Cécile!" wrote Mother Cécile to Father Rabussier on September 4, 1885. "I had always thought that Madame Abbess of Stanbrook would see you one day. I care very much for her health, but her soul is a hundred times dearer to me. . . . Our Lady of Consolation of Stanbrook is destined to spread." Indeed, through Stanbrook, the influence of Sainte-Cécile would later reach into Latin America with foundations made in Brazil, Argentina and Uruguay during the twentieth century.

The two monasteries were continuously in communication. The famous "Declarations" which had caused such difficulties for the community of Sainte-Cécile when presented to Bishop d'Outremont for his acceptance, would be equally a source of distress for Stanbrook, though for a different reason. At the same time that the abbess of Stanbrook sent the document to Rome for approval, her prioress submitted, in the name of the community, a request seeking perpetual tenure for the abbess. This, however, was not in accord with the custom of the English Congregation, whose superiors had held three-year terms since its foundation in the seventeenth century. Moreover, the president of the Congregation had not been consulted on the matter. He reacted with harsh vigor, imposing drastic sanctions on the abbess, the prioress and the community as a whole.

Nonetheless, the "Declarations" were approved by Rome for usage at Stanbrook within the English Benedictine Congregation even before they were approved for the Congregation of Solesmes. After

---

Dourgne, southern France, founded in 1890; St. Hildegard of Bingen's abbey in Eibingen, Germany was repopulated by nuns of the Abbey of St. Gabriel in Prague in 1904, a century after its closure by the state in 1803.—Trans.

the death of Mother Cécile, the nuns of the Congregation of Solesmes had to ensure that the Declarations were in agreement with the new Code of Canon law, promulgated in 1917. They therefore submitted the document to the Holy See for the first time. In their application, they simply requested to use the "Declarations" already approved for Stanbrook, thus avoiding further delays and further revisions to the text.

The relationship of Solesmes with the Abbey of Saint-Nicolas in Verneuil, in the region of Évreux, had been solidly established even before the foundation of Sainte-Cécile. Saint-Nicolas was founded in 1627 by Charlotte de Hautemer, widow of Pierre Rouxel de Médavy. It managed to survive the French Revolution, despite its suppression and dispersion in 1792. To justify their existence, the sisters opened a boarding school in 1796; then, in 1802, they took over the care of the hospice in their small town, thus becoming teachers and hospital sisters. It was not until 1824 that they finally took possession again of their cloistered monastery.

Dom Eugene Gardereau of Solesmes preached retreats at Saint-Nicolas, and after the foundation of Sainte-Cécile, Mother Saint-Augustine Delvigne, its abbess, began exchanging letters with Mother Cécile. Following a very brief abbacy, cut short by her premature death at twenty-eight (at the end of 1870), she was replaced by Mother Anastasie Grandineau (1871–1892).

After consulting with the community, Bishop François Grolleau, the ordinary of Évreux, decided to have Saint-Nicolas adopt the Declarations as well as the Ceremonial[3] of Sainte-Cécile (1888), soliciting Mother Cécile's aid in re-establishing full traditional monastic observance at the abbey. He requested that the abbess and three nuns of Saint-Nicolas spend some time at Sainte-Cécile in order to observe the daily life of the community, and then that two nuns from Solesmes be sent to Saint-Nicolas for an extended period of time. This appeal coincided in time with the foundation at Wisques, the first to be made by Sainte-Cécile.

---

[3] The Ceremonial of a religious congregation is the book that contains in detail the order of religious ceremony and solemn worship as observed in the liturgical functions of that particular religious congregation. —Trans.

"No one will doubt me," wrote Mother Cécile, "when I say that this latest undertaking weighs upon me even more than the foundation in the north; it is a more difficult and more delicate affair. So I am urgently asking for prayers for me before God so that we will not fail our well-beloved Lord as He calls for a more generous fidelity from us."[4]

Mother Cécile sent her subprioress, Mother Agnes Bouly, one of the first professed nuns of Sainte-Cécile, accompanied by a younger nun. "May it please you, Madame Abbess, to recognize in this latest decision the true and profound devotion that I have for you and for your abbey! Just as you have well understood, at this moment, when these painful separations are multiplying for us, I was questioning myself whether I would be able to keep my promises to you. I have sent along with our Mother Subprioress, our dear Sister Madeleine Landeau, who has all the maturity and wisdom of a true religious. I could not have made a more deeply felt sacrifice for you, nor given you a more intelligent assistant."[5]

She also promised to come to Verneuil to visit them on her return from installing the nuns at the new foundation in Wisques. She did so for a few days before the feast of the Assumption in 1889, accompanied by Dom Couturier who received three professions at the abbey. An alarming surprise awaited her there; she discovered that Bishop Grolleau was ready to have Mother Agnes nominated coadjutor to the abbess, who was frequently ill. Mother Cécile just narrowly was able to preempt the blow.

Mother Cécile's aid was also requested for another foundation—a projected monastery of nuns of the Congregation of Beuron in Maredret, Belgium, which would be the female double of the Abbey of Maredsous. This time what was asked of her was much easier to grant and did not involve her sending out yet more religious. The request was that the foundress and first nuns be formed at Sainte-Cécile, making their novitiate and spending the first few years after their profession there.[6]

---

[4] Delatte, "Vie," chap. 10.

[5] Ibid.

[6] The Congregation of Beuron was established by the brothers Dom Maurus and Dom Placidus Wolter, founders of the Abbey of Beuron in 1863 and disciples of Dom Guéranger

A preliminary meeting was arranged in 1888, about which Mother Cécile wrote to the abbess of Stanbrook: "You ask for news? . . . Last week we saw the Count de Hemptinne and his daughter Agnes. She has everything needed to make for a great nun; the foundation is there. He asked me for nothing more than that I talk with his young daughter. I gave her the Constitutions and the Customary of the novitiate to read, and I supplied her with all the information I could. She is simple, has no pretentions of being a foundress, and will do all that she is told. In this respect, she has greater understanding of monastic life than I had when I was nineteen under Dom Gueranger's direction. . . . I merely stated with all clarity that if ever I were needed, there should be no hesitation in putting me to work for the monastic cause."[7]

Nothing was decided upon at this first visit; Agnes de Hemptinne awaited the conclusion of other affairs before coming to Solesmes for her novitiate. She was admitted on May 5, 1889 and wished to take the name "Cécile." On August 13, 1889, along with Agnes Henardt, another Belgian postulant, she received the habit from Mother Cécile upon her return from Wisques and Verneuil. Her brother, Dom de Hemptinne, future abbot of Maredsous and future first primate [elected administrative head] of the Benedictine Order, came for the ceremony. After he returned to his monastery, he commented on the joy he had experienced during his brief stay by the banks of the Sarthe River:

"Madame Abbess, despite my long silence and my delay in thanking you for your kindness, I do not feel guilty at all, as it seems to me that my debt to you is in no wise old, so lively is the joy I still feel when I think of Sainte-Cécile. No wonder, for everything there was so beautiful! . . . It all seems to me to be a mysterious and delectable compendium of all that paradise and the world hold of the

---

(see chap. 12, p. 122, n. 17). Among the several foundations made by Beuron is the Abbey of Maredsous in Belgium, established in 1872 at the prompting of one of its Belgian monks, Dom Hildebrand de Hemptinne, brother of the "foundress" mentioned here. Perhaps the best-known member of the Abbey of Maredsous is Blessed Columba Marmion, an Irishman, who entered Benedictine life at the Belgian abbey after studies in Rome, becoming its abbot in 1909.—Trans.

[7] Letter dated October 3, 1888.

great and beautiful. . . . Please accept my profoundest gratitude and know that I will never forget the hours I spent at Sainte-Cécile."[8]

The monastic profession of the first nuns of Maredret was made on August 15, 1890, received at the hands of Dom Placidus Wolter, archabbot of Beuron.[9] Three years later, the young foundress moved into her monastery of Saint-Jean & Sainte-Scholastique on September 7, 1893,[10] along with the five companions who had come join her in Solesmes during her four-year sojourn there.

On October 23, 1885, the young princess Marie of Loëwenstein entered Sainte-Cécile. It had not been possible for Mother Cécile to decline to receive such a determined vocation solely because of her social status, but the abbess was not at all charmed by her entrance. She later confided, "With regards to Princess Marie, I was nearly upset. The prospect of having princely vocations did not please me at all. I had no desire of this for my house."[11] However, Princess Marie's entrance was only the first hint of a future that would bring similar surprises, for the holy family of Loëwenstein had several branches, and vocations among them began to multiply.

Princess Marie's own vocation was sure and unfailing. It was not for nothing that the young woman had left her country, her family and her mother tongue, to come to Sainte-Cécile and place herself under its abbess. Mother Cécile was quickly reassured of the spiritual mettle of the young woman the Lord had sent to her, regardless of social and national boundaries. One of the princess's sisters, Agnes, would soon join her as well.

Their father, Prince Karl—who would spend his last years as a Dominican, donning the habit in 1908, and whose sister, the Duchess Adelaïde of Bragança, herself obtained entry to Sainte-Cécile—had conceived of the idea of reviving the ancient monastery of the mystic Saint Hildegard in Eibingen, which faces Bingen on the Rhine, in the Diocese of Limburg. The saint founded an abbey there in 1165 to house the nuns that her own monastery of Rupertsberg could no longer hold for lack of space. The project was only in its conceptual

---

[8] Feast of Saint Michael, September 29, 1889.
[9] See note 6 above.—Trans.
[10] The monastery was newly built on land donated by the Desclée family.—Trans.
[11] Delatte, "Vie," chap. 8.

stage and did not begin to take shape until the two princesses, Marie and Agnes had entered Sainte-Cécile.

"I know that Monseigneur the Prince of Loëwenstein is going to offer me, within two years . . . Saint Hildegard's monastery and custody of her holy relics!!!" wrote Mother Cécile to the prioress of Bonlieu. "Even before the vocation of his daughters, this is all the prince thought about. . . . He will not die in peace unless he endows his country with a veritable abbey of daughters. He has made the arrangements; he has reached an agreement with the bishop, and now is only awaiting my consent. This [the relic] will be one of our greatest monastic bequests; I can almost sense the thrill of joy that would have filled Dom Guéranger to the very marrow of his bones. I will accept . . . but you are guessing at my thoughts. I hide all that in your soul."[12]

The foundation would be delayed. Marie of Loëwenstein, now Sister Benedict, was more concerned with acquiring the experience of years in community life than with being abbess to realize her father's dream. She died prematurely on July 2, 1896, before anything had yet concretely begun.

The revival of Eibingen came about, nonetheless, in 1904, but in a way different from that originally foreseen. It was another abbess who took the initiative, Mother Aldegonde Berlinghoff, from the monastery of Saint Gabriel in Prague, which had been founded in 1889 by the Congregation of Beuron, following the observances of Sainte-Cécile. Mother Aldegonde, who visited Solesmes in 1893, asked Mother Cécile to consider Eibingen an indirect foundation of Solesmes.

Similarly, in 1890 Dom Romain Banquet, founder of the monastery of En Calcat, addressed himself to Mother Cécile asking her to receive his spiritual daughter, Marie Cronier, at Sainte-Cécile for a sojourn of two weeks with the community. He had plans of creating a monastery in Dourgne, in the diocese of Albi, with Marie Cronier as foundress.[13]

---

[12] Letter dated October 28, 1888.

[13] Dom Romain Banquet entered the Benedictine monastery of Pierre-qui-Vire in 1864, and took charge of the spiritual direction of Marie Cronier, a gifted soul, in 1874, when she was seventeen. Dom Banquet founded the monastery of St. Benedict, for monks, in 1890 in his

"As far as we are concerned," replied the abbess of Solesmes to Marie Cronier, "there are no obstacles to your visit, which will give us much joy. I would be very thankful, however, if you would let me know a little ahead of time when you intend to arrive once everything is confirmed with certainty, as it will be necessary for us to obtain the bishop's permission in order to open our doors to you, and I do not want to ask him for this without having complete assurance. I need not tell you, my very dear sister, with what fraternal support we look upon your foundation project, and with what great affection we will place at your disposal all information that may be useful or pleasing to you." [14]

Marie Cronier arrived in Solesmes on June 23 with one companion, her young sister Clémence. Two other foundresses came to join them a few days later. Mother Cécile's personality made a very strong impression on the future superior of Dourgne:

"I can tell you that Madame Abbess is one of the souls with whom I have the completest empathy," she wrote to Dom Romain. "We talk together, and I am delighted, because she is very much the ideal superior. You would like her very much, I am sure. I am astonished at the similarity of our thoughts, views, and way of seeing things. If she were not a person so far superior in all things, I would have dared to tell her so, but I am afraid this would be very pretentious of me. . . . Oh! truly, in every way Jesus has brought us here, it is so good that I have come here! The interior good that this is doing me for the Work is immense, and I would have never found anywhere else what I have found here. . . . There are coincidences that fill me with delight and it is incredible how many parallels there are between our two works. . . . If you could only see this beautiful

---

native village of En Calcat, while at the same time securing Mother Cécile's aid and orientation for a women's foundation to be made in Dourgne the same year, the monastery of St. Scholastica, with Marie Cronier as foundress. As an interesting aside, the monastery of Pierre-qui-Vire has a story similar to Solesmes, with parallels between its founders. It was established in 1850 by Fr. Jean-Baptiste Muard (1809–1854) of the diocese of Sens, who discovered the riches of the rule of Saint Benedict on occasion of a sojourn at the Benedictine Abbey of Subiaco in Italy. Upon his return to France in 1848 with plans of founding a Benedictine monastery, he and two companions went through their novitiate training at the Trappist abbey in Aiguebelle. Thus, Dom Banquet's foundation in En Calcat was not part of the Congregation of France founded by Dom Guéranger. — Trans.

[14] Letter dated June 9, 1890.

community, the air of happiness, and at the same time, of fervor. . . . I believe it is Madame Abbess who animates everything; she is a superior woman. I will tell you a thousand things that will please you."[15]

Following this initial meeting, the relationship between the two foundresses continued without interruption. The progress of the new monastery was accompanied with solicitude from Solesmes: the pilgrimage to Rocamadour, the arrival at En Calcat, the first clothing ceremony, the construction work, the professions on September 24, 1891, the election of the prioress, the permanent installation of the community in the monastery, its erection as an abbey in 1896. Mother Cécile came to Dourgne to attend the abbatial blessing, as did Dom Delatte, who was then the abbot of Solesmes.

It was at the request of Mother Cécile that Marie Cronier, now an abbess, wrote her autobiography. Written between 1896 and 1907, it unfortunately only covers the first nineteen years of her life; it is a colorful, lively, precise account composed with the encouragement of Dom Romain Banquet, out of friendship for the abbess of Sainte-Cécile.

In his own memoirs of Marie Cronier, Dom Romain testifies to the affinity between these two souls: "Without prior arrangement on either side, they noted with pleasure their agreement on fundamental ideas, on principles to be kept, and on how to proceed. Their identity of spirit thus corroborated and cemented forever the kinship of these two hearts. The uninterrupted relationship which followed is evidence of this. . . . The abbess of Sainte-Cécile penetrated the soul of her new sister and, from the first instant and forever, there was between the two one of those friendships that come directly from the Heart of Our Lord and that are guarded by Him. To describe the encouragement that our sisters received from Sainte-Cécile would not be an easy thing."

Sainte-Cécile's influence continued spreading, directly or indirectly, after the death of Mother Cécile. Monasteries desiring to follow the traditions of the nuns of Solesmes were founded just about all over the world. In addition, many religious institutes received

---

[15] Letter dated June 26, 1890.

both guidance and support from Mother Cécile. During all her life she was interested in the work of the Servantes des Pauvres (Servants of the Poor)[16] whose first superior general had once been a guest at Coudreuse; Mother Cécile helped them with drawing up their constitutions. Mother Marie de la Passion, foundress of the Franciscaines Missionnaires de Marie (Franciscan Missionaries of Mary), made a trip to Sainte-Cécile in 1880, and the abbess surrounded the budding congregation and its work with all her solicitude. Mother Cécile had, in fact, opened her community to the missionary dimension of the Church, as Dom Guéranger had done at Saint-Pierre. She personally occupied herself with missions in the Antilles, in West and North Canada, Mexico, South Africa, Sri Lanka (then Ceylon), Australia, Korea, China, Japan, etc., and the nuns followed her example with fervor.

---

[16] The Servants of the Poor came about on the initiative of Dom Camillus Leduc, a monk of Solesmes, whose father on his deathbed expressed the desire that his house be used for charitable purposes (1870). Dom Leduc decided upon helping the destitute of war, and a small community of Franciscan sisters was officially installed at his paternal house in 1872 to carry out this mission. At the recommendation of the local ordinary, the Bishop of Angers, Dom Leduc formed the sisters as Benedictine regular oblates. In 1874 the Bishop of Angers established the regular congregation of the Servants of the Poor, Regular Oblates of St. Benedict. Dom Leduc was encouraged in this charitable mission by Dom Guéranger. His cause for canonization was introduced in June 2009.—Trans.

Chapter 27

Notre-Dame de Wisques in Artois

THE FOUNDATION OF THE MONASTERY of Sainte-Cécile had been preceded by that of the priory of monks of Sainte-Madeleine in Marseilles, close to the chapel of the Great Catechism of Canon Coulin. The vocations that had sprung up among the circle of young women associated to the Great Catechism had enabled Dom Guéranger to divert Monsieur Bruyère's alarm at preparations being made for a new foundation in Solesmes.

Now that Sainte-Cécile had taken wing and was growing "in merit and in number,"[1] the possibility of a new establishment was emerging for a not too distant future. The nuns from Marseilles dreamed of a new monastic center under the sun of their native Provence, and Mother Cécile also was tending toward this prospect.

Created in July 1856, the priory of monks of Sainte-Madeleine had experienced troubles of all sorts and its growth had been slow and difficult. In 1871, Dom Guéranger had even considered simply closing the monastery: "Three years ago I was thinking of recalling you from this foundation back to Solesmes," he said in December 1874, during his last visit to Sainte-Madeleine. "It seemed to me that the hopes that I had nurtured when I drew up the priory's charter of foundation and consecrated the place to Saint Mary Magdalen, would never be realized. But now I see clearly that God has answered our prayers. He has done such strange and surprising things here, that it is obvious that God has blessed us."

It was not through Dom Guéranger himself that the priory was made into an abbey, but rather through Cardinal Pitra, who took it upon himself to obtain the abbatial status for Sainte-Madeleine. The monastery had thirteen priests and four brothers when Bishop Charles Place of Marseilles proceeded with the abbatial erection on

---

[1] Reference to the final prayer said after a conference given by an abbot or abbess: "Grant us, O Lord, we beseech Thee, the grace to persevere in the service of Thy will, so that in our days the people that serves Thee may grow in merit and in number. Amen." —Trans.

March 28, 1876 and Dom Christophe Gauthey was appointed its first abbot on April 4 by Dom Couturier.

The new abbot was close to Mother Cécile and considered himself somewhat of her spiritual son, which, however, did not preclude some significant differences in opinion, particularly in what concerned contemplative practice at his own monastery. By virtue of the circumstances of its foundation, the monastery was linked to Canon Coulin's apostolate and was thus involved in urban ministry, which was very demanding of the small community. It was not an easy thing to meet the demands of monastic life and at the same time provide the services the canon expected of them. A number of the monks longed for an existence such as they had had at Solesmes, free from the multitude of works and ministries that now occupied their time. However, Dom Gauthey believed that his duty as abbot was to preserve the form of life adopted by Dom Guéranger for this urban foundation, cost what it may.

"I dream (granted, a castle in the sky), I dream of the priory of Sainte-Madeleine," wrote Dom Joseph Rabory in 1873, "occupied by those charged with the ministry, with the work of the Catechism and the monks of the schola, and three or five or fifteen miles from Marseilles, a beautiful and grand monastery where the regular life could unfold in all its magnificence and where the monks of Sainte-Madeleine could come to replenish themselves."

This was akin to Mother Cécile's own thoughts. She did not believe that a new monastery of nuns should be erected in an urban center. Therefore, if Sainte-Cécile were to make a foundation in Marseilles, it would have to be at a certain distance from the great city. If assigning two monks for the service of the nuns was not a desirable option, it would be necessary to transfer the priory of Sainte-Madeleine as well to a location outside Marseilles, keeping the residence in the city at the rue d'Aubagne only as a secondary base.

The relocation of the entire community to the countryside where conditions would be more favorable to monastic life was a matter repeatedly raised. Dom Couturier would have happily opted for the Maussan estate in Cassis, known as the Sainte-Croix hermitage, an ancient country house of Canon Coulin's family that sat upon a hill by the sea, a splendid site. The house had already been offered to

Dom Guéranger, who, for lack of enough monks decided to decline what would amount to a second foundation in the area. Dom Gauthey found himself facing the same problem: not enough men.

At the time of the expulsions in 1880, the monks of Sainte-Madeleine were taken in by the family of Brother Cécilien Fabre, a young monk of Solesmes. Their home was in Saint-Barnabé, a country manor in the verdant environs of Marseilles, three miles from the rue d'Aubagne. Cardinal Pitra believed the community should remain in that area for the future, but Dom Gauthey was not at all favorable to a permanent transfer, whatever the desires of certain of his monks might have been.

Therefore, the conditions that would enable Sainte-Cécile to make a foundation in Provence were not in place and there was nothing to indicate that they would be in the near future. Another indispensable requirement for the establishment of a new monastic house was the agreement of the bishop. It would be necessary for him to accept without difficulties the canonical arrangement instituted by Dom Guéranger for Sainte-Cécile. We have seen that at Le Mans difficulties arose when dealing with Bishop d'Outremont about the subject, and measures taken in Rome had only succeeded in maintaining the status quo without obtaining any other form of guarantee. Thus, a bishop that would accept the nuns into his diocese would have to be well-disposed toward them. This was the case with Bishop Jean-Marie Bécel,[2] of the diocese of Vannes, in Brittany, who was always happy to visit Sainte-Cécile. However, the first foundation would not be made in his diocese, but rather in the north of France.

Soon after his profession on March 21, 1885, Brother Paul Delatte, now become Dom Delatte, had to visit his family home to take care of affairs related to goods he had bequeathed to the monastery. Dom Couturier took the opportunity to entrust him with the mission of visiting a property that had been offered him for a foundation of monks and nuns in the vicinity of Douai, in Wagnonville, in the archdiocese of Cambrai. The newly professed monk was very enthusiastic about what he saw: a property of 110 acres with a vast

---

[2] Jean-Marie Bécel (1825–1897) was bishop of the diocese of Vannes, in northwestern France, from 1866 to his death. —Trans.

building, called "The Roman House" because of its architectural design.

But the project was not well received by the bishop of Cambrai, Archbishop François-Edouard Hasley.[3] Just recently installed, he was little inclined to risk provoking the local government at a time of such difficulty for religious. He also feared diverting vocations from the Bernardines of Esquermes. This convent was a diocesan institution approved in 1827, formed by a few Cistercian nuns who had come together in the wake of the Revolution. Thus, there was no room for the nuns of Sainte-Cécile in the diocese of Cambrai.

This seemingly negative outcome was actually favorable to plans harbored by Mother Cécile and friends from Saint-Omer—the Dambricourt family and the Graux brothers. For a long time Mother Thérèse Bernard, who belonged to the Dambricourt family, had her heart set on the chateau of Wisques, close to Wizernes and five miles to the south of Saint-Omer. Upon the death of the proprietor on April 15, 1879, the two edifices on the estate, that is, the large and the small chateaux, along with the surrounding acreage, was acquired by the Desclée family of Tournai. Following the disappointment in Wagnonville, hopes for a foundation turned toward Wisques.

Perhaps it behooves us to retrace our course and speak again about Mother Thérèse Bernard, since her childhood memories are linked to the region of Wisques, where she had long dreamed of having a foundation from Sainte-Cécile. In a letter of 1896, she recalled how she had organized her first trip to Solesmes for the profession of Dom Augustin Graux, and described her first meeting with Mother Cécile at the nuns' monastery in 1872:

"Terce, then the Mass. I found the chant most beautiful. The gradual was sung by our Mother, who had a splendid voice then, so weakened after her pleurisy. . . . The Mass ended, Sext followed, and then there we were at the door. Madame Abbess received me, took me to the choir, and then had me put on the bonnet.[4] Time between Mass and dinner flew by, but all had been accomplished and I went

---

[3] François-Édouard Hasley (1825–1888) was bishop of Beauvais from 1878 to 1880, archbishop of Avignon from 1880 to 1885, and archbishop of Cambrai, in northern France, from 1885 to his death.—Trans.

[4] The bonnet was worn by postulants.—Trans.

down to the refectory feeling as attached to our Mother as I am now. After having spoken about everything, we came to recounting little anecdotes. My surname was unfamiliar to our Mother; however, that of my aunt, Madame Dambricourt, evoked some childhood memories. Our Mother was of the same age as some of our cousins in Paris, and they frequently saw each other from age eight up to twelve. My great-grand-aunt seemed a phenomenon to our Mother, because of her vivaciousness, her originality and her faith. She always spoke of "my son Benoît"[5]; this uncommon name seemed quite singular to the little girl. In fact, one of the indelible experiences of our Mother's early childhood happened within our family. She was at the thermal waters in Enghien with her mother, and my aunt invited Madame Bruyère, indeed, the whole Bruyère family, to her chateau in Saint-Brice. Our Mother was then four or five years old. Great was her surprise when she beheld a priest at table; she had never seen priests except while performing the holy ministry of their office; the child was dumbfounded and did not dare to speak. This priest was a venerable old man, the pastor at Saint-Brice. After dinner, the children were running about the lawn, while the priest promenaded to and fro with the other guests. At one point, when the priest was with Monsieur Bruyère, he walked toward Jenny, stopped her, and blessed her, laying both hands on the head of the little girl. He addressed to her some words to the effect that she must serve Our Lord well. Monsieur Bruyère never forgot this incident any more than did his daughter, and he used to remind the little one about it. It had been the first time that she had received a priestly blessing, and it always gave her the impression that this priest had discerned something beyond what could be apparent in a little girl of five, playing and running about."

Thérèse Bernard spent another four years with her family, awaiting her majority. She entered Sainte-Cécile at Easter 1877, received the habit on November 21 of the same year, and made her profession one year later, on the patronal feast of the monastery[6] in 1878.

---

[5] Benedict.—Trans.
[6] That is, on the feast of Saint Cecilia, November 22.—Trans.

Even before her entrance to the monastery, the prospect of a foundation in her native area was imprinted in her heart. She confided this to a friend on July 19, 1894: "One of my aunts (Anna Dambricourt), a pious widow, and I desired this double foundation, even before I was at Solesmes."

Though some restoration work was done to the castle of Wisques before 1883, the Desclées never stayed at their new estate in the Artois region. When they learned that the nuns of Sainte-Cécile were looking for property in the diocese of Arras, they gladly ceded Wisques to them. The indispensable consent from the bishop of Arras was secured through Father Henri Graux. He was never able to obtain permission from his bishop to leave the diocese and enter religious life in Solesmes, as his two brothers had done. But Bishop Joseph Dennel had made him his Vicar General, and in this position he was able to advance the preliminary arrangements for the foundation.

Mother Cécile then presented an official request to the bishop. The objective of the foundation, as she wrote on March 25, 1889, was to "erect also in Wisques the double work that goes on in Solesmes: establish the monks, who will serve God and the Church in their holy retreat and will welcome the clergy that will come to them; to establish the nuns to celebrate the divine praises and affirm that the Church of our times is the same as that of ancient times, for consecrated religious continue as always the same work of perfection."

The bishop put up no difficulties to accepting the arrangements regarding jurisdiction over the nuns, sharing it with the abbot of Solesmes, whose powers would be the same as at the monastery of Sainte-Cécile. The community of nuns was informed of the project on April 26, and Mother Cécile proceeded to make the first nominations for offices, as it was necessary to provide for the vacancies that would be left at Solesmes after the departure of the foundresses.

A trip to the site of the foundation became imperative in view of the preparations and adjustments that needed to be made to the buildings. The chateau had been unoccupied for a long time and the distribution of rooms in a dwelling of this kind was not immediately suited to monastic life. At the beginning of June, the prior of Saint-

Pierre, Dom Delatte, brought the abbess, the cellarer of Sainte-Cécile, and Mother Thérèse Bernard on a reconnaissance expedition.

"God went before us," wrote Mother Cécile to the future foundresses, "and I am convinced that there is a great apostolate to be carried out here. The natural beauties that abound here call for voices that will repeat unceasingly: *Benedicite omnia opera Domini Domino* (Bless the Lord all ye works of the Lord);[7] they need consecrated voices and lips so as to be complete."[8]

The Abbey of Saint-Pierre was preparing the foundation of Saint-Maur de Glanfeuil, on the banks of the Loire in the region of Anjou, and, for the moment, could only send a small group of monks to Wisques—a type of expanded chaplaincy, which would remain a simple *cella*[9] for several years. However, the idea of a future foundation of monks in Wisques was accepted.

Eight choir nuns, one choir postulant, and three lay sisters were chosen as foundresses to join Mother Thérèse Bernard, who was designated the prioress of the new foundation. The canonical act of erection, signed on July 2, 1889 at the bishopric of Arras, was sent to Sainte-Cécile and read at the chapter. The new monastery would be immediately autonomous, with the rank of a conventual priory and the faculty of having its own novitiate. On July 14, feast of Saint Bonaventure and anniversary of the abbatial election of Mother Cécile, she handed the seal and keys of the new monastery to the new prioress, after having solemnly appointed her to her future charge. The group departed in the evening of July 21. After Matins, which was said at an earlier hour, Mother Cécile crossed the threshold of Sainte-Cécile with her daughters to board a night train for Paris. Dom Couturier had preceded the little troop, traveling by short stages. The community settled in quickly, and, on July 24, the first conventual sung Mass was celebrated by the abbot in a provisional chapel.

---

[7] Dan 3:35, first verse of the "Canticle of the Three Youths" which is part of the psalmody for Lauds on Sundays and major feast days.—Trans.

[8] Letter dated June 6, 1889.

[9] A *cella* is the small contingent of monks or nuns that is sent to begin a foundation; it remains under the direct control of the abbot or abbess of the founding abbey until established as a priory.—Trans.

"Our Lord and His holy Mother were very much here; and they continue to be here visibly sustaining all their dear daughters," wrote Mother Cécile to Mother Agnes Bouly who was still in Verneuil. "They have worked so hard that everything has now been unpacked and put in place; our conventual life is fully established as of yesterday, Sunday. As to the Office, since the twenty-fourth when the Blessed Sacrament was reserved in our chapel, all goes on as at Solesmes. Imagine that on the evening of the twenty-third, after Reverend Father Abbot had kept me for a while, I still had to line the tabernacle with Sister Cécile, and we couldn't get to bed until two thirty in the morning. The nails wouldn't stay, we didn't have any glue . . . But when Our Lord had taken possession of his little abode, we felt well compensated and consoled for all our troubles."[10]

To Dom Logerot she wrote: "We are beginning to see more clearly through the upheaval of the move, and as of today (and I think from now on) we had our first complete conventual day. We only gradually resumed regular monastic observance, except for the Office, which we have kept to with exactitude from the first day. As to the remainder, I see with joy that everything is returning to regularity, falling into place as if by its own weight. We have made only very sparing use of the dispensation from silence and from other observances that was given us. What strong serenity in these souls. God is undeniably here. Isn't our Father Abbot in heaven smiling at all this? I was thinking about it on the feast of Saint Anne.[11] I am well; I am in our cell, the huge window is open, and I hear not a sound, which gives me repose. Pray much for Madame Prioress."[12]

Dom Couturier departed on August 8, having presided at the establishment of the small monastery of monks in the eighteenth-century villa by the park, at a respectable distance from the chateau. The abbess left the new priory in the morning of August 9. She was to return at a future date. For now, her way back would take her to the Abbey of Saint-Nicolas in Verneuil.

---

[10] Letter dated July 29, 1889.
[11] July 26, also the anniversary of the monastic profession of Dom Guéranger.—Trans.
[12] Letter to Dom Logerot dated July 28, 1889.

Chapter 28

The Abbess and Her Community

DOM GUÉRANGER HAD DETECTED the treasures of maternal tenderness concealed in the young superior's heart, and worked at drawing them out over a long period of time. When his last moment was approaching and the nuns, gathered around their abbess, awaited news of his death, Sister Scholastica said to her: "If Father Abbot was our father and mother for a long time, now you will be our mother and father." And Mother Cécile responded: "Yes, I sense that."[1]

Her motherliness and virility had reached full maturity by the time Dom Guéranger passed away, he who had patiently worked at forging the soul of Saint-Pierre and then of Sainte-Cécile. With Dom Guéranger gone, the abbess became truly the center and core of her own community and an anchor for the monks themselves.

For a preliminary idea of what Mother Cécile was for her nuns, there can be nothing more informative than to refer to witnesses from outside the community. After returning from a long stay at Sainte-Cécile, the abbess of Stanbrook wrote to Cardinal Pitra:

"What can I tell you, most Eminent Lord, of my sojourn at Sainte-Cécile? Quite simply, it was three months of heaven on earth, which is what best and most fully can convey the impression that has stayed with me. I tasted with delight of the overflowing friendship, as holy and as true as can be had on earth; I imbibed in long drafts the treasures of doctrine, light and love that the Spouse has deposited in His well-beloved bride. I was able to observe all that Our Lord demands of her and the admirable way in which she cooperates with Him, carrying out the enormous task that He requires of her love. I drank from the *flumen aquæ vivæ* (stream of living waters) with which Our Lord inundates the blessed holy city of Solesmes; never and nowhere have I experienced such a supernatural current so manifestly become the natural atmosphere, the natural element of all these beings who aspire so truly, so generously, to the Sovereign

---

[1] Annals: continuation, January 30, 1875.

Good. And Saint-Pierre benefits from all that, drawn, as it is, in the same current."[2]

Mother Cécile received many of her first companions from the hands of Dom Guéranger, particularly her sisters from Marseilles. But for the greater part of the nuns, she herself accompanied them from the beginnings of their vocations with an untiring affection, as bear witness so many letters sent by her to the young women preparing to take the final step.

From Jouarre, she wrote to the young Sister Dorothée Daniel on December 13, 1875: "It is by moving forward in peace, in joy and in serenity that, after having been happy on earth, you will find Our Lord's smile again when you leave this world, as happened to our Domitille.[3] Live in peace, in joy, and know that I love you with all the tenderness of my heart."

With the alumnates,[4] she showed her maternal tenderness even more: "How grown I will find you, my little one!" she wrote from Wisques on July 29, 1889 to Anne Blanchon-Lasserve. "She will even have shed those little singularities, which are but her childish ways, and will have acquired that reasoned bearing that I wish her to have. ... Have a good day, Annette, my dearly beloved little daughter; I embrace you with all my mama's heart; you well know that the good God has cast a mother's heart in a special mold."

In her memoirs, Mother Agathe de la Fougère underlines Mother Cécile's capacity to adapt to the needs of each one: "She had an immense heart for her daughters that enabled her to embrace all the different characters, in the measure that each one allowed. There was no personality, no education, no nationality that our mother did not understand and welcome. Not only did she make herself all for all, but she felt and understood the sorrows, joys and difficulties of each one. Nothing could be told her that would cause her astonishment; yet there were a thousand things that were in themselves opposed to her natural character, her habits, to that which she had experienced in her own milieu: 'I am from every land,' she would say at times, 'I love all.' This was so true that each one of us could feel as if she

---

[2] Letter dated December 12, 1885.
[3] Young nun who had died on the preceding November 12.
[4] Girls living in the alumnat. (See chap. 20, p. 200, n. 13.—Trans.)

were more understood by her than the others were. We could say anything to our mother; nothing we confided to her could be troublesome to her because her own personality was never involved. I mean by this that she referred everything to the Lord and considered each person and each thing in relation to Him and not to herself."[5]

A few weeks before the death of Dom Guéranger, in a letter to Étienne Cartier dated December 27, 1874, Mother Cécile revealed the secret of the transformation that had enabled her to become open and receptive to everyone: "I was born with a *sharp* and *trenchant* personality that caused many a struggle during my childhood because I wanted to be a saint. Well, a religious superior, above all an abbess, can no longer have a 'me.' She is a cement that binds all the stones together, softens their angular contours, etc., etc. She herself must not count, and the measure of her success is the measure of her abnegation. When she exerts her authority—and it is necessary that she do so to maintain order in the family—it must never be for her sake or to defend her personality. The Master, in placing me there (in my charge) is therefore taking good care of me; He has done so to make me progress along the way, to correct me, and to tame me—not to elevate me."

Thus, it was the exercise of her role as a superior itself that forced her to overcome her own limitations, to forget her preferences, her way of seeing things, and to submit herself to the real needs of her daughters. Referring to her abbatial charge, she commented in the same letter: "As you know, I have often remarked to you that it [the abbacy] seemed heavy to me. Well, when I've said something like that, it was out of self-love. When I am being reasonable, I find that this is the most precious grace that Our Lord has ever accorded me."[6]

Again in her memoirs, Mother Agathe de la Fougère speaks with admiration of the discretion Mother Cécile possessed. She was attentive to everything at the monastery, making sure not to be irksome when intervening: "No one was less suspicious than our abbess; she did not know what it was to inquire into something or to

---

[5] Memoirs of Mother Agathe de la Fougère, p. 396.
[6] Letter to Étienne Cartier dated December 27, 1874.

keep a distrustful watch over things. Still, her eyes were constantly wide open and nothing escaped them. However, she did not reprimand anyone for trivialities; she let incidents without importance pass by and reserved the force of her authority for fundamentals or for details that might have undermined a principle or an observance. How many times we heard her say: 'My daughters have a conscience. As to those who would elude authority, all the worse for them; I tell Our Lord: it is You that this concerns, let them deal with You.'"[7]

"She noted how a cloister had been swept, how a garment had been mended or cared for," wrote Mother Aldegonde Cordonnier in her "Chronicles." "No detail escaped her. I remember having heard her say one day: 'I can discern the character of my daughters simply by the way they place the pins in their veil. I immediately identify those who could not be bothered.'"[8] The result of Mother Cécile's being present to all and everything, while being careful not to be inquisitorial, was that each nun conducted herself with great liberty of spirit, while keeping the observance of the Rule and of the customs of the monastery.

Always attentive to preserve the orientation set by Dom Guéranger, she forever reminded her nuns of the essentials and pointed out how privileged they were to have been led by the abbot to give priority to the great current of tradition which embodies the wisdom of the Church: "If there were any better practices for our sanctification than those of the Church, She would point them out to us. Thus, the soul must be docile to Her inspirations. . . . Our little devotions are nothing at all, this divine food (the Eucharist) operates without our closing our eyes, without our holding our heads in our hands. . . . When we are attentive to what the Church prescribes— barring any adulteration—we are sure that treasures of graces are reserved for us. It is in this way that we will reach union with God."[9]

In addition, Mother Cécile wanted her nuns to give pride of place to the Office, rendering it with all possible solemnity. In the first years, they gradually increased the number of chanted pieces of the

[7] Memoirs of Mother Agathe, p. 420.
[8] April 25, 1877, p. 467.
[9] Conference on June 19, 1897.

Office,[10] progressing without haste but steadily: "It is true that it will be laborious for us," she would say when they were to begin a new phase, "but since it is for the good God, so much the better."[11]

When there were large projects that mobilized the entire community, Mother Cécile was always at the forefront, setting the example. In the Annals of 1885, a letter by Mother Eulalie Ripert dated January 18 is transcribed, describing the abbess in the thick of the action of the moment: the season when at Sainte-Cécile, as well as at the surrounding homes and farms, the pigs were slaughtered:

"Picture Madame Abbess these last few days making sausages, headcheese, blood sausages, rillettes, etc., etc., and assuredly acquitting herself better than the most skillful of butchers. I should say that we fattened a pig with the worst leftovers, which we could not use for anything else, and we were most successful. *Herodiade*[12] was the name of the poor beast, more innocent, no doubt, than her namesake! A gentleman came to slaughter it for us and the adept members of the house, our mother at the head, have done marvels with it. Mother Scholastica is full of enthusiasm before her seventeen huge pots of rillettes. All this did not keep Madame Abbess from writing perhaps seventy letters since the beginning of the year, without mentioning all the other things she has done; and she laughs with all her heart at the thought of the diversity of her tasks, going from a letter to a bishop to making sausages."

Manual labor was conducted in silence, as much as possible. However, recreations were a moment of intense and animated family life. The entire community came together as one group for one common conversation, just as it was at Saint-Pierre during Dom Guéranger's time. The particular circumstances in which the monks lived during the time of their expulsion necessitated changes, and the excessive size of the community thereafter decided Dom Delatte to sanction the newly-acquired habit of holding recreation in smaller groups. With the nuns, however, Mother Cécile insisted upon this gathering of everyone into one great family. In 1871 there were about

---

[10] As opposed to chanting them in monotone.—Trans.

[11] Annals: continuation, January 1886.

[12] Latin for "Herodias," the unlawful wife of Herod, infamous foe of St. John the Baptist.—Trans.

twenty at recreation, but in 1889 the numbers had grown beyond seventy-five and in 1899 there were more than ninety!

"Our recreations were in general quite lively," wrote Mother Agathe de la Fougère in her memoirs. "We were all of one heart and one soul, and our young prioress [she is speaking of the first few years after the foundation of Sainte-Cécile], so perfectly kind and gracious, had a way of bringing out the charm of a thousand little incidents in life. With her we were happy, everything was colorful, animated, everything became easy.... We all came from different provinces, varied climates, each one of us had her own character. ... Madame Prioress, by dint of her consummate virtue, her good judgment, the perfect equilibrium of her entire person, and by this gracious and kindly attitude that immediately charmed everyone, created among us a bond of sisterly affection that nothing could alter. It can be said that she was no one in herself, but a true lieutenant of Our Lord in the monastery; all that our blessed Father[13] expected of an abbot was realized in her in every respect."[14]

Recreations in monasteries are often an opportunity to accomplish conventual tasks that are out of the ordinary and fall somewhere between work and play. The chronicles of Sainte-Cécile include these when they bear mention. Thus, in 1872 they describe the transfer of the carp from a small pool to the pond in the garden, which the nuns called the "lake," and also the miraculous fishing ventures in this big pond when the carp had reached their full size. The community would often come feed the fish during recreation. Mother Domitille de Marquié recalls: "At recreation, Madame our Mother loved to give bread to this portion of her domain. The carp, already tamed, would gather next to the bridge as soon as they heard the sound of voices and they did honor to the bread we threw to them. The aquatic 'abbess' frequently scandalized us with her voracity and selfishness. Taking advantage of her large fins, she would use them to hit the less well-armed carp so as to devour the largest piece of bread all by herself." Mother Agathe remembers that "out of all this, our Mother

---

[13] Saint Benedict.—Trans.
[14] Memoirs of Mother Agathe, p. 37.

knew how to draw charming and subtle comparisons that she gaily pointed out to us."[15]

There was also the memorable hunt in 1890 when the invasion of junebugs in that particular year had reached unsettling proportions: "During recreation, and also at other times, we wage war on them to the extreme, because of the future larvae whose ravaging work in our vegetable garden would be disastrous. We shake the tree branches and the insects fall into a piece of cloth stretched out below them; then we put them all inside some buckets and throw them into a pit, where the lime quickly takes care of them. This reminds us of a text from Isaiah: '*Et congregabuntur spolia vestra sicut colligitur bruchus velut cum fossæ plenæ fuerint de eo.*' (And your spoils shall be gathered together as the locusts are gathered, as when the ditches are full of them. Is 33:4)[16]

"Of all of us, Madame Abbess is the most daring; she never stays behind when it is a matter of departing for battle. What a warrior our Mother is! And then, she will not tolerate the childish fright that some of us feel with insects and other animals. She absolutely insists that we have control of ourselves on this point—it is imperative that we be mistresses of ourselves in all areas, otherwise we must renounce becoming saints. Each one of us shows great courage. During Compline, one and another have to leave choir to free ourselves from these unpleasant guests, which have lodged themselves just about everywhere."[17]

"At recreation," writes Mother Germaine de Marquié, "our Mother would give us abundant instruction, but she never preached at us." In the same memoirs, the nun underscores the equanimity of the abbess's temperament: "Often enough, our recreations were for her and for us an opportunity to generously practice patience. . . . I have sometimes seen our Mother repeatedly resuming a letter she was reading to us. There was always someone interrupting her at each instant to make a silly or useless remark, to give a long explanation that didn't explain anything, or still, to tell a boring story that we already knew by heart for having heard it a hundred times.

---

[15] Annals: continuation, September 1872.
[16] This translation and numbering as in the Vulgate/Douay-Rheims.—Trans.
[17] Annals: continuation, May 1890.

... Our Mother ... feigned not to notice anything. ... At recreation we consistently observed to what extent our Mother practiced this self-dismissal of which she spoke so often. She, who was unlike anyone else, did not have her own particular character. She had no personality other than that of the Lord."

Recreations contributed greatly to build up the community and give a common soul to the monastery, "almost as much as her conferences," wrote Mother Aldegonde Cordonnier. Mother Cécile took care "that these moments unfold as the 'Declarations' prescribe, that is, in a manner so as to preserve the family spirit. ... All types of subjects were discussed during recreation: the beauties of the Divine Office, current events, books that we read in community or individually, etc. There was not a single family event that wasn't brought up in conversation. We often remembered events of the past. At recreations on every January 30, for example, Dom Guéranger was always the exclusive subject.[18] We also laughed enough, even to tears, especially when, for example, we had a letter from Father Schliebusch to read. ... Our recreations were of an incomparable charm, and when the bell sounded, we would think: 'Already!' Also, recreation time was often extended. Thursdays were sacred in this regard. We always had longer recreations for the great feast days, and also for smaller feasts, for example, ten minutes more for feasts of the apostles, and then certain anniversaries would come to mind just at the right moment."

The Abbey of Sainte-Cécile was a united body with a well formed head. Mother Cécile kept vigilance over everything. Several of her character traits are reminiscent of "la Madre Teresa d'Ávila," such as her energy, her presence of mind, her extreme liveliness, her sense of humor, her dynamism, unaffected by her poor health. There was no affectation in her, no ceremoniousness; she communicated with candidness and in all simplicity, at the same time being very demanding in what concerned politeness and good manners. She insists on this point in her "Commentary on the Rule":

"When a person has good manners, the body is kept in check because the soul always has control over the body. Life in society is

---

[18] January 30 was the anniversary of Dom Guéranger's death. —Trans.

not possible without good manners. The relationship of persons who render to each other that which is their due is full of charm. Nowadays we no longer know politeness in our poor France, once renowned for its refinement."[19]

On more than one occasion, she pointed out how the nuns should relate to each other: "We must render to each one that which is her due, and not intervene in the lives of others except with politeness. ... We must never invade another's territory, but have perfect discretion. Lack of consideration is the ruin of a religious house; when we begin to lose this beautiful exterior garment of charity, a host of things of a higher order very quickly is lost."[20]

In her individual relationship with each member of the community, Mother Cécile was yet even more motherly, if that is possible. She knew by experience how painful separations at the time of entrance into a monastery can be, and she took it to heart to help the postulants at these moments. The half-sister of Dom Delatte, Honorine Barbier, the future Sister Thècle, received these lines from her on April 16, 1884, in view of the approaching farewells. "How dearly has He purchased you and of what great price is your dowry! He wishes—and this out of respect and delicacy toward you—He wishes you to contribute the sum of your own efforts, so that it may seem that you also are giving Him something on the day of your betrothal. Hoard your goods while you are there, suffer a little while you can suffer, for a time will come when you will no longer be able to suffer and, if you are still in this world then, your only suffering will be to no longer be able to suffer."

As to private exchanges, we only know what comes from the testimony of sisters who left written accounts of their experience: "In spiritual direction," writes Mother Agathe de la Fougère, "this soul so close to God worked to bring us closer to Him, and for this she made herself everything to everyone. Her fine sagacious eyes quickly discerned the strengths and weaknesses of each and their aptitudes, as diverse as the souls that she guided. She would rather exceed in discretion, never drawing out confidences or forcing an openness

---

[19] Commentary on the Rule, chap. 55.
[20] Ibid., chap. 53.

from those who were a bit on the reserved side," —in this she followed the pattern that her father abbot had applied to herself— "but when someone opened her heart completely to her and she felt that this soul was now 'her' territory, she labored upon it with such a mixture of firmness and sweetness that it could only be the attribute of someone moved by the Holy Spirit. No revelation seemed to astonish her. It was said that she had experiential knowledge of all the weaknesses and all the miseries of a soul. She knew how to delicately cause to resonate the string that is the essence of our life, and which our ritual of profession translates into such sublime language. This perspective, which our Mother always impressed on us, was capable of obtaining any sacrifice. For the novices, it was expectation of the Beloved; and after our profession, the bond created between Our Lord and ourselves was a sacred obligation. Each one can recall what [our Mother] said to her in particular, and a thousand references in her conferences dwell upon this reality, that is, of our belonging to the Lord, which makes us the *adjutorium simili sibi* (a helper like unto himself; Gn 2:18)."[21]

Encouragement never took the form of flattery: "If our Mother made few particular remarks, she complimented us even less," remembers Mother Germaine de Marquié. "This moderation extended to the whole of life. She had the custom of saying that, since duty is but something due, there is no reason to point it out when it is accomplished."

As it happens, trust inspires trust, and openness inspires affection. Mother Agathe wrote in her memoirs: "She confided to me one day that the greatest defect could not disturb her and that she suffered little from those who had explosive personalities, but what was a daily chore for her was dealing with the spirit of 'contradiction,' someone who almost always expressed an idea opposed to her own, be it by word or by look."[22] However, even in these situations, Mother Cécile succeeded in overcoming her own difficulties: "Never, I believe, has a religious superior fulfilled, as did our Mother, this advice given by Saint Benedict to an abbot: '*Multorum servire moribus*'

---

[21] Memoirs of Mother Agathe, p. 85.
[22] Ibid., p. 88.

(Adapt himself to many dispositions).[23] Through grace and a courageous struggle, her character, naturally obstinate and independent, had become supernaturally supple."[24]

Mother Cécile was always succinct when counseling her nuns and did not uselessly prolong her conversations: "In general, our Mother said that we had little need of direction," wrote Mother Aldegonde Cordonnier, "as Saint Benedict already had wisely ordered all things. The text of the Rule and the Divine Office are for the nun a source of light that resolves many a problem, or even better, that prevents problems from arising. Our Mother commented on this subject in her conference on Saint Benedict in 1890: 'If you are in need of a good word, open your breviary, your Old Testament, your psalms; therein is our spiritual direction, and it is guaranteed by the Holy Spirit; we do not have need, as elsewhere, of so many spiritual directors.'"[25]

The abbess did not easily let herself feel pity for those who had too much self-complacence toward their own interior sufferings; she did not like dolorism:[26] "All these self-crucifixions, in the end, what do they prove? That the 'old man' is still there and still strong; things would seem less crucifying if this weren't so."[27] She did not want her daughters to dwell upon their trials, however real they might be: "Saint Benedict does not want people who are sorry for their lot and who are in any way sad. All must be contented; in a nutshell, no one should make a martyr of himself. . . . Saint Benedict wants us to feed on misery with an air of good cheer."[28]

Life at Sainte-Cécile under the governance of the abbess excluded all pretense and useless spiritual fineries, like the abbess herself: "The ways of God are simple and no one has the right to complicate them at will; this serves for absolutely nothing. When a person enters religious life, she often has some false notions about humiliations—she imagines that they will make her walk on all fours, eat hay, kiss another's feet; all that feeds the imagination, she wishes to be a great

---

[23] See "Rule," chap. 2, 31.
[24] Memoirs of Mother Agathe, p. 94.
[25] March 4, 1906.
[26] Indulgence in pain, suffering and despondency. An actual philosophical current in France in the early twentieth century.—Trans.
[27] Commentary on the Rule, chap. 58.
[28] Ibid., chap. 35.

soul! She will accept all that. But no, you will have much simpler opportunities to humble yourselves, to which no one will pay attention. You see everyone working, and you are clumsy, you break everything that you take in hand—behold the opportunities offered by the Lord. He sends them to you from a divine return address, and you will not even have the little glory of having your virtue noticed."[29]

The telling characteristic of true penance and humility is that they go unperceived, otherwise their value is null or of very little worth.

Nonetheless, Mother Cécile knew how to partake in the genuine sufferings and trials of her daughters, and how to use comforting words. We know this through letters she sent while away and those addressed to nuns who had left for foundations: "I am particularly happy with your good disposition in your present trial," she wrote from Jouarre to Mother Flavie Jaubert. "Our Lord will bless your courage, your humble submission, and everything will be well inside this dear little soul for whose good I would give all my blood. You know well, my little child, that I love you, no? But I love you exclusively for our dear Master, wishing to see you entirely and forever with Him. ... Good-bye, my dear child; you would not believe the effort I had to make to write to you as busy as I am all day long, but still, I cannot deprive myself from being with you. Farewell and courage!"[30]

When she had to be stern, Mother Cécile did not hesitate to be both firm and loving at the same time, without ever mincing her words: "My good little daughter," she wrote to a nun, "you cause me very deep and very poignant sorrow when I find in you neither the humility nor the seriousness that befit a spouse of Our Lord. Can it be, my dear daughter, that you forget what it is you are and that you cannot give to your Beloved that which He has the right to expect from his N. [name omitted] whom He has so much loved and whom He loves so much?! Examine your heart and see if it is such as it should be. I do not judge you, I want you to judge yourself. ... I can assure you that it is with profound pain that I see that such things are

---

[29] Ibid., chap. 58.
[30] Letter dated December 11, 1875.

possible. Ah, my child! When, then, will you love yOur Lord alone, so gracious as He is? What will He have to do for you in order to touch your heart? Do not come to me until you have been touched in this way, for I do not want to say any more harsh things to you, and I would have to do so if you are not good, for I am the guardian of the honor of the Lord."[31]

Mother Cécile knew how to wait for God's good time; she was patient and preached patience: "A sign of an independent spirit and self-centeredness is *impatience*. We become impatient because we cannot get used to the slow pace of God; we become impatient because we cannot accept the circumstances of time, surroundings and contacts in which God has placed us. A docile soul, a soul that is respectful of God and a true adorer of His Majesty is necessarily patient with herself, with others, and with the Lord. As much as she may desire the good, she does not desire it more than, nor more quickly than, God will have it; and as long as God is satisfied, she embraces what He determines with docility."[32]

She had some merit in practicing this patience herself, since she had a very acute consciousness of the quality of service due to God: "I was made to gaze upon God, nothing but God with His absolute Beauty," she once wrote to Dom Delatte in a letter she had been tempted to destroy before sending to him. "Everything else makes me suffer, and while I perhaps do not lack in love for souls, I might lack in equity towards them, demanding more than they can give. Even less could I apply to them the measure that I apply to myself, for they would not be able to bear it for a week's time. With myself, I am pitiless without any trouble apart from a veritable and unmitigated repugnance for my own imperfection."[33]

In the final years of her life, infirm and communicating only with difficulty, Mother Cécile remained the heart and core of the community. The sight of her invalid carriage was enough to bring all the community together around her. She had given so much to each and every one in the course of her years as prioress and abbess, which were the entirety of her religious life!

---

[31] Undated.

[32] Letter dated December 20, 1895

[33] Letter dated January 19–22, 1892.

Chapter 29

Daily Lessons

MOTHER CÉCILE'S NOTES ON the "Life of Dom Guéranger," numbering thousands of pages, as well as her book *The Spiritual Life and Prayer*, constitute *written* works. Beyond any doubt, they are definitely reflective of Mother Cécile, and she would be the first one to affirm this. But they are not Mother Cécile in her totality. Tone and style are always different when addressing an audience ad hoc and without pressure, than when composing a text, aware that one's writing will be exposed to a reading public.

The copious "Life of Dom Guéranger" is essentially a collection of documents destined to serve as source for whomever would write the biography of the abbot, be it Bishop Pie or another person; in the end it was Dom Delatte. Mother Cécile could not bring herself to write it for the public. As she had told Bishop Pie in 1877, she had too much to say and her own memories of her spiritual father were too different from the commonly held image of "Dom Gueroyer[1]."

The book *On Prayer*[2] was written quickly, but had been thought out at length beforehand. "In one minute I saw the totality of the text, and the only time I opened any book was to look up the references needed. I wrote it in three weeks and reread it in another three weeks," she told Father Schliebusch.[3] And to the prioress of Bonlieu: "The book was a rushed job (five or six weeks)."

Mother Cécile wrote with ease and in a carefree manner; had it been otherwise, she would not have found the time to leave so many

---

1 Moniker by which Dom Guéranger was playfully referred to in Rome, "guerroyer," in French meaning "to wage war." It referred to his reputation in the Roman Curia for habitually taking the pen to defend orthodoxy, particularly against Gallicanism, with a certain ardor. In a letter dated May 16, 1863, Cardinal Pitra writing from Rome told his abbot ". . . more than once I have heard you referred to here as "Dom Guerroyer." Information provided courtesy of Dom Louis Soltner, archivist of Saint-Pierre of Solesmes.—Trans.
2 This refers to the original version of the book, the title of which began with the words "*On Prayer*." It is later, when published for the general public and expanded by a number of chapters, that the title of the book opens with the words "*Spiritual Life*."—Trans.
3 Letter dated August 8, 1886.

pages behind as she did. Her already limited time was continuously interrupted, whether by the Office and conventual functions, or by visits at the parlor, by urgent letters, or by the nuns who came to see her . . . at any moment a sister could knock at her door to ask for permission, to report a small domestic drama that had just occurred, or to present a problem above her own authority to decide. Mother Prioress had no qualms about coming in at any instance under the pretext of watching over the abbess's health, to advise that she rest a while.

Even if matters were resolved quickly and the interrupted line of thought easily reassumed, the prospect of having to produce a volume for publication compelled her to be attentive about how she crafted her texts, keeping in mind the rules of grammar, works she had read, and models that served her as reference. She applied herself to write well, for Dom Guéranger had told her not to neglect these details, deemed important by him.

However, her finished writings are not many. Besides the two major works already mentioned, there are several articles that appeared anonymously in a few periodicals, the small "Commentary on the Canticles" penned for the nuns of Stanbrook, memoirs, memoranda on different subjects (on the abbatial charge, for example, for Mother Thérèse Bernard), a customary for the lay sisters, etc.

Her correspondence constitutes a genre apart, from which we have drawn many an extract in the course of the preceding chapters. These quotations allow us to directly appreciate the tone of her confidences. The abbess of Stanbrook, the prioress of Bonlieu, Mother Thérèse Bernard, Dom Delatte, Father Schliebusch, all had the privilege of being privy to her spontaneous written reactions to different happenings and situations.

With regard to her conferences, Mother Cécile was often caught unprepared, without even a quickly penned outline to follow. For the greater part, they were impromptu talks from the heart in which she communicated to the nuns, in raw form, the object of her meditation and prayer. Some of the religious, working from memory, wrote down the tenor of her conferences; however, these texts were never revised by the abbess. The same occurred with the "Conferences" of

Dom Guéranger, and it is for this reason that Dom Delatte ordinarily did not want them circulated outside the monastery.

"Despite the good will of the nuns who put the conferences in writing, it is possible that they did not always exactly understand the thoughts of our Mother," writes Mother Aldegonde Cordonnier in the introduction to a manuscript volume. "Madame Abbess told us once: 'Those who speak in public and who have the pleasure of seeing what they say put in writing, should leave behind a document at the time of their death, declaring that they are not responsible except for what they have written themselves. ... We will affirm something in one conference, and in the next conference we will say something to the contrary. All of that depends on the circumstances in which we are speaking, on the listeners we have before us, etc., etc.' And again: 'On a given day I will say some words about such and such a fact, and then, when I am no longer thinking about the subject, one of you will repeat to me what it was I said, sometimes expanded and embellished.'"[4]

If Mother Cécile did not revise the transcriptions made by her nuns, it did happen that she would occasionally glance through them. When she did not recognize her exact thoughts therein, she would say: "You will make me hang with all this gibberish!" But, at the end of her life, when she could no longer teach, at times she would point to the volumes containing her conferences and say: "I have said everything. Let my daughters go to these books; they will find everything . . ."

Just as with her correspondence, her conferences allow us to uncover many aspects of her spiritual life: "These are precious pages because they fully contain the soul of our Mother and we can accompany her spiritual ascent in them—in the first years, it was the exuberance of life which characterizes the beautiful season of spring, then comes autumn with its graver aspect, but marked also by a greater maturity."[5]

These talks are also historical documents, a witness to the life of the community, at least in a negative fashion: "We also find reflected

---

[4] Conferences of Questions: introduction, vol. 1, p. 3.
[5] Ibid.

in these conferences of our Mother the full identity of her monastery; they provide almost enough material to trace its history. But one must keep in mind that our Mother was always intent on calling the attention of her daughters to potential abuses that might have occurred; she did not emphasize what was going well."[6]

In the "Commentaries on the Rule," there is more than one page that is in fact an anthology of the daily life of the nuns at Sainte-Cécile. Mother Cécile had the masterly ability of flinging these effective little darts: a word, an original comment that remained etched in one's memory; and she was not below seasoning her explanations with some delightful words taken from the local dialect,[7] after the example of Dom Guéranger.

The texts of her conferences were shared, in confidentiality, with a few other monasteries—Stanbrook at first, and later Wisques, from its foundation. Their recipients attested to finding in them a faithful echo of the teachings they themselves had heard directly from Mother Cécile.

Out of the treasury emanating from Solesmes, the abbess of Stanbrook had a preference for the conferences given to the nuns: "You were telling me that you were going to gather a bouquet of the conferences of the Right Reverend Father [it would have been Dom Delatte at this time]. Well, that is very good, and I believe that I have already savored some of your harvest. But that should not keep you from occasionally gleaning from our Mother's field, no? Her unique gift is so singular, so extraordinarily a gift that we cannot keep from, and certainly should not keep from, gathering it in as she throws it into the furrow."[8]

From a letter written in 1879, to her Ursuline friend, Mother Saint Catherine of Siena, we learn that the abbess applied herself to giving a conference every day, without exception: "At this moment, our week is arranged as follows: on Mondays, commentary on a psalm; on Tuesdays, commentary on the prophet Isaiah; on Wednesdays, the history of the Church or a translation of Dom Martène's work on

---

[6] Ibid.
[7] The author specifies "patois manceau," the dialect of the area around Le Mans.—Trans.
[8] Letter dated April 4, 1891.

monastic practice;[9] on Thursdays, since the lay sisters attend the conference that day, we talk about the saints whose feasts will be celebrated in the following week. . . . At times I ask questions in order to jolt the attention of the sisters and verify whether I am being understood. On Fridays I rest, which is to say that each sister in her turn can ask me whatever question she wishes about all manner of subjects. Finally, on Saturdays, we read and comment on a spiritual treatise, and on Sundays I 'preach,' as my daughters teasingly say."[10]

Even during Holy Week, Mother Cécile did not excuse herself from what she considered to be her solemn duty: "Madame Abbess almost never omitted a spiritual conference which, according to the text of our "Declarations," should be given every day. In the beginning it would even happen that she would change the time of the conference rather than omit it altogether, such as on the day Cardinal Pitra departed from Solesmes. . . . Far from taking advantage of the least pretext to omit the conference, she found a thousand ways not to deprive the souls of her daughters of this most precious grace. She never took into account the additional activities of certain feast days. . . . This is because, for our Mother, her duties of state took priority above all else, and she considered that of imparting doctrinal knowledge to her daughters as the primary one.

"It often happened that when the bell rang for conference time, Madame Abbess would be at the parlor or dealing with some important matter for the fifth or sixth time in the day, or else she was in the midst of writing her tenth letter, and was left without a single minute to prepare for her talk. She would say with a smile that she had just had enough time to reflect on what to say while descending the stairs, and we would congratulate her on having at least one landing on her way down!"[11]

---

[9] Dom Edmond Martène (1654–1739), Benedictine historian and liturgist of the Abbey of Saint-Rémy at Rheims, a house of the Congregation of Saint-Maur. In the course of his scholarly work he resided in several monasteries of his order, particularly in Rouen. The work that Mother Cécile is referring to here is most likely the French translation of *Commentarius in regulam S. P. Benedicti litteralis, moralis, historicus ex variis antiquorum scriptorum commentationibus, actis sanctorum, monasticis ritibus aliisque monumentis cum editis tum manuscriptis concinnatus.* (Paris, 1690 & 1695).

[10] Letter dated January 6, 1879.

[11] Chronicles of Mother Aldegonde Cordonnier, March 4, 1906.

Once, on the feast of Saint Julien, patron of the diocese—whose office has never elicited much enthusiasm from either the monks or the nuns, with the exception of those native to the area—at the end of her conference she playfully added: "It was on the first landing of the staircase that these ideas came to me, for the staircase . . . that is where I find my inspiration! It is the moment of revelation as to what I am supposed to say at the conference, and the operations of the Lord are so prompt that this one moment suffices. Admit, my children, that it is not much to have two landings at my disposal! And isn't it also very good that the divine operations are so prompt? For, what would I do since I never have time to prepare?"[12]

Mother Cécile was well aware that this lack of preparation could be a liability, but it serves to highlight the particular gifts that made her the out-of-the-ordinary superior so admired by Father Schliebusch.

Friday was the day of the "conference of questions," a practice instituted by Dom Guéranger at Saint-Pierre. Each monk desiring to pose a question would write it on a note which he then placed on the small table by the abbot's chair in the chapter room. Dom Guéranger conducted the same type of conference at Sainte-Cécile, and the abbess continued this practice after his death.

"At times there are many such pieces of paper on the little table before the conference begins," noted the prioress of Bonlieu after a sojourn at Sainte-Cécile in 1887. "Madame Abbess begins by reading one of them out loud and mentioning the name of the nun who wrote it; she then immediately responds to the question, resolving what are often very complex questions in the most natural way in the world, without an inkling of difficulty or hesitation. . . . These are true conferences, serious and elevated, with no room for futility and pretentiousness. These are discussions full of instruction, which exclude any idle subtleties and where mutual courtesy and form is always observed with great care, so that no hint of discord ever surfaces. I imagine that this form of conference will never become a tradition,[13] but will remain a precious memory of the great lights that

---

[12] Chronicles of Mother Aldegonde Cordonnier, March 4, 1906.
[13] That is, it will never be perpetuated as a tradition since it is uniquely a product of Mother Cécile.—Trans.

God bestows on this utterly eminent woman who has the mission of distributing them to others."[14]

It is impossible to render in a few pages an account of thirty years of daily teaching. A proper assessment would require a dedicated study based on thorough examination of the subjects discussed, the themes that recurred, and Mother Cécile's style of teaching. In lieu of citing additional multiple quotations, it is best to refer the reader to those already contained in *In spiritu et veritate* (In spirit and in truth), a compilation published on occasion of the first centenary of the foundation of the Abbey of Sainte-Cécile.[15] Only a work of this kind can adequately introduce the reader to this vast field that remains unknown to those who do not have access to the relevant manuscript sources. We must content ourselves here with a few very brief points. The overall impression we can gather is of an overabundant wealth that reflects the oral and spontaneous character of Mother Cécile's instructions; her mode of address is simple, familiar, clear and original. One can discern a profound intelligence, acute and non-conformist, served by great facility of expression. If need be, Mother Cécile did not shy away from creating her own words, not to be found in any dictionary.[16] Gone were the days of that surprise conference at Little Sainte-Cécile which ended in tears.[17]

Besides her commentaries on the Rule and the question-conferences, Mother Cécile covered a multitude of topics. We cited above how subject areas were distributed in a weekly cycle during 1879, which gives an idea of the variety of themes treated by Mother Cécile. Nonetheless, it was to the Holy Scriptures that she allotted a greater portion of her attention, as can be verified in the same list of days of the week previously cited: Mondays were dedicated to the psalms and Tuesdays to Isaiah. The abbess thus commented on nearly all the books of the Old Testament, one after the other.

---

[14] Mother Marie de la Croix, "Mon voyage à Sainte-Cécile de Solesmes" (My trip to Sainte-Cécile of Solesmes), p. 95.

[15] *In spiritu et veritate*, Solesmes : Abbaye Sainte-Cécile de Solesmes, 1966.—Trans.

[16] For example, "recoquillé sur soi," "il serait industrié, " etc. [A non-existent verb "recoquiller," based on the word "coquille", i.e, shell, meaning supposedly "enclose oneself within one's shell"; "industrier," another non-existent verb, based on "industrie," i.e., industry, literally "he would be industricized." The latter's context is not clear.—Trans.]

[17] See chap. 12, p. 120.

During their stay at Sainte-Cécile in 1871, two sisters from the abbey of Stanbrook noted that the Solesmes nuns had not only a psalter and a copy of the New Testament for their personal use, as did many a religious, but also a small complete Bible. The monastery's financial situation was far from brilliant and the community was constantly curtailing expenses in all areas. But the nuns of Sainte-Cécile had such an ardent desire for also having their own Bible that their young abbess put aside economy and decided to purchase a copy for each. In the Annals, one reads that "some sisters, in their initial enthusiasm, did not want to be separated from their Book and took it with them wherever they went. At night, they would devoutly place it on their beds so as to remain in its company even during their sleep!"[18]

Meditation on the divine Scriptures, so cherished in monastic tradition, was well nurtured at the abbey. Mother Cécile "repeated to her daughters that Sacred Scripture is the Word hidden under symbols, as He is hidden in the Holy Eucharist under the appearance of the species. And she encouraged them to delve into the Word of God and make of it the object of their continual study and meditation, reminding them that the fathers of the desert considered the gift of understanding of the Scriptures to be the most precious of rewards, the fruit of the most fearsome mortifications and of the most heroic virtue."[19]

We can haphazardly pick almost any passage in which she broaches the subject; for example, the conference on the feast of Saints Peter and Paul, on June 29, 1893: "[In our day], devotion to Sacred Scripture is limited to considering it not more than a useful museum, an arsenal where one can find weapons with which to fight the enemies of religion. This is the only use that the good find for Scriptures. . . . And the best of Catholics, do they think of searching for the Divine Word in the Scriptures, the food of their souls, and for what the Spirit of God has to say to men?"

The Bible used by the nuns was the text of the Vulgate in Latin, which Mother Cécile preferred to translations, for which she had no

---

[18] Annals: continuation, October 1871.
[19] Ibid.

liking; she preferred "the language of the Church" and found translations to be incomprehensible without reference to the text by Saint Jerome.[20] It is this version of the Bible that she expounded and of which she knew many passages by heart.

Her commentaries dwelt primarily upon the literal sense of the text and upon historical discussions, using the rather imperfect instruments that were then at the disposal of Catholic exegetes. Nonetheless, Mother Cécile's approach followed the tradition of the Fathers of the Church and, in particular, the thought of Gregory of Nyssa in his *Life of Moses*, from whence her particular interest for the Canticle of Canticles.[21]

"It was toward the end of the year 1875 that our Mother began her first commentary on the Canticle of Canticles, a true little masterpiece of grace and spontaneity," writes Mother Agathe de la Fougère in her memoirs. "Her commentary was in two parts. In the first explanation, she concentrated on the literal sense of the text. Our Mother brought to bear all her understanding of the Holy Scriptures and the knowledge she had of the ways and customs of the people of God."[22]

Her teachings were, in fact, a continuous inducement to a return to the primary sources of sanctification. The normal path leading to contemplation is the loving and cognizant celebration of the liturgy and the sacraments, and knowledge of the Scriptures and of the doctrine of the Church: "That is the reason for our existence, we who are daughters of Saint Benedict. We must prefer this life of the Church to all possible and imaginable devotions. To live from the life of the Church; to observe above all what the Church enjoins us to do, to desire but one thing: to live this life to the fullest. This is what must be the object of our efforts, of our most ardent desires. What would you say of someone who, being able to satiate himself in the ocean, prefers to drink from a bottle? He would say: 'but this is water from the sea, it is enough for me.' Well! I myself prefer the ocean! If you prefer the bottle, I leave it to you." [23]

---

[20] That is, the Vulgate, the Latin translation by St. Jerome of sources in Greek. —Trans.

[21] St. Gregory of Nyssa wrote fifteen homilies on the "Canticle of Canticles." —Trans.

[22] Memoirs of Mother Agathe, p. 361.

[23] "Commentary on the Rule," chap. 58.

She never ceased to return to this thought under diverse forms throughout her life—in her conferences, her private conversations, and in her writings. She insisted on the importance of faith, on the spirit of adoration, on peace, on the unity attained by the soul entirely given to God.

In her conferences on prayer, Mother Cécile relates that in 1866, Bishop Fillion—having come for the first time to visit the postulants in their provisional monastery, Sainte-Cécile-la-Petite—asked them if they were "young women of prayer"; they stood there as silent as clams.[24] Just as Monsieur Jourdain had been speaking in prose without ever knowing it,[25] unbeknownst to them, they had not ceased to pray, like Thérèse Martin praying behind curtains and between two doors.[26]

"Meditation is a personal prayer, an interior conversation that, as any human action, must take place in the understanding and the will. . . . We must not become used to awaiting the breath of God and doing nothing ourselves. First of all, we must equip our minds with wholesome and strong things so that it may more easily settle itself before God. . . . If the Holy Spirit doesn't feed your soul Himself, you must look for food by reading the Holy Scriptures."[27]

"Monastic life consists of the thought of God in the heart, of intimacy with God. And if a monk or nun could escape God for more than a quarter of an hour, one could rightly say: 'the habit does not make the monk!' . . . We need intimacy with God, we need to be with Him, to think of Him. . . . Let us never leave the environment of faith within which we are to move about as freely as a fish in water and a bird in the air. This is our own element; let us establish ourselves in

---

[24] See Conference of May 10, 1885.

[25] Monsieur Jourdain is the protagonist of Molière's play *Le Bourgeois Gentilhomme*, 1670 (*The Bourgeois Gentleman*). In an exchange with the "Philosophy Master" he learns that there is no other way of expressing oneself than by either prose or verse. This is a great revelation to Monsieur Jourdain who replies, "By my faith! For more than forty years I have been speaking prose without knowing anything about it, and I am much obliged to you for having taught me that." Molière (Jean-Baptiste Poquelin, 1622–1673) was the master playwright of Louis XIV's court.—Trans.

[26] A reference to St. Thérèse's own description in her autobiography (*Story of a Soul*) of her unwitting practice of mental prayer as a child.—Trans.

[27] Commentaries on *The Conferences* of John Cassian, August 29, 1889.

this element in such a way that our soul will no longer be able to leave it."[28]

The cognizant and loving practice of the liturgy, celebrated by one's entire being, should place the nun before the grandeur, the beauty, and the purity of God, and gradually make of her a "true adorer." This teaching placed the sisters constantly before the sole object of their lives: to unite their hearts and their voices to the loving adoration which the Word Incarnate raises from the earth up to the Father:

"The true adorers on earth are the contemplatives; we are made exclusively for God. . . . The enclosure, by which nuns can be apart from all the things of this world, is so that they may understand these words of the Gospel: 'But the hour cometh, and now is, when the true adorers shall adore the Father in spirit and in truth.' (Jn 4:23) It is rightfully just that God should find upon this earth people who think of nothing but Him. . . . I can assure you that if there were true adorers in this world, the planet would also find its place and things would go much better for all."[29]

This adoration is compatible with all the activities of monastic life, even the most absorbing: "There is no need to isolate yourselves in order to find Him; do what you have to do, but only do it having God in mind. This was Dom Guéranger's doctrine and I cannot think of things in any other way. The spirit of recollection consists of seeing God in everything, at the washhouse, at the kitchen, in your storage boxes, in your clothes, etc. . . . Never should these things hamper the spirit of prayer. It also consists of lending ourselves to everything without ever totally giving ourselves away."[30]

To better fulfill this office of adorer, one must learn to understand what God has said of Himself in the Scriptures and in the teachings of the Church, which has not ceased to comment on the Word of God through the Fathers of the Church, its spiritual masters, its theology, and to apply what one knows to daily life, in complete fidelity. "In the rite of consecration of virgins, the Church desires that the nun come before the Lord *secura cum lumine* (serenely bearing her lamp).

---

[28] Conference on the fourth Sunday of Lent, 1890.

[29] Conference on March 7, 1891.

[30] Conference on March 9, 1891.

The Church insists upon this light, this knowledge of God. *Secura cum lumine,* the two words [*secura* and *lumine*] are in perfect accord with each other because the light of God pacifies, renders serene, while gentleness and tranquility are indispensable for keeping the lamp lit—a strong wind will very quickly blow out the flame. Therefore we must seek to be penetrated by light, by knowledge of divine things; we must strive to come close to God in order to grasp the eternal truth. We must not be attached to passing knowledge, but be centered on that knowledge that remains unto eternity. . . . How much pettiness comes from our not living within vast thoughts . . . We nuns are not upon this earth to do *little holy things,* but to do little things in a way to make them great. That is what happens when the light of doctrine illuminates all our actions."[31]

At the close of this chapter, how can we resist the pleasure of quoting from yet one more conference, this one on Our Lady, which shows to what point Mother Cécile's intuition corresponds to that of Thérèse of Lisieux, regarding the grandeur of daily life and the extraordinary character of the ordinary within the supernatural order? It was given on Assumption day, when the Gospel reading of the feast was formerly the episode of Martha and Mary:

"We would need to penetrate eternity in order to grasp with what great torrents of beatitude and glory the Lord rewarded the way Our Lady lived the [contemplative] life of Mary. I am, nonetheless, quite convinced that heavenly rewards also adorn the perfection with which she fulfilled her [active] life of Martha. Who can say how much merit and recompense God has reserved for us by our accomplishment of the most humble of our daily duties? We belittle these things too much. Who has organized our life as it is? Was it not the Creator Himself? . . . If the good God had wanted something else for us, he would have made us differently. Well, it so pleased Him to thus organize our existence after the fall of our first parents; it so pleased Him that this life should be that of His mother, and He did not disdain partaking of this way of life when He came into this world, not even providing for Himself the extraordinary conditions that occur in the lives of certain saints. Our Lady led the common life

---

[31] Conference on July 14, 1880.

of a Jewish woman; we see in it not a trace of anything extraordinary, nothing is said of her fasts. She assumed the most common form of life, the simplest. But then this life of Martha came to an end. . . . In order for us to understand the nobility of the external material life we would have to comprehend how Our Lady lived it herself."[32]

---

[32] Conference on August 15, 1873.

Part IV

The Way of the Cross
1890–1909

Chapter 30

Dom Delatte, Abbot of Saint-Pierre

AS TIME WENT ON, MOTHER CÉCILE continued accumulating ever more material for a complete biography of Dom Guéranger, transcribing documents at her disposal and gathering everything into a compilation which followed strict chronological order. In her zeal for objectivity, she went into great detail, even including episodes that were not very flattering of the monks of Solesmes. Cardinal Pitra, from his distance in Rome, was anxious over this particular point, for he had been the superior of the house in Paris at the time of its financial collapse in 1845, and therefore felt himself responsible for the unfortunate outcome of the foundation. He did not have direct knowledge of the work of the abbess, but he knew something about it through Dom Gauthey of Marseilles, with whom he kept up close correspondence.

In February 1886, when the cardinal came to Marseilles for the funeral of his sister, superior of the Filles de la Charité de Nîmes (Daughters of Charity of Nîmes), Dom Gauthey put three volumes of Mother Cécile's notes at his disposal. He passed the night reading the material. Upon leaving the Abbey of Sainte-Madeleine, he requested that Dom Gauthey ask Mother Cécile to pass more lightly over several of the unpleasant episodes and to destroy the notes that contained the more embarrassing details. Upon his return to Rome, he spoke about this to his secretary and confidant, Monsignor Battandier, who fully agreed with him. The cardinal desired to read the documentation more carefully and with more time than he had had in Marseilles, and so applied to Sainte-Cécile for a copy of the work as it stood.

At Solesmes, after considering the request, Dom Couturier and Mother Cécile decided that nothing would be done about it. An impartial historical account gains nothing by the elimination of vexatious documentation, much less by its destruction. They were in the right, but the cardinal was profoundly hurt by this refusal. Perhaps Mother Cécile was too harsh in communicating the decision, for the financial disaster in Paris had left wounds that ran deep and were still smarting.

Henceforth the cardinal would distance himself from the abbey of Sainte-Cécile, towards which he had shown such great solicitude until this point. He wrote his own recollections of the episode and entrusted them to Monsignor Battandier; his objective was to delimit the part he had played in the events that had been so detrimental to the subsequent development of Solesmes. Unfortunately, his recollections do not perfectly coincide with the letters that he himself had written at the time, as well as with other archival documentation which he did not have at hand in Rome. These latter documents refute his version of the events on several points. The account of the episode as related by Mother Cécile more accurately reflects the reality of the facts.

Thanks to the good offices of Dom Gauthey, Cardinal Pitra finally received, in 1887, the volume concerning the foundation in Paris. However, he still could not reconcile himself to the stark presentation of the facts. Thus, when he died two years later he was interred in Rome according to his final wishes, and not in the small cemetery of the nuns, as he had so keenly desired at first.

Before him, other cherished friends of the monastery had already departed for eternity: Dom Laurence Shepherd, the English disciple of Dom Guéranger and the spiritual father of the nuns of Stanbrook; Canon Coulin, who had been the catalyst for the foundation of Sainte-Madeleine in Marseilles and whose Great Catechism had given Sainte-Cécile its first nuns; Étienne Cartier, who had generously come to the aid of the monastery during its most difficult years.

The monastery of Sainte-Cécile had an abbess, and it had recently made a foundation at Wisques, but it still had not been erected as an abbey. Bishop Guillaume Labouré,[1] as ordinary of the diocese of Le Mans, thought the moment had arrived, and joined Mother Cécile in applying for the favor from the Holy See. Dom Couturier sent one of his monks, Dom Cabrol, to Rome to negotiate both the abbatial erection as well as sanction of the statutes drawn up by Bishop Fillion

---

[1] Guillaume-Marie-Joseph Labouré (1841–1906) was Bishop of Le Mans from 1885 to 1893, when he was appointed metropolitan archbishop of Rennes. — Trans.

and Dom Guéranger, which had been a point of contention during the tenure of Bishop d'Outremont. The request was granted on January 29, 1890 by the Congregation of Bishops and Regulars, and Bishop Labouré proceeded to publish the decree by a letter dated February 20. He wrote to Dom Couturier: "It is with sentiments of great joy that I send you my most heartfelt congratulations. I am happy that your wishes and the ardent desires of your daughters have been gratified. And if I was able to lend any help in this matter, I will consider myself amply rewarded by the prayers, by the public prayer that the *abbey* will be lifting up to Heaven for the diocese of Le Mans and its bishop."[2]

In autumn of 1889, following the foundation of Wisques, Dom Couturier's health began to steadily decline. He seldom left his cell, even on the great feast days when he felt too weak to officiate over the ceremonies of the day. During Christmas 1889, he seemed to have regained some of his strength, but this did not last long. More and more, the community of Saint-Pierre, dispersed among the village homes, was *de facto* governed by the prior, Dom Delatte. There were those who did not take kindly to his being invested with such great responsibility so soon after his profession, and some resented his exerting the authority given him without taking into account certain situations that had taken on a permanent status.

For many years, Dom Couturier had been lovingly preparing the foundation at Saint-Maur de Glanfeuil,[3] located between Angers and Saumur. The saint venerated there was, as then believed, the disciple

---

[2] Letter dated January 29, 1890.
[3] According to Abbot Odo of Glanfeuil (ninth century), St. Maurus, the disciple of St. Benedict, having come to France, founded a monastery on land donated by King Theodebert and died there in the year 584. Thus Glanfeuil claimed to be the oldest Benedictine abbey in Gaul. The scholarly view, however, is that it was founded in 824 by Rorgon I of Maine. Having been rebuilt after Norman devastation, the abbey was once more suppressed in 1790 by the Revolution, and would not come to life again until its refounding by Dom Couturier one hundred years later. The foundation was made in 1890 and raised to the status of abbey in 1894, with Dom Édouard du Coëtlosquet as abbot. Upon the exile of religious imposed by the French government in 1901, the community of St. Maur took refuge at first in Beauraing, Belgium, and later in 1909, transferred to a property acquired in the Grand Duchy of Luxembourg, close to the town of Clervaux. A decree of the Holy See dated May 3, 1909 declared the Abbey of Saint-Maur extinct while the Abbey of Saint-Maurice et Saint-Maur de Clervaux in Luxembourg was erected in its place. —Trans.

of Saint Benedict of whom St. Gregory the Great speaks in the second book of his *Dialogues*. The last stages of the long preparation for the foundation coincided with the final weeks of the life of the first successor of Dom Guéranger. In September 1890, Dom Couturier was still able himself to install his monks upon the banks of the Loire, after which he returned to Solesmes never again to leave. He gave his last conference on the feast of Saint Michael. On October 5, Dom Delatte administered the last rites; it was the feast of St. Placid,[4] patron of the novitiate at that time. On the eighth, the community gathered to recite the prayers for the dying, recommending his soul to God. However, the agony was prolonged for yet two more weeks.

"Our Very Reverend Father is still here, always dying, with no signs of either improvement or deterioration, for a fortnight," wrote Mother Cécile to the prioress of the Norbertine nuns in Bonlieu. "He is always calm and serene; his mind is lucid and perfectly balanced. You well guess that these days are somber ones and that the devil is raging a battle against the angels, some sparks of which have been reaching us. . . . Help us to ever so gently conduct our venerated father to the bosom of God, and to obtain here below a head who will be a true elect of God."[5]

Mother Cécile no longer could communicate with Dom Couturier except by writing: "You have amply paid your debt toward the Congregation," were words sent to him in his last days. "Now cast everything into the Sacred Heart of the Lord—the anxieties, the fears, the burdens . . . You belong exclusively to God at this hour, and the measure of grace that you will draw upon us is certainly the measure

---

[4] The only factual source of information on St. Maurus and St. Placid is found in the cited second book of the *Dialogues* of St. Gregory the Great, his biography of St. Benedict (*Life and Miracles of St. Benedict*). Both St. Maurus and St. Placid came from Roman patristic families and were entrusted at an early age to St. Benedict for their education. They are famed for the miraculous incident related by St. Gregory whereby St. Placid, drowning in a lake, was saved by the young St. Maurus who, at a command of St. Benedict, ran upon the waters and pulled the boy out by his hair, without ever noticing that he had left firm ground. The reader is referred to *The Life of Little Saint Placid* by Mother Geneviève Gallois (1888–1962) of the Abbey of Saint-Louis du Temple (trans. Monks of Mount Saviour, New York: Pantheon, 1956) in which the little that is known of St. Placid is the point of departure for a most imaginative, powerful and engaging exposé on contemplative monastic life, illustrated with line drawings by the Benedictine nun and artist herself.—Trans.

[5] Letter dated October 16, 1890.

by which you will belong to that sovereign Beauty which you are going to contemplate unveiled."

The hour of eternity tolled for the abbot on October 29, 1890, after First Vespers of the feast of the Holy Relics.[6] The authorities refused to allow the community to celebrate the funeral services in the abbey church at Saint-Pierre, still empty and guarded by the police. Instead, they took place at Sainte-Cécile where, since 1882, Dom Couturier had presided at pontifical ceremonies on great feast days. One hundred men of the parish took turns keeping watch over the abbot's body during the night. On November 4, the feast of Saint Charles, Bishop Labouré of Le Mans came to conduct the funeral ceremonies. The body was interred in the old chapel of Saint-Aquilin at the village's cemetery. There it would rest, with the monks who had died during the eviction years, until October 1899, when it was finally possible to transfer them to the abbey church.

There was little doubt as to who would be elected as Dom Couturier's successor. The majority of monks of Solesmes had already designated Dom Paul Delatte for the charge, but this was not a unanimous stance. Many members of the chapter dreaded him because of his strong-handedness and the measures he had taken to recall certain monks to a better understanding of their vocation. The particular conditions of life within the village—around the walls of the abbey rather than within them—had, in fact, given occasion to certain abuses.

Dom Delatte's greatest handicap was his few years in monastic life. None of the superiors of the Congregation—the abbot of Ligugé, Dom Bourigaud, the abbot of Marseilles, Dom Gauthey, the prior of Silos, Dom Guépin, the prior of Saint-Maur, Dom Chamard—had had him as their brother at Solesmes or knew him personally. Dom Delatte had only twice met with Dom Guéranger. How could he, they wondered, assure transmission of the founder's heritage? Dom

---

[6] The feast of the Holy Relics, according to Dom Guéranger in his *The Liturgical Year*, was at his time commonly celebrated on the Sunday within the octave of the feast of All Saints (thus, after November 1), though the exact date could vary from diocese to diocese. The day was later fixed to November 5. In this year of 1890, the feast was observed at Solesmes on October 30, two days prior to the feast of All Saints. On this feast, parishes and monasteries honor in particular the saints whose relics are in their custody, a practice still retained in some dioceses and churches, particularly in Europe.—Trans.

Couturier and Mother Cécile saw things differently, but one was no longer in this world and the other lacked any voice in the chapter.

Moreover, at the time of the General Chapter in 1889, the superiors had deemed that the young prior had gone overboard in fulfilling his role (according to the Constitutions at that time, he had taken part in the chapter as a delegate for Saint-Pierre). It was difficult for him to act any differently, since Dom Couturier, hampered by his poor health, required much of him with regard to the government of the community. Dom Delatte had no inclination to mold his future, having not a trace of desire to be elected the third abbot of Solesmes, and he did nothing to allay those who were opposed to his election. Some resented him; so much so that there was much agitation during the days that preceded the election. And if Dom Delatte was chosen in the end with two-thirds of the vote, this was not without contention. Many of those who opposed him did not accept the ballot count, and the superiors of the Congregation who were voting at the chapter at Saint-Pierre thought this result placed the abbey in a precarious situation, as it would now be entrusted to someone they believed to be inexperienced. Some of the monks had sought to have Dom Delatte solemnly declare at the opening of the ballot that he would not accept the abbatial charge, and to ask his supporters to place their vote on another candidate. As the opinion of Mother Cécile would be decisive for him, some requested that she act along these lines. She refused to do so and publicly denounced the maneuver.

The opponents of Dom Delatte had supported Dom Logerot, who was first among those who wanted to see the prior elected to the abbacy. One of the difficulties raised came from the imprecision of the Congregation's legislation. Each autonomous monastery of the Congregation had two votes, that of the superior of the community and that of a delegate. However, the monks sent to Wisques, though they resided at a distance, were still part of the chapter of Saint-Pierre of Solesmes, since their monastery was not yet autonomous but still entirely dependent on the founding abbey. Dom Delatte, as prior of Saint-Pierre, had convoked them to the election. The General Chapter of 1898 would make the necessary precisions for such a situation and would ratify the practice of summoning monks of dependent monasteries for abbatial elections. But for the moment, in 1890, the convocation of the monks of Wisques was not well taken by some, since the addition of their votes assured the two-thirds majority which brought about the election of Dom Delatte.

On the evening following the election, November 9, Mother Cécile wrote to her nuns at Notre-Dame de Wisques. "The Lord Who continues to enrich His own according to His infinite munificence, did not wish to prolong our wait, and the Father of lights, from Whom comes all fatherhood, has chosen His elect, thus making His divine fatherhood visible to our eyes in the person of the Right Reverend Father Dom Paul Delatte, previously the prior of the Abbey of Saint-Pierre, now elected the abbot of the same abbey. You have long known the doctrine and the holiness of life of the one who will now take the place of Christ among us, for he has had the singular charity of accepting the heavy load of the abbacy. I have no doubt that you will render to him 'that humble and sincere love,'[7] of which the holy patriarch speaks, and that you will, in as much as you are able, render the *procuratio animarum* (government of souls) less difficult and arduous for him. Neither will you neglect, my dearly beloved daughters, your duty of gratitude toward God for His having prepared for us, over a long period of time, a true abbot, a tender father and a teacher enlightened in the ways of God, realizing that so excellent a gift completely surpasses our merit and will be the strength, the prosperity and the supernatural consolation of the entire Congregation."

Because of the three-year tenure of the abbots of Monte Cassino— this limited term was a measure taken in the fifteenth century to curb the abuses of commendatory abbots[8]—its elected abbots had the privilege of assuming office without having received the abbatial blessing. Following the norm of the Italian Congregation, Dom

---

[7] Rule of Saint Benedict, 72:10.—Trans.

[8] A practice common in the Middle Ages, by which the abbatial charge was bestowed by ecclesial or secular authorities upon persons, religious or lay, who did not reside at the appointed abbey, but held its title and benefited from its revenue; canonically this was done on a provisional basis, "*in commenda*" meaning "in custody." This was originally an arrangement made in the case of vacancy of an abbacy, but became an abuse to the point where one individual would hold several abbacies *in commenda*. Such was the case with Jean-Armand de Rancé, founder of the Trappists. (See chap. 23, p. 220, n. 1)—Trans.

Guéranger had at first been abbot for three years at a time; it was only later that he obtained the abbacy for life for the abbey of Solesmes. The other abbots of the Congregation of Solesmes in the beginning had been elected and approved for ten-year terms, so that none of them had received the abbatial blessing. The "particular law" of Monte Cassino, by dint of circumstances, had become the particular law for Solesmes as well.

But Dom Guéranger, always strongly attached to the rites of the Church and their efficaciousness, had been most satisfied that Mother Cécile could be blessed as an abbess, even before the canonical erection of her monastery to the status of an abbey. Seeking to be faithful to Dom Guéranger's intentions, Dom Delatte asked that he too receive the abbatial blessing.

As the only church available for the larger ceremonies of the monks during their years of banishment, Sainte-Cécile served as the setting for the first blessing of a Solesmian abbot, on December 8, 1890. However, Dom Delatte's innovation caused some surprise among the other superiors of the Congregation.

For Mother Cécile, the election and blessing of Dom Delatte was a sign that her own role vis-à-vis Saint-Pierre had come to an end, and she rejoiced in this without any reservations. It is paradoxical, to say the least, that Rome's intervention regarding her influence upon Saint-Pierre (which we will address further on) would happen at a time when it already was so reduced. Already in 1888, as prior, Dom Delatte, had invited her to grant less generously the interviews at the parlor that the monks of Saint-Pierre asked of her. One of his first measures as the new abbot was to name the novice master, Dom Logerot, for the office of subprior at the newly founded monastery of Saint-Maur, established only a few months previously, and to designate another monk to be responsible for the novitiate. Later, in 1899, Dom Logerot would be elected the conventual prior of Sainte-Anne de Kergonan.

The proof of Dom Delatte's intervention in limiting communication between Saint-Pierre and Sainte-Cécile, taken six months after his nomination as prior in 1888, is found in a letter that Mother Cécile addressed to him on December 8, the feast of the Immaculate Conception. "Everything that you told me yesterday morning I myself have had in mind, but I was awaiting the right moment to communicate it to you—either that you would have assumed the fullness of the authority that pertains to you, or that I would be given a sign as to what I should do. Your words yesterday showed me that the hour has come, but nonetheless, I did not want to act upon a first impulse. This morning, our Immaculate Queen pressed upon me to act, and our father abbot as well [father abbot in Heaven, Dom Guéranger]—the blessing of March 12, 1874[9] must pass to your head, the deposit that I received then I must give to you, and this must be today. ... This is God's hour which I've awaited for thirteen years [1875–1888]. Now we launch upon a new phase. I ask pardon of God, of Our Lady, of my father abbot in Heaven and of you, my well-beloved son, for all my faults, all the negligences I committed in the exercise of this mandate. May they not have caused harm to the kingdom of God here below. Yet a little more time and, ever so gently and tranquilly, that which the Spirit of God establishes in principle at this moment will be fully realized."

On the day following Dom Delatte's abbatial blessing, she wrote him once again. "When Dom Guéranger died, he so strongly commended Saint-Pierre to me that I took the monastery into my heart, and with that, each and every monk, known or unknown to me, friendly or hostile, all were enclosed in a unity that pertained to no one to undo. My affection and my devotion—not having their source here below—withstood all disappointments and all suffering. I was not asking for recognition which was not my due. I did not expect anything from anyone, because it was for no one in this world that I was acting. To those who wanted my friendship, I gave it with fidelity, I believe; I have given without counting my time, my effort, and my prayers. There were those who, after having disparaged me, have approached me of themselves; others, after having for a long time confided in me, turned against me. My heart remained the same, bearing no rancor, in fact, without retaining a thought of these unpleasant episodes. I had no attraction for intervening in government; I desired only silence and obscurity. I was asked for counsel, and I gave it in loyalty to God, timidly and despite myself.

---

[9] See chap. 18, p. 181.

Indeed, I have always experienced the affectionate confidence and esteem of those who love monastic life. Dom Couturier showed me a most fatherly trust. He well discerned that my devotion was limitless and my discretion, total; he gave proof of this to me.

"Moreover, when I am responsible for anything, I pursue matters to their very end so that I may be able to answer for them before God and before men; and the ease with which I abstain from judging that which, before God, is not placed upon my shoulders is almost unbelievable. A lively awareness of my impotence, a timidity greater than one would imagine, a horror of interference, often hold me back from extending a hand or from encouraging a confidence. I believe that prayer makes up for everything, replaces everything, without the disadvantages of direct intervention. You now have my confession to the full; it is complete."

It was thus that Mother Cécile acted with regard to Saint-Pierre, from the death of Dom Guéranger to the abbatial election of Dom Delatte. The time of her direct intervention had come to an end. Henceforward, Dom Delatte would often come himself to ask for her counsel, but it is astonishing that it was under his abbacy, deemed by certain monks to be too severe, that some began to draw comparisons between Solesmes and the order of Fontevrault,[10] which set in motion the action of the Roman authorities against him and against the abbess.

---

[10] The Abbey of Fontevrault was founded by Blessed Robert d'Arbrissel (1047–1117) in 1100, in the region of Anjou. It was the first double abbey, with two separate monasteries, one of nuns and one of monks, functioning within the same property under the governance of the abbess. The abbey attracted mostly members of royalty and the high nobility. Robert d'Abrissel, a charismatic itinerant preacher by mandate of Urban II, adopted the Rule of Saint Benedict for Fontevrault with modifications and adaptations providing for the particularities of a double abbey, placing emphasis on fasts and austerities. Considered a religious order unto itself, the abbey made numerous foundations throughout Europe. In d'Abrissel's Rule, the function of the monks of the order of Fontevrault was primarily to serve the nuns, which gave occasion to discontentment and rebellion throughout the turbulent and sometimes scandalous history of the order. Fontevrault was disbanded by the French Revolution, arising again in 1804 as a teaching order of sisters alone.—Trans.

30. Mother Cécile Bruyère (1889)

31. View of the two monasteries in the nineteenth century

32. The monastery of Sainte-Cécile of Solesmes

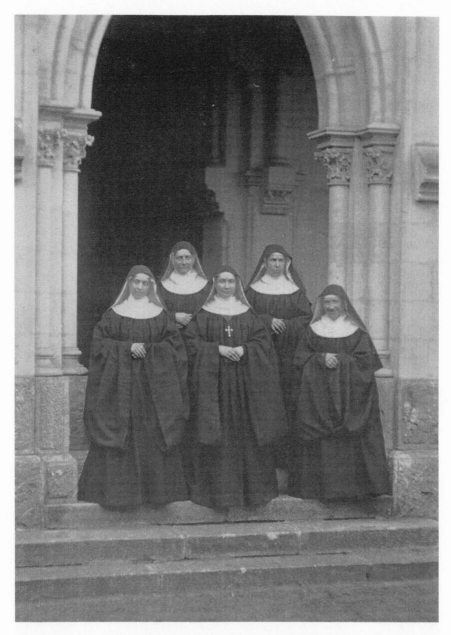

33. The five foundresses of Sainte-Cécile (1879)

Sainte-Cécile le 23 Juillet 1872

Mademoiselle et très chère fille,

Le courage et la fermeté dont
vous faites preuve dans la question
de votre vocation religieuse m'ont
grandement touchée. Laissez-moi
vous en féliciter, et permettez-moi
aussi de compatir aux souffrances
inhérentes à un pareil moment.
Notre Seigneur vous soutiendra,
mais il se glorifiera en même temps
de vous laisser sentir le poids
de sa croix, et de mettre à
l'épreuve votre fidélité.

[...] moi [...]
affection avec laquelle je suis toute votre
Sr. Cécile J. Bruyère, abb.

34. Letter written by Mother Cécile Bruyère

35. Mother Cécile Bruyère at her desk

36. Dom Paul Delatte (1848–1937)

37. Mother Cécile Bruyère (1895)

38. The community of Sainte-Cécile

39. The community of Sainte-Cécile (detail)

40. Mother Cécile with the lay and extern sisters in 1891

41. The choir of Sainte-Cécile

42. Mother Thérèse Bernard (1856–1940) and Mother Cécile Bruyère (in 1897)

43. Mother Lucie Schmitt
(1849–1938)
and Mother Cécile Bruyère
(in 1898)

44. Mother Cécile in 1895 and Mother Gertrude d'Aurillac Dubois (1842–1897)

45. Mother Marie Cronier
(1857–1937)

46. Mother Marie de la Croix
(1840–1905)

47. Mother Cécile de Hemptinne (1870–1948) and Mother Cécile Bruyère
in 1893

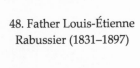

48. Father Louis-Étienne
Rabussier (1831–1897)

49. Cardinal Jean-Baptiste Pitra
(1812–1889)

50. Father Yves-Marie
Schliebusch (1827–1904)

51. Cardinal Édouard Pie (1815–1880)

52. The Abbey of Sainte-Cécile of Solesmes in its definitive form

53. The cloister of the Abbey of
Sainte-Cécile of Solesmes

54. Northwood in the Isle of Wight

55. Appley House in Ryde, Isle of Wight

56. Tomb of Mother Cécile Bruyère at Solesmes

57. Plaque over the entombed heart of Dom Guéranger,
at Sainte-Cécile of Solesmes

30. Mother Cécile Bruyère at age forty-four, at the time of the foundation of Notre-Dame de Wisques (1889).

31. Panoramic view of Solesmes, taken from the right bank of the Sarthe. Between the monasteries of Saint-Pierre (at left) and of Sainte-Cécile (at right, in the background) is the house used for Sainte-Cécile-la-Petite. In the foreground, to the right, are the marble workshops owned by Léon Landeau.

32. Sketch of the monastery of Sainte-Cécile as it was when finished in 1870. In the foreground, the entrance to the church and the nave of the faithful. To the far left, the chapel of Our Lady, which faces the choir of the nuns. Extending from the nuns' choir is the chapter. The cloister can be seen in the background. The building to the right contains the portery area and the parlors.

33. The foundresses standing on the steps of the cloister in 1879. From left to right: Mother Gertrude de Ruffo-Bonneval, Mother Agnès Bouly, Mother Cécile Bruyère, Mother Mechtilde Foubert, Mother Scholastique Meiffren. Dom Guéranger used to call them "My incomparable five!"

34. Letter from Mother Cécile Bruyère to Élise Tissier, future Mother Domitille, dated July 23, 1872.

35. Mother Cécile Bruyère in her office. The photograph most likely dates from around 1891.

36. Dom Paul Delatte (1848–1937), third abbot of Solesmes. He made his monastic profession on March 21, 1885, was named prior in 1888 and then elected as the successor of Dom Couturier in November 9, 1890. His abbatial blessing, the first for an abbot of Solesmes, took place at Sainte-Cécile on December 8, 1890.

37. Mother Cécile Bruyère in 1895.

38. The community of Sainte-Cécile in 1891. In the foreground, on either side of the sheep, are the young alumnates brought up in the monastery.

39. Detail of the same photograph.

40. Recreation close to the farm with the lay and extern sisters of Sainte-Cécile, in 1891. To the left of Mother Cécile sits her cellarer, Mother Lucie Schmitt, future foundress of Kergonan.

41. The nuns' choir according to a miniature that appears in the illuminated lectionary of the monastery. This lectionary, used for the great feasts, was crafted in the art studios of Sainte-Cécile, to which Mother Cécile gave great impetus.

42. Mother Thérèse Bernard (1856–1940), foundress and first abbess of Notre-Dame de Wisques at the side of Mother Cécile in 1897.

43. Mother Lucie Schmitt (1849–1938), foundress and first abbess of Saint-Michel de Kergonan, on a walk with Mother Cécile. The photograph was taken at Saint-Michel in 1898.

44. Mother Gertrude d'Aurillac Dubois (1842–1897), abbess of Stanbrook in Great Britain, with Mother Cécile. This abbess spent two extended sojourns at Solesmes and considered herself a spiritual daughter of Mother Cécile.

45. Mother Marie Cronier (1857–1937), foundress and abbess of the Abbey of Sainte-Scholastique de Dourgne. She kept up copious correspondence with Mother Cécile, who attended her abbatial blessing.

46. Mother Marie de la Croix Odiot de la Paillonne (1840–1905), abbess of the Norbertines of Sainte-Anne de Bonlieu, in the diocese of Valence. She and Mother Cécile were very close friends.

47. Mother Cécile de Hemptinne (1870–1948) spent four years in formation at Sainte-Cécile, joined by companions from Belgium, before founding the Abbey of Maredret (Belgium). The photograph with Mother Cécile was taken in September 1893, at the moment of her departure from Solesmes.

48. Father Louis-Étienne Rabussier, S.J. (1831–1897), who greatly helped the abbess of Sainte-Cécile with his counsels after the death of Dom Guéranger.

49. Jean-Baptiste Cardinal Pitra (1812–1889), monk of Solesmes under Dom Guéranger, raised to the cardinalate in 1863; illustrious correspondent of Mother Cécile.

50. Father Yves-Marie Schliebusch (1827–1904), rector of Kerentrech, the "great original friend" who preached several highly appreciated retreats at Sainte-Cécile.

51. Édouard Cardinal Pie (1815–1880), great friend of Dom Guéranger, who asked Mother Cécile to write biographical notes on the abbot in view of a future biography.

52. Abbey of Sainte-Cécile. The ever-growing number of nuns required that the monastery be enlarged, a work undertaken in several stages starting in 1881. What is seen in this image dates from 1893.

53. Abbey of Sainte-Cécile, an angle of the cloister.

54. Northwood in the Isle of Wight, first place of exile of the community of Sainte-Cécile, from 1901 to 1906.

55. Appley House in Ryde in the Isle of Wight, second place of exile beginning in the spring of 1906. Here it was that Mother Cécile Bruyère died on March 18, 1909. Her body would remain here until 1930.

56. Tomb of Mother Cécile Bruyère, in the crypt chapel of Sainte-Cécile of Solesmes. Her body was brought to Solesmes from Ryde in March 1930.

57. Plaque before the altar of the abbey church at Sainte-Cécile of Solesmes marking the place where the heart of Dom Guéranger is entombed. It is on this plaque that the nuns of Sainte-Cécile of Solesmes pronounce their solemn vows. The inscription reads: "The Very Reverend Father in Christ / Dom Prosper Louis Paschal / Guéranger / Abbot of Solesmes / to his well-beloved daughters at Sainte-Cécile / bequeathed his heart / which is placed here / in peace." — Trans.

Chapter 31

The Storm of 1893

AN IMAGE CARRIES AN inestimable power. It penetrates the spirit and, once indelibly engraved in the mind, will withstand all attempts at reasoning. At what date did people begin to speak of Solesmes as a "double monastery"?

Mother Bénédicte de Gobineau, speaking to her brother about the situation created by the second expulsion of the monks of Saint-Pierre (March 23, 1882), wrote: "On Sundays and particularly during Holy Week and Easter all the offices are solemnly celebrated at Sainte-Cécile. It is magnificent! It seems that we have returned to the seventh and eighth centuries, when the abbeys of our order were double."[1]

This image took root. One finds it echoed by Dom Cabrol and others, including journalists. However, historians of the double monasteries of the past would not agree—the two monasteries of Solesmes presented nothing that could resemble that institution, apart from the psalmody done in two choirs on certain days when the parish church was not available to the monks.

One of the criticisms leveled against Mother Cécile was that she had wanted to bring back to life the monasticism of Fontevrault, in which the abbess was the head of the order, having the monks as well under her jurisdiction. In actuality, not even Fontevrault was, properly speaking, a double monastery. After the first generation, the men's branch comprised only the chaplains of the nuns and lay brothers who served the nuns' monastery. Nonetheless, the image took hold and hid the reality of things.

The story of what unfolded in 1893 at Solesmes has only partially been told, as the monks have been careful not to compromise the unity of their monastic family by reopening old wounds. For, while the protagonists of the crisis were two members of the community of Saint-Pierre, Dom Sauton and Dom de la Tremblaye, they were heeded by superiors of other monasteries of the Congregation, who

---

[1] Letter dated April 11, 1882.

themselves might have been great and holy religious, but who took the two monks' grievances to heart and supported them in their complaints.

In addition, the clearest exposé of the crisis and its development, if not the most well substantiated, is paradoxically found in the writings of Albert Houtin, who cites the names of all involved. The principal difficulty with this source is that it systematically presents an unfavorably biased image of Solesmes, of Dom Delatte and of Mother Cécile. In this, the author acted with a certain hypocrisy since, at the time of his writing, he was little concerned about orthodoxy and the Christian faith, let alone Roman condemnations and ecclesiastical discipline. He had, by then, long dismissed what were for him relics of the past that no longer held any interest. But he had an account to settle with the hierarchical Church, with the condemnations that had been directed to the group of modernists of which he was a part, and with all of Christian society, which he had known at the time of his young clerical years.

Born at La Flèche on October 4, 1867, Albert Houtin entered the major seminary of Angers in 1886, at nineteen. He then tried a vocation at Solesmes spending one year in the novitiate (1887–1888), after which he returned to the diocese of his incardination where he was ordained a priest in June 1891. His career as an historian began during his first years as professor at the minor seminary of Mongazon in Angers. Having retained great veneration for Dom Couturier, he set upon writing a biography of the second abbot of Solesmes, for which he was given ample access to the archives at Solesmes. There, he transcribed copies of numerous documents that were closely related to his subject, and others that were only remotely so. His biography of Dom Couturier remains a good reference work.

However, it did not take long for Father Houtin to find himself in difficulties with the ecclesial authorities of his diocese over the controversy touching his work on the apostolicity of the churches of France.[2] He questioned the received belief about the origins of the church in Angers, based on later legends, bringing upon himself the

---

[2] In 1901 Albert Houtin published a book entitled *La controverse de l'apostolicité des Églises de France* (The controversy over the apostolicity of the churches of France).—Trans.

hostility of those who upheld what was traditionally taught as the history of Angers. He was correct from an historical viewpoint in his analysis, but, nonetheless, he had to leave his teaching post at Mongazon.

He thus came to work in Paris and quickly became involved in the modernist debate, successively publishing two books in which he adopted radical positions: *La question biblique chez les catholiques de France au XIXe siècle*[3] (The Biblical question among Catholics of France in the nineteenth century) and a more personal work entitled *Mes difficultés avec mon évêque*[4] (The difficulties I have with my bishop). Both books were placed on the Index at the same time as were the works of Father Loisy.[5]

From this point on, he openly took the side of the modernists in his books and articles. The widow of the former priest Hyacinth Loyson[6] requested he write the biography of her husband, which gave him the opportunity to question the practice of clerical celibacy. This was also the subject of his book about Canon Charles Perraud, *Un prêtre marié (A married priest)*.[7] He also published what he thought he knew of the private lives of Fathers Perreyve and Gratry,[8] two

---

[3] Paris : Picard & Fils, 1902 (March).—Trans.

[4] Non-commercial printing, April 1903.—Trans.

[5] Alfred Firmin Loisy (1857–1940), ordained in 1879, theologian and professor, was a force for Biblical Modernism in the Catholic Church, and questioned whether Jesus Christ had intended to found a structured Church. His views eventually led to his excommunication in 1908.—Trans.

[6] Charles Loyson (1827–1912), in religion named Hyacinthe, was born in Orleans, and studied at the seminary of Saint-Sulpice in Paris, where he was ordained in 1851. He subsequently entered the Discalced Carmelite order in 1860. A powerful preacher, he increasingly entertained Gallican views and liberal convictions which led him to be excommunicated in 1869, after which he collaborated with the Old Catholic Church (a group of small national churches separated from Rome). In 1897 he married an American widow whom he had converted to Catholicism. In 1878, he founded the Gallican Church in Paris, an independent church supported by the Anglican Church through the Archbishop of Canterbury.—Trans.

[7] *Un prêtre marié : Charles Perraud, chanoine honoraire d'Autun, 1831-1892*, Paris: A. Houtin, 1908, trans. by John Richard Slattery, Boston: Sherman, French & Co., 1910.—Trans.

[8] August-Joseph Alphonse Gratry (1805–1872) was a scholar, theologian and professor of great influence in Paris, elected to the French Academy in 1867. He, along with others, worked to restore the Oratory in France, establishing the Oratoire de l'Immaculée Conception in Paris. Among his circle was the younger Henri Perreyve (1831–1865), likewise a scholar and university professor, in his case, at the Sorbonne.—Trans.

great spiritual authors of the nineteenth century whose influence was and remains considerable.

Albert Houtin definitively abandoned the clerical state on April 24, 1912. He continued to write about modernist issues, about Loyson and about Father Hébert. At the time of his death, on July 28, 1926, he had just published his autobiography *Une vie de prêtre: mon experience (1867–1912)*,[9] (*The life of a priest: my own experience, 1867-1912*) having left the second part of the work in manuscript form, which was published by his literary heir, Félix Sartiaux, with the title *Mon experience. Ma vie laïque (1912–1926)* (My experience. My secular life).[10] Albert Houtin was given a civil funeral service and his body was cremated.

According to Émile Poulat—the historian of Modernism who identifies himself as an agnostic—Albert Houtin was always interested in the question of mysticism. He had led a hard life in poverty. His stubborn character and his intransigent judgments caused him many a distress, but he refused to acquiesce to anything that might seem to him a form of compromise.

His work about Mother Cécile Bruyère, *Une grande mystique, madame Bruyère, abbesse de Solesmes, 1845–1909* (A great mystic: Madame Bruyère, abbess of Solesmes) was finished on October 4, 1924, two years before his death. A second edition appeared in 1930 through the offices of Félix Sartiaux. In the mind of the author, this was but a partial study, intended to be part of a larger work. As he explained in his preface, "For more than thirty years, I have been preparing a history of the Congregation of Solesmes. My first contribution to this project, written while yet young, was the biography of Dom Charles Couturier, printed in 1899. Twelve years later I wrote some biographical notes on the first eighty-one professed monks of Solesmes, published as an essay in the *Province du Maine*. Now I believe I should publish certain documents related to the influence exerted over the Congregation by the abbess of Sainte-Cécile, Madame Bruyère."[11]

---

[9] Paris : F. Rieder & Co., 1926, trans. Winifred Stephens Whales, London: Watts & Co., 1927.—Trans.

[10] Paris, 1928.—Trans.

[11] Albert Houtin, *Une grande mystique, madame Bruyère* (Paris: Alcan, 1925), p. v.

The book is effectively a collection of documents, preceded by a very brief biography that runs twenty-four pages. The bulk of the work is made up of a "Memorandum on Solesmes" written by Dom Joseph Sauton, which takes up more than two hundred pages. This memorandum is precisely the document that was addressed by the monk to the Holy Office in 1892, at the origin of the events that unfolded as a result.

However, besides the archival pieces that Albert Houtin quotes, which are of some value in themselves, the book also contains several transcribed oral testimonies that ring more of malicious gossip than of historical documentation. He did not have to look very far for these, obtaining them from individuals in Le Mans who were hostile to Solesmes, notably Father Ambroise Ledru.

His biographical notes on the professed monks of Solesmes during Dom Guéranger's time are characteristic of his style. They are almost uniformly negative and partial. Each biographical sketch begs to be completed, placed into context and corrected. Taking a reverse approach to the typical hagiographical style used in death notices, Albert Houtin plunges into a caricature that approximates calumny.

His life of Mother Cécile is of the same stripe. The very same documents Houtin cites could be used to propose an interpretation surprisingly different from that given in his book. Once all the systematically unfavorable commentaries and interpretations have been omittted, we are left with the skeleton of a biography, quite poor and insufficiently substantiated. Thus, the essence of Albert Houtin's book is actually and decidedly made of Dom Joseph Sauton's text.

Dom Sauton (1856–1916) was a young medical doctor who studied at Salpêtrière[12] before entering Solesmes. As a monk-doctor, he would have a brilliant career after his departure from Solesmes. His works on leprosy, which was his specialty, held great authority in his time. While still a novice, he was referred by Dom Logerot to Mother

---

[12] The Pitié-Salpêtrière Hospital is a world-renowned teaching hospital in Paris. Built by mandate of Louis XIV, it was the largest hospital in the world by the time of the French Revolution, serving a capacity 10,000 patients, many of them mental patients. In the nineteenth century the first humanitarian reforms in the treatment of the violently insane were initiated there. Under Dr. Jean-Martin Charcot (1825–1893), considered the founder of modern neurology, the Salpêtrière became the foremost center of psychiatric treatment in the world. His reputation as an instructor drew students from across Europe.—Trans.

Cécile, as the master of novices thought she could do him some good and help him develop a liking for prayer and the interior life. After some hesitation, he was conquered by the abbess's personality and became one of her admirers. But, being a doctor, he wanted to exert certain authority over her regarding her health, which was not his purview. Upon realizing that Mother Cécile had no intention of receiving medical directions from him, he gradually developed a grudge against her, eventually believing he could diagnose a case of hysteria, analogous to cases he had observed at Salpêtrière. He actually placed her in the second category defined by Doctor Jean-Martin Charcot: "those who are hysteric from a psychological standpoint only, i.e., moral hysteria."

From that point on, this perspective colored any information he could glean about Mother Cécile, her family, her abbacy, her influence with Dom Couturier, Dom Logerot and Dom Delatte. And he shared his views with Dom de la Tremblaye (1856–1909), whose vocation was not solid. The latter had come to Solesmes encouraged by his parents—devout to the extreme—more than by personal choice. He had dreamed of becoming a navy officer. Frustrated, he harbored profound bitterness about his fate and later accused his parents of having forced him, so to speak, to become a monk. Naturally, he never entirely entered into the spirit of his religious profession. Some time after the events of 1893 he left the monastic state in order to marry. He, as well, did not accept the firm authority of his abbot.

In 1890, Dom Sauton had done everything in his power to obstruct the election of Dom Delatte, in whom he saw the abbess's candidate and against whom he was in open revolt. He did not accept the abbot's election. His complaints found an echo with the abbots of the abbeys of Marseilles and Ligugé. For the sake of peace in the community and to give him a chance to resume a normal monastic life in a new environment, Dom Delatte sent Dom Sauton to Ligugé. It is there that he composed his memorandum addressed to the Holy See. In the end, the apostolic visitation in the summer of 1893 did not uphold his accusations. However, Dom Sauton would not assent to Rome's verdict; he never accepted any judgment other than his own.

When he died on August 14, 1916, he had only one thought, that "this memorandum be published after his death as soon as possible."[13] The archbishop of Albi, Eudoxe Mignot, who visited him shortly before his passing, promised him that this would be done, without having any knowledge of the contents of the text. Archbishop Mignot was a friend of Loisy and of Baron von Hügel,[14] and his sympathies lay with the modernists. However, upon reading the memorandum of Dom Sauton, the archbishop realized that he could not publish it. Nonetheless, he kept the document in his files, of which another copy existed at the archives of the Holy See in Rome. It is probably after the death of the archbishop, on March 18, 1918, that Albert Houtin inherited the "Memorandum on Solesmes." He set about having it published.

The historical value of the text should not be underestimated. Dom Sauton related his personal experience as he had lived it—he would not have dared to provide the Holy Office with his witness if he did not believe himself to be in the right. However, a reading of the memorandum with the known facts in mind reveals that the person afflicted with mental illness was the author himself, rather than the abbess. In the absence of other sources of information and without examining the parties involved, the document may seem to be objective. However, the conclusion to which the inquisitor from Rome arrived after having questioned the witnesses was very different from what Dom Sauton had expected.

The memorandum, as well as the long introduction by Albert Houtin, would not at all please the feminists of our days. In their male prejudices, Joseph Sauton and Albert Houtin seem incapable of conceiving that Mother Cécile would have had the right to say nothing when she was consulted and when an opinion was asked of her. An extract from the introduction is revealing of this attitude:

"Having become the spiritual mother of the principal monks who held office, the abbess did not take long to become the true superior of the entire Congregation. She did not interfere with the details of

---

[13] Houtin, Une grande mystique, p. v.
[14] Baron Friedrich von Hügel (1852–1925), Austrian lay Catholic thinker and writer, naturalized English citizen in 1914. He was a modernist, receiving an honorary Doctor of Divinity degree from the University of Oxford in 1920.—Trans.

smaller affairs and did not even express the desire to know about them. However, when consulted about important matters, she knew how to make her opinion prevail, even if seemingly acquiescing to the authority of those who asked for her counsel."[15]

In other words, what does this mean, if not that Mother Cécile gave judicious counsels when they were asked of her, but did not concern herself with matters she was not asked about; she took care not to substitute herself for the legitimate authorities in place.

Curiously, the abbess, who was the principal object of Dom Sauton's memorandum, was not as affected by its repercussions. While the storm raged at Saint-Pierre and Dom Delatte was the object of the more serious sanctions, Mother Cécile only felt the residue of the crisis. The canonical status of the Abbey of Sainte-Cécile bore upon the situation. The abbey, in fact, was under the jurisdiction of the bishop of Le Mans, who was well aware of where things stood and had no need of extensive inquiry. It was to him that it pertained to oversee the governance of Sainte-Cécile. The Abbey of Saint-Pierre, on the other hand, was under the Holy See and therefore under the immediate purview of the Congregation of Bishops and Regulars. The monastery of nuns, which, like Saint-Pierre, received an apostolic visitation, would not be directly involved until after examination of the writings of Mother Cécile by the theologians of the Holy Office.

When the first measures of the Holy See were taken, they were not entirely unexpected by Dom Delatte, the principally concerned party. Their way had been prepared by a certain number of developments about which he had no direct knowledge, but of which he had suspicions.

On December 17, 1890, the Congregation of Bishops and Regulars published a stern decree concerning spiritual direction in religious communities, determining that it should be dealt with as in the seminaries and houses of formation, that is, it should be completely separate from the temporal government of the house. This was to avoid confusion between the internal and external forums, and to allow for full liberty of conscience on the part of the members of a community. Also, women religious superiors should not occupy

---

[15] Houtin, *Une grande mystique*, p. 15.

themselves with the direction of souls, which should be left entirely to the care of approved confessors.

As it had often happened, Dom Guéranger's intuition had led him to adopt the practices of ancient monasticism without further ado. His notion of the abbatial charge was based upon the image drawn by St. Benedict, heir of the traditions of the fathers of the desert. The head of a cenobitic community was above all a spiritual father. The abbatial charge, as conceived by St. Benedict, arose from the practice of spiritual formation—disciples would seek an elder and place themselves under his direction. Thus, the abbacy was not in principle a juridical role.

However, this did not correspond to the view commonly held elsewhere. The code of canon law of 1917 would sanction the common practice of the time as outlined in canon 1358. The new code of 1983, however, is more respectful of the particular traditions of each religious family (canon 630).

There were well-grounded reasons for the precautions informing the 1890 decree. Several abuses had been committed within religious communities—particularly in women's communities—in the name of obedience and a manifestation of conscience. There was, indeed, a certain confusion between the internal and external forums, so that some superiors did not sufficiently respect the freedom of conscience of their charges and encroached upon the prerogatives proper to confessors.

Dom Guéranger had determined things in such a way that the nuns of Sainte-Cécile were fully immersed in that ancient monastic tradition by which the abbess is both the spiritual and temporal mother of the community, according to the Rule of Saint Benedict. However, Dom Bourigaud, abbot of Ligugé, believed there was a discrepancy between the Roman decree and what was practiced in the Congregation of Solesmes. He had long been a secular priest before entering Solesmes as a late vocation. He was thus less familiar with the thoughts of Dom Guéranger on this point. He spoke about his concerns with Cardinal François Richard, the archbishop of Paris, who suggested he refer the matter to Rome.

On his part, Dom Sauton considered the decree of December 17, 1890 a formal condemnation of the practice in usage at Sainte-Cécile;

much more condemnable, then, were the spiritual counsels Mother Cécile gave to this or that monk of Saint-Pierre. He revealed his thoughts to Cardinal Léon Thomas, archbishop of Rouen, who delegated the matter to his auxiliary Bishop de la Passardière. Dom Sauton also spoke about it to the archbishop of Bourges, Jean-Joseph Marchal. According to Albert Houtin, the two prelates imposed upon him an obligation of conscience to inform Rome of the affair. In the recent past, the predecessor of Archbishop Marchal had allowed himself to be misled by the superior of the Société de Marie-Auxiliatrice (Society of Mary Our Help) who sought to expel the foundress, Mother Marie-Thérèse de Soubiran. Thus, the archbishop believed he knew something about the tyranny of certain women religious superiors.

Again according to Albert Houtin, Dom Sauton and Dom de la Tremblaye, with whom the former had shared his secret, "began separately to write down their experiences. Their memoranda were finished by the month of November 1891 and substantiated by supporting documentation. . . . They then wrote a case of conscience to be sent to the pope himself, under the seal of confession: 'Such a monk, knowing of and seeing such things, is he obligated by conscience to denounce them?' Were they to receive an affirmative response, they would then send the memoranda to the pope."[16]

The archbishop of Bourges had offered to be the intermediary to bring the affair to Rome's attention. However, he died. The auxiliary bishop of Rouen, Bishop Jourdan de la Passardière, had no particular reason to go to Rome in the near future. Thus, the abbot of Ligugé "took it upon himself, without informing the two monks, to write to Rome and point out the existence of the documents that were in the hands of Bishop de la Passardière."[17] In response, the Holy Office requested they be sent to Rome. They were dispatched to Cardinal Monaco La Valetta[18] on April 24, 1892.

---

[16] Houtin, *Une grande mystique*, p. 55.
[17] Ibid., p. 56.
[18] Cardinal Raffaele Monaco La Valetta (1827–1896) was Secretary of the Supreme Sacred Congregation of the Holy Office, Dean of the Sacred College of Cardinals, and Major Penitentiary of the Apostolic Penitentiary.—Trans.

These were substantially the facts reported by Albert Houtin. The exactitude with which he speaks is impressive, but his factual statements call for verification, for there are several anachronisms in the very same pages. We can especially point out three instances. The first concerns the description of Saint-Maur de Glanfeuil in 1890 that does not correspond to the actual state of that foundation which had only recently been established, carefully prepared by Dom Couturier. The second is the projected foundation of Sainte-Cécile in Marseilles in 1892, placed at a date when the idea had already been abandoned for many years in favor of a foundation in Wisques. The third chronological mistake is the date of erection of Sainte-Cécile as an abbey. Albert Houtin is not always as well informed as it may seem at a first reading.

Through a procurator he had sent to Rome for a variety of matters, Dom Delatte learned something about the developments that were underway. The abbot asked his delegate to inform the pope, on occasion of an audience, that Dom Sauton and Dom de la Tremblaye, who had become unbearable at Solesmes and had been received by the abbot of Ligugé, did not merit any credit given the behavior they had shown for some years at the monastery. That was the full truth. Leo XIII ordered that the matter be dropped.

Nonetheless, a canonical inquiry was opened on the two monks. Dom Sauton appeared before the bishop of Poitiers on October 18, 1892; he sent a supporting memorandum on November 3 and was called to Rome in January 1893. The Holy Office sought permission from Leo XIII to resume the process of investigation. The two monks and Dom Bourigaud were summoned several times to give their testimony. In his turn, Dom Gauthey—after a disagreement with the General Chapter—made known to the Congregation of Bishops and Regulars his doubts about the fidelity of Dom Delatte to the heritage of Dom Guéranger.

In April 1893, Dom Delatte came to the Eternal City with his prior, Dom Cabrol, for the laying of the first stone of the church at the College of Saint Anselm on the Aventine Hill. All Benedictine abbots had been called to Rome on this occasion, as the Holy Father intended to officially create the Confederation of the Benedictine Order and to proceed to the election of an abbot primate.

On April 8, the abbot of Solesmes received an invitation from the Holy Office to come in person in order to provide certain explanations. In actuality, the measures to be taken had already been set and the explanations required of Dom Delatte were only a matter of form. He was declared suspended from his functions and assigned to a residence in Italy. The provisional government of Saint-Pierre would be assumed by Dom Gauthey, abbot of Sainte-Madeleine. The Abbey of Sainte-Cécile was removed from the authority of the abbot of Solesmes and placed under the sole jurisdiction of the bishop of Le Mans, who would appoint secular priests as confessors to the nuns. All relations between the two monasteries were interdicted, including communication between monks and nuns related by blood. These decisions were submitted to Leo XIII for his signature on April 14.

On May 5, Bishop Labouré of Le Mans came to Solesmes to promulgate these measures in the name of the Holy See and install Dom Gauthey as administrator of Saint-Pierre. The abbey's council entreated the prelate to listen to each monk individually. Though he did not have the mandate for this, nonetheless, he consented to do so out of friendship, limiting himself to listening to the monks. He then saw Mother Cécile, who explained the situation to him as she saw it. The bishop knew in whom he should believe. He was personally convinced of the fundamental inanity of the accusations and decided thenceforward to do whatever was within his capacity to bring the matter to an end. However, he had no power beyond his jurisdiction over the nuns. To assist them, he designated Fathers Lepelletier and Blot, chaplains of Notre-Dame-du-Chêne, who fulfilled their mandate most admirably.

Naturally, in such cases, the public immediately suspects the worst. Rumors circulated calling into doubt the morality of Mother Cécile and Dom Delatte, despite the fact that the denunciations of the Holy Office contained nothing of the sort. The families of the nuns were indignant at such insinuations.

Prince Loëwenstein, with two daughters at Sainte-Cécile, had a primary vested interest in the affair and put his entire family in motion. He interceded with the Holy Father, addressing letters to him and to Cardinal Rampolla,[19] as well as to Cardinal Ledochówski.[20] He asked his sister Adelaïde, married to Miguel de Bragança, the Infante[21] of Portugal, to intervene. She involved her daughter in the action, the Infanta Maria-Antonia, wedded to Robert, the Duke of Bourbon-Parma. Prince Loëwenstein also entreated his nieces, the archduchesses of Austria and Bavaria, to support him in his cause.

Maria Cristina of Habsburg-Lorraine, widow of Alfonso XII and regent of Spain, had great affection for a French nun who was a friend of Sainte-Cécile—Mother Marie-Célestine of the Good Shepherd, prioress of the convent of the Assumption in Madrid. The ties between Solesmes and the Congregation founded by Father d'Alzon and Saint Marie-Eugénie Milleret de Brou, [22] dated from the time of Dom Guéranger. Mother Marie-Eugénie had spent some time at Solesmes in 1888, accompanied by Mother Marie-Célestine. The latter, then, alerted by Mother Cécile as to the alarming proceedings affecting Solesmes, involved the queen regent of Spain as well. However, the insistent entreaties of Queen Maria Cristina before the Holy See did not reap their effect until mid-July. In the meantime, Dom Delatte was given permission to accept the friendly hospitality of Father Schliebusch, with whom he spent the month of July.

---

[19] Cardinal Mariano Rampolla (1843–1913), born in Sicily, was Secretary of State to the Holy See at this time.—Trans.

[20] Cardinal Mieczysław Halka Ledóchowski (1822–1902), born in Górki, Poland, was the Prefect of the Sacred Congregation for the Propagation of the Faith at this time.—Trans.

[21] Infante (infanta, feminine), title of the child of the king/queen of Portugal or Spain who is not the heir to the crown.—Trans.

[22] Saint Marie-Eugénie of Jesus (1817–1898), born Anne Marie Eugénie Milleret in Metz, France, was the daughter of agnostic parents, her father being a wealthy banker and liberal follower of Voltaire. When tragedy beset and rent asunder her family, she moved to Paris where, at age nineteen she attended a Lenten mission retreat preached by Father Lacordaire at Notre-Dame cathedral which brought about her conversion. Under the spiritual guidance of Father Théodore Combalot, apostolic missionary preacher at Saint-Eustace church, she founded in 1839 the Religious of the Assumption, a teaching order whose aim was to spread the reign of Christ in society and in its religious members by evangelizing minds, making families truly Christian and thus transforming the society of her time. She and her companions were assisted in this mission at the beginning by Madame de Chateaubriand, Father Lacordaire, Count de Montalembert and others. Her spiritual director in religious life, Father Emmanual d'Alzon, founded the Augustinians of the Assumption in 1845 with the same mission. Saint Marie-Eugénie was beatified in 1975 and canonized in 2007. As she had not yet been canonized at the time the present book was written, the author refers to her as "Blessed."—Trans.

To find an honorable solution to the crisis, Leo XIII considered granting a post in Rome to Dom Delatte. Under this scenario, Dom Delatte would submit his resignation as abbot of Solesmes and a new election would supply the abbey with another superior. Dom Delatte's response to this possibility was that such a resignation would have a deplorable effect—he had already moved to resign in April and the Holy Office had refused him then (until that point he had only been suspended from his functions). Under the current circumstances, such an action would immediately have the effect of lending weight to the rumors that were already circulating, giving them an appearance of truth, to the great detriment of the two monastic families.

At long last, at the slow pace customary to similar cases, an apostolic visitor, Archbishop Cesare Sambucetti, titular archbishop of Corinth,[23] was sent to conduct an inquiry at Solesmes. He lodged himself at the house of the Mssionaries at Notre-Dame-du-Chêne, and began his work on August 11, 1893. He started with the community of Saint-Pierre, questioning the monks during two weeks, a longer period than is usual for canonical visitations. Following the monks, he inquired with lay individuals, and then passed on to the nuns, finally meeting with Dom Delatte in Paris. His conclusions were ready on September 18. It had taken him six weeks to complete the inquiry—hardly a "sham investigation" as Albert Houtin described it.[24]

In the memoirs of Dom Joseph Blanchon-Lasserve, at the time still a young postulant come from the navy, we read: "After the monks, a great number of friends and enemies of Solesmes, priests, lay men and women, religious men, religious women, came to give their testimony and protest against the errors committed and the events that had been transpiring over the past eight months. Italian diplomat that he was, the archbishop let nothing show, not an impression; he said nothing, reflected within himself, was amiable but very distant."

---

[23] Archbishop Cesare Sambucetti (1838–1911), born in Rome, was a high-ranking diplomat for the Holy See; in 1893 he was made Secretary of the Sacred Congregation of Ceremonies.—Trans.

[24] Houtin, *Une grande mystique*, p. 62.

Once the inquiry was finished, Archbishop Sambucetti entrusted the youngest member of the chapter, as was the custom, Father Georges de Longueau de Saint-Michel, to bring his report to the sovereign pontiff, and then awaited the result. His report was entirely favorable to Dom Delatte and his monks, as well as to the community of Sainte-Cécile and its abbess. From that moment, the pope resolved to keep the two superiors at the head of their respective monasteries *ad nutum Sanctæ Sedis.*[25]

However, the press became involved. On November 13 a scandalous article appeared in *Le Matin* which drew a fulminating rebuttal by Édouard Drumont in *La Libre Parole.* Other periodicals in Paris published articles on the subject, and then those in the provinces entered the fray. To bring a stop to the controversy, which was verging on becoming a scandal, Leo XIII ordered the bishop of Le Mans to immediately reinstate Dom Delatte in his abbatial charge.

But the troubles were not yet all over for Sainte-Cécile. Communication between the abbey and the monastery of Saint-Pierre still remained barred, the monks did not have permission to resume hearing confessions there, and the abbot of Saint-Pierre did not have any jurisdiction over the nuns. There was even talk of assigning a permanent chaplain from the secular clergy to Sainte-Cécile. Bishop Labouré, who in the meantime had become the archbishop of Rennes, actively applied himself to having the links between the two monasteries reestablished. The hoped for resolution did not come about until February 1894.

During this time, the Holy Office had undertaken a thorough examination of Mother Cécile's book about prayer. In *La Cathédrale,* in a dialogue between Durtal and Father Plomb, Huysmans alludes to this meticulous inquiry into the orthodoxy of the doctrine expounded in the abbess's work:

---

[25] Expression in canon law which signifies that a decision taken has no other limit in time than that given by the Holy See. ["At the disposition of the Holy See." It refers to any circumstance where the Holy See decides to take a matter under its own jurisdiction and reserves to itself the right to make a final judgment on the matter. Definition from Fr. John Hardon's *Modern Catholic Dictionary*—Trans.]

"Isn't she the author of a *Treatise on Prayer* which I perused some time ago at the Trappist monastery, but that, I believe, wasn't looked favorably upon by the Vatican?"

"Yes, it is she indeed. But you are roundly mistaken in imagining that her book might have displeased Rome. As with all works of the kind, it was examined under a microscope, passed through a sieve, line by line, turned inside out, and the theologians charged with conducting this pious screening recognized and certified that this work, conceived according to the surest principles of mysticism, is learnedly, resolutely, totally orthodox."

There was nothing that could be said against Mother Cécile's book. However, an account of mental prayer included in Dom Sauton's files caught the attention of theologians of the Holy Office. It was an inaccurate copy made by him of a document dated October 12, 1886, written by Mother Cécile solely for her confessor, Dom Logerot. The latter had shown it to some of his novices so that they could share in his admiration. The text dealt with the mission of spiritual motherhood. Five propositions judged to be questionable were drawn from it which every monk and nun was required to reject. Bishop Labouré came in December to have each member of the two communities sign in secrecy the Roman document condemning the propositions judged to be inexact. All of them complied without hesitation.

Undoubtedly through Dom Sauton, the document came to the hands of Albert Houtin who innocently comments: "The signing of the formulary, kept extremely confidential, . . . was divulged, *I believe*, for the first time in a small, little-read journal, the *Revue de l'Anjou*, in its July-August 1901 issue."[26] Interestingly, this is the journal to which he contributed his own articles at this period on regional history, and it was he, most probably, who occasioned the disclosure he writes about!

To reproduce the censured document and the propositions drawn from it, would entail too long an explanation here. The text evokes a very ancient spiritual doctrine, that of the birth of God in man, of

[26] Houtin, *Une grande mystique*, p. 69.

which Mary is the model. It has its source in Origen[27] and the Fathers of the Church who adopted the notion from him, a theme well-known by the mystics. It is next found in Saint Augustine and Saint Bernard, and is developed by Meister Eckhart[28] and the German theological school. It is magnificently illustrated by Angelus Silesius.[29] But isolated from its context and rendered as propositions, it alarmed the Holy See's theologians and called for rectification.

In its essence, thus went the crisis that assailed the two monasteries during the eight months from April to November 1893. Compared to what may be found in the history of many other congregations, this crisis was altogether relatively limited; however, it left deep marks upon its victims.

The ensuing deterioration of Mother Cécile's health seems to have been the sequel to the crisis. The Lord used this distressing episode to render her even more detached, to plunge her even more deeply into humility, and thus imbue her actions with even greater fecundity.

---

[27]Origen of Alexandria (185–254), biblical exegete, mystical writer, considered one of the most brilliant Christian apologists of his time; he died probably as a result of severe torture which he suffered for the faith. He was much admired and consulted by a great number of his contemporaries and beyond, as alluded to in this paragraph. However, several of his theories were condemned by the Second Council of Constantinople in 553, including the notions of inequality among the divine Persons of the Holy Trinity and of the existence of human souls prior to the creation of man, the theory that the supreme and essential sense of the Scripture is allegorical, and the claim that the devil and those in hell will eventually be saved, absorbed by the one Fount of Beauty.—Trans.

[28] Eckhart von Hochheim (c. 1260–c. 1328), Dominican theologian, philosopher and mystic, was born in Gotha, central Germany, and held several charges as superior in the Dominican Order in Germany. Referred to contemporarily as "Meister" or Master because of his academic title *Magister in theologia* obtained at the University of Paris, he is a controversial figure, whose mystical writings were alternately considered heretical, then exonerated as orthodox by the Holy See in 1327, and then again condemned in a Bull of 1329. He himself made a profession of faith, repudiated any error, and submitted himself to the judgment of the Holy See. The problematic traits in his sermons and writings were reflective of quietism and pantheism.—Trans.

[29] Angelus Sibelius (1624–1677), born Johann Scheffler in Silesia (Breslau/Wrocław), was the son of a Lutheran Polish nobleman and a German mother. He completed doctorates in philosophy and medicine in Padua, and entered the Catholic Church in 1653, taking "Angelus" as his confirmation name. In 1661 he was ordained a priest and retired to the monastery of the Knights of the Cross in Breslau, where he died. A mystic and poet, many of his poems were set to music as religious songs, some of which have allusions that have been considered pantheistic or quietist even during his lifetime, but which he defended as orthodox. His *The Cherubim Pilgrim* was published with an imprimatur, and includes a preface in which he explains his paradoxes.—Trans.

Upon the outburst of the storm, she wrote to the prioress of Bonlieu: "Nothing gives me either pleasure or pain. For one month I thought that a defamatory memorandum written by two monks of Solesmes who were my children and took advantage of me for many years . . . would have grave consequences for me vis-à-vis the Holy Office in Rome. It was all so horrible, so malicious, so perverse that the Right Reverend Father became ill, and our prior was out of himself when he discovered this secret affair on the day of St. Anne, on the occasion of a visit to Rome for another matter. As for myself, I told the Lord without any emotion: 'It is your business; my reputation is Yours like everything else.'"[30]

Around the same time, she wrote to the abbess of Stanbrook: "It seemed to me that care for my honor belonged much more to the Lord than it did to me, and after having spent a long period of my life concerned more about honor than about life, I realized that I was no longer concerned about either one or the other, and that this type of deprivation was not without its joy. . . . You know this better than I, Madame Abbess and very dear daughter, having advanced on this path with distinction before we did."[31] Mother Cécile is alluding here to the tempest that assailed Stanbrook because of the actions taken by her nuns to obtain the abbacy for life for their superior directly from Rome.

At the height of the crisis, Mother Cécile told Father Schliebusch: "We are quite simply in the divine hands of Him who has deigned to take seriously the offering of all our being which we so often renew. Isn't it only just that among the members of Our Lord Jesus Christ there be some who consent to be attached to the same cross as He, to die with Him, according to the will of the Heavenly Father and for the adorable purposes of His intentions? . . . It simply seems to me that we do not have a future, or better, that we have only the future that God will fashion for us. I expect everything and I expect nothing at all. The Lord is sufficiently powerful to bring us back to life if He so desires. I prefer to abandon everything to Him, to owe everything to Him, He knows well what we need in order to live."[32]

---

[30] Letter dated September 23, 1892.
[31] Letter dated November 4, 1892.
[32] Letter dated May 20, 1893.

"For me it is obviously much more than my mode of existence that is at risk, seeing the existence (of Solesmes) at risk" she wrote to Father Schliebusch some time later. "Still, the Lord knows well that it is without being troubled, without anxiety that I would watch everything collapse at one sign, not of His will, but by His good pleasure. I perceive most distinctly that, if the natural and supernatural world would be annihilated at one blow, nothing would be missing to the Being, to Him Who fills everything and Who is all beauty, all truth, all perfection. Nothing that has been created has added or can add a single iota to the Infinite. This sentiment, when it runs deeply and has been experienced, is the source of a certain firmness that nothing can move."[33]

But the blow from the trial was beyond what the physical constitution of Mother Cécile could bear. She emerged from it exhausted from so much suffering. Her health was forever sapped of its vitality and strength.

---

[33] Letter dated June 28, 1893.

Chapter 32

And There Was a Great Calm

THE EVENTS OF 1893 LEFT their mark. It is not unusual to find in random publications some echo of the accusations made by Dom Sauton and spread by Albert Houtin. However, the monk-doctor demonstrated by his writings that his intelligence was little more than mediocre. The text in which he speaks of the first years of Dom Delatte and his teachings to the community is a catalogue of misinterpretations and lack of understanding of the spiritual doctrine expounded by the abbot. This can be verified rather easily by those who are familiar with Dom Delatte's thought and know his writings, a great portion of which has been published. Dom Sauton accumulated misinterpretation upon misinterpretation with such ease, it would seem he did so deliberately. His dislike for Dom Delatte distorted his own judgment—he saw in the teachings of Dom Delatte a type of quietism! As to women's psychology, it seems to have escaped him altogether.

If the community at Saint-Pierre was generally united around its father abbot, it became even more so after the trial. During the last weeks of the interim abbacy at Solesmes of Dom Gauthey, he himself took away most of the monks who were still hostile to Dom Delatte. Dom Joseph Blanchon-Lasserve writes in his memoirs: "In October we learned of the departure of Dom Gauthey for Marseilles; he will take Dom Rigaud with him. Other monks are leaving for Ligugé."

At Sainte-Cécile, the denunciations made in Rome had surprised and scandalized everyone. The nuns were deeply pained by it all. Mother Thècle, the half-sister of Dom Delatte, who did not even have permission to write him, was the most affected. At the height of the trial, Mother Cécile wrote to Father Schliebusch: "Things here are going gently and in peace. Time seems very slow, but no one complains. All are behaving very well. We are learning the psalms in such a way that it seems that their meaning is given to each nun. In particular, I am keeping my eye on my little Mother Thècle, for I well know how much tenderness is enclosed within her fortitude; but she is doing well. Someone who is very much changed is Mother Bénédicte of Loëwenstein. I would never have imagined that she could be so affected. In the beginning, tears streamed unceasingly from her eyes and everyone noted (some with astonishment) the tenderness and delicacy of this soul so pure. She is almost able to express herself to me now. Her solicitude surrounded Mother Thècle on all sides; it seemed she wanted to place herself between her and anything that might affect her. And thus each one of us continues on."[1]

Unlike the situation at Saint-Pierre, at Sainte-Cécile not a member of the community would have thought of contesting the government or teaching of the abbess, nor that of Dom Delatte. Mother Cécile remained in charge during the crisis with the total support of Bishop Labouré.

To certain select correspondents, she spoke of the dispositions of her soul even before the fury of the storm had erupted. She was filled with a profound peace, beyond sufferings and joys. Writing about it, she points out the apparent contradiction: "I have not had time to be distressed; moreover, when I intend to capture this intolerable torture that would make one cry out *Tristis est anima mea usque ad mortem* (My soul is sorrowful even unto death. Mt 26:38), it all disappears, and by the time it goes from my heart to my pen it has become the image of perfect contentment. Everything causes me an intolerable repugnance, and nothing weighs upon me or bothers me; I can no longer suffer from anything or anyone, and everything seems to me as light to bear as a feather. I am flat and colorless with regards to the things of God, and I have no desire for any of the favors once received. Isn't this so strange?"[2]

Her correspondent, the prioress of the Nobertines of Bonlieu, did not think this was surprising, because the experiences of her own life held many similarities to those lived by Mother Cécile. Their friendship dated from 1883. Mother Marie de La Croix was slightly older than the abbess, having been born in Toulouse on March 18, 1840, to the family of Colonel Odiot. She spent her childhood at a

---

[1] Letter dated July 9, 1893.
[2] Letter to Mother Marie de la Croix, March 29, 1892.

family property near Avignon, where she exercised an influence similar to that of Jenny Bruyère at Chantenay. At age thirty, in 1870, after a novitiate at the Trappistine nuns of Maubec, close to Montélimar, she made her profession in the Order of Norbertines (Premonstratensians) at the hands of the bishop of Valence. She and some companions took up quarters in the Cistercian abbey of Bonlieu,[3] a few miles from Maubec, attaching their monastery to the Norbertine province of Brabant which was under the jurisdiction of the abbot of Tongerloo.

It was the Cistercian abbot of Aiguebelle,[4] Dom Marie-Gabriel, a great friend of Solesmes, who advised her to seek the help of Mother Cécile and spend some time at the Abbey of Sainte-Cécile. The first visit occurred in the fall of 1887. Perhaps excepting the abbess of Stanbrook, there were few people with whom Mother Cécile felt such great affinity.

"When you tell me these confidences about your soul, my dear and good Mother," wrote Mother Cécile to Mother Marie de la Croix, "I so identically recognize myself in what you say that I could use your letters to describe myself. What great force the sacrament of baptism has; it is like the root of the soul that is thus stripped, isn't it so? Then, there is the need to be patient in everything and wait for everything from God, taking refuge deeply in Him. The accidentals fade away and the light, now uniform, no longer highlights anything. What a singular existence this is, which definitely is no longer in time, but which is not yet eternity! This often makes me think of the stylites[5] lifted between the earth and the sky, immobile on their

---

[3] The abbey of Bonlieu, in the region of the Rhône-Alpes, was established in 1171 by the Viscountess of Marsanne for a community of Cistercian nuns, passing to the hands of Cistercian monks in the sixteenth century. It had been abandoned since the dissolution imposed by the French Revolution. —Trans.

[4] The abbey of Aiguebelle was founded in 1137, by monks from the abbey of Morimond, the fourth daughter house of the abbey of Citeaux, cradle of the Cistercian Order. After the dispersion of 1791, its buildings were pillaged and then sold as national property. In 1815 a group of Cistercians originally from La Trappe, returned from their exile in Switzerland to resettle the abbey of Aiguebelle, led by Abbot Augustin de Lestranges. —Trans.

[5] The stylite was a solitary, or hermit, who lived at the top of a pillar, performing great austerities and mortifications as penance for the corruption of society, and also preaching to the people from his stark abode. It is a phenomenon of the Middle East and Eastern churches, having emerged in Syria in the fifth century. —Trans.

columns, having no space and, nonetheless, having a solid rock on which to support themselves, with all the solitude and isolation of the desert and yet all the inconveniences of a crowd. It is like a crucifixion with a type of resurrection, for there are no ties or nails. It is like the beginning of an ascension without leaving the rock of faith. Often I think of my Saint Cecilia lying below the altar, neither dead, nor alive, her head turned to the side, away from all that is created, performing only one act—a confession of the Holy Trinity; no longer moving, her neck half-cleaved, and obtaining, in this way, the consecration of her house as a church."[6]

Whoever calls to mind the statue of Saint Cecilia[7] by Maderno, a replica of which was under the main altar of the abbatial church, immediately will understand what Mother Cécile means. Her face is enveloped in a veil, her head is turned on its side, toward the back of the altar, and the neck shows the large wound cut by the two-edged sword that was unable to sever her head. The three extended fingers of the right hand signal confession of the Trinity, with the fourth and fifth fingers bent against the palm, as in the gesture of the Christ-Pantocrator as he appears in the early Roman churches, at the entrance door or on the vault above the apse.

Thirty-three years had gone by since Mother Cécile had received the abbatial blessing, and it had been thirty-seven years since she had been governing the community which continued to grow, despite the reduction brought about by the foundation of Notre-Dame de Wisques in 1889.

---

[6] Letter to Mother Marie de la Croix, May 7, 1892.

[7] Saint Cecilia, young Roman noblewoman of the early centuries (date unknown), was martyred after having defended the tenets of the Christian faith before the Prefect of Rome. After surviving an attempt to suffocate her in the baths of her house, she was beheaded; but the hesitant executioner could not sever her head after having struck three times and left her yet alive. It took three days for her to die, during which the faithful came to pay their homage. She finally passed away with a statement of faith, signaling her belief in the Holy Trinity, as the author explains, with three fingers extended in the right hand, and one finger extended in the left. Because of her high position, her execution was carried out in her own house that then became a church of the early Christians, which is what Mother Cécile alludes to here. In the crypt chapel immediately below the high altar of her church is enshrined her body, which was still incorrupt when her tomb was opened in 1599 (as noted in chap. 17, p. 166, n. 4). Maderno's statue, based on her own figure as it appeared then, is located below the high altar.—Trans.

When Bishop Labouré came in name of the Holy See to reinstall Dom Delatte as abbot of Solesmes, the time was nearing for his departure from the diocese of Le Mans. When he returned a little later to have members of Saint-Pierre and Sainte-Cécile sign the formulary required by the Holy Office, he was already the archbishop of Rennes. According to the *Memoirs* of Cardinal Ferrata, Leo XIII saw to it that the new bishop of Le Mans be chosen carefully, because among the clergy there were those who had sided with Solesmes, and those who had been against it, so that the clergy was still divided on the issue. The choice was for Msgr. Charles Gilbert,[8] vicar general of Limoges. "He could not be more considerate, more intelligent and more self-assured," wrote the abbess about him.

At the beginning of 1894, Mother Thérèse Bernard made the trip to Solesmes to settle several matters related to Notre-Dame de Wisques, which was rapidly growing. "Even though it is late, I cannot bear it any longer, and am going to talk a little with you, as I have done during the day with my big daughter of Wisques, for she is here," wrote Mother Cécile to the abbess of Stanbrook. "You know it, and you are happy about it, I am sure. It is like a dream for me, a beautiful dream, because after these long months, there was so much to talk about! Vainly did we keep up a continuous flow of letters; there are a thousand things that escape us, which in conversation come to mind and pour forth. If only you were here, it would be perfect indeed. Your name is always coming to our lips. . . . You have all prayed so much for us that truly all have behaved as chosen souls. We are mighty calm. Our health has been more affected than our souls. Mere children, such as your little dove (the very young Mother Anne-Cécile Blanchon-Lasserve), have shown firmness and serenity to a heroic degree. . . . Truly, they have progressed by giant steps, quietly, in all simplicity, in all profundity. I myself can barely explain it; I wish you could see it yourself."[9]

We are fortunate to have some words from Mother Thérèse Bernard about the monastery of Sainte-Cécile at that time. They are directed to a Carthusian monk: "I speak of what I've seen. The

---

[8] Charles-Joseph-Louis-Abel Gilbert (1849–1914), bishop of Le Mans from 1894 to 1897, when he resigned.—Trans.

[9] Letter dated January 16, 1894.

attitude of our venerated mother is ineffable, sweeter than ever and always calm. The unity of the community has increased, for all have suffered with one heart and one soul. What I see here is truly the consecration of suffering settling upon the walls of Sainte-Cécile. A phrase from Saint Cecilia's office keeps returning to me, in that passage where the martyr dedicates her dwelling to God—*Virginali cruore consecratam* (consecrated by virginal blood)."[10]

At Wisques, unbeknownst to its prioress, the members of the chapter had written Mother Cécile to inquire whether it would not be good to take the necessary measures in order to erect their monastery as an abbey, since now the chapter had thirteen perpetually professed nuns. Mother Cécile thought it was still early, but Dom Delatte was of the opinion that she should move ahead with this, perhaps to show the Congregation of Bishops and Regulars that there had been no basis for the alarm felt at Rome in the previous year, and that the work of God was progressing. Therefore, it was to deal with this matter that Mother Thérèse—now informed of the desire of her nuns—came to Solesmes for the first time since she had left Sainte-Cécile for the foundation.

The project came together in May, when Dom Hildebrand de Hemptinne, the new primate of the Order, made his canonical visit to Notre-Dame de Wisques, accompanied by Dom Delatte. Leo XIII had charged him with visiting all the monasteries of the Congregation of France and with preparing the General Chapter himself, so as to eliminate any possible sequels to the crisis of the previous year. The new ordinary of Arras, Bishop Alfred Williez,[11] approved the abbatial erection of the monastery.

On July 7, 1894, the nuns of Wisques departed from the large chateau where they had begun their foundation, leaving it to the monks. They settled in the already finished section of their new monastery, which was being built at a certain distance, at the top of the hill that dominates the valley of the Aa river and the town of Saint-Omer.

---

[10] Cited by Dom Delatte in "Vie," chap. 12.
[11] Alfred-Casimir-Alexis Williez (1836–1911), bishop of Arras from 1892 to his death.—Trans.

On July 14, the Bishop of Arras came to Wisques to perform the blessing of the new monastery and its regular places.[12] He established the enclosure and then proceeded to the provisional chapter room to preside over the election of the first abbess. As expected by all, it was Mother Thérèse who was elected. Some days later, Mother Cécile wrote to the nuns of Wisques: "My very dear daughters, it seems that I love you even more since the election, when you spontaneously and readily ratified the choice made five years ago of whom you should have for your mother. Truly, the Church has been so gracious toward you in calling you to render such a resounding witness in favor of her who has generously given you of her cares and her efforts. The abbatial blessing of September 16 will crown and confirm the graces of this year."[13]

Dom de Hemptinne had come to Sainte-Cécile for his first visit as primate in February of the same year. On that occasion, he spoke with Mother Cécile about the crisis of the previous year, a conversation which she rendered in playful terms in a letter dated April 16 to Mother Marie-Célestine, religious of the Assumption:

"The Very Reverend Dom de Hemptinne is haunted by my illuminism. He vigorously questioned me on this point, which is the principal reason for the miseries assailing the Congregation of France!!! But where can this illuminism be found? Where is the proof of it? At the Holy Office they repeatedly went through *L'Oraison* with the intent of finding errors therein, and had to give it a full certificate of orthodoxy (a negative and moral certificate, of course). If my so-called doctrine is anywhere, it is in that book. But, says the primate, this book does not have the charm of the writings of Saint Teresa. He cannot find any mention of personal experiences. Instead of relying on herself, Madame Abbess is relying on Sacred Scripture and the Fathers! That was indeed my intention, my dear Mother, believing that my personal testimony would have little to offer compared to those sources. There is another reproach that the primate presented to me. 'What do you want? You have a reputation for sanctity (I started laughing) . . . people consult you, all that makes for trouble, etc., etc.' I

---

[12] The "regular places," (from the Latin *regula*, "rule") of a monastery are the choir, chapter, refectory, cloister and dormitory.—Trans.
[13] Letter dated July 16, 1894.

would like to know what I should do to avoid this regrettable reputation, and I have never been able to understand how to go about it. How much I wish that you could see the good primate so that you could prove to him that I am not at all saintly, that I do not desire any reputation, that, of myself, I would love people to leave me tranquilly alone and that this would be the fulfillment of my desires."

However, at the end of his canonical visitation to Saint-Pierre and Sainte-Cécile, Dom de Hemptinne stated: "I will have to tell the Holy Father that at Solesmes I have found one hundred monks and nuns who say the same thing. It is an imposing unanimity."[14] In his report on his visitation to the nuns he stated that Sainte-Cécile was a chosen garden reminiscent of Eden, and acknowledged that the perfection of monastic observance he encountered there was principally due to the prudent government of the abbess. Dom de Hemptinne's secretary clarified further: "The Right Reverend Primate was enchanted with his visit to Sainte-Cécile, much more so than he lets transpire in his letter of visitation."[15] Following his report to the Holy Father, the accusations of 1893 were definitively closed in Rome.

At Saint-Pierre, the monks were able, at long last, to re-enter their walls, after fourteen years of harassment including twelve years of siege in the village. No longer would there be the liturgical celebrations in two choirs—imposed by circumstances—that had triggered such anxieties in Rome the previous year.

Mother Cécile, like Dom Delatte, was delighted without reservation. In 1891, upon returning from his first canonical visit to the other monasteries of the Congregation of France, the abbot had said that "this trip had been a revelation to him, as never before had he had the opportunity to observe the *regular* monastic life, and that he was happy to have been able to form an idea of it now by visiting Saint-Maur, Ligugé, Silos and Marseilles."[16] In effect, when Dom Delatte entered Solesmes, the monks were living after the manner of a *laura*[17] in the village. Despite his efforts, he had not been able to

---

[14] Delatte, "Vie," chap. 12.

[15] Ibid.

[16] Houtin, *Une grande mystique*, p. 267.

[17] Laura: monastery formed by cells dispersed around a church and conventual buildings. [First spoken of in Palestine, in the fifth century, the laura comprised individual hermitages

transform the community, dispersed outside the walls of the abbey, into a homogeneous body, as can only happen under the normal conditions of life led in the interior of a monastery. That is why, starting in 1891, he began his efforts to have the interdiction on their monastery lifted.

"Gradually the monks all returned," writes Dom Joseph Blanchon-Lasserve in his memoirs, "and we took possession of the abbey, the entire church and the buildings. For some time the police remained there, supposedly to see if there would be any problems, but they lodged themselves by the print shop; then they left after a farewell visit. We were back home now, and people could come to our Offices and our Masses."[18]

Mother Cécile went to Wisques for the abbatial blessing of September 16, 1894, accompanied by Sister Bénédicte of Loëwenstein. She brought along with her a small volume she had written for use of the new abbess—"Recommendations to a newly elected abbess"—which she had begun at the time of the establishment of the foundation at Wisques, but had not had the time to finish until this point.

Upon returning, she wrote to Mother Thérèse: "My thoughts have unceasingly dwelt on that grand beautiful Sunday of inexhaustible memories. What joy you have given me, sweet daughter, for yourself, for your daughters, for the beautiful white walls, and what acts of thanksgiving should be raised to Him Who has done everything in you and by you! Surely, I cannot leave such a place; I joyfully remain there with you."[19]

Since 1889, Sainte-Cécile had more than filled the places vacated by the sisters who had first departed for Wisques. Many candidates had presented themselves during the years that followed the first foundation. The number of actual members of the community at Sainte-Cécile was now approaching one hundred. The earlier problem of an overpopulated monastery, with the consequent mounting expenses, was again weighing upon the abbess. The bishop

built around a church where the hermits gathered periodically for liturgical functions celebrated in common.—Trans.]
[18] In actuality, things did not unfold that simply. See *Lettre aux amis de Solesmes*, 1996, p. 3.
[19] Letter dated September 23, 1894.

of Rodez, Joseph Bourret,[20] made a cardinal in 1893, had submitted his request for a foundation, but his diocese was no doubt a bit too close to that of Albi where the monastery of Dourgne was being erected.[21] Moreover, Bishop Bécel of the diocese of Vannes, a long time friend, had long been clamoring for a house of Sainte-Cécile. Preference was given to the latter, in Brittany.

Mother Cécile was making slow but steady progress in her monumental work of collecting materials intended for a biography of Dom Guéranger. Before the crisis, she had estimated that two years would be sufficient to arrive at the end of the project, when, in fact, it took her seven years to complete it. Once this work were finished, she planned on finding some time to write the Annals of Sainte-Cécile. Previously, in 1891, she had summarized the conferences that Dom Guéranger had given at Sainte-Cécile into one large volume, using notes taken by sundry sisters on loose sheets of paper. She then proceeded to compose a customary for the extern sisters,[22] providing in detail for all the circumstances of their life.

---

[20] Joseph-Christian-Ernest Cardinal Bourret, C.O. (1827–1896) was Bishop of Rodez, in the south of France, from 1871 to his death, and was elevated to the cardinalate as cardinal-priest of Santa Maria Nuova in 1893.—Trans.

[21] See chap. 26, p. 258 ff.—Trans.

[22] "Coutumier des Oblates du tour" literally a "Customary for the oblates of the turn." In current terminology, these would be the "extern sisters" of a cloistered community, who deal with external matters and with the public, functioning outside of the cloister. "Turn" refers to the rotating, cylindrical device opened on one side, used in cloistered monasteries for conveying objects from the public area into the cloistered area and vice versa.—Trans.

Chapter 33

The Foundation of Kergonan

A LETTER FROM MOTHER CÉCILE to a friend, the prioress of the Carmel of Niort, written around the time we are examining, shows to what point she was convinced that she was only a mere tool for the work that God had made spring forth from her hands. "Something which greatly amuses me is the idea you have that I have done all that! Never has that thought come to me and I am still stunned and astonished that it could have occurred to you. In the beginning, during the first eight years, I was but a docile little girl, very obedient, who, having used up all my energies to be able to leave the paternal hearth, was reduced to the state of rice pudding. I was, thus, only the executor of the intentions of Dom Guéranger. After him, I continued to maintain the impulse he had given, day by day, without initiative or spontaneity, as if he were to return the following day. Around me and with me I had daughters much more capable than I, and to whom I only had to say: 'Yes, that is fine.' Truly, dear Mother, when I look around myself I could well exclaim with the doge of Genoa, 'What astonishes me the most, is to find myself here!'[1] I have no more the sense that I have anything to do with what is accomplished here than that I have lived at the other side of the globe. And I am astonished at times—when I think about it, which is very rare—that the Lord should have guarded me so well so as not to allow me to hinder anything."[2]

Those who were close to Mother Cécile and truly knew her well, would know that these sentiments were not rote formulas learned

---

[1] This refers to a historic audience the Doge of Genoa had with King Louis XIV at the Versailles palaces, an event celebrated in a painting by Claude-Guy Hallé. After Genoa had broken faith with France by supporting Spain in the French-Spanish war, Louis XIV insisted that the doge come to Versailles to beg his pardon in person. This was done on May 15, 1685. In order to come to the king, the doge and his retinue had to make their way through large crowds gathered in the several rooms that had to be crossed before reaching the king's apartments, which was accomplished with some difficulty.—Trans.

[2] Letter dated February 21, 1897.

and repeated without conviction. She was and wished to be the disciple and continuator of Dom Guéranger, nothing else.

In the first days, she had dreaded the possible coming of Princess Catherine of Hohenzollern, whom Dom Guéranger had succeeded in redirecting away from Sainte-Cécile. Later, her fears were renewed with the entrance of the two Loëwenstein princesses. However, she was then able to appreciate their profound religious sensibility. Their aunt, the sister of Prince Charles of Loëwenstein and widow of Dom Miguel de Bragança, Infante of Portugal,[3] was a fervent admirer of Mother Cécile's book on prayer and the spiritual life. She, in turn, asked to join her two nieces at Sainte-Cécile.

"In two weeks I will be receiving H.R.H. the Duchess of Bragança, widow of Dom Miguel and mother of Maria Teresa, the future empress of Austria!!!" she wrote to the abbess of Stanbrook. "In no way did she want to hear about Prague, nor of any other monastery. . . . I did my best to prove to her that the republic would separate her even more from her children . . . it was of no use. This place is 'unique'!!! And her trust in the abbess unmatched!!! This is all so singular, on both counts."[4]

The relationship between Solesmes and Bishop Bécel of Vannes dated from the years immediately following the death of Dom Guéranger—almost as long-lasting as the friendship with Father Schliebusch. The Bishop once invited Dom Couturier to the shrine of Sainte-Anne d'Auray for a celebration in March 1877 that would inaugurate the proper office of Saint Anne which had been approved for the diocese of Vannes. On this occasion, he named Dom Couturier honorary canon of his cathedral, and himself communicated the fact to Mother Cécile: "I do not want to leave to anyone else the task of

---

[3] Dom Miguel de Bragança (1802–1866), was King of Portugal and the Algarves between 1828 and 1834. He was the son of King João VI of Portugal, who fled to Brazil during Napoleon's occupation. There, his eldest son and heir, Dom Pedro I, declared the independence of Brazil from Portugal in 1822 and made himself Emperor of Brazil. This situation weighed upon Dom Miguel's claims to the throne of Portugal when João VI died, as Dom Pedro abdicated in favor of his seven-year-old daughter Maria II. Supported by the conservatives in the Cortes, Dom Miguel assumed the throne in 1828. In 1833, Dom Pedro sailed from Brazil to lead a fleet that defeated Miguel's forces when the English joined the conflict in favor of Dom Pedro. Dom Miguel went into exile in 1834, married Princess Adelaide of Loëwenstein in 1851, and died in Karlsruhe, Germany in 1866.—Trans.

[4] Letter to Mother Gertrude d'Aurillac Dubois dated September 21, 1895.

announcing to you that I have forged ties of honor, if not of jurisdiction, between Solesmes and Vannes."[5]

The project of a foundation in Brittany, in his diocese, dated from the month that Dom Delatte had spent in exile in July 1893, at the home of Father Schliebusch in Kerentrech. The initiative came from Bishop Bécel, but it would seem that the curate of Kerentrech had much to do with it, in his great friendship for the two abbeys.

Bishop Bécel's principal interest was for a future monastery of nuns. However, the monks would be the first to arrive and would expedite the nuns' arrival by assuring their spiritual assistance. In the chronicles of the foundation of the monastery of Sainte-Anne[6] it reads: "For the bishop of Vannes, one monastery was not sufficient; two were needed. Perhaps the first was only a means to arriving at the second. For many years already Bishop Bécel had not been shy about openly expressing, at every occasion, his affectionate veneration for Sainte-Cécile and his desire to receive an issue from that house in his diocese." The crisis of 1893 had not cooled his sentiments, quite the contrary.

The difficulty with twin foundations was having enough space for them both. At Wisques, the property extended over 250 acres, enough for the two monasteries to be set totally apart from each other. In his book *L'Oblat* (*The Oblate*), Huysmans had a bit of criticism for Solesmes through the figure of his character Durtal, who states to the monks of the fictitious Val-des-Saints, which stands for Ligugé: "You are happily poor and, consequently, are not disturbed by a fixation for building palaces and buying parks." The "palace," was the great Mellet building[7] dominating the Sarthe river which Dom Delatte had had erected; the "parks" were the properties of Wisques and Kergonan. But it is difficult to make a foundation without enough land.

---

[5] Letter dated March 7, 1877.

[6] This is the monks' monastery.—Trans.

[7] Dom Jules Mellet, a Benedictine, and his brother Henri, both architects from Rennes, partly rebuilt the Abbey of Saint-Pierre starting in 1895—an enlargement undertaken to accommodate the ever-growing community. The old lodgings of the abbot and the guest house were demolished, and massive buildings were erected to house a new kitchen, refectory, cells, scriptorium and the abbot's chamber.—Trans.

Two estates were proposed at first: the chateau of Kergonan, looking over the village of Trinité-sur-Mer, and a chateau by the Auray river, once owned by the celebrated Breton penitent of the seventeenth century, Pierre Le Gouvello de Kériolet,[8] friend of Monsieur de la Dauversière.[9] But both "parks" were too small to satisfy the "greed" of the monks and the nuns of Solesmes. Divided in two, there was not much left for either community.

The curate of Plouharnel, aware of the project, let them know that the estate of Kergonan was available—185 acres of land with the ruins of a chateau. The property belonged to an officer of the cavalry stationed at Sedan, Monsieur Latour-Lavigerie, who wanted to sell it. They would need to move quickly before another buyer might present himself.

The proposal had its attraction, given that the property included quarries of granite that would only have to be extracted to provide sufficient material for the construction of the two monasteries. But the estate's high price gave pause to Dom Delatte, who was at this same time beginning a campaign to build at Saint-Pierre. The Abbey of Sainte-Cécile, in its turn, was temporarily in a difficult situation following a bad investment. Mother Cécile thought of commending the affair to the Infant Jesus of Prague; the stocks then rose at the exchange, permitting them to acquire Kergonan.

On April 18, 1895, Dom Delatte came to Kergonan accompanied by Dom Bouré, a monk of old Breton stock. Upon his return on April 22, he submitted the project to the chapter of Solesmes. As had occurred with Wisques in 1889, Sainte-Cécile, more affluent than Saint-Pierre, offered a part of the land reserved for the nuns to the monks. The transfer of deed was signed at Carnac on June 4, 1895, the

---

[8] Pierre Le Gouvello de Kériolet (1602–1660) born to a family of the low nobility in Brittany, grew to be a notoriously egregious personality: arrogant, proud, violent, dishonest, and licentious. At one point he set off for Turkey to become a Muslim, but was diverted on his way; at a later date, he apostatized as a Huguenot so as to obtain money from his family to return to the Catholic Church. He was involved in satanic rites. Ironically, it was his presence at the exorcism of a community of Ursuline nuns in Loudun, an historic case of possession, that finally brought about his lasting conversion. He was eventually ordained a priest and was a frequenter of the Shrine of St. Anne in Auray, where the Carmelite friars, custodians of the shrine, had a cell for him in permanence and where his remains are now entombed.—Trans.

[9] Jérôme Le Royer de la Dauversière (1597–1659) was a founder of the city of Montreal.

price having been settled at seventy thousand francs, so that the total paid, including registration fees, amounted to eighty-one thousand.

The person who had let the monks use his name as buyer, wrote in a letter of June 29, 1895: "The location is superb, with a magnificent view. From a terrace, one can see the ocean to one side, and to the other, the belfry of Sainte-Anne's shrine with its golden statue. The terrain surrounding the old manor is well cultivated; it is your portion of the land [the nuns' portion], I believe, and, according to my mother, it is certainly the best. The portion reserved for the fathers, that is, *my property*, is somewhat less lush with some moors and woods of maritime pines. But the soil is good."

Kergonan is in the heart of the great megalithic region of Brittany, with the alignments of menhirs of Carnac to one side, and the numerous dolmens between Plouharnel and Erdeven to the other side. A dolmen sits at the entrance of the way that leads to the nuns' monastery.

Within the 185 acres of the estate, there were three farms whose buildings were located on the tract of land destined for the nuns. The latter, however, were not yet ready to begin construction of their monastery, so cancellation of the farm leases was left to a future date. The monks would be the first to build on the property and move in, arriving before their sisters.

Mother Cécile had not as yet explored the site and the bishop urged her to do so without further delay: "If it pleases the Lord, Our Lady and Saint Anne, in one month we will be seeing each other," wrote Mother Cécile to Father Schliebusch. "For me, such a trip is solemn; it is worth a procession. To take possession of such a land in order to establish there the praises of God, is a solemn thing. Just the thought of it recollects my soul more than anything else; for, after all, it is as if we were to fulfill the first three petitions of the Our Father. . . . I will come ask for your blessing for this little germ of an abbey which will be very much your own, for it will be the daughter of your prayers, of your work and your sufferings. Yes, venerable father, the two foundations of Kergonan will look at you as their patriarch. Come now, I know well where their foundations will rest: besides the profession of July 26, 1837[10] [on the feast of Saint Anne], and the love of Dom Guéranger for your Brittany, there is your own love, Father Schliebusch, for Solesmes. There is our common faith without alloy, and our love for the Church, . . . there are also the tears of our Right Reverend Father in 1893. All of that is as if alive for me, and attracts me to the place to begin there the work of God."[11]

The abbess was on location in Kergonan from July 21 to 25, 1896, in company of her prioress, Mother Gertrude de Ruffo-Bonneval, and of Mother Pudentienne Marsille, who was from the region. Her goal was to determine the site of the buildings of the future monastery. The monk's construction was at this time already in full motion:

"One hundred and eighty five acres of fir trees, arable soil with water springs nearly at the surface of the terrain. Soil that produces famous vegetables, all species of trees in the sheltered areas. The bay at front, less than half a mile away, visible on three sides. The entire Quiberon peninsula, then the islands at its extremity, Belle-Isle and Houat. Then, beyond, the open sea . . . Sainte-Anne already rises proudly. It is beautiful, well designed, well executed. In grave Romanesque style, but not somber, built of good granite with no plaster coating, which would not withstand the salt air."[12]

The plans and design of the nuns' monastery, Saint-Michel, was entrusted to Monsieur Caubert de Cléry, brother of one of the nuns of Sainte-Cécile and a relative of the Marsille family. He had been working in Rennes for some time, at the firm of Henri Mellet, brother of the monk architect, Dom Jules Mellet, which gave him the opportunity to consult with the two brothers on the project. The structure he conceived of rivals the architectural design of Dom Mellet: a sober neo-gothic that gives an impression of strength and harmony, but is not suggestive of later developments in the art of construction.

As to the patronage of the monastery, Father Schliebusch would have liked Mother Cécile to have chosen the name of Our Lady under the mystery of her Assumption, in memory of the day when the first

---

[10] July 26, 1837 was the day Dom Prosper Guéranger made his monastic profession at the hands of the abbot of Saint Paul-Outside-the-Walls in Rome, Dom Vincenzo Bini.—Trans.
[11] Letter dated May 17, 1896.
[12] Letter to the community of Wisques dated July 29, 1896.

professions at Sainte-Cécile were made. The patronage of Saint Anne had been appropriated by the monks. The abbess decided in her heart to dedicate the monastery to Saint Michael, whose great abbey juts out of the perilous sea at the northern coast of France, where Normandy and Brittany meet: "For Kergonan, at first I was a bit saddened that Sainte-Anne would be the men's abbey; then, I was consoled," she wrote to the sisters at Wisques on May 12, 1895. "I promised Saint Michael and the angels that I would give them this abbey of daughters, if I were free to do so; and I well sense that it will be the case. This corresponds to a combination of things that you will understand and that goes back quite some time."

Mother Cécile did not return to the Abbey of Sainte-Cécile for some weeks. She, as well as Dom Delatte, were expected at Dourgne for the abbatial blessings of both Dom Romain Banquet, abbot of Saint-Benoît d'En Calcat, and of Mother Marie Cronier, abbess of Sainte-Scholastique, on September 23 and 24. Bishop Gilbert, of Le Mans, had pressed her to accept the invitation.

She went through Albi to make a pilgrimage to the only cathedral in France dedicated to her patroness, Saint Cecilia, and was received at Dourgne as she would have been received at Wisques: "My Mother, here you are at home," were Mother Marie Cronier's welcoming words. "It is you who are the abbess, it is to you that it belongs to speak, to teach, to reprove, to correct, as you would do amidst your daughters at Sainte-Cécile." Of course, this was not to be taken literally, but it demonstrates the closeness of these two souls and the accord of their monastic doctrine.

At a certain point there was some question whether it would not be necessary to postpone the foundation in Brittany. It seemed to be an ill-appointed time for a new monastic establishment in France. Religious congregations were being crushed by special taxes that were sapping their assets, as if with the intent of rendering their life impossible. And besides, there was the infamous image of double monasteries which already had given enough grief to Solesmes.

Despite the reassurance that Dom de Hemptinne might have had by the example of the abbeys of Maredsous and Maredret,[13] he had to inform Dom Delatte, in veiled terms, of concerns that were percolating in high places. "I hope that this will not be a double foundation in the same vein as that of Wisques," he wrote, "for, after the communications made at Solesmes in the name of the Holy Office, it is necessary that you abstain from making such types of foundation. I believe with certainty, and *I have the most serious reasons to tell you so*, that if you were to persevere along this path despite everything, you would be calling some most disagreeable troubles upon yourselves. This is due to circumstances you well know. From this standpoint, I highly regretted your presence alongside that of madame the abbess of Sainte-Cécile at the blessings that were just celebrated at Dourgne. I strongly hope that this will not create new incidents. The concurrence of the two blessings is already a matter to excite the forces that were ignited in Rome by the affairs of Solesmes. And both your presences will only have accentuated that perception. Know well that I have positive reasons to fear it."[14]

Indeed, the bishop of Albi, being the ordinary of Dourgne, had received from Rome a reminder of the standing prohibition on double communities and the need for the nuns to be under the jurisdiction of the local bishop. Bishop Bécel of Vannes received a similar communiqué, which highly disconcerted him. Dom Delatte had to act quickly to dissipate his scruples—the canonical situation of the monasteries of nuns in the Congregation did not in any way deprive the bishop from his jurisdiction over them; as to double monasteries, that was plain fiction since each community would have its own cloister and its own oratory. Bishop Bécel was thus able to respond to the Holy Office:

"All precautions have been scrupulously taken to avoid any criticism: the two establishments will be separated by nearly half a mile without any common walls, and encircled by public ways. Within that space of half a mile, there will be two worker's homes,

---

[13] The two Beuron foundations made in Belgium, Maredsous being Dom de Hemptinne's own monastery, and Maredret the foundation made by his sister, Mother Cécile de Hemptinne. See chap. 26.—Trans.

[14] Letter dated October 14, 1896.

another for the gardener, a guest house, and a hamlet of about twenty roofs, while very close by, the towns of Carnac and Plouharnel. . . . To suspend the work now would be to incur onerous contractual claims and to be exposed to the most regrettable commentaries, which the bad press will not hesitate to abuse. This would, no doubt, result in a lamentable scandal."[15]

Upon his *ad limina* visit in Rome, the bishop gave the necessary explanations and applied himself to reassuring those concerned. Kergonan would not be a Thélème.[16] After this, it seems no one heard again of any apprehensions in Rome regarding foundations of this type. However, Bishop Bécel would not have the joy of receiving the nuns in his diocese—he died on November 6, 1897, from typhoid fever.

The foundation was made the following year. At the beginning of May 1898, a final trip was made to the location for arrangement of the last details. After some hesitation, Mother Cécile chose the cellarer of Sainte-Cécile, Mother Lucie Schmitt as superior of the new monastery, who was privately given the news on May 24. On August 10, feast of Saint Lawrence, Mother Cécile announced to the entire community the name of the prioress and the nuns who had been designated for the foundation.

Mother Cécile had the presentiment that Kergonan would be the last of her great works. On June 11, at Vespers, she had a first bout of indisposition, then, in the evening, during Matins, a small attack of paralysis ensued. The abbess was unable to return to her cell that night without help; she was only fifty-three then. She recovered from the attack to a degree, but not completely.

Come July, the house of Saint Michael was not yet ready, so that the departure of the foundresses was delayed until August 17. The postponement was welcomed, as it allowed Mother Cécile to recover enough to be able to bring the group of founding nuns to Brittany herself, and to stay with them for one month. Conventual life was

---

[15] Letter from Bishop Bécel to the assessor of the Holy Office, dated October 16, 1896.
[16] Refers to the fictitious Abbey of Thélème, in François Rabelais's first book, *Gargantua et Pantagruel*, in which the only rule is "Do what thou wilt." Rabelais (1494–1553) was initially a Franciscan, then a Benedictine monk, and eventually left religious life to become the well-known humanist and writer of fantasy, satire, and the grotesque.—Trans.

established on August 18: "You might imagine how these beginnings of Kergonan take me back nine years,"[17] wrote Mother Cécile to the abbess of Wisques, "though these little ones here are singularly more spoilt. The eldest had indeed to show her strength of will . . ."[18]

Some time later, André Hallays[19]—a critic well known for his works about the Marchioness of Sévigné and the impressions he recorded of his trips to places consecrated by literature—wrote in a style typical of the times, about his enthusiasm for the chanting of the nuns of Sainte-Cécile:

"The mysteriousness of this invisible choir lends to the chant a distant accent that moves and ravishes the listener. Then, the pious and innocent delight of Gregorian melodies, how well rendered by these female performers! These religious have a clear timbre, almost child-like, as if the years, having been gentle upon the pale visages of the nuns, respect also, along with the freshness of their features, the freshness of their voices. All is grace and purity. The antiphons sweetly roll away like the light clouds from a censer. The long melismas[20] of the alleluias blossom open like the rose touched by a breeze. The psalms unfold as the murmuring, clear waters of a brook. And when the chanting ends and a lower and faster voice recites a versicle, one would say that a swarm of bees is humming in the sun."[21]

---

[17] To the time of the foundation of Notre-Dame de Wisques.—Trans.

[18] Letter to Mother Thérèse Bernard dated August 30, 1898.

[19] André Hallays ((1859–1930), journalist and author.—Trans.

[20] A group of more than a few notes sung to a single syllable. In Gregorian chant they are particularly characteristic of the Alleluia, the Gradual and Tract.—Trans.

[21] *En flânant*, Solesmes, June 1899. (*Les idées, les faits, les œuvres. En flânant*, Paris, s.d. [1900]).

Chapter 34

The Close of a Century

SINCE 1830, RELATIONS BETWEEN Church and State had been difficult each time that the Church attempted to free itself from the harsh control imposed by the concordat of Napoleon, following the French Revolution, in exchange for religious peace. They were particularly poor at the time of the Third Republic. The most difficult period was without doubt the years between 1879 and 1914, which coincided with the abbacy of Mother Cécile. There was a temporary respite starting in 1890, during which Dom Delatte negotiated with the administration for the return of the community within the walls of the abbey of Saint-Pierre. His opponents reproached him for this: "Solesmes witnessed the erosion of the nobility and firmness that Dom Couturier, of regretted memory, had been able to safely preserve from all assaults until his last breath," wrote Dom Joseph Sauton, giving proof, once again, of his lack of comprehension of where problems truly lay. He continues: "The expulsion, by having dispersed us all, gave us legitimate pride in accomplishing our duty and putting up a resistance that became famous. Today, the return to our dear abbey has left all of us with an impression of defeat . . . we could not understand how the new abbot could have waited so little to undermine the valiant conduct of his predecessor."[1] Dom Delatte was even accused in 1893 of being a Freemason, and some suggested that the Holy Father's action in suspending him from his powers had no other reason!

In the course of the long fight undertaken by the state to limit the influence of the Church upon society and to control it more closely, republican attacks were concentrated on three strategic objectives: the religious, education, and the concordat.

The expulsion of religious men and women from their monastic homes in 1880 had been made possible not by a new law, but by governmental decrees reaffirming revolutionary laws that had fallen

---

[1] Houtin, *Une grande mystique*, p. 243.

into disuse. There was need for legislation that would define the role of associations within the state, and it was on this occasion that new regulations concerning religious were drawn up.

A law dated July 1, 1901, gave official recognition to the existence of not-for-profit associations for the first time since the promulgation of the Napoleonic Code.[2] They could now be established by agreement of several persons who desired to hold in common, in a permanent fashion, their intellectual knowledge or their activities, for a purpose other than that of sharing the benefits thereof. The law recognized three categories of associations: undeclared free associations, declared associations, and associations of public utility.

It would seem that within the framework of such a law, religious communities would have found their legal place in society. This was not the case, however. On the contrary, the new legislation drew a distinction between congregations and associations. Associations did not involve a particular type of life for its membership, which continued to live like everyone else. A congregation, on the other hand, created a special type of life for its membership, keeping them apart from society and, for this reason, greater control was necessary in order to avoid abuses and to protect individual liberty.

In principle, the law would not affect those congregations that had been legally recognized and authorized; but all non-authorized establishments that were dependent on these congregations would have to apply for authorization, and would have to do so individually. In the absence of such an application, closure of the delinquent establishment would be declared by decree of the Council of Ministers.

Since no religious community could be formed without a specific legislative authorizing act, the non-authorized congregations would have to apply for this authorization. The application should be addressed to the Minister of the Interior, signed by all the founders, and should be supported by a certain number of documents. One of these would be a declaration on the part of the bishop of the congregation's diocese, committing himself to maintain jurisdiction

[2] Established in 1804, the Code proscribed privileges based on birth, allowed freedom of religion, and determined that governmental positions be assigned according to qualification. —Trans.

over the congregation and its members. The Minister would then have the application examined, requiring in particular the opinion of the municipal council of the town where the congregation was established, and a report from its mayor. The application would then be submitted to the two Chambers, that is, the Chamber of Deputies and the Senate.

The elaboration of this law and related preliminary discussions are the background against which the circumstances experienced by Solesmes unfolded during the years preceding the law's promulgation. Thus an explanation, at least in summary form, was necessary here for a better understanding of this troubled period of time. The law was obviously extremely restrictive in its intent and it would be even more so in its application. This explains why so many religious families chose exile over submitting themselves to the narrow control of a treacherous government that, in the end, was only seeking to hamper and limit them as much as possible.

By an interesting paradox, this law was prepared principally in Masonic lodges—by a secret society that had no intention, as far as it was concerned, of submitting itself to any form of governmental regulation.

The two years preceding the twentieth century were for Mother Cécile the threshold into the passive and suffering phase of her life. Since her childhood, the Lord had not spared her, but she had proved to have an incredible vitality. She found a way of having time and energy for everything—for governing Sainte-Cécile, teaching the nuns, preparing foundations, writing prolific notes on the life of Dom Guéranger, and preparing her book on prayer. However, after the foundation of Saint-Michel de Kergonan, it no longer was possible for her to undertake great projects. She had to reserve her limited strength for the day-to-day affairs of the monastery: "I am fashioning a very reasonable life for myself and I rest as soon as I feel any fatigue," she wrote to the prioress of Bonlieu. "If you were to see me, you would find me extremely well behaved. . . . Kergonan gives me no concern now. Mother Lucie surpasses my hopes—she has been able to capture the hearts of her daughters and everything there goes joyously, simply, peacefully."[3]

The respite following the first alert of June 1898 allowed Mother Cécile to give a definitive form to her book on prayer. Until this date, the work in its French original version had been privately circulated among monasteries in simple manuscript form. An English translation had been in progress in 1890, with an introduction and notes by Cardinal Manning, but it never saw the light of day because of the prelate's death. The German edition, patronized by the bishop of Mainz, was published in 1896. In France, many bishops, as well as religious and spiritual authors, knew the book and wished to see it published.

At this point, it would have been difficult to keep the work within the private domain. But before definitively publishing it, Mother Cécile deemed it necessary to make several changes. Her first attempt at addressing this need was to collect her thoughts into one small tract, the *Épilogue du livre de l'oraison* (Epilogue to the book on prayer), which she had some friends read. But this was not sufficient to some, who regretted the chosen format of a simple addition, as if it were an addendum written to correct a work that had been disputed. Therefore, Mother Cécile rearranged the whole in a more logical order and wrote four new chapters, which were incorporated into the body of the work, thus completing her teachings. She also changed the title of the book to *La vie spirituelle et l'oraison d'après la Sainte Écriture et la tradition monastique* (*The Spiritual Life and Prayer According to Holy Scripture and Monastic Tradition*). The completed treatise appeared in 1899 and was received with enthusiasm.

In its preface, she wrote: "This book does not aim at science or at erudition. It contains nothing new; on the contrary, the author's ambition is to be wholly traditional and ancient. The end proposed will be fully gained if God should deign to make use of these pages to kindle some sparks of divine love in souls who, in the midst of our dark times, are truly seeking Him."[4] Under its definitive form, the treatise comprised twenty-three chapters. Father Rabussier, who had

---

[3] Letter dated December 13,1898.
[4] Cécile Bruyère, *The Spiritual Life and Prayer According to Holy Scripture and Monastic Tradition*, trans. Benedictines of Stanbrook (Eugene, OR : Wipf and Stock, 2002) p. xi.—Trans.

so helped Mother Cécile in her spiritual life, was no longer there to rejoice at its publication. He had died at Poitiers, on December 9, 1897, prior to the foundation of Saint-Michel in Kergonan. Another great friend, Bishop Freppel, passed away in 1891, before the crisis of 1893.

At this time, the prioress of the Norbertines of Bonlieu was preparing for her abbatial blessing. She had a copy of the "Recommendations to a newly elected abbess," which had been written for Mother Thérèse Bernard and then communicated to the abbess of Stanbrook.

"Your retreat resembles mine," wrote Mother Cécile to Mother Marie de la Croix. "When I wanted to make a retreat the Right Reverend sent me on my way telling me that I did not have the time for such a thing, that it was fine for others, but that I had only to occupy myself with my daughters as usual and that Our Lord thought it was fine this way. In reality, the weight of our duties and the importance of this blessing are quite enough, my dear good Mother, to supply all the gravity and recollection desired. I would add most humbly that, in those days, I had, besides, such a repugnance for the charge that it was better I not look too closely lest I be invaded by a type of internal convulsion. I applied all my will to wanting what God wanted and to abandoning myself to Him."[5]

On the occasion of the inauguration of a monument honoring Bishop Freppel at the cathedral of Angers, Bishop Touchet[6] of Orléans came to Solesmes to request a double foundation in his diocese. However, neither Saint-Pierre nor Sainte-Cécile could think of it in these years that were still so close to the foundations in Kergonan, other offers having also been previously made to them.

Most importantly, the situation in France was becoming more and more difficult as the elaboration of the bill on associations progressed. In parliamentary debates, there was continuous talk about seizure of real estate belonging to non-authorized congregations. From financial considerations, discussions passed imperceptibly to putting into question the very existence of the religious congregations themselves.

---

[5] Letter dated October 10, 1899.
[6] Stanislas-Arthur-Xavier Touchet (1848–1923), bishop of Orléans from 1894 to his death.— Trans.

Invitations began to arrive from England, in case forced expulsions should occur: "You know, my Mother, that Stanbrook is yours," wrote Mother Gertrude d'Aurillac Dubois. "You will come here, or Notre-Dame or Saint-Michel, as you judge best."[7] But the precaution was still premature. The situation had not yet arrived at that extreme point in 1898: "The present circumstances only require of us the law of a more profound attachment to our religious life, so persecuted by these miscreants," Mother Cécile would say. "After all, we are not at the mercy of men, but in the hands of God. Nothing will happen to us except what the Lord wills. Let us just realize that we will only merit the special protection of God in the measure that we have no other concern than Him alone."[8]

Among the foundresses in 1866, Mademoiselle Foubert had been unable to arrive during the very first days to begin her monastic life at Sainte-Cécile-la-Petite. She joined the group some weeks later, and received the name of Sister Mechtilde. First chantress,[9] she was also the personal secretary of the abbess. Her monastic pilgrimage, however, was now drawing to a close. "My venerable Father, one of our first sisters is very seriously ill and asks for your prayers," wrote Mother Cécile to Father Schliebusch. "It is Mother Mechtilde Foubert. She had a bout of influenza in the spring, and did not recover. The name of her illness, which has become very serious, is quite complicated [a pancreatic neoplasm] and means nothing to you nor to me. But what concerns us is that she is very much afflicted and that if Our Lord and the Blessed Virgin do not put things back in order, it will not be long. Therefore, Father, I have again great need of your devotion if God so wills and I beseech you to tell this to Our Lord and His Mother . . ."[10]

Mother Mechtilde had been a precious helper to Mother Cécile and the witness of her intimate life for thirty-five years. She went to God on September 3, 1900: "I do not know whether, in one life, one

---

[7] Delatte, "Vie," chap. 13.

[8] Ibid.

[9] This is an office within a monastic community, such as that of novice mistress and subprioress.—Trans

[10] Letter dated August 20, 1900. In her correspondence with Father Schliebusch, Mother Cécile often uses the familiar tone that he himself employed with his flock.

can encounter twice a heart like that which has just been frozen by death," wrote Canon Graux. . . . "I will pray for the daughter, being infinitely grateful for all the services she rendered her mother. But I will not forget the mother either, who is plunged into piercing sorrow by this trial."[11]

Mother Cécile wrote on October 9 to the abbess of Bonlieu: "As for me, I am moving forward a bit like those people who close their eyes when on a train so as not to become dizzy by the speed of things going by, and I feel myself seated despite the pace. The absence of Mother Mechtilde is felt ever more greatly, but I do not pay attention. I think of her repose in beatitude where she has taken her devoted and practical spirit, and where she does not forget anything, I am convinced. I never thought I would survive her, but I am not astonished that it was so, because it seems to me impossible to be astonished at anything that God does. Quite simply, she has departed, with a course so sure that it is impossible to find therein any matter for surprise. . . . It was to be this way and nothing more."[12]

Some weeks later, the three women superiors of the Congregation[13] were reunited at Kergonan for the laying of the cornerstone of the church on September 24, 1900. The building would remain unfinished for seventy years, its walls exposed to rain and wind, to storms and the sun, before a roof could be put in place to make of it a true sanctuary, and no longer a sort of picturesque ruin.[14]

The friends of Solesmes at the Élysée[15] tried to reassure the monks as to the results of the bill on associations. They thought that it would not secure enough votes in the Chamber or that the Senate would reject it. However, the totality of the bill's provisions obtained a majority vote on March 31, 1901.

Thus, the General Chapter, customarily held during Eastertide at the end of April, had to deal with this question that had now become urgent. To submit an application for authorization was out of the

---

[11] Letter dated September 6, 1900.

[12] Letter dated October 9, 1900.

[13] That is, Mother Cécile Bruyère, Mother Thérèse Bernard and Mother Lucie Schmitt.— Trans.

[14] A little more than a century later, on April 19, 2007, the abbey church was destroyed by fire and rebuilt in five years, having been consecrated on April 29, 2012.—Trans.

[15] That is, the friends of Solesmes in government.—Trans.

question; it went completely against the stance that Dom Guéranger had consistently held from the beginnings, since 1833. They would have to renounce pontifical exemption and accept the close supervision of a government that would control its personnel, its recruitment, its foundations, and its budget. Moreover, nothing guaranteed that the vote of the Chamber—required to obtain authorization for each of the houses individually—would be favorable. It was, therefore, decided that no application would be submitted, and, to avoid finding themselves in a situation worse than that of 1880 and 1882, without the means of maintaining regular conventual life, departure abroad was foreseen.

Indeed, the Senate, in its turn, ratified the bill and Émile Loubet,[16] president of the Republic, affixed his signature to it on July 1, 1901. The new law was published in the official journal the following day. Applications for authorization would have to be submitted by October 1.

---

[16] Émile Loubet (1838–1929), eighth president of the French Republic from 1899 to 1906.— Trans.

Chapter 35

Northwood

BY JUNE 1901, IT SEEMED going into exile would be imperative in a matter of a few months, given that nothing could be done to change the proposed legislation. When Dom Delatte spoke to Mother Cécile about this possibility on June 30, she reacted with caution. She did not feel ready for such a thing. The expulsions of the 1880s had only affected communities of men, and she did not see the future in the same way as the abbot of Solesmes did. The nuns had had their share of administrative harassment within the fiscal arena, but they had not suffered directly the weight of persecution.

Why hasten the hour of departure? If the police were to proceed to evict them again, including the nuns as well, it would be enough to act as Dom Couturier had done in his time. But Dom Delatte, who knew firsthand the unfortunate consequences of a rupture in community life, even if temporary, had no desire to experience the dispersion of the monks yet again. An impromptu departure could be planned: the monks would take with them their books, their furniture, their work tools, and the most needed objects. Otherwise, everything would be placed under seal, and they would have to resume daily life with nothing, and under very difficult conditions. While this would be excellent for fostering complete detachment and a spirit of poverty, the inconveniences it would pose to community life and the tasks that had been undertaken for the Church also merited some consideration.

Mother Cécile's hesitation did not last very long, only a few days of reflection and prayer. Thus, it was decided that they would seek a refuge abroad. The exile would probably not be long-lasting, for the dispositions of the new law as they applied to congregations, authorized or not, were impracticable. And wouldn't there be a surge in public opinion against it? On this point, the monks were roundly mistaken. Huysmans noted this in his *L'Oblat*, when he had his character Monsieur Lampre say: "The Benedictines imagine that France knows them and will be desolate to see them leave! How deluded! If they only knew how little this sorry country—which is unaware of them—cares if they stay or flee, they would gape in wonder!"

This was exactly the case. As to a change in legislature, there could be no prospect of this while the majority remained as it was, and it had been the same for twenty-five years. Only a great social upheaval could effect the prerequisite changes that would alter the factors impacting the situation and bring about the transformation in attitudes and stance that would be needed.

In exile, there would be no need for the two monasteries to be separated by long distances, thus, the arrangements being made by Saint-Pierre shaped those made by Sainte-Cécile. While the two communities in Wisques and in Kergonan could each go their way, with regards to Solesmes, Mother Cécile would not easily resign herself to a radical separation of the two monasteries that Dom Guéranger had erected in close proximity to each other.

"Luxembourg is too small. It seems they are already very tight there," wrote Dom Delatte to Dom Cabrol at Farnborough[1] on June 21, 1901. "I have been offered the Jacobsberg castle, near Boppard on the Rhine. It is German country, but Catholic and friendly. They are offering it for 70,000 marks. That is feasible. Nonetheless, I would prefer a rental rather than a definitive purchase. So, I'll be coming your way. Do you have anything for me in England or in Ireland? ... Speak of my English project to Madame Abbess of Stanbrook. I know she thinks Ireland is a possibility; as for me, Ireland would be best."

However, it was to England—particularly the south of the island country, still close to the French coast—that first choice was given. In the end, the two monasteries found an abode on the Isle of Wight, the nuns to the north, the monks to the south.[2] "I have written to Archbishop Sambucetti,[3] who in a diplomatic letter expressed his

---

[1] With Dom Cabrol as prior, Solesmes made a foundation in Farnborough in 1895, by invitation of Empress Eugénie, who had built a monastery on the grounds of her property in exile, in memory of her husband, Napoleon III and her son, killed in the Zulu War. This is St. Michael's Abbey, about 30 miles from London.—Trans.

[2] The Isle of Wight is within the diocese of Portsmouth, where the abbey of Farnborough is located.—Trans.

[3] See chap. 31, p. 322, n. 23.—Trans.

desire to know from me what will be happening to us," Dom Delatte told Mother Cécile on August 27, 1901. "I wrote him yesterday, not without mentioning that there will be the whole length of the island between you and us. That is always reassuring to Rome . . ."

At this date, Mother Cécile had already preceded the abbot to England—there where she would be installing her daughters. She sent Dom Delatte an account of what she had been doing. "Thank you for finding the time, amidst your comings and goings, amidst all the cares pertaining to the move, to write us letters that help us follow your actions," he wrote again on August 31, 1901. "I say 'us' because I pass your letters on to Sainte-Cécile just as they are. It cannot hurt me that they should know how you speak to me—they will all be jealous. All the better; I will thus have my revenge. At least in your heart, I will be . . . of the family."

Northwood, the property rented by the nuns at the north of the island, was located between Cowes and Newport, on the left bank of the large estuary of the Medina River, at the foot of a hill. It belonged to Edmund Ward[4] and included at its center a vast building where the community would find space enough, though they would still be somewhat constricted. The property lay two miles away from the sea. Cowes was then the capital of yachting. Not far, on the other side of the estuary, rose the royal castle of Cowes built by Henry VIII, which now houses the Royal Yacht Squadron. One mile further east stood Queen Victoria's Italian villa, Osborne House. This was her residence of preference during the last years of her life. A bit further north was Norris Castle, where Victoria had stayed with her mother when she was still a young princess.

Newport, in the center of the island, lay only a very few miles from Northwood—a small bustling village, close to the castle of Carisbrooke, an ancient Roman village. There the Normans had built an impressive fortification, giving it the new name Beaucombe, which remained the symbolic seat of the governor of the island.

---

[4] Edmund Granville Ward (1853—1915), was the son of William George Ward (1812–1882), one of the more vehement Tractarians, who converted to the Catholic Church in 1845, before John Henry Newman. William Ward was the grandfather, and Edmund Ward, the uncle, of Maisie Ward, who married Frank Sheed and founded with him the Catholic Evidence Guild and the famed Catholic publishing house, Sheed & Ward.—Trans.

Mother Cécile was in the first party to leave Solesmes, accompanied by Mother Thècle, her cellarer, and two other nuns. Before departing on the evening of August 19, 1901, she went to the little cemetery of Sainte-Cécile for a few moments of recollection where her parents lay, along with many much-loved nuns. In the crypt was the tomb of Mother Mechtilde Foubert, the first of the foundresses to have left for eternity. As the time approached to part from her community for a few weeks, she said: "I will not leave you long, my children, without calling you close to myself; you will quickly come to rejoin us. There will be no peace or happiness for me until we are all together on the other side of the strait."[5] She would not see Sainte-Cécile again.

Without having planned it, she came upon the prioress of Saint-Michel de Kergonan on the train in Sablé, who, with a companion sister, was also en route to England to look for a temporary refuge close to London.

The community of Sainte-Cécile arrived in Cowes by groups traveling one after the other. The first nuns set off for the Isle of Wight in the beginning of September. "The first detachment of nuns is preparing to leave on Monday," wrote Dom Delatte on August 31, 1901. "The monks will depart without doubt in eight or ten days."

"How happy I am to think that I will soon see some of you again," wrote Mother Cécile to the first group of travelers. "I have a tremendous desire to see each of your dear faces; each arrival will be a feast of the first order. I am happy that I will be receiving you in a mild and healthy climate. Each of your places is already determined and reserved. I think that you will be as well as one can be outside of Sainte-Cécile."[6]

During their entire sojourn in Northwood, the nuns had no church—at first, it was only an oratory arranged as best could be in a huge dance hall, and then a wooden chapel. This was a great sacrifice for them: "I was hoping to write you for our celebration of October 12," wrote Mother Cécile to the abbess of Bonlieu, who, for her part, was on her way to Prinsenkasteel, close to the Norbertine abbey of

---

[5] Delatte, "Vie," chap. 13.
[6] Ibid.

Grimbergen in Belgium. "We commemorated our feast of the dedication just the same. The high point of the dedication of the temple in Jerusalem was indeed the day when the Divine Majesty filled it in such a way that even the priests had to remain outside.[7] This text haunts me when I think of our consecrated churches, which I believe to be filled more than ever now. This apparent solitude, no doubt, concludes their consecration, I believe."[8]

"While awaiting, we chant our office in a provisional oratory where we are a bit like sardines, but the altar is very close . . . At the moment, the grille is being placed in the real oratory where the office will be given proper dignity. Our house—no doubt Saint Cecilia wanted it thus—is of Roman design; it is a curious thing to be under this sky with paintings in Pompeian style. . . . Truly everyone is in good health, including myself, despite the tiring efforts we've had to make. We drink beer, like you, and some tea to counter the humidity. Otherwise, the weather of the island is very mild. The garden is full of holm oaks, cork oaks, oleanders, rhododendrons, and flowering myrtles, as in areas of southern France. The birds on our trees are numerous and familiar to us. Though close to the town, we are in true solitude. The sea is below the park, and its borders are lined with greenery, just like a Swiss lake. We can see the coast of England.

"The population is kindly, very honest, and very religious. The people are enthusiastic for prayer and respect religious and priests. The children are beautiful, so beautiful that I always think about St. Gregory when I see them.[9]

---

[7] See 2 Chronicles 5:13b-14.—Trans.

[8] Mother Cécile is referring to the anniversary of the consecration of the church of Saint-Pierre in Solesmes (originally on October 12, 1010) as well as that of Sainte-Cécile (October 12, 1871), which the community commemorated "just the same," despite being away in exile. She then reflects on the fact that, though those churches are now empty, they remain buildings that are in the service and for the glory of God, and the vicissitudes suffered by those who should be occupying them crown their consecration.—Trans.

[9] A reference to the episode narrated by the historian St. Bede (ca. 672–735) which, according to him, prompted Pope St. Gregory to send St. Augustine of Canterbury (d. 604) and a group of his Benedictine monks to England as missionaries. The story relates that St. Gregory came upon English slave-boys being sold at the marketplace in Rome. Struck by their handsome and fair features, he inquired about their nationality and was told that they were Angles. "Good," he said, "they have the faces of angels, and should be coheirs with the angels in heaven."—Trans.

"The bishop is very kind to us and to our fathers. He places great hope in prayer, *'for the people of the island,* he said, *'have more need of prayer than of controversy.'* The Ten Commandments are seriously observed here, and if you could only hear these religious songs! Close by to us there is a Ritualist temple called Saint Mary's Church[10] where there are services every Sunday. These Protestants ask us for medals of St. Benedict! If we get to see any conversions, how consoled we would be! I hope so, if you help us . . ."[11]

Mother Cécile shared the same experiences as her correspondent, who wrote to her from Belgium: "One thing I find strange, that during the first days, and still, I lost memory of Bonlieu to the point where I had to make an effort of mental reconstruction, physical and moral, in order to retrieve something again of that poor Bonlieu, even the places most frequented—the cells, the regular places, parlors, hallways, etc., etc., . . . I was able to remember the church more easily, but again, not without some effort. I told myself: 'Does the Lord want me to forget everything, even the place of my stability?' And I asked myself, 'Then, is there something for me to do here, and what is it?' I found no answer to give myself other than to keep myself in perfect peace, without desire, nor any project, nor any curiosity; in the hands of God for the present, the past and the future. It should be enough for us that God manifests his divine designs as He wishes and step-by-step."[12]

The abbess of Sainte-Cécile did not adapt to the climate of England; because of her state of health she was having difficulties adjusting to a new environment. "I feel that I am not acclimatizing at all," she admitted one day. But she admired and slightly envied the religious fervor of the Protestants of the island. On occasion they would come to assist at the offices of the nuns. This was especially the case after 1903, when the sisters had a wooden chapel built—after the example of the monks in Appuldurcombe[13]—the belfry of which was

---

[10] A High Anglican church.—Trans.

[11] Letter dated October 12, 1901.

[12] Letter dated November 9, 1901. [From Mother Marie de la Croix, abbess of Bonlieu to Mother Cécile.—Trans.]

[13] Appuldurcombe was the property where the monks of Solesmes first installed themselves in 1901, moving to Quarr Abbey House, in Binstead, in 1908. Quarr is still a house of the Congregation of Solesmes, a contingent of monks having remained there after the greater

fitted with the bells brought from Sainte-Cécile. There were many conversions, which filled the heart of the abbess with immense joy each time.

The vocation of the Loëwenstein sisters had led to that of Mother Adelaïde de Bragança; and the vocation of Mother Adelaïde, in her turn, attracted her grandchildren to Sainte-Cécile, daughters of the Duke and Duchess of Bourbon-Parma. The nuns' proximity to Cowes occasioned a visit to the monastery from Edward VII and his queen.[14] The latter came first unannounced to see Mother Adelaïde. The king, in turn, stated 'I will also go see the good Duchess of Bragança who has come to take refuge in my realm." He came on August 19, 1902, ten days after his coronation. The atmosphere among the authorities in England differed from that in France.

It seemed that Mother Cécile had left the last of her strength behind in Solesmes. Each nun was aware of this, though she herself did not speak to anyone of her exhaustion. Those who had known her before the first alert suffered just prior to the foundation of Saint-Michel de Kergonan, were grieved to think that she was but fifty-seven. At the end of 1901, the doctor diagnosed anemia and prescribed complete repose for her.

There was an improvement in the course of 1902; Mother Cécile was able to reassume some of her daily duties in the government of the community and to give her conferences. Nonetheless, it was not like before. Nothing was lacking in her teaching, but now her speech was slow, sometimes encumbered, whereas before the nuns were used to clear, precise and quick words from her. A new threshold would be crossed in 1906.

The community of Saint-Michel de Kergonan had temporarily found asylum at Blake Hall, close to Snaresbruck in the outskirts of London. Other lodgings were located for them in the immediate vicinity of Sainte-Cécile in East Cowes, on the other side of the estuary, but only a little over a mile from Northwood as the crow flies.

---

part of the community returned to their abbey in Solesmes in 1922. Quarr was elevated from a priory to an abbey in 1937.—Trans.

[14] Alexandra, born Princess of Denmark.—Trans.

Notre-Dame de Wisques settled at Oosterhout, close to Breda in Holland. From there, Mother Thérèse came to visit Sainte-Cécile-in-exile (August 1 to 11, 1902), to speak about Saint-Nicolas de Verneuil, whose abbess with a group of nuns were requesting refuge in a Solesmian monastery. Northwood was barely large enough for the community of Sainte-Cécile, so the nuns from Verneuil were directed to Oosterhout.

During that period in France, the government of Combes, which had succeeded Waldeck-Rousseau,[15] rejected forthright all applications for authorization without examination, thus forcing five hundred religious congregations into exile. Sainte-Cécile increasingly dispensed its alms to assuage the plight of thousands of exiles.

The climate of the Isle of Wight enjoys a reputation for being the mildest in England. However, the doctors believed it to be the cause of the deterioration of Mother Cécile's health. During winter she suffered further decline: "Yesterday I saw Madame Abbess somewhat weighed down by the relapse, not yet having fully recovered the strength sapped from her by the bout she suffered, but in good disposition, nonetheless," wrote Dom Delatte on February 20, 1903 to his friend Doctor de Backer. "It seems to me, besides, that this incident is an epiphenomenon; only that in a state of advanced weakness such as hers, the effects of a mere flick can be felt."

It was recommended that she take some time to rest away from the community. The abbess resisted the idea as best she could, but Dom Delatte made it a duty of conscience for her to go and attempt to recover at Oosterhout for one month, from September 3 to October 6 in 1903. There she saw again not only Mother Thérèse, but also the abbess of Verneuil, who was already very ill.

The nuns of Notre-Dame did the impossible to strengthen Mother Cécile's condition, and she submitted to everything, not without some discomfort at times. She was at ease when she visited the

---

[15] Pierre Waldeck-Rousseau (1846–1904) was the 68th Prime Minster of France, from 1899 to 1902, during Émile Loubet's presidency. Émile Combes (1835–1921), a radical and avowed occultist, succeeded him as Prime Minister from 1902 to 1905. To his credit, Waldeck-Rousseau emerged from his retirement to protest in the Senate against the obstruction Combes had put to the law of July 1, 1901, rejecting en mass all applications for authorization submitted by teaching and contemplative congregations.—Trans.

infirmary and conversed here and there with the sick nuns who were there.

To the prioress of Kergonan, who wrote inquiring about the outcome of this prolonged repose, Mother Thérèse responded: "Now, our Mother? What has improved the most is her countenance. Her face has recovered all its animation, especially at certain hours, and her color is very good. As to her strength, my Mother, that is another story. . . . I believe our Mother is better because resting and repose is the only pace of life she can have from now on. Once she reassumes the government in small doses, her concerns in infinitesimal doses, she will again be overwhelmed. . . . I tell you what I think. Keep it to yourself."[16]

But the abbess of Sainte-Cécile was in haste to return to her home: "I do not know whether my daughters have need of me, but I have need of my daughters!" she would say upon returning. The abbess of Bonlieu had hoped for a visit at Grimbergen, located north of Brussels, when Mother Cécile would depart from Oosterhout. It would have amounted to only a detour of some sixty miles into the Belgian Brabant. If that were not possible, she herself could come to Oosterhout with permission from her superiors. But Mother Cécile did not want to delay her return:

"I must confess that, for some days, Our Lord had already been preparing me for this sacrifice, impeding me from asking Him for this grace," wrote the abbess of Bonlieu. "I was astonished at this attitude of the Lord, so much did it seem to me a just and good thing to desire this good for my daughters and for myself. And still the Lord positively put obstacles to my prayer, even to my desires, and in my soul some words kept resurfacing, words that I saw I do not remember where: 'there is no good thing of which the sacrifice isn't better.' Then, upon learning for certain that you had left this land of our exile and that I would not see you here, I told myself interiorly: 'I well knew it!'"[17]

---

[16] Letter to Mother Lucie Schmitt dated September 28, 1903.
[17] Letter dated October 12, 1903.

Mother Marie de la Croix would die less than two years later, on January 15, 1905, in the place of refuge put at the disposal of her community by the Mérode family.[18] The chateau was burnt down by the Germans in 1944.

---

[18] Ancient princely family of Belgium.—Trans.

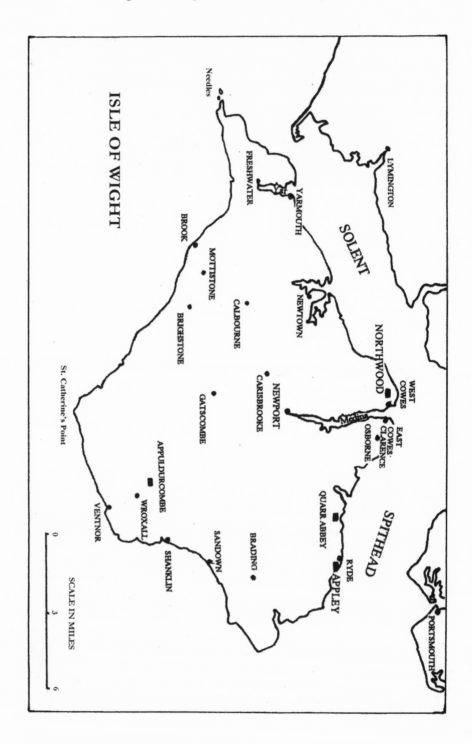

Chapter 36

Appley House, Sainte-Cécile of Ryde

THOUGH MOTHER CÉCILE EXTENDED HER stay in Holland until October 6, 1903, she returned to Northwood without any tangible improvement having been made. Now she had to reckon with her waning strength and to establish a rhythm of life and government to suit her declining health. For a superior spirit such as hers, capable of facing any type of intellectual challenge, this impoverishment asked of her by God required a most crucifying type of detachment. Mother Marie Eynaud[1] noted that the abbess's last conference at the chapter was given on March 4, 1906, Ash Wednesday, and that she was obliged to cease her correspondence on January 10, 1906.

On July 20, 1903, Leo XIII's long life came to an end. A new pope was elected to succeed him—Cardinal Sarto, of Venice,[2] an admirer of the traditional chant of the Church. On November 22, 1903, the feast of Saint Cecilia, he published a *motu proprio* about sacred music that gave pride of place to Gregorian chant.[3] The long work of restoration undertaken by Solesmes was now being recognized and encouraged.

As to the daily use of chant, many preferred the nuns' singing to that of the monks. That is what Dom Jean de Puniet[4] said in a talk given in England in 1901, which brought upon him the amused protests of Dom Delatte. "He had the gumption of saying that the Benedictine nuns sing better than we do," wrote the abbot to Mother Cécile on August 27, 1901. "I definitely contest this assertion. There are days when no one in the world sings better than our monks. I will only concede that these days are not every day. Father Jean will have

---

[1] Mother Cécile's niece, daughter of her sister Lise Eynaud.—Trans.

[2] Pope St. Pius X (1835–1914), né Giuseppe Melchiorre Sarto, was elevated to the cardinalate and named Patriarch of Venice in 1893, and elected as supreme pontiff in 1903. He was canonized in 1954.—Trans.

[3] *Tra le Sollecitudini.*—Trans.

[4] Dom Jean de Puniet (1869–1941), monk of Solesmes and master of novices. Dom Delatte sent him to Oosterhout (the Netherlands) as prior of Saint-Paul de Wisques when the community was in exile. He became abbot of Saint-Paul in 1910, and when part of the community eventually returned to Wisques, he chose to stay in Oosterhout.

to make satisfaction for his appraisal, especially for having revealed it to the public!"

Following the issuance of the pope's *motu proprio* and his decision to celebrate the Mass of Saint Gregory himself, sung in Gregorian chant at the Basilica of Saint Peter on March 12, 1904, the Abbey of Sainte-Cécile resolved to commemorate the event by presenting the Holy Father with a booklet for this Mass, copied and illuminated by the nuns. The piece was sent to Rome through the Austrian embassy and delivered to Pius X, in the name of the abbess, by three monks of Solesmes who had been invited for the event. A copy of *The Spiritual Life and Prayer* was sent as well. The response to the gift came in the form of a pontifical letter dated May 5, 1904, which was a ray of sunshine for Mother Cécile and her nuns.

However, bereavement steadily assailed the abbess with the departure of loved ones, one after the other: the good Father Schliebusch, the abbess of Saint-Nicolas de Verneuil, the abbess of Bonlieu, and her brother-in-law Léo Eynaud, who had just entrusted his daughter to Sainte-Cécile.

In the chronicles of the novitiate of the priory of Sainte-Anne de Kergonan, which at that time was in the diocese of Namur in Belgium, the entry for May 8, 1905 reads: "Today the nuns of Saint-Michel de Kergonan, in exile in the Isle of Wight (England), are in great joy. His Holiness Pius X, by request of the Right Reverend Father Abbot of Saint-Pierre de Solesmes, agreed to elevate the priory of Saint-Michel to the abbatial dignity and himself designated the abbess—Mother Lucie. The blessing of the elected abbess was fixed for this magnificent date, the feast of the apparition of the great Archangel.[5] Our father prior assisted at the ceremony, which was *undique splendidissima* (splendid in every way). The bishop of Portsmouth presided, accompanied by another prelate, by the Right Reverend of Solesmes, and the Right Reverend of Farnborough. Also present were the monks of Solesmes, distinguished friends, Madame Abbess of Sainte-Cécile, Madame Abbess of Wisques and the nuns of both monasteries."

---

[5] In the calendar then in use, May 8 is the feast of the "Apparition of the Archangel St. Michael," which commemorates the day when the archangel visibly manifested himself in a cave in Mount Gargano, Italy, in 492.—Trans.

The tone is somewhat solemn, but it lends an idea of the general joy that was the nuns', a joy which Mother Cécile was the foremost to savor. There was no room for the ceremony at East Cowes in the house where the community of Saint-Michel was lodged, while the situation of the nuns of Sainte-Cécile was somewhat better at Northwood, on the other side of the Medina estuary. Thus, the wooden church accommodated both communities and their guests on that day. The abbatial erection of Saint-Michel was the crowning of the monastic work begun in 1866 at Sainte-Cécile-la-Petite. From a distance, the monasteries that had benefited from Sainte-Cécile united themselves to the celebration: Stanbrook, Maredret, Dourgne, Saint-Gabriel in Prague, Eibingen . . .

"Those who were witness to this feast," wrote Dom Delatte, he himself having been among them, "the most complete and most joyous, but also the last in her life [Mother Cécile's], will not forget that she was the radiant beauty of the event. The Archduchess Maria Teresa, her daughter the Archduchess Maria Annunziata, the Grand Duchess of Luxembourg . . . honored the function with their presence. The three eldest daughters of the Grand Duchess of Luxembourg wished to be the assistants of Madame Abbess of Sainte-Cécile: the future Grand Duchess of Luxembourg (Maria Adelaïde) bore the crosier, and her younger sisters, the Princesses Charlotte and Hilda, the book. The nuns' choir, augmented by the nuns from Saint-Michel, was arranged in three rows. The abbatial blessing was performed by Bishop Cahill[6] of Portsmouth in the presence of his auxiliary,[7] Bishop Cotter."[8]

Solesmes has been reproached for too easily mobilizing the nobility. But these friendships came to them without their having been sought. In fact, they revolved around one family: the daughters, the sister, and the grandnieces of the Prince Loëwenstein, who himself would be making his profession as a Dominican on August 4,

---

[6] John Baptist Cahill (1841–1910), born in London; bishop of Portsmouth from 1900 to his death.—Trans.

[7] William Timothy Cotter (1866–1940), born in Cloyne, Ireland; auxiliary bishop of Portsmouth from 1905; appointed bishop of Portsmouth upon Bishop Cahill's death, remaining in the see until his death.—Trans.

[8] Delatte, "Vie," chap. 14.

1908. Dom Guéranger was the son of a school director, Dom Couturier, of a village wool craftsman, Dom Delatte, of a drill worker and a domestic helper. . . . As to Mother Cécile, she belonged to the bourgeoisie ennobled by Napoleon. The greater part of the monks came from the petty or middle bourgeoisie and from peasant families; only a few were from the aristocracy. Catholic princely families came to Solesmes for reasons other than aristocratic relations.

After the abbatial blessing of Mother Lucie, Mother Cécile entered little by little into the silence that would envelop her during the last four years of her life. "Henceforth, the abbess of Sainte-Cécile would be only the attentive spectator—often anxious but powerless—of what went on about her," wrote Dom Delatte. "Weakness gave place to total exhaustion, her movements became increasingly painful. It was no longer possible to retain her attention for long."[9] The state of health that the abbot of Solesmes describes here in its extreme form was arrived at gradually, as her condition deteriorated month by month.

On July 16, 1905, at the renewal of charges,[10] Mother Cécile told her daughters: "You see, my children, my health is not the best, but we must accept what God is giving us and bow down our heads. The days are evil, we must redeem the times. Let us observe our Rule with fidelity. I ask for your pardon for speaking to you like this, I, who can no longer observe it. But I have followed it as much as I was able to; and if I can no longer follow it today, I still do love it forever."

A new incident occurred on March 18, 1906, the Third Sunday of Lent. Mother Cécile had another small attack of paralysis when pronouncing the blessing for the reader of the week[11] at the end of the Mass; then again in the evening at First Vespers of St. Joseph, during

---

[9] Ibid.

[10] This is the "deposition and renewal of charges," which in the female branch of the Congregation of Solesmes occurs every three years, according to the "Declarations." All of the officials (those in charge of a department or task, such as cellarer, subprioress, kitchen, linen room, garden, choir mistress, novice mistress, etc.) are "deposed," i.e., relieved of their charge; officials are then newly appointed or re-appointed after the council and the abbess meet and consult. From the time of the deposition until the renewal, the former official does not exercise her charge in any way, so for necessary charges (e.g., infirmarian, cellarer, novice mistress, portress, sacristan) an interim official is named.—Trans.

[11] The nun who will be in charge of doing the reading in the refectory for the week.—Trans.

the chanting of the collect for Sunday. From that point on, the progress of the illness was inexorable, without any hope of recovery.

Mother Pudentienne Marsille had hoped that Mother Cécile would stop at Clarence House (Saint-Michel de Kergonan) when the community of Sainte-Cécile moved to Appley House. But Mother Agnes Bouly had to explain the reason why the invitation was declined: "She speaks with such great difficulty that perhaps she was afraid of the impression she might have given the community, for she is alert to everything about her, and savors each incident caused by her weakness. What treasures of grace she must be meriting for us in this way! She continues to be the dearly beloved center of our lives."[12]

The exile was extending itself more than had been expected, and the cramped situation at Northwood could not be sustained beyond a few years. Besides, it was not possible to keep renewing the lease indefinitely. Thus, if they should have to stay in England for yet some time, it would be necessary to acquire sure property.

The two locations of greater significance in the northeast portion of the island were Brading and Ryde. Brading, at the end of its own estuary, had been an important marketplace in the Middle Ages because of the advantageous location of its ancient port, now drained and landlocked. Ryde had been the principal point of access to the island since the fourteenth century, by reason of its immediate proximity to Portsmouth, only five miles away on the other side of the Spithead strait. A jetty was constructed in 1813–1814 to allow for boarding during low tide; it was then lengthened and completed by a second jetty in 1857–1864, to facilitate access to the port. In the beginning of the twentieth century, Ryde was still a large town grown around a village of fishermen, extended by its new resort village built upon a hill. Ryde, more than all other places on the island, bore the mark of the Victorian age. The wide five-mile long sand beach that surfaced when the tide ebbed attracted vacationers, and the town put on its best garb to receive them.

At some distance to the east, outside of Ryde, lay Appley House amidst thickets of trees which at that time were still plenty, as shown in old maps. It was a spacious mansion overlooking the sea, which

---

[12] Letter dated May 22, 1906.

had been enhanced by the erection of a long building in the grounds, intended to house a small school. In February 1906 the nuns of Sainte-Cécile became the owners of the property.

Under the guidance of Mother Cellarer, a monastery emerged by combining the existing structures with the construction, between them, of several new and properly conventual buildings which together formed a whole vaguely reminiscent of the abbey in Solesmes. The removal of the community to Appley House was diligently planned, and the first group of nuns, with Mother Cécile at its head, moved in on May 19, 1906. Three weeks later, on June 12, the entire community was reunited in its new abode by the sea, and monastic observance resumed with its usual perfection.

Another attack in the beginning of 1907 aggravated Mother Cécile's state: "Some days ago our venerated mother again suffered a crisis from which she is recovering, they say, little by little, but it has completely taken away her ability to speak," wrote the abbess of Kergonan to the abbess of Stanbrook on January 7, 1907. Mother Cécile had to concede that her legs no longer could bear her; from that moment she had need of a wheelchair to move about.

The community at Ryde still lacked a church. However, on June 30, 1906, Bishop Cahill came to lay the cornerstone of the new church, which was finished by the following year and blessed by Dom Delatte on March 28, when they took possession of it. The church was consecrated on October 12, 1907, on the thirty-sixth anniversary of the consecration of the abbatial church of Sainte-Cécile in Solesmes, and nine centuries after that of Saint-Pierre.

"I will not begin to tell you of the splendid function that was the consecration of the church of Sainte-Cécile," wrote Mother Lucie to the abbess of Stanbrook. "I will leave that pleasure to madame the abbess of Wisques. Likewise, should I tell you of the state of our venerated mother? No, by the spoken word you will know better than by letter to what state of incapacity our beloved Mother has been reduced, the image of a holocaust that silently consumes itself in honor of the sovereign Master of all things. Everything has been turned over to God and the Lord seems to be pleased with the acceptance, so total and so complete, of this soul, of this body, of this entire being. With the eyes of faith, it becomes a beautiful sight."[13]

Mother Cécile still found some strength to copy the offertory antiphon of the Mass of dedication: "Lord my God, in the simplicity of my heart, I have offered everything in joy . . ." She followed all the rites with great attention and in her heart lived intensely that grand liturgical function which sings of the mystery of the Church.

"Glorious is the spectacle that this soul presents to the eyes of faith, this soul silently consuming itself in adoration before the Divine Majesty," wrote Mother Lucie to the abbess of Dourgne. "And the image of the altar ablaze at the moment of the final consecration— when the clouds of incense placed upon the five parts of the altar form but one fragrant flame—well reflects the image of that holy soul. It is incense; but no one sees the puffs of cloud rising toward the sky in the temple; instead, it is rather the flame of the Spirit of love consuming the incense in honor of the divinity. If our supernatural eyes gloried at this indelible spectacle, what can be said at the sight of that body, utterly weighed down? Those lips, once so eloquent, proffer but a few words, barely distinct. The body is no longer sustained by its legs, which refuse nearly all service."[14]

Bishop Cahill officiated at the ceremony. In 1912, it would be his successor[15] who would consecrate the church Our Lady of Quarr, west of Ryde, built on the site of an ancient Cistercian monastery. Thanks to the generosity of the Abbey of Sainte-Cécile, the monks of Solesmes were able to purchase the property in 1907.

Once again the two monasteries were reunited, though at a distance of nearly three miles one from the other. For Saint-Pierre, this meant that there would no longer be the need to have two monks detached away from the community, residing close to the nuns to serve them as chaplains; for Sainte-Cécile, it meant that their liturgy could more easily be solemnized. Each community gained.

With the advance of her illness, Mother Cécile came to depend completely on her nurses. Even reading had become difficult for her. "Her speech was almost completely silenced," wrote Dom Delatte.

---

[13] Letter dated October 18, 1907.
[14] Letter dated October 17, 1907.
[15] Bishop William Cotter; see note 7 above.—Trans.

"The paralysis progressively reached her limbs, making it impossible for her to walk. Anxiety, a growing anxiety spread over her features. Nonetheless, it was enough to arouse her attention to obtain from her withered lips a witness of her hidden adoration and acceptance of the will of God. 'Whatever God wills,' she would repeat, 'as God wills.' The resignation of her soul was perfect."[16]

"Be assured that our Mother feels and tastes all the bitterness of the chalice that God has her drink to the dregs," wrote Mother Agathe de la Fougère, in her turn, to the abbess of Kergonan on June 8, 1906. "This sacrifice brings you [the community of Saint-Michel] closer still to us for you thus partake of the cup from which we daily drink."[17]

"One of her daughters, on her way to adoration at the feet of the Most Blessed Sacrament, asked her:

'Do you wish me to tell the Lord for you, my Mother, that you love Him very much?'

'Tell Him,' she replied, 'that I want to love Him very much.'"[18]

"She delivered herself up with the docility of a child to all the measures taken out of a desire to better or to maintain her health. It was said that she was nothing but submission. 'And now,' she would say, 'what do you want to do to me?'"[19]

In a letter of August 19, 1907 to his great friend Dr. de Backer, the abbot wrote: "At Sainte-Cécile, persons and things are going as usual. Madame Abbess has only a very few words."

News of the death, on April 15, 1908, of Dom Athanase Logerot, prior of Sainte-Anne de Kergonan and former confessor of Mother Cécile, reached her shortly after it occurred. She was "very occupied with this death," according to the words in the monastery's chronicles.[20] It was he who had brought her into contact with Blessed Marie-Eugénie Milleret de Brou,[21] the foundress of the Religious of the Assumption, whose spirituality was very similar to that of Dom

---

[16] Delatte, "Vie," chap. 14.

[17] Letter dated June 8, 1906.

[18] Recollections of Mother Praxède Boisseau.

[19] Delatte, "Vie," chap. 14.

[20] Chronicles written by Mother Aldegonde Cordonnier.

[21] Mother Marie-Eugénie Milleret de Brou (1817–1898) was canonized on June 3, 2007, after the publication of the original of this book. See chap. 31, p. 321, n. 22 for biographical notes.

Guéranger. The closeness of Sainte-Cécile to the religious of the Assumption did not wane after Mother de Brou's death in 1898, and the convent in Auteuil had welcomed the Benedictine nuns on their way to exile.

Bishop Cahill came personally for the canonical visitation of the abbey in August 1908. The state of incapacity of Mother Cécile made the government of the house difficult for the prioress, who carried responsibility for everything without having defined powers outside of her own charge. The community felt orphaned. At that time—after so much effort had been spent to obtain for themselves the privilege to conform to the Rule of Saint Benedict and secure the right to the abbacy for life—there was some hesitation toward considering the resignation of the superior as a solution to problems of governance. Dom Bourigaud, abbot of Ligugé, however, did submit his resignation when he became blind. On the other hand, Dom Delatte—who himself was so inclined to resign himself in periods of crisis—did not accept the resignation that Mother Cécile had offered him in 1903 after her return from Oosterhout. The nuns would have hardly consented to the idea that their abbess not remain their mother until death.

Mother Cécile's cell was in the area of the house that had been built before the school building—a "mansion" filled with light streaming through the large overhanging windows, English style. She almost never left her place, except in an invalid carriage.

The first of the young princesses Bourbon-Parma, a family of numerous children, entered Sainte-Cécile during this period, and received the habit on October 23, 1908. It was the sixty-third anniversary of the baptism of Mother Cécile, who would have no more than six months to live.

Chapter 37

Toward the Liturgy of Eternity

"ILLNESS IS A VERY GREAT TRIAL for a monk and I compassionate with you with all my heart," wrote Mother Cécile to a correspondent on May 14, 1890. "Still, my reverend and most dear Father, our life is so entirely given over to God, body and soul, that I cannot help but think that there is a type of providence that exists particularly for it. Sometimes this providence may seem to be the slumber of the Lord in Peter's boat. Nonetheless, His slumber should not disconcert us — He still watches.

"Nothing can keep us from rendering our interior life the more intense in the measure that our physical strength is more restricted. We must seek for more heart-to-heart conversations with God, more faith, more love. Don't you think that Our Lord often tears down the surroundings of a soul in order that she concentrate upon herself and that she become accustomed to finding in herself the Divine Guest Who is therein? It is a device that the Master uses to free us, to release us from exterior things, even good things, which tend to scatter us. . . . I am convinced that all the trials that you have just gone through are so that you may seek, even more, a more completely contemplative life."[1]

In the silence of her final years, when a veil seemed to separate her from the world of the living and she became remote, Mother Cécile entered upon the state that she described so well to the monk who had come to confide his distress to her. The time of man was no longer hers, the hour of God approached.

"I have often thought that the grace of martyrdom is a grace of fortitude, as is often said" she commented on November 28, 1890, "but above all it is a grace of extreme meekness. I am surprised that this aspect isn't pointed out more frequently. *Tanquam agnus coram tondente se* (as a lamb before his shearer, Is 53:7). It is a science to

---

[1] Letter to Dom Henri Beauchet-Filleau.

know how to offer a perfect holocaust, that is, an offering without alloy and without blemish, keeping nothing of oneself back."[2]

Her total powerlessness, which left her dependent on the care of others at the end of her life, was an effect of this grace—the patience of one who lets it be done to her, for the love of God. She had to suffer moments of incomprehension on the part of Mother Prioress, who, from the beginnings of the foundation, had been charged by Dom Guéranger with taking care of her health. In the final months, Mother Gertrude de Ruffo-Bonneval did not understand to what point Mother Cécile was aware and conscious of the least thing, even as she was enveloped in the silence imposed by her illness. More than once, the prioress made decisions with regard to the patient that were unwittingly cruel. The Empress Zita, who was then seventeen and had obtained permission to spend some months at Sainte-Cécile where her sister Maria Benedetta of Bourbon-Parma was a novice, attests: "It was enough to look at her extraordinary gaze to realize that she saw and understood everything!" By a curious judgment, Mother Prioress decided that Mother Cécile would only receive communion when she was in choir for the Mass of communion. Thus, she was often deprived of Holy Communion, and at times could be heard murmuring, "I am hungry, I am hungry!"[3]

She often feared to lack courage and at night she would cry "My God, my God, have mercy on me!" But she did not consent to be relieved of God's will for her. When she was asked to pray to be healed, relying on the intercession of Dom Guéranger, she would say: "No. You ask, if you so wish. As for myself, I will not ask for it."[4]

One of her joys was to be taken to the park on the grounds, where she passed long hours when the weather so permitted. There was a pavilion there, which was arranged so that she could be sheltered while benefitting from the open air. "Today she is still in the garden in her little house, which has been enlarged and organized so well

---

[2] Letter to Dom Athanase Logerot.

[3] Testimony collected from the Empress Zita of Austria by a nun of Sainte-Cécile during summer 1971. In 1909, when her marriage with the Archduke Charles of Hapsburg was already being contemplated, her mother wished that she complete her instruction at the alumnat at Sainte-Cécile.

[4] Delatte, "Vie," chap. 14.

that our dearly beloved mother can settle herself there without any fatigue and without any danger of being cold. Since she began spending several hours each day outside in this way, she has regained some appetite and strength."[5]

At the end of January 1909, Dom Delatte once again preached the annual retreat at Sainte-Cécile.[6] His first retreat was in 1889, when he was still the prior, after which he preached in turn successively at Saint-Pierre, at the Religious of the Assumption in Auteuil, at Saint-Michel de Kergonan, etc. This year, at Sainte-Cécile, he started with Gideon's summons to form an army and the selection of combatants made by the Lord.[7] Then he spoke of life as an apprenticeship for eternity: "We are heading toward God; some day we will arrive before Him, that is a fact. . . . Soon, at the threshold of eternity, we will find ourselves face to face with Him. That is what makes for joy in our present life: to feel that, supported by Jesus Christ, we are heading towards the Light, towards the Truth, towards Tenderness, Purity, towards Justice."

The only reasonable use we can make of this life is to prepare ourselves for this encounter, or better, to let God prepare us, as He pleases, without our putting up any resistance to Him: "All of life is joyous suppleness, deferent docility. We are but instruments, a force to be deployed as God desires; workers of God, because we labor for Him; instruments of God, because we are in His hands. And our joy is to belong to Him. . . . Let us allow God to think in us, will in us, love in us, act in us."

Mother Cécile was too fatigued to attend the conferences, but she thanked the abbot for offering her daughters what she could no longer give them. "For both preacher and retreatants," wrote Dom Delatte, "no words could in any way be equaled to the example that their venerated mother, hidden inside the monastery, gave them. She once told her daughters what the attitude of a nun should be during all her life, standing before God alone: 'The soul,' she said, 'is

---

[5] Letter from Mother Agnes Bouly to Mother Lucie Schmitt dated April 24, 1908.

[6] In monastic life, each year a community holds a week-long retreat within its monastery, preached by a guest preacher. Mother Cécile had often asked Dom Delatte to preach community retreats at Sainte-Cécile.

[7] Judges 6 and 7.—Trans.

occupied with God alone and uninterested in everything else—herself as well as all external realities—seemingly living already in eternity and seeing things only in God, having lost from sight their earthly aspect, like someone for whom everything is finished and for whom there is no tomorrow. For the nun, likewise, the created, the perceptible, the exterior are over. For her, there is only God.'"[8]

Her life was that state of peaceful contemplation that she had once described in a conference: "This atmosphere of prayer must penetrate all aspects of our life, from our waking in the morning to our retiring at night, and even while we sleep, we do so in the arms of God. It is a continuous prayer, and when everything seems to be dormant, this prayer penetrates all our being like incense penetrates the objects that it has touched—its perfume remains in the flowers and in the sacred vestments at the altar. That is the very image of this perfume of prayer, which must emanate from a nun. One does not attain to this constant prayer of the entire being through workings of the brain, but through harmony of the will with God, through the total deliverance of one's life into His hands." Such had been her life for many long years; her illness had only served to take away the distractions germane to her charge of governance. Mother Cécile was ready to meet her Lord.

A few months before the death of Mother Gertrude, the abbess of Stanbrook, Mother Cécile wrote to her: "There is no need of enthusiasm[9] to go directly to God. I do not believe that the sweet Queen of Heaven ever rendered this type of coin to God. Isn't profound adoration, which is the perfect blossoming of divine charity, the downfall of enthusiasm? The latter is the fruit of a lower world, while all that is divine is dignified. It is said that deep lakes which lie on the elevated flats of high mountains have no waves. Waves touch only the water's surface, while the abyss of the ocean knows them not. My dearly beloved daughter, when the soul advances toward the abyss of the Divinity, what invades her is peace, an unspeakable peace that nothing can submerge; not the thought of our sins, nor our sorrows, nor those of others, nor anything in the

---

[8] Delatte, "Vie," chap. 14.

[9] It must be clarified that the word "enthusiasm" here has the sense of a superficial emotion, inconsequent and ephemeral.

world, because it is the dawn of eternal life that begins to gleam. One cannot yet discern the source of this invincible peace, but experiences it nonetheless."[10]

"Death seems to me to be the easiest, the simplest of all the actions of our life. It is the most complete and most joyous giving of ourselves to God," she once said in a conference, the date of which has not been noted. "Doesn't a child sleep confidently in the arms of his father, even when he has just been disobedient? Isn't it easier to lay out our lives before Him than to break our heads?"

On March 5, 1909, Mother Cécile attended a meeting of the chapter called the "chapter of novices," in which the mistress of novices presents the candidates for profession to the community, with their qualities and their weaknesses. This was the last time she would attend a conventual gathering. She steadily continued to decline, without its being possible to discern whether the end was close or not. She was habitually in a state of prostration from which it was difficult to arouse her. Dom Delatte conferred the sacrament of extreme unction on her and gave her viaticum on March 15. Two days later, in the evening of the seventeenth, he returned to speak to the nuns about the imminent departure of Mother Cécile, preparing their souls for that solemn moment.

"My children, my children, there is only one thing in which you must be interested," the abbot said to the community, "the soul of your mother; there is nothing else, no memories, except to remember the devotion, the tenderness which were shown us during her long life. All thoughts, all worries, all solicitude, all prayers must be for her; this is only gratitude and justice on our part. Everything, absolutely everything must be offered for the soul that is about to depart to God. . . . This soul, who has loved us and whom we love, must present herself before God guarded by our prayers, adorned by us, enveloped by our filial piety, by our supernatural tenderness, clothed, as it were, by all the souls whom she labored to keep for God. . . . Most surely, the Lord will help us in a special way during these solemn and absolutely unique days. We will have, no doubt,

---

[10] Letter dated October 5, 1897.

only one occasion in our lives to make a sacrifice such as the one God will be asking of us. . . .

"A monastery has only one center: its abbot or abbess. During these days the abbess must be abbess more than ever; she must be loved more than ever, obeyed more than ever. All souls must be but one soul with hers. Her lips are still, her voice no longer reaches us, but her thoughts are known to us."

That night, the nuns took turns watching and praying by Mother Cécile. In the middle of the night, the prioress sent a message to Dom Delatte to forewarn him that the abbess's death seemed imminent. However, the following day found them still in expectation. "The dying one had lost consciousness and no longer showed to anyone the signs of the previous night," wrote Dom Delatte. "Her breath, faint and short during the entire afternoon, became fast and labored in the evening. The agony had set in, but gently, interrupted by one sigh. Her face, which until then had been flushed with fever, took on a hue white as ivory; a few very sweet moans escaped from her tortured breast."[11]

"The agony only lasted a half hour," wrote Mother Agnes de Puniet, "and then she was again very calm. At the end, her breathing was labored, and there were long moans that seemed to be calling to the Lord."[12]

Then, came the passage of death. It was about half past ten at night on March 18, 1909; the feast of Saint Joseph had begun with First Vespers. After the chanting of the *Subvenite,*[13] the nuns came to show their obedience one last time, kissing the hand of their abbess and mother. During the three days that followed, March 19, 20 and 21, the body remained exposed upon the funeral bier. Her features were relaxed and tranquil.

The Princess Zita of Bourbon-Parma, who would wed the Archduke Charles of Austria in 1911, kept her recollections of the

---

[11] Delatte, "Vie," chap. 14.

[12] Letter to Mother Michael Maillard, March 19, 1909.

[13] Traditional responsory sung immediately after death and at burial services, which begins: *Subvenite sancti Dei, occurrite angeli Domini: suscipientes animam ejus, offerentes eam in conspectu Altissimi.*(Come to her assistance, ye saints of God, meet her, ye angels of the Lord, receiving her soul, offering it in the sight of the Most High.) — Trans.

death of Mother Cécile: "I was almost face-to-face with Father Abbot
Dom Delatte, on the other side of the bed, and Mother Prioress was
by my side, so that I witnessed the last moment of Madame Abbess. It
was very impressive, for, despite the great difficulty with which she
breathed, a profound peace reigned about the bed of agony. The
following day we spent much time praying by her, and that
expression so serene, so *having arrived*, was profoundly striking. I
very much shared the sorrow of all the community, we felt like
orphans. While she was there, it was our mother who was there.
When she left, we felt completely abandoned, even myself who had
been there for such a short time." [14]

And Mother Agathe de la Fougère wrote on March 19: "Our
mistress and mother acquitted herself of this her last liturgical
function on earth with the majesty of a queen. She was glorious in
this calm that called to mind Saint John's repose upon the breast of
the Master. Her eyes, shut, seemed to contemplate within, her head
was slightly turned toward the left and her right arm, extended upon
the bed, seemed to offer itself for our kiss of homage. . . . Immediately
after her *dormitio*,[15] our mother became very beautiful; all traces of her
final sufferings disappeared and she donned an expression of
youth." [16]

The funeral was celebrated on March 22 by Dom Delatte, in the
presence of Dom Marsille, prior of Kergonan, Dom de Puniet, prior of
Wisques, and Dom Cabrol, abbot of Farnborough. The body was
interred in a sarcophagus of white marble in a crypt next to the nuns'
church, which could only be accessed from the side of the enclosure.

Upon his return to Oosterhout, Dom Jean de Puniet spoke of the
events of those days to the nuns of Notre-Dame de Wisques. "The
first impression one had in the presence of those venerable remains
was very different from what we feel at the side of our own dead,
even those most loved. It was an impression of joy—everything was
simple, peaceful, calm and recollected. There was something
luminous about Madame Abbess's bearing, an atmosphere of peace
that invited one to prayer. I say that we prayed, because the attitude

---

[14] Notes written during summer 1973.
[15] Her "falling asleep," that is, her death. —Trans.
[16] Letter to Mother Lucie Schmitt, March 19, 1909.

of Madame Abbess was such that we could do nothing else. One would think that Madame Abbess held the Lord between her hands, truly present, and that she contemplated him at her leisure. And, at the same time, it was an attitude of trust, of repose, as that of a small child sleeping on her mother's bosom."[17]

In that same year, Dom Delatte published the biography of Dom Guéranger for which Mother Cécile had amassed notes and material in the course of twenty years. The abbot had reached the end of his own work on the biography amidst his numerous occupations; however, it is probable that he had not wished to issue the book to the public, out of discretion, before the death of Mother Cécile, to whom he was indebted for the greater part of the material he had used. Neither did he consent to signing his own name to the work, simply indicating that it had been written "by a monk of the Congregation of France." Mother Cécile had not worked in vain to make known him of whom she had only desired to be the most faithful disciple. Yet, by the sanctity of her life and by the monasteries she founded, isn't she, even more eloquently, one of the most beautiful titles to glory of the first restorer of Benedictine life in France?

In March 1930, the remains of Mother Cécile were taken to her monastery in France at the beginning of the abbacy of Mother Madeleine Limozin. They now repose in the crypt of the church. Here the nuns come daily to ask their foundress for the grace to keep faithfully the legacy they have inherited, and to benefit from the charism that allowed her, in this life of faith, to see eternity already present.

"We already possess everything that we will later have. Our faith can succeed in reconstructing for us everything that paradise will be. An unlimited faith would nearly attain to the [beatific] vision, so much do these two things border on each other. When faith has attained its culminating point, the passage on to vision is nearly imperceptible; it is traversed without shock, as a regular, normal thing. That is how it should be and it is easy to arrive at this point through the reception of the sacraments. If we attentively consider all

---

[17] Chronicles of Notre-Dame de Wisques, March 1909.

the means we have for our sanctification, we must acknowledge that everything is there for us, in perfect harmony. God never does anything abruptly. Rather, it is like an uninterrupted chain, from our first initiation through baptism up to our entrance into glory."[18]

In a conference given on Easter Sunday, April 14, 1895, Mother Cécile said: "What is our present life? It is a passage, a means of testifying to our fidelity toward the Lord and of completing what is lacking in His Passion, as St. Paul says. We must complete in ourselves all the mysteries of the Lord, the resurrection included. If there are those who, here on earth, continue to complete in particular the passion of Our Lord, we may, if we devote ourselves to it, apply ourselves to completing His resurrection, to having the ways of the truly risen again, which is not forbidden us. . . .

"All we must do is to live from this life with which we are inoculated through the Holy Eucharist; for in It, Our Lord, while immolated, is also risen again, living and glorious. In receiving Holy Communion, we are filled with light, and the blood of the Lord runs through our veins. And this light which inundates us, this blood which vivifies us, it is the light and the blood of the Resurrected One. Our conduct, then, must be imbued with the strength of the Resurrection."[19]

---

[18] Notes taken at a spiritual conference on November 19, 1901.

[19] With the death of Mother Cécile Bruyère, the appointment of a new abbess had to be made. The choice fell on Mother Claire de Livron (1865–1928), a professed nun of Sainte-Cécile who had been sent to Notre-Dame de Wisques as foundress in 1889. She received the abbatial blessing on April 13, Easter Tuesday, from the hands of Bishop Cahill. The nuns of Sainte-Cécile made their gradual return to Solesmes in 1922, beginning in May, with Mother Claire leaving Ryde on September 28. What brought about the possibility of a return to their home was a change in the political climate of France, best explained by the author in his *Introduction to the History of the Congregation of Solesmes* (p. 73):

"When the war was over something had changed in France; the atmosphere of religious tension which marked political life from 1880 to 1914 had given way to a different climate. The anticlericalists had not all given up the battle, far from it, but the virulent anticlericalism of the founders of the Third Republic ('The Republic will be secular or will not exist at all') now seemed outmoded to many; the years of common national effort during the Great War had made it obsolete and a little absurd. The first assembly elected after the war adopted a compromise between left and right; the motto was 'Religious peace before everything.' A vague text of agreement stated that the fact of secularism had to be reconciled with the liberty and rights of all citizens, regardless of their beliefs, for only in this way could religious peace be assured.

"Nothing in the legislation against congregations was changed; they continued to be banned and excluded, but the republic's eyes were kept closed and they were ignored. The 'republican laws' re-emerged during election campaigns when there was nothing else to mobilize the left, but normally they were kept in the cupboard like cast-off clothes. The authorities did not want to see, and the communities were left to enjoy the freedom they would not be granted officially but which was theirs for the taking. It was time, therefore, in all the monasteries to think about returning."

Mother Claire was succeeded by Mother Madeleine Limozin (1873–1949) who received the abbatial blessing on January 21, 1929. It was under her abbacy that the remains of Mother Cécile were brought back to Solesmes, in 1930. Twenty-four of Mother Cécile's daughters died in exile and are interred in the cemetery at the monastery in Ryde, which has been the home of the Benedictine community of Pax Cordis Jesu since the departure of the nuns of Solesmes.

The priory of Pax Cordis Jesu was founded in 1882 at Ventnor, in the south of the Isle of Wight, by the Abbey of Paix Notre-Dame of Liège, Belgium, itself established in 1627. When the Solesmes communities took refuge in the Isle of Wight, the nuns of Pax Cordis Jesu, who ran a small boarding school, assisted the exiles in a variety of ways. Conversely, the monks of Saint-Pierre were able to provide for the spiritual needs of the Ventnor nuns. Dom Cozien was assigned as their chaplain and encouraged them in adopting the fully contemplative life toward which they tended. This process was given impetus when the nuns of Solesmes returned to France in 1922, vacating their monastery in Ryde which the community of Pax Cordis Jesu then took up, in time discontinuing their boarding school and becoming fully enclosed. In 1926 the priory was raised to the rank of an abbey, with Mother Ambrosia Cousin as its first abbess and in 1950 it became a house of the Congregation of Solesmes. The monks of Quarr Abbey (the Solesmian community that remained on the Isle of Wight) continue to celebrate daily Mass for the Pax Cordis Jesu nuns and function as their regular confessors. While their monastery in Ryde is more properly named Pax Cordis Jesu, it is also known as Saint Cecilia's Abbey by virtue of the property it occupies, first built by the community of Sainte-Cécile.—Trans.

Postscript

THE FINAL YEARS OF Mother Cécile Bruyère, viewed from the exterior, may seem to have been sad. Communication with those about her waned little by little; her illness gradually enveloped her in deep silence and the solitude of physical incapacity. Her personality, so assured, seemed to hide behind a cloud, making it no longer possible for others to reach her. The hour of the Passion had arrived, which was one of greater intimacy with God.

From 1900, she ceased to labor in a visible and tangible way at the work for which God had prepared her from her very infancy by bestowing on her uncommon graces that place her among the great spiritual masters. If effacement came upon her at a seemingly early time in life, at fifty-five years of age, the period of her blossoming, on the other hand, had begun quite early, upon reaching her majority in 1866. Moreover, during the twenty-five years that followed the death of Dom Guéranger, from 1875 to 1900, she gave of her full measure, which can be appreciated in the work she left behind.

Perhaps her message was heard and received so well that her person has been forgotten, except within the limited circles of her monastic family. She made her message known to those about her; it then spread from person to person, without her having prompted this in anyway, and in the end, the entire Church came to know it.

In 1925, in an article of the *Dictionnaire des connaissances religieuses* (Dictionary of religious understanding), A. Molien could still write: "A considerable number of devotions arises each year and nearly every day. They are attached to one of the main devotions to better explain it, or to place it within reach of a greater number of people by simplifying it, or, at times, to complicate it to the point where a person can no longer discern the actual object of the devotion and the Church is obliged to intervene in order to regulate or repress it. . . . This multiplicity must not lead to dissipation. Many devotions must not obliterate *the* devotion, instead of fostering it. As a guide to dealing with the very great number of devotions that exist, we can categorize them as necessary, optional, superfluous. . . ."[1]

As she described it herself in imagery, Mother Cécile had always preferred the ocean and its infinite horizons to seawater distributed in bottles. In face of the situation described by Molien, which was already true of her times, she never ceased to recall that it was necessary above all to return to the essentials, to the primary sources of the true Christian spirit: the sacraments, the liturgy, *lectio divina*.[2] Beyond the many devotions of her century, which she did not reject, there was the living contact with the great sea: Holy Scripture, the prayers of the liturgy, the writings of the saints, beginning with those by the Fathers of the Church and the fathers of monasticism.

Today, at the close of the twentieth century, all of that has again become—or is in the process of becoming—the common good of the Church, that is, this return to the sources so encouraged by the documents of the Second Vatican Council. But things were not yet there in 1899—quite the contrary. When Mother Cécile published her book, *The Spiritual Life and Prayer According to Holy Scripture and Monastic Tradition*, circulated to a wider audience for the first time by theologians and bishops of Germany, she was deemed a pioneer.

Except for the external influence she exerted through her book, Mother Cécile labored only at the monastic work to which Providence had called her by leading her to Dom Guéranger: the foundation of the Abbey of Sainte-Cécile de Solesmes, and then of its daughter houses, Notre-Dame de Wisques and Saint-Michel de Kergonan. She likewise counseled those who came to her, but without concerning herself with having her teachings known beyond her religious family. To her religious sisters and her brothers at Saint-Pierre de Solesmes, she reminded them that their vocation consisted primarily of being fully what they were—consecrated souls, daughters and sons of Saint Benedict, to whom the Church entrusted as primary duty the solemn and faithful celebration of the liturgy.

---

[1] "Dévotion et Dévotions," in A. Molien, *Dictionnaire Pratique des Connaissances Religieuses,"* ed. J. Bricout, vol. 2 (Paris, Librairie Letouzey et Ané, 1927) col. 803.

[2] *Lectio divina* is a traditional practice of prayerful reading of Holy Scripture intended to engender communion with God and ever more profound knowledge of His Word.—Trans.

Simplicity and a return to the essentials; these are the fundamentals which she dedicated herself to transmitting and that epitomize her message. Dom Guéranger had shown her the way. From his teaching she drew the necessary conclusions, especially with regard to the religious family to which she belonged and whose contemplative character she resolutely upheld. She never sought to have any influence beyond this limited circle. The rest followed spontaneously of itself.

There are not many women from the turn of the nineteenth century whose teachings have had such repercussions. That is why it was high time that she be given due attention in a book which should have been written much earlier, so as to avert the oblivion and misunderstanding from which she suffered after her death in the land of exile.

Chronological Table

Exterior/Background Events	Year	Events in the Life of Mother Cécile Bruyère
July Monarchy (1830–1848)	1830	
POPE GREGORY XVI (1831–1846)	1831	
July 11: Dom Guéranger restores Benedictine life at Solesmes	1833	
July14: Dom Guéranger appointed Abbot of Solesmes	1837	
September: closure of the priory in Paris	1845	Oct 12: birth of Jeanne-Henriette Bruyère (Jenny) in Paris Oct 23: Jenny's baptism in the church of Saint-Roch
POPE PIUS IX (1846–1878)	1846	
Pope flees to Gaeta *Fall of Louis-Philippe, Paris Revolution Second Republic is established (1848–1851) with Louis-Napoleon as President of the Republic of France*	1848	
	1849	Jun 29: birth of Lise Bruyère, only sister of Jenny
Second Empire (1851–1870)	1851	
Napoleon III, Emperor of the French	1852	Nov 23: death of Jenny's grandfather, Jean-Jacques Huvé First Confession
Foundation of the monastery in Ligugé	1853	Aug 14: acquisition of the Manor of Coudreuse
Dogma of the Immaculate Conception	1854	
	1856	The Bruyère family moves to Coudreuse
	1857	May 19: Jenny's first meeting with Dom Guéranger May 28: Jenny's First Communion in Sablé

Exterior/Background Events	Year	Events in the Life of Mother Cécile Bruyère
	1858	Apr 15: Jenny's Confirmation at the parish church in Chantenay Dec 12: Jenny first reveals to Dom Guéranger her desire to consecrate herself to God
Second War of Italian Independence (1859–1860)	1859	
	1861	Oct 12: vow of virginity made at Saint-Pierre
Encyclical *Quanta cura* and *Syllabus*	1864	
Foundation of the monastery in Marseilles	1865	
	1866	Oct 8: blessing of the cornerstone of the monastery of Sainte-Cécile by Bishop Fillion Nov 13: Cécile Bruyère arrives at Sainte-Cécile-la-Petite Nov 16: monastic life is established. Sister Cécile Bruyère is nominated superior
Creation of the International Workmen's Association	1867	Aug 12: episcopal decree of erection of the monastery of Sainte-Cécile Aug 14: clothing of Sister Cécile and the first six postulants with the Benedictine habit
	1868	Aug 15: monastic profession of Mother Cécile and the first six novices Aug 16: election of Mother Cécile as prioress
First Vatican Council (1869–1870) Constitution *Pastor æternus* defines the dogma of papal infallibility	1869	
Franco-Prussian War (1870–1871)	1870	Jul 14: rescript of Pius IX elevating Mother Cécile to the dignity of abbess
The Paris Commune (1871) *The Third Republic (1871–1914)* *Foundation of Catholic Worker circles*	1871	Jul 14: abbatial blessing of Mother Cécile Jun 10 – Jul 5, 1872: sojourn at Sainte-Cécile of two nuns of Stanbrook, one of whom is Mother Gertrude d'Aurillac Dubois Oct 12: dedication of the abbatial church of Sainte-Cécile
	1872	Jan 2: death of Madame Félicie Bruyère Feb 12: death of Monsieur Léopard Bruyère

Exterior/Background Events	Year	Events in the Life of Mother Cécile Bruyère
Jul 28: death of Bishop Fillion	1874	Mar 11: Dom Guéranger entrusts Mother Cécile with a maternal mission toward Saint-Pierre of Solesmes
Jan 30: death of Dom Guéranger *Feb 11: Dom Couturier elected second abbot of Solesmes* *Aug 7: Cardinal Pitra visits Solesmes*	1875	Jan 27: Dom Guéranger's last visit to Sainte-Cécile Dec 8–21: Mother Cécile visits the abbey of Jouarre
POPE LEO XIII (1878–1903)	1878	
Encyclical *Æterni Patris* (on Thomism)	1879	Jun 2: death of Lise Eynaud, Mother Cécile's sister
Law against religious congregations *Nov 6: first expulsion of the monks from Saint-Pierre*	1880	
Mar 22: second expulsion of the monks	1882	
Sep 7: Father Delatte enters the novitiate at Saint-Pierre of Solesmes	1883	
Encyclical *Immortale Dei*	1885	Mother Cécile writes her book on prayer
	1887	Sep 24–Oct 26: sojourn at Sainte-Cécile of Mother Marie de la Croix, prioress of the Norbertines of Bonlieu
	1888	Dec 8: Mother Cécile passes on to Dom Delatte the mission she had received from Dom Guéranger on March 11, 1874.
	1889	Jul 24: foundation of Notre-Dame de Wisques Aug 9–13: Mother Cécile visits Verneuil.
Oct 29: death of Dom Couturier *Nov 9: Dom Delatte elected third abbot of Solesmes* *Dec 8: abbatial blessing of Dom Delatte at Sainte-Cécile*	1890	Jan 29: erection of Sainte-Cécile as an abbey Jun 23–Jul 7: sojourn at Sainte-Cécile of the foundresses of the Abbey of Dourgne Aug 15: profession at Sainte-Cécile of the first nuns of Maredret
Encyclical *Rerum Novarum* (on social issues)	1891	Jul 19–Aug 7: Mother Cécile travels to Wisques and to Stanbrook.

Exterior/Background Events	Year	Events in the Life of Mother Cécile Bruyère
April: Dom Delatte leaves for Rome. He is suspended from his functions. *August: apostolic visitation at Saint-Pierre* *November: Dom Delatte is reinstated in his functions as abbot of Saint-Pierre.*	1893	Apr 12–Jun 5: sojourn at Sainte-Cécile of the Benedictine prioress of Prague, Mother Aldegonde Berlinghoff August: apostolic visitation at Sainte-Cécile Sep 7: the Belgian nuns leave to establish the foundation at Maredret.
Gradual return of the monks to their monastery in Solesmes	1894	Sep 16: abbatial blessing of Mother Thérèse Bernard
	1898	Aug 18: foundation of Saint-Michel de Kergonan
	1899	Publication of *The Spiritual Life and Prayer According to Holy Scripture and Monastic Tradition* in its definitive form
The radical republic (1900–1914)	1900	
Law of associations *Saint-Pierre goes into exile at Appuldurcombe (Isle of Wight)*	1901	Sainte-Cécile goes into exile at Northwood (Isle of Wight)
POPE PIUS X (1903–1914)	1903	
Nov 22: *motu proprio* on sacred music	1903	Sep 3–Oct 6: extended stay in Oosterhout for a period of rest
Separation of Church and State declared in France	1905	May 8: abbatial blessing of Mother Lucie Schmitt (of Kergonan) at Northwood
	1906	May: the community moves to Appley House in Ryde
Encyclical *Pascendi* (against Modernism)	1907	Oct 12: dedication of the church in Appley
Saint-Pierre monks move to Quarr	1908	
	1909	Mar 18: death of Mother Cécile Bruyère at Appley House in Ryde

Illustration Sources

Archives of the Abbey of Sainte-Cécile: cover, 4, 5, 8, 11, 15, 16 (Photo Constantin), 23, 27, 28, 29, 33, 34, 35, 37, 38, 39, 40, 41, 42, 44, 47, 48, 50 (Photo Fonteneau), 54, 55 (Areofilms and Aero Pictorial Ltd.), 56

Archives of the Abbey of Saint-Pierre: 12, 13, 14, 17, 18, 19, 20, 21, 22, 24, 25, 26, 31, 32, 36, 49, 53

Archives of the Abbey of Saint-Michel in Kergonan: 43

Archives of the Abbey of Saint-Scholastique in Dourgne: 45

Archives of Our Lady of Clear Creek Abbey: 57

Photo Archives of Bonlieu: 46

Photo Archives of P. Huvé: 3, 9

Archives of the Eynaud Family: 10

Archives of the Church of Saint-Roch: 6 (photograph taken April 1997 by kind permission of Rev. Fr. Thierry de l'Épine, pastor of Saint-Roch)

Revue Historique et Archéologique du Maine, 1895: 1

Panthéon des illustrations françaises au XIXe siècle, Paris, 1866: 51

Photo CIM: 52

Photo Luc: 2

Photo Becquereau, Saint-Omer: 30

Bibliography

Works by Mother Cécile Bruyère

Manuscript Sources

"Cahiers de réflexions" (Notebooks of reflections)
"Enfance et jeunesse de mère Cécile Bruyère." Written at the request of Dom
      Guéranger. 1864.
"Les Annales: origines, 1ère et 2e années" (Annals: origins, first and second
      years)
"Souvenirs sur dom Guéranger." 1875. (Recollections on Dom Guéranger)
Notes on Dom Guéranger for Bishop Pie. 1875
Notes on Dom Guéranger for Bishop Freppel, 1887.
Conferences by Dom Guéranger given at Sainte-Cécile. Collected by Mother
      Cécile.
"Coutumier des Oblates du tour" (Customary for the extern sisters)
Biography of Sister Apolline Martin
Biography of Sister Augustine Bignon
Notes on the life of Dom Prosper Guéranger, abbot of Solesmes. 1878–1900.
"Commentaires de l'Ecriture Sainte." (Commentaries on Holy Scripture)
"Commentaires de la Règle de saint Benoît." (Commentaries on the Rule of St.
      Benedict)
Conferences on Sundays and feasts of the liturgical year.
"Commentaire des *Conférences* de Cassien." (Commentary on the *Conférences* of
      John Cassian)
Conferences on prayer.
"Quelques remarques sur le chant sacré et ses différences avec la musique
      modern." (Some remarks on sacred chant and how it differs from
      modern music.)
Counsels to a newly elected abbess. Written for the abbesses of Stanbrook and
      Wisques.

Published Works

"Lettre à un père de famille." Paper read at Cercles catholiques d'ouvriers of
      Albert de Mun.
"La morale de deux histoire." *L'Univers*. April 1, 1882.

"Sommes-nous chrétiens, oui ou non?" *L'Univers*. October 16, 1882.

La vie spirituelle et l'oraison d'après la Sainte Ecriture et la tradition monastique. Solesmes 1886, 1895 ; Tours, 1920. German translation, Mainz, 1896 and Düsseldorf, 1953. English translation: *The Spiritual Life and Prayer According to Holy Scripture and Monastic Tradition*, trans. by the Benedictines of Stanbrook, London, 1900 and New York, 1905. Dutch translation, Amsterdam, n.d. Italian translation, n.p., n.d. [Rome, 1903] and Milan, 1976. Spanish translation, Barcelona, 1959.

Le Cantique des Cantiques. Commentaire de madame Cécile Bruyère. Published *pro manuscripto* by Stanbrook Abbey. Worcester, 1913.

In Spiritu et Veritate. Solesmes: Abbey of Sainte-Cécile, 1966.

Works related to the life of Mother Cécile Bruyère

"Le mémorial des Fondateurs." In *Selon ta Parole*. For the hundredth anniversary of the abbeys of Saint-Benoît d'En Calcat, Sainte-Scholastique de Dourgne. Lavaur, 1988.

Battandier, A. *Le cardinal Jean-Baptiste Pitra: Bibliothécaire de la Sainte Église romaine (1812–1889)*, Paris, 1893.

Bellune, (Canon). *Monseigneur Hector d'Outremont. Sa vie et sa doctrine spirituelle*. Tours, 1900.

Bernard, Ch.-A. *Le Dieu des mystiques*. Paris, 1994.

"Récit de madame Bruyère sur l'enfance de sa fille Jenny." Notes by Félicie Bruyère written at the request of Dom Guéranger. 1867.

Bruyère, L. *Études relatives à l'art des constructions*. 2 vols. Paris, 1823–28.

Bulletin de Saint-Martin. Ligugé. Diverse articles on Dom Sauton's work on leprosy. vol. 2, pp 35–41, 54–60; vol. 7, p. 338 ; vol. 9, p. 358 ; vol. 10, pp. 89, 279.

Buschmann, J. *Beuroner Mönchtum. Studien sur Spiritualität, Verfassung und Lebensformen der Beuroner Benediktinenkongregation vom 1863 bis 1914*.

Cabrol, F. *Histoire du cardinal Pitra, Bénédictin de la Congrégation de France*. Paris, 1893.

Cartier, E. *Les moines de Solesmes: Expulsions du 6 novembre 1880 et du 22 mars 1882*. Solesmes, 1882.

Clair, R. "Une fondation urbaine de dom Guéranger, Sainte-Marie-Madeleine de Marseille." Paper presented at the Colloquium on Dom Guéranger. Solesmes, 1975.

Delatte, P. *Dom Guéranger, abbé de Solesmes*. 2 vols. Paris, 1909-1910. Solesmes, 1984.

———. *Lettres*. Compiled by Dom Lucien Regnault. Solesmes, 1991.

———. "Vie de madame Cécile Bruyère." Manuscript. 1915–1916

Doyere, P. "Madame Thérèse Bernard, abbesse de Notre-Dame de Wisques." Manuscript source.

Edwards, E. "Dom Guéranger vu par un disciple anglais (Dom Laurent Shepherd)." Paper presented at the Colloquium Dom Guéranger. Solesmes, 1975.

Eynaud de Fay, J. "Louise Bruyère. Travaux descendance (1758–1831)." *La Province du Maine*. vol. 70 (1968), p. 170 ff.

Eynaud de Fay, A. "Bruyère-Huvé. " Manuscript source.

Freppel, Ch.-E. *Discours sur l'ordre monastique prononcé dans l'église abbatiale de Solesmes à l'anniversaire des obsèques de dom Guéranger, le 16 mars 1876.* Angers, 1876.

Gazeau, R. "Une nouvelle vie." In *Histoire de Sainte-Croix de Poitiers. Quatorze siècles de vie monastique*. Société des Antiquaires de l'Ouest. Poitiers, 1986, p. 435-485.

Gobineau, Arthur and Bénédicte de. *Correspondance, 1872–1882*, edited by A.-B. Duff and R. Rancœur. Paris, 1958.

Guépin, A. *Dom Guéranger et madame Durand*. Poitiers, 1911.

Guéranger, P. *De la monarchie pontificale*. Paris : 1870.

———. *Sainte Cécile et la société romaine aux deux premiers siècles*. Paris, 1874.

———. *Le Règlement du noviciat*. Solesmes, 1885.

Guerny, R. du. "Les seigneurs de Chantenay d'après les anciens registres paroissiaux." *Annales fléchoises* 11 (1910): p. 227–289.

Hourlier, J. "Dom Couturier, témoin de la pensée monastique de dom Guéranger." Colloquium Dom Guéranger. Solesmes, 1975.

Houtin, A. *Dom Couturier, abbé de Solesmes*. Paris, 1899.

———. *Une grande mystique, madame Bruyère, abbesse de Solesmes*. Paris, 1925, 1930.

Huvé, J.-Cl. *Un architecte des lumières, Jean-Jacques Huvé (1742–1808). Sa vie, sa famille, ses idées*. Paris, 1994.

Huysmans, J.-K. *La cathédrale*. Paris, 1898.

———. *L'Oblat*. Paris, 1903.

Marsille, J. *Dom Athanase Logerot*. Amay, 1909.

Maury, J. "Dom Guéranger et la fondation de Sainte-Cécile de Solesmes." Colloquium Dom Guéranger. Solesmes, 1975.

Metz, R. *La consécration des vierges dans l'Église romaine. Étude d'histoire de la liturgie*. Paris, 1954.

Moreau, H. *Dom Hildebrand de Hemptinne*. Maredsous, 1930.

Navier. *Notice sur M. Bruyère*. Paris, 1833.

Oury, G.-M. *Introduction à l'histoire de la Congrégation de Solesmes*. Solesmes, 1995.

———. *L'abbaye Notre-Dame de Wisques*. Wisques, 1989.

———. "Recherches sur les tentatives de restauration de l'Ordre de saint Benoît en France au début du XIXe siècle." *Collectanea Cisterciensia* 57 (1995): 181–189.

Pie, E. *Oraison funèbre de dom Guéranger*. Poitiers, 1875.

Puniet, J. de. "Bruyère, Jeanne-Henriette-Cécile." In *Dictionnaire de Spiritualité*, vol. 1. Paris, 1937, col. 1972–1974

Regnault, L. "Portrait de dom Delatte." *Lettre aux Amis de Solesmes*, 1987, no. 3, 7–28.

Robert, L. *Dom Guéranger et la fondation de Sainte-Cécile*. Conference to Les Amis de Solesmes, 1959.

Savaton, A. *Dom Paul Delatte, abbé de Solesmes*. Paris, 1954. Solesmes, 1975.

Soltner, L. *Solesmes et dom Guéranger*. Solesmes, 1974.

Tissot, G. *Solesmes en Angleterre*. Conference to Les Amis de Solesmes, 1959.

———. "La pensée monastique de dom Delatte." *Revue Mabillon* 50 (1961): 111–122.

———. *Le rayonnement de Sainte-Cécile de Solesmes*, Conference to Les Amis de Solesmes, 1967.

Tissot, H. *Dom Charles Couturier, deuxième abbé de Solesmes, 1817–1890*. Conference to Les Amis de Solesmes, 1961.

Triger, R. "Les travaux publics au Mans à l'époque de la Révolution et l'ingénieur Bruyère." *Revue historique et archéologique du Maine* 8 (1895).

Works of General Interest

Anson, P. *The Religious Orders and Congregations in Great Britain and Ireland*. London, 1949.

Baunard, L. *Histoire du cardinal Pie, évêque de Poitiers*. 2 vols. Poitiers, 1901.

Best, G., ed. *The Permanent Revolution: The French Revolution and its Legacy, 1789–1989*. London, 1988.

Bienvenue, J. M. *L'étonnant fondateur de Fontevraud, Robert d'Arbrissel*. Paris, 1981.

Chastel, G. *Huysmans et ses amis*. Paris, 1957.

Chastenet, J. *Histoire de la Troisième République*. Vol. 1, *L'Enfance de la Troisième, 1870–1877*. Paris, 1952.

Chaussy, Y. *Les bénédictines et la Réforme catholique en France au XVIIe siècle*. Collection documents et textes spirituels. Paris, 1975.

Combe, P. *Histoire de la restauration du chant grégorien*. Solesmes, 1979.

Dansette, A. *Histoire religieuse de la France contemporaine*. Paris, 1965.

Debidour, A. *L'Église catholique et l'État sous la Troisième République, 1870–1906*. Paris, 1906–09.

Dicks, B. *The Isle of Wight*. London, 1979.

Dreyfus, R. *La république de M. Thiers (1871–1873)*. Paris, 1930.

Fleury, M. and L. Sonolet. *La société du Second Empire*. Paris, 1911.

Guillemin, H. *Histoire des catholiques français au XIXe siècle (1805–1905)*. Geneva, 1947.

Johnson, C. "Prosper Guéranger (1805-1875): a liturgical theologian. An introduction to his liturgical writings and work." Rome, 1984.

Lachapelle, G. *Le Ministère Méline*. Paris, 1928.

Lafrance, J. *Un regard tout en Jésus. Essai sur la spiritualité de Marie-Eugénie*. Paris, 1976.

La Gorce, P. de. *Histoire du Second Empire*. 7 vols. Paris, 1899–1905.

Latreille, A. and R. Remond. *Histoire du catholicisme en France*. Vol. 3, *La période contemporaine*. Paris, 1962.

Lecanuet, E. *L'Église en France sous la Troisième République, 1870–1878*. Paris, 1907.

Lemeunier, F. "L'année terrible: Souvenirs d'un Israélite (1870–1871)." *La Province du Maine* 74 (1972): 369–

Lemoine, R. *Le droit des religieux du Concile de Trente aux Instituts séculiers*. Paris, 1956.

Linage Conde, A. *San Benito y los Benedictinos*. 7 vols. Braga, 1993.

Maurain, J. *La politique ecclésiastique du Second Empire de 1852 à 1869*. Paris, 1930.

Mejean, L.-V. *La séparation des églises et de l'État*. Paris, 1959.

Metais-Thoreau, O. *Un simple laïc, Léon Papin-Dupont, le saint homme de Tours, 1797–1876*. Cholet, 1993.

Oury, G.-M. *Dom Camille Leduc, 1819–1895*. Pionniers de la charité. Paris, 1974.

———. "La Tradition monastique toujours vivante." In *La Part des moines. Théologie vivante dans le monachisme français*. Le point théologique. Paris, 1978.

Prou, Jean, and the Benedictine nuns of the Solesmes Congregation. *Walled About with God: the history and spirituality of enclosure for cloistered nuns*, trans. & ed. by Br. David Hayes, OSB, Herefordshire, [Gracewing], 2005.

Rouelle, O. *La république absolue. Aux origines de l'instabilité constitutionnelle de la France républicaine, 1870–1889*. Paris, 1982.

Rousseau, O. *Histoire du mouvement liturgique*. Lex orandi. Paris, 1945.

Schmitz, P. *Histoire de l'Ordre de saint Benoît*. Vol. 4, *Histoire externe du Concile de Trente au XXe siècle*. Maredsous, 1948.

Siegfried, A. *Tableau politique de la France de l'Ouest sous la IIIe République*. Paris, 1913.

Sifflet, A. *Les évêques concordataires du Mans, Mgr Fillion*. Le Mans, 1928.

Terrien, E. *Monseigneur Freppel*. 2 vols. Paris, 1931–32.

Veuillot, E. *Louis Veuillot*. 4 vols. Paris, 1913–.

Vogüe, A. de. *La communauté et l'abbé dans la Règle de saint Benoît*. Textes et études théologiques. Paris, 1960.

Index

U. I. O. G. D.

Printed in Great Britain
by Amazon.co.uk, Ltd.,
Marston Gate.